The Europeanisation of International Law

The Status of International Law in the EU and its Member States

Jan Wouters / André Nollkaemper / Erika de Wet
Editors

T·M·C·ASSER PRESS

Published by T·M·C·ASSER PRESS
P.O. Box 16163, 2500 BD The Hague, The Netherlands
<www.asserpress.nl>

T·M·C·ASSER PRESS' English language books are distributed exclusively by:

Cambridge University Press, The Edinburgh Building, Shaftesbury Road,
Cambridge CB2 2RU, UK,
or
for customers in the USA, Canada and Mexico:
Cambridge University Press, 100 Brook Hill Drive, West Nyack, NY 10994-2133, USA
<www.cambridge.org>

ISBN 978-90-6704-285-7

PRINTED IN THE NETHERLANDS

PREFACE

This book explores some consequences of European integration for the application of public international law in the European Union and its Member States. While in the early stages of the European integration process these consequences were rather modest, in recent years they have become increasingly important. As a consequence of the combination of expansion of the regulatory domain of international law and the increasing scope of competences of the EU, much of international law becomes part of the legal order of the EU and in that sense is 'europeanised'. It is becoming a system that is distinguishable from general international law.

The book focuses on one set of characteristics of europeanisation in particular: the consequences of europeanisation for the effects of public international law within the national legal orders of EU Member States. Normally, the constitutional law of each State determines the implementation of international obligations and the status and effect of such obligations on the national law level. However, for the Member States of the EU this 'classic' legal relationship between international and national law is modified into a new triangular relationship: international law, EU law and national law. Europeanisation of international law means that EU law determines how international law is to be applied in the EU Member States.

The scope and consequences of this process have not been subjected to much scholarly analysis. It also seems that, to a large extent, they have not been recognised in practice. This book aims to fill part of the gap and contribute to our understanding of the europeanisation of international law, in particular as it affects the domestic law of the Member States.

The chapters in this book were originally presented at a conference held at the Amsterdam Center for International Law, University of Amsterdam and co-organised with the Universities of Leuven, Ljubljana and Pecs, in the Netherlands, on 2 September 2005. They were reworked on the basis of the discussions at the conference and in light of later developments. The conference was made possible by contributions from the Research School Ius Commune, the Universiteit van Amsterdam, Amsterdam Center for International Law, the Netherlands Organization for Scientific Research (NWO) and the Royal Netherlands Academy of Arts and Sciences (KNAW).

For the Amsterdam Center for International Law, the conference and the book are part of the project *Interactions between Public International Law and National Law*. The project, funded by the Netherlands Organization for Scientific Research, has explored several legal questions arising from the increasing and changing interactions between international law and national law. The process of Europeanisation of international law and the emergence of a triangular relationship: international law, EU law and national law, is one of these new forms of interactions. For the

Leuven Centre for Global Governance Studies and Institute for International Law of Leuven University, these interactions belong to its core research focus on the role of the European Union in multilateral governance and legal processes.

We would like to thank Emily Bell, Stefanie Küfner and Caitilin McGivern for their excellent editorial assistance in the preparation of the book

April 2008 Jan WOUTERS, André NOLLKAEMPER and Erika DE WET

SUMMARY OF CONTENTS

TABLE OF CONTENTS

LIST OF ABBREVIATIONS

ACP	African, Caribbean and Pacific countries
AcP	Archiv für civilistische Praxis
AFDI	Annuaire Français de Droit International
AG	Advocate General
AJIL	American Journal of International Law
BGB	Bürgerliches Gesetzbuch
BYIL	British Yearbook of International Law
BVerfG	Bundesverfassungsgericht
CC	Constitutional Court
CFI	Court of First Instance
CFSP	Common Foreign and Security Policy
CMLR	Common Market Law Reports
CML Rev.	Common Market Law Review
DŐV	Die öffentliche Verwaltung
EC	European Community
ECHR	European Convention on Human Rights
ECJ	European Court of Justice
ECR	European Court Reports
ECtHR	European Court of Human Rights
EEA	European Economic Area
EEC	European Economic Community
EELR	European Environmental Law Review
EFA Rev.	European Foreign Affairs Review
EFTA	European Free Trade Association
EJIL	European Journal of International Law
EU	European Union
EuR	Europarecht
EWS	Europäisches Wirtschafts- und Steuerrecht
FAO	Food and Agriculture Organisation
FRY	Former Republic of Yugoslavia
GATT	General Agreement on Tariffs and Trade
GYIL	German Yearbook of International Law
ICC	International Criminal Court
ICCPR	International Covenant on Civil and Political Rights
ICJ	International Court of Justice

ICLQ	International and Comparative Law Quarterly
ICTY	International Criminal Tribunal of the former Yugoslavia
IGC	Intergovernmental Conference
IHR	International Health Regulations
ILM	International Legal Materials
ILO	International Labour Organization
IMF	International Monetary Fund
IMO	International Maritime Organization
IOs	International Organisations
JIEL	Journal of International Economic Law
JZ	Juristenzeitung
Leiden JIL	Leiden Journal of International Law
MARPOL	International Convention for the Prevention of Pollution from Ships 1973
NJCM	Nederlands Juristen Comité voor de Mensenrechten
NJW	Neue Juristische Wochenschrift
Nordic JIL	Nordic Journal of International Law
NWO	Netherlands Scientific Research Organization
OECD	Organisation for Economic Cooperation and Development
OJ	Official Journal of the European Communities/Union
PCIJ	Permanent Court of International Justice
PICT	Project on International Courts and Tribunals
PJCC	Police and Judicial Cooperation in Criminal Matters
Rev. trim. dr. eur.	Revue trimestrielle de droit européen
Rev. trim. dr. h.	Revue trimestrielle des droits de l'homme
Rev. univ. dr. h.	Revue universelle des droits de l'homme
SEW	Sociaal-Economische Wetgeving
SPS	Agreement on the Application of Sanitary and Phytosanitary Measures
TBT	Agreement on Technical Barriers to Trade
TEC	Treaty establishing the European Community
TEU	Treaty on European Union
TRIPS	Agreement on Trade-Related Aspects of Intellectual Property Rights
UN	United Nations
UNCLOS	United Nations Conference on the Law of the Sea
UNECE	United Nations Economic Commission for Europe
UNO	United Nations Organisation
UNTS	United Nations Treaty Series

UST	United States Treaties and Other International Agreements
VAT	Value-added tax
VCLT	Vienna Convention on the Law of the Treaties
WEU	Western European Union
WIPO	World Intellectual Property Organization
WTO	World Trade Organization
ZaöRV	Zeitschrift für ausländisches öffentliches Recht und Völkerrecht
ZeuP	Zeitschrift für Europäisches Privatrecht
ZöR	Zeitschrift fur öffentliches Recht (Austrian Journal of Public and International Law)

Chapter 1
INTRODUCTION: THE 'EUROPEANISATION' OF INTERNATIONAL LAW

Jan Wouters, André Nollkaemper and Erika de Wet*

1. Background of the book

Some ten years ago, Christaan Timmermans, Judge at the European Court of Justice (ECJ), pointedly observed that '[t]he relationship between European Community law and public international law is a complex one.'[1] This complexity has multiple dimensions. On the one hand these relate to the contribution of the EU to the development of international law, in particular through its intensive treaty-making practice, in which tenuous issues regarding the relationship between the Member States and the EU arise. On the other hand, these relate to the effect of public international law on and within the European Union and its Member States.

The complexities are increasing with the larger responsibilities that the EU has taken *vis-à-vis* international relations and international law. In the Lisbon Treaty one finds among the core objectives of the newly shaped Union in Article 3(5) TEU:

> 'In its relations with the wider world, the Union shall uphold and promote its values and interests and contribute to the protection of its citizens. It shall contribute to peace, security, the sustainable development of the Earth, solidarity and mutual respect among peoples, free and fair trade, eradication of poverty and the protection of human rights, in particular the rights of the child, as well as to *the strict observance and the development of international law*, including respect for the principles of the United Nations Charter.'[2]

* Jan Wouters, Professor of International Law and International Organisations and Director, Leuven Centre for Global Governance Studies and Institute for International Law, KULeuven; André Nollkaemper, Professor of Public International Law and Director of the Amsterdam Center for International Law, University of Amsterdam; Erika de Wet, Professor of International Constitutional Law, University of Amsterdam.

[1] C. Timmermans, 'The EU and Public International Law', 4 *EFA Rev.* (1999), p. 181.

[2] Treaty of Lisbon amending the Treaty on European Union and the Treaty establishing the European Community, signed at Lisbon, 13 December 2007, OJ 2007, C 306/1 (emphasis added). See also the commitments to international law in the new Art. 21(1), first para. and Art. 21(2)(6), TEU: 'The Union's action on the international scene shall be guided by the principles which have inspired its own creation, development and enlargement, and which it seeks to advance in the wider world: democracy, the rule of law, the universality and indivisibility of human rights and fundamental freedoms, respect

J. Wouters, P.A. Nollkaemper, E. de Wet (eds.), The Europeanisation of International Law

One of the results is that the EU is bound by an ever increasing body of international law. While the initial strive for autonomy of the Community legal system made the ECJ, at least during the first decades of the European Community's existence, reluctant to accept arguments based on international law, this wariness has meanwhile given place to a much more open attitude *vis-à-vis* international law in the ECJ's ever-evolving case-law.[3] But it remains an openness with a distinctly European perspective. Indeed, in practical terms, the ECJ case-law 'absorbs' international agreements – both mixed and non-mixed[4] – to which the Community is a party[5] and even, up to a certain degree, decisions of international organisations and customary international law, into the Community legal system. As far as international agreements are concerned, this case-law is based on the old provision of Article 228(2), nowadays Article 300(7) TEC,[6] according to which international agreements concluded under the procedure laid down in that article 'shall be binding on the institutions of the Community and on Member States.'[7]

---

for human dignity, the principles of equality and solidarity, and respect for the principles of the United Nations Charter and *international law*'; 'The Union shall define and pursue common policies and actions, and shall work for a high degree of cooperation in all fields of international relations, in order to [...] consolidate and support democracy, the rule of law, human rights and the principles of *international law*.' See also, on the EU's humanitarian aid policy, Art. 214 Treaty on the Functioning of the European Union: 'Humanitarian aid operations shall be conducted in compliance with the principles of *international law* [...]'. The new Treaty also induces the Member States to respect international law: see, e.g., Art. 77(4) Treaty on the Functioning of the Union: 'This Article shall not affect the competence of the Member States concerning the geographical demarcation of their borders, in accordance with *international law*' (emphases added).

[3] See, *inter alia*, J. Wouters and D. Van Eeckhoutte, 'Enforcement of Customary International Law through European Community Law', in J.M. Prinssen and A. Schrauwen (eds.), *Direct effect. Rethinking a Classic of EC Legal Doctrine* (Groningen, European Law Publishing 2002) pp. 183-234. At the time this book goes to press, important questions on customary international law and its relationship to treaties to which the EC is (UNCLOS) or is not (MARPOL) a party as well as to secondary EU law (Directive 2005/35/EC on sanctions against pollution by ships) were to be addressed by the ECJ in Case C-308/06 *Intertanko* v. *Secretary of State for Transport*, Judgment of 8 June 2008. Likewise, important problems of principle on the relationship between UN Security Council Resolutions and EU law are before the ECJ in the appeal in the *Kadi* case in which Advocate General Maduro has delivered his opinion on 16 January 2008 (Case C-402/05 P *Yassin Abdullah Kadi* v. *Council of the European Union and Commission of the European Communities*). The latter case is discussed in the chapter by Nikolaos Lavranos in this volume.

[4] See ECJ, Case 12/86 *Demirel* [1987] ECR 3719, para. 9 and Case C-13/00 *Commission* v. *Ireland* [2002] ECR I-2943, para. 14: 'mixed agreements concluded by the Community, its Member States and non-member countries have the same status in the Community legal order as purely Community agreements, as these are provisions coming within the scope of Community competence.'

[5] See already ECJ, Case 181/73 *Haegemann* [1974] ECR 449, para. 5, where it is held that the provisions of an international agreement concluded by the Community 'from the coming into force thereof, form an integral part of Community law.'

[6] One finds a somewhat adapted version of this clause also in Art. 111(3), 2nd para. EC.

[7] See ECJ, Case 104/81 *Kupferberg* [1982] ECR 3641, para. 13, where it is derived from this provision that '[i]n ensuring respect for commitments arising from an agreement concluded by the Community institutions the Member States fulfill an obligation not only in relation to the non-member country concerned but also and above all in relation to the Community which has assumed responsibility for the due performance of the agreement.' See also ECJ, Case 12/86 *Demirel* [1987], *supra* n. 4, para. 11; Case C-13/00 *Commission* v. *Ireland* [2002], *supra* n. 4, para. 15.

The processes through which an ever increasing body of international law becomes binding on the EU and through which distinct qualities and features are given to such international law within the EU, constitute core facets of the phenomenon of 'europeanisation of international law' that forms the subject-matter of this book. The contributions focus, in particular, on the distinct effects that international obligations have upon the EU institutions as well as within the Member States (after having entered the domestic legal order via the EU legal order). By doing so, the contributions address the important, but largely unexplored consequences that European integration has on the position of international law in the EU and its Member States. To the extent that it is binding upon the EU institutions, international law becomes part of the EU legal order and is therefore 'europeanised'. Thus, it follows that the application and interpretation of such international norms by EU Member States are no longer solely a matter for the constitutional order of the latter, but in the very first place for EU law, notably with a view to its uniform application and interpretation.[8] Thus, we see the emergence of a complicated triangular relationship between international law, EU law and domestic law. International law continues to bind Member States directly. However, the EU is increasingly placed in between international law and domestic law.[9]

The contributions to the book aim to illuminate critical questions pertaining to this triangular relationship. Such questions include: are we dealing with the emergence of a distinct European system of public international law? To what extent do EU Member States recognise the effect of this 'europeanisation' of international law? What is the specific role of the ECJ with respect to the application and interpretation of 'europeanised' international law? And: what are the consequences of 'europeanisation' for the unity and coherence of public international law?

First, this introductory chapter will give an indication of the broad context in which the narrower concept of 'europeanisation' as defined above, is situated. It will explain the phenomenon of 'europeanisation' in general (section 2) and its application to international law (section 3). Thereafter it provides a roadmap of the different contributions (section 4).

---

[8] See again ECJ, Case 104/81 *Kupferberg* [1982], *supra* n. 7, para. 15: 'It follows from the Community nature of such provisions that their effect in the Community may not be allowed to vary according to whether their application is in practice the responsibility of the Community institutions or of the Member States and, in the latter case, according to the effects in the internal legal order of each Member State which the law of that State assigns to international agreements concluded by it. Therefore it is for the Court, within the framework of its jurisdiction in interpreting the provisions of agreements, to ensure their uniform application throughout the Community.'

[9] See for (rare) general discussions of this phenomenon: D. Bethlehem, 'International Law, EC Law, National Law: Three Systems in Search of a Framework', in M. Koskeniemmi (ed.), *International Law Aspects of the European Union* (The Hague, Kluwer Law International 1998) pp. 169-196; N. Lavranos, *Decisions of International Organizations in the European and Domestic Legal Orders of Selected EU Member States* (Groningen, European Law Publishing 2004) pp. 3-10.

2. The phenomenon of 'Europeanisation'

Whether one agrees or not with the thesis that modern international law is to a large extent a European invention,[10] it remains a fact that European States have had a dominant influence on the development of international law for many centuries in contemporary history.[11] Especially since World War II, this influence has been reduced to a considerable extent. The emergence of new global powers outside Europe, the weakening of European States due to two successive devastating world wars, the dissolution of colonial empires and the emergence of nearly 100 new States, in general developing countries in the southern hemisphere, have profoundly impregnated the course of the evolution of international law.

Over the last decades, however, a new specific European contribution to international law has emerged. The most fundamental development in this respect is the breathtaking pace and depth of the European integration process since the 1950s. The coming into being of the European Communities (first the European Coal and Steel Community in 1952, later the European Economic Community and European Atomic Energy Community in 1958), each of them international organisations with legal personality and important internal *and* external powers, has given rise to the development of a new level of law-making and governance: European Community law and policy. The uniqueness of the 'Community method' of law-making and law enforcement has been stressed time and again. There is the well-known pivotal position and role of the European Commission, a supranational institution with both the exclusive right to table legislative proposals, the power to enforce existing laws *vis-à-vis* Member States before the ECJ and considerable powers in socio-economic policy areas stretching from competition policy to external trade policy. But there is also the 'Luxembourg factor': the ECJ – now together

---

[10] See, *inter alia*, M. Koskenniemi, 'International Law in Europe: between Tradition and Renewal', 16 *EJIL* (2005) pp. 113-124. As to the development of international law in the course of the 19th century, see the nuanced view of W.G. Grewe, *The Epochs of International Law* (Berlin-New York, De Gruyter 2000) at p. 466: '(…) the European law of nations gradually grew into a global legal order, the members of which were, it is true, only the "civilised nations". This development cannot be interpreted as a "regionalisation" or "Europeanisation". Rather, the dualism of the Christian-European law of nations and the natural law-based universal law of nations dissolved into a single, universal legal system, albeit one which had been deprived of its natural law foundation by the rise of positivism.' Compare, in very strong terms, A. Orakhelashvili, 'The Idea of European International Law', 17 *EJIL* (2006) p. 315, at p. 347, who rejects the idea that international law is a European tradition, holding that it 'has from the outset been a racist idea that misrepresented the real character of international law', that 'European international law is an ideology based not on evidence, but on prejudice and chauvinism generated from a sense of racial, cultural and religious superiority over those who are different' and that 'international legal reasoning should be rid of the clichés of European international law and the related implications of the continuous tradition of Eurokitsch based on the misinterpretation of legal institutions right up to the end of the 20th century.'

[11] See as to the '*jus publicum europaeum*' and its foundering, C. Schmitt, *The* Nomos *of the Earth in the International Law of the Jus Publicum Europaeum* (New York, Telos 2003); S. Laghmani, *Histoire du droit des gens du* jus gentium *impérial au jus publicum europaeum* (Paris, Pedone 2003), at p. 186 even states explicitly: 'Le droit international classique aura pour mission d'organiser l'hégémonie multiforme qu'exerçaient l'Europe et les Etats d'origine européenne sur le reste du monde.'

with the European Court of First Instance – has played and still plays a pivotal role in the interpretation and further development of EC law. Basic principles and doctrines, such as the supremacy of EC law over conflicting national laws of Member States, direct effect and State responsibility *vis-à-vis* individuals for failure to implement EC law, have been elaborated by the ECJ and are nowadays the cornerstones of a fully-fledged legal order which, unlike classical international law, is deeply rooted in the national legal systems of EU Member States.[12]

The expansion of EC law into an ever greater variety of policy and legal areas, which has continued unabatedly since the Maastricht Treaty created the European Union in 1993 (of which the Communities continued as the 'first pillar' until the Lisbon Treaty, which formally abolishes the pillar structure and integrates the EC into the EU[13]), and the continuing consolidation and further development of this legal order through a very intense law-making practice and case-law, has lead to paradigmatic changes in the European legal and political arena. National law and policy-making have become so much under the influence of EU law in multiple areas that one can say they have become 'europeanised'. These areas stretch from company and financial to environmental law and, increasingly, to a great diversity of legal areas which were shielded for a long time from EU influence, such as private,[14]

---

[12] Cf. already ECJ, Case 26/62 *Van Gend & Loos* [1963] ECR 1, where the ECJ stressed that 'the Community constitutes a new legal order of international law for the benefit of which the States have limited their sovereign rights, albeit within limited fields, and the subjects of which comprise not only Member States but also their nationals', and ECJ, Case 6/64 *Costa* v. *ENEL* [1964] ECR 585: 'By contrast with ordinary international treaties, the EEC Treaty has created its own legal system which, on the entry into force of the Treaty, became an integral part of the legal systems of the Member States and which their courts are bound to apply. By creating a Community of unlimited duration, having its own institutions, its own personality, its own legal capacity and capacity of representation on the international plane and, more particularly, real powers stemming from a limitation of sovereignty or a transfer of powers from the States to the Community, the Member States have limited their sovereign rights, albeit within limited fields, and have thus created a body of law which binds both their nationals and themselves.' See also, forcefully, ECJ, Opinion 1/91, *European Economic Area* [1991] I-6079: '[T]he EEC Treaty, albeit concluded in the form of an international agreement, none the less constitutes the constitutional charter of a Community based on the rule of law. The Community treaties established a new legal order for the benefit of which the States have limited their sovereign rights and the subjects of which comprise not only Member States but also their nationals. The essential characteristics of the Community legal order which has thus been established are in particular its primacy over the law of the Member States and the direct effect of a whole series of provisions.' More recently, see ECJ, Case C-15/00 *Commission* v. *European Investment Bank* [2003] ECR I-7281, para. 75: '[T]he European Community is based on the rule of law, inasmuch as neither its Member States nor its institutions can avoid a review of the question whether the measures adopted by them are in conformity with the basic constitutional charter, the EC Treaty, which established a complete system of legal remedies and procedures designed to permit the Court of Justice to review the legality of measures adopted by the institutions'.

[13] See new Art. 1, third para. *in fine*, TEU: 'The Union shall replace and succeed the European Community'.

[14] See, e.g., R. Zimmermann, 'Comparative Law and the Europeanization of Private Law', in *The Oxford Handbook of Comparative Law* (Oxford, Oxford University Press 2006) pp. 539-578; P. Nebbia, 'Law as Tradition and the Europeanization of Contract Law: a Case Study', 23 *Yearbook of European Law* (2004) pp. 363-382; C. Joerges, 'The Challenges of Europeanization in the Realm of Private Law: a Plea for a New Legal Discipline', 14 *Duke Journal of Comparative & International Law* (2004)

administrative and constitutional,[15] criminal and asylum law.[16] Increasingly, the term 'europeanisation' has indeed been used to reflect this impact of EU law on domestic law.[17]

The phenomenon, and the concept, of 'europeanisation' is not limited to law exclusively. A variety of definitions of 'europeanisation' circulate in the social science literature. Let us briefly explore them in order to see what legal scholarship can learn from this. The term 'europeanisation' is referred to in different contexts, but is invariably seen as a process: a historical process, a cultural process, a process of institutional adaptation, and the adaptation of policy and policy processes.[18] The last two categories are especially relevant from the perspective of public international law. 'Europeanisation' as institutional adaptation refers to 'domestic adaptation to the pressures emanating directly or indirectly from EU membership.'[19] Such institutional adaptation is the consequence of another form of 'europeanisation', namely 'the emergence and the development at the European level of distinct structures of governance.'[20] As adaptation of policy and policy processes, 'europeanisation' has different sub-connotations. First, it is used to refer to the constraints on domestic policy posed by EU law. Second, it refers to the reorientation of the direction and shape of national politics and policy-making through EU political and economic dynamics[21] (whereby the EU becomes an increasingly important point of political reference for the actors at the level of the Member States[22]). Finally, it refers to the recognition of domestic inputs into EU policy-making, and to the increasing coordination at EU level of national policies, such as foreign policy.

---

pp. 149-196; W. Pintens, 'Europeanisation of Family Law', in K. Boele-Woelki (eds.), *Perspectives for the Unification and Harmonisation of Family Law in Europe* (Antwerp, Intersentia 2003) pp. 3-33.

[15] See recently J.H. Jans, R. de Lange, S. Prechal and R.J.G.M. Widdershoven, *Europeanisation of Public Law* (Groningen, Europa Law Publishing 2007); J. Ziller, M. Marquis and H. Taoufiqi (eds.), *L'europeanisation des droits constitutionnels à la lumière de la Constitution pour l'Europe* (Paris, L'Harmattan 2006).

[16] See, e.g., E. Guild, 'The Europeanisation of Europe's Asylum Policy', 18 *International Journal of Refugee Law* (2006) pp. 630-651; J. van Selm, 'The Europeanization of Refugee Policy' and N. Ghanea, 'Europeanization of Citizenthip and Asylum Policy: a Case Study of the U.K.', in *New Regionalism and Asylum Seekers: Challenges Ahead* (New York, Berghahn 2007) pp. 79-109 and pp. 111-135 respectively; S. Lavenex, 'The Europeanization of Refugee Policies: Normative Challenges and Institutional Legacies', 39 *Journal of Common Market Studies* (2001) pp. 851-874.

[17] See the references in nn. 14-16 *supra*.

[18] See K. Featherstone, 'Introduction: In the Name of 'Europe'', in K. Featherstone and C.M. Radaelli (eds.), *The Politics of Europeanization* (Oxford, Oxford University Press 2003) p. 3, at pp. 5-12.

[19] K. Featherstone, *supra* n. 18, at p. 7.

[20] T. Risse, M.G. Cowles and J.A. Caporaso, 'Europeanization and Domestic Change: Introduction', in M.G. Cowles, J.A. Caporaso and T. Risse (eds.), *Transforming Europe: Europeanization and Domestic Change* (Cornell University Press, 2001) p. 1, at p. 3.

[21] Cf. the definition of R. Ladrech, 'The Europeanization of Domestic Politics and Institutions: The Case of France', 32 *Journal of Common Market Studies* (1994) p. 69.

[22] See K. Hanf and B. Soetendorp, *Adapting to European Integration: Small States and the European Union* (Longman, 1998) p. 1.

3. 'EUROPEANISATION' AND INTERNATIONAL LAW

How does this reflect on the relationship between EU and international law? The aforementioned social science approaches can help us in trying to identify the various types of 'europeanisation'. A first type of 'europeanisation' concerns the influence of the EU on international law. One could argue that today's development of international law is 'europeanised' in the sense that EU political dynamics, especially the EU's external policies, attempt to increase their influence on the shaping of international law and the laws and policies of international organisations more and more. There is an increasing EU 'international law practice' in this sense.[23] Furthermore, a growing body of political scientific research deals with the role of the EU as a 'normative power'[24] in exporting some of its normative preferences to other countries, especially, but not uniquely, those linked to it in the context of the European Economic Area, the Neighbourhood Policy and association agreements,[25] regional and even global multilateral organisations and regimes.[26] On the other hand, a certain measure of 'europeanisation' may follow in a much more indirect, and not necessarily sought-after, manner from the fact that EU law in specific policy-making fields is becoming quite influential as a model for a number of countries. A side-effect of such countries adopting bits and pieces of EU law in their own legal

[23] See, *inter alia*, J. Wouters, F. Hoffmeister and T. Ruys (eds.), *The United Nations and the European Union: An Ever Stronger Partnership* (The Hague, T.M.C. Asser Press 2006); F. Hoffmeister, 'Outsider or Frontrunner? Recent Developments under International and European Law on the Status of the European Union in International Organizations and Treaty Bodies', 44 *CML Rev.* (2007) pp. 41-68; F. Hoffmeister, 'The Contribution of EU Practice to International Law', forthcoming in *Proceedings of the Academy of European Law* (2008); J. Wouters and R.A. Wessel, 'The Phenomenon of Multilevel Regulation: Interactions between Global, EU and National Regulatory Spheres', 4 *International Organizations Law Review* (2007) pp. 169-201; J. Wouters, R. Wessel and A. Follesdal (eds.), *Multilevel Regulation and the EU. The Interplay between Global, European and National Normative Processes* (Leiden-Boston, Martinus Nijhoff Publishers 2008).

[24] See generally, *inter alia*, T. Diez, 'Constructing the Self and Changing Others: Reconsidering "Normative Power Europe"', 33 *Millenium: Journal of International Studies* (2005), pp. 613-636; S. Lucarelli and I. Manners, *Values and Principles in European Union Foreign Policy* (London, Routledge 2006); I. Manners, 'Normative Power Europe: A Contradiction in Terms?' 40 *Journal of Common Market Studies* (2002), pp. 235-258; Id., 'Normative Power Europe Reconsidered: Beyond the Crossroads', 13 *Journal of European Public Policy* (2006), pp. 182-199; M. Pace, 'The Construction of EU Normative Power', 45 *Journal of Common Market Studies* (2007), pp. 1041-1064; R. Youngs, 'Normative Dynamics and Strategic Interests in the EU's External Identity', 42 *Journal of Common Market Studies* (2004), pp. 415-435. For strong critiques, see, *inter alia*, M. Merlingen, 'Everything is Dangerous: A Critique of 'Normative Power Europe'', 38 *Security Dialogue* (2007), pp. 405-453; H. Sjursen, 'The EU as a Normative Power: How Can This Be?', 13 *Journal of European Public Policy* (2006), pp. 235-351.

[25] See, *inter alia*, S. Gstohl, 'Political Dimensions of an Externalization of the EU's Internal Market', *EU Diplomacy Papers 3/2007* (2007); S. Panebianco and R. Rossi, 'EU Attempts to Export Norms of Good Governance to the Mediterranean and Western Balkan Countries', *Jean Monnet Working Papers in Comparative and International Politics* (October 2004), JMWP n° 53.

[26] See, as applied to the setting up of the International Criminal Court and the elaboration and implementation of the Kyoto Protocol, S. Scheipers and D. Sicurelli, 'Normative Power Europe: A Credible Utopia?', 45 *Journal of Common Market Studies* (2007), pp. 435-457.

systems may well be that in the process of international standard-setting, the EU norm becomes a kind of preferred model *de facto*. These various processes explain why in the eyes of some a phenomenon of European 'regulatory imperialism'[27] is on the rise, whereas in the view of others much of this has to do with 'unintended consequences of European power'.[28]

A second form of 'europeanisation' is that which constitutes the main theme of this book, namely the distinct qualities and features that international law acquires once it enters the domain of the EU. As indicated above, as bits and pieces of public international law become part of the sphere of competence of the EU, they become part of the EU legal order. This is even true in instances where the EC/EU is not a party to a treaty as such. For example, although the European Community was not a party to the GATT 1947, it effectively assumed the powers of EU Member States due to its exclusive competences in the area of common commercial policy (Article 133 TEC) and hence became bound by GATT 1947.[29] At the same time the ECJ made abundantly clear that the question of possible invocability and direct effect of GATT was to be addressed on the Court's own terms, i.e., based on its own analysis of the nature and scope of GATT obligations and on its own doctrine of direct effect.[30] In such cases, substance and procedure of public international law as it applies within the EU are influenced and transformed by EU law. One may argue that public international law is 'europeanised' to this extent, and becomes a system that is distinguishable from general international law.

Increasingly, this development also seems to have an impact on the status of public international law within the national legal orders of the EU's Member States. Normally, the constitutional law of each State determines the implementation of international obligations and the status and effect of such obligations on the national law level. However, for EU Member States, this 'classical' dual legal relationship *international law / national law*, is gradually becoming replaced by a new triangular relationship, *international law / EU law / national law*. The 'europeani-

---

[27] See the editorial 'Regulatory Imperialism', *Wall Street Journal* 25 October 2007, citing the Microsoft Affair, the ban on chlorine-rinsed poultry, the Reach legislation on chemical products, the plan to tax airline companies as part of EU climate change policy.

[28] See Z. Laidi, 'The Unintended Consequences of European Power' <http://www.portedeurope.org/spip.php?article3563> (last visited on 1 April 2008).

[29] See, *inter alia*, ECJ, Joined Cases 21-24/72 *International Fruit Company* [1972] ECR 1219, para. 18, where reference is made to the fact that 'the Community has assumed the powers previously exercised by Member States in the area governed by the General Agreement'; ECJ, Joined Cases 267/81, 268/81 and 269/81 *Societa Petrolifera Italiana and Michelin Italiana* [1983] ECR 801, para. 17.

[30] It is interesting to recall the two defining considerations of the ECJ from the *International Fruit* case: 'Before the incompatibility of a Community measure with a provision of international law can affect the validity of that measure, the Community must first of all be bound by that provision' (para. 7; this question was answered affirmatively later in the judgment); 'Before invalidity can be relied upon before a national court, that provision of international law must also be capable of conferring rights on citizens of the Community which they can invoke before the courts' (para. 8; this question was answered negatively).

sation' of international law means that it is EU law that determines how international law is to be applied in the EU Member States. [31]

This also means that the ECJ typically determines the status and direct effect of 'europeanised' international instruments, from treaties to decisions adopted by international organisations and bodies.[32] As far as status is concerned, a corollary of being part of Community law means that there will in any event be primacy over conflicting provisions of national law, irrespective of the position of these provisions in the national legal system,[33] and that even in the hierarchy of sources in the Community legal system proper, there will be primacy over instruments of secondary Community law.[34] Furthermore, national courts and authorities will be under EU law obligation to interpret provisions of national law in conformity with such international instruments or norms.[35] Apart from this obligation of consistent interpretation of national provisions in light of EC law, the ECJ has also recognised the obligation to interpret EC law itself in conformity with such international law instruments since 'the European Community must respect international law in the exercise of its powers.'[36] The fact that in the hierarchy of norms, international instruments and norms occupy an intermediate position, i.e., in between primary and secondary EU law, also implies that such international instruments and norms can be used as part of the ECJ's and/or the Court of First Instance's control of the validity of EU norms, either as part of a direct challenge based on Article 230 TEC, or as part of a validity check through the preliminary procedure of Article 234 TEC. Direct effect is not required for this and the international norm may be both

[31] N. Lavranos, *supra* n. 9, pp. 3-10.

[32] See, e.g., decisions of the Association Council in the context of the EC-Turkey Association Agreement: ECJ, Case C-192/89 *Sevince* [1990] ECR I-3461.

[33] See K. Lenaerts and T. Corthaut, 'Of Birds and Hedges: the Role of Primacy in Invoking Norms of EU Law', 31 *EL Rev.* (2006) p. 287, at p. 289, with interesting reflections on the relationship between primacy and direct effect at pp. 289-291. See also J.M. Prinssen, *Doorwerking van Europees recht. De verhouding tussen directe werking, conforme interpretatie en overheidsaansprakelijkheid* (Deventer, Kluwer 2004) at p. 11.

[34] ECJ, Case C-61/94 *Commission* v. *Germany* [1996] ECR I-3989, para. 52. See R. Holdgaard, 'Principles of Reception of International Law in Community Law', 25 *Yearbook of European Law* (2006) p. 263, at pp. 266-267. No such primacy is recognised over instruments of *primary* Community law: see, with arguments, A. Peters, 'The Position of International Law Within the European Community Legal Order', 40 *GYIL* (1997), p. 9, at pp. 38-40; see also I. Cheyne, 'International Agreements and the European Community Legal System', 19 *EL Rev.* (1994), p. 581, at p. 586.

[35] See, *inter alia*, ECJ, Case C-61/94 *Commission* v. *Germany, supra* n. 34, para. 52, where the ECJ holds explicitly that 'the primacy of international agreements concluded by the Community over provisions of secondary Community legislation means that such provisions must, so far as is possible, be interpreted in a manner that is consistent with those agreements'; see also ECJ, Case C-53/96 *Hermès* [1998] ECR I-3603, para. 28 (TRIPS Agreement). See in general terms on the obligation of consistent interpretation in Community law ECJ, Joined Cases C-397/01-403/01 *Pfeiffer* [2004] ECR I-8835, para. 115: 'The requirement for national law to be interpreted in conformity with Community law is inherent in the system of the Treaty, since it permits the national court, for the matters within its jurisdiction, to ensure the full effectiveness of Community law when it determines the dispute before it.'

[36] See ECJ, Case C-286/90 *Poulsen and Diva Navigation* [1992] ECR I-6019, para. 9.

treaty-based[37] or custom-based.[38] In this respect Lenaerts and Corthaut correctly stress:

> 'As long as an obligation can be identified, as long as a behavioral norm for the Community can be derived from an international agreement, this agreement can serve as a norm for reference when the validity of EC law is at stake. As a result the ECJ can also, even in the interest of individuals, assess the validity of Community law in the light of international custom, without having to wonder whether those customary norms create rights which individuals can rely on directly before the courts.'[39]

The 'europeanisation' of international law may also affect the means and methods for the enforcement of international law. The fact that an international instrument or norm forms part of the Community legal order means that the Commission can – at least theoretically – bring infringement proceedings against Member States that are not in compliance with it[40] and, at least theoretically, that individuals could bring damages claims against the Community based on breaches of such international instrument or norm.[41] Finally, it can be submitted that the non-compliance with 'europeanised' international law – whether treaty-based or customary in nature – may imply that Member State authorities can be held responsible under the ECJ's *Francovich* case-law on state liability – provided of course the conditions for such state liability as developed by the ECJ are fulfilled.[42]

The aforementioned corollaries of 'europeanisation' have profound effects, not just in terms of the role of the ECJ in regard to public international law, but also for the reception, interpretation and application of public international law within Europe in general, both at the EU and national level. It is remarkable that these effects seem to have been recognised only to a relatively limited extent in the actual

---

37 See, e.g., ECJ, Case C-377/98 *Netherlands* v. *European Parliament and Council* [2001] ECR I-7079, para. 54, where the Court holds, concerning the Convention on Biological Diversity, that even if it 'contains provisions which do not have direct effect, in the sense that they do not create rights which individuals can rely on directly before the courts, that fact does not preclude review by the courts of compliance with the obligations incumbent on the Community as a party to that agreement'.

38 Case C-162/96 *Racke* [1998] ECR I-3655.

39 K. Lenaerts and T. Corthaut, *supra* n. 33, at p. 298.

40 See, e.g., ECJ, Case C-61/94 *Commission* v. *Germany, supra* n. 34, on Germany's failure to comply with the International Dairy Arrangement; ECJ, Case C-13/00 *Commission* v. *Ireland, supra* n. 4, on Ireland's failure to adhere within the prescribed period to the Berne Convention for the Protection of Literary and Artistic Works.

41 See the chapter by P.J. Kuijper in this volume.

42 See, *inter alia*, ECJ, Joined Cases C-6/90 and C-9/90 *Francovich* [1991] ECR I-5357; Joined Cases C-46/93 and C-48/93 *Brasserie du Pêcheur* [1996] ECR I-1029. For an interesting linkage between the international and EC doctrine of state liability, see ECJ, Case C-224/01 *Köbler* [2003] ECR I-10239, para. 32: 'In international law a State which incurs liability for breach of an international commitment is viewed as a single entity, irrespective of whether the breach which gave rise to the damage is attributable to the legislature, the judiciary or the executive. That principle must apply *a fortiori* in the Community legal order since all State authorities, including the legislature, are bound in performing their tasks to comply with the rules laid down by Community law which directly govern the situation of individuals.'

practice at domestic level.[43] However, it is also true that the processes at hand may have been insufficiently understood and that, at the same time, little research has been done into their actual scope and manifestations. It is against this background that the various contributions to this book study the phenomenon of 'europeanisation' of international law and its consequences.

4. Structure of the book

The ten contributions to this book, all from recognised experts, are structured around two axis. The first part focuses on the **phenomenon of 'europeanisation'**. *Rainer Wahl* provides an opening shot by looking into the complexities of 'europeanisation', which, in his view, goes far beyond the principle of supremacy of EU law and has generated a profound metamorphosis of the legal systems of the Member States, creating an intimate entanglement between national and EU law. *Bruno de Witte* poses the question of 'europeanisation' of international law in different terms: he investigates whether a European system of public international law with distinctive features exists, differentiating between the way in which international law develops and is practiced in EU Member States and the rest of the world. His search for an answer involves the doctrine of subjects of international law. Based on the extensive treaty practice of the EC and, increasingly, the EU, he argues that EU Member States are no longer sovereign States to the same extent as other States in the world: the EU *and* its Member States have become 'strange subjects' of international law together that do not match classical textbook categories.

The following three contributions deal with the position of international law in EU law, paying attention to the case-law of the ECJ. *Christian Tietje*, in outlining the legal framework governing the EC's treaty-making activity, tackles three complex issues: (i) the relationship between the law of the World Trade Organization (WTO) and EU law and the haziness of the case-law of the ECJ in this respect, (ii) mixed agreements, i.e., agreements to which both the EC and (at least some) EU Member States are a party and the problems of responsibility under international law; and (iii) briefly, the status of international instruments by which the EC is not bound in the ECJ's case-law.

ECJ judge *Allan Rosas,* for his part, situates international law norms, both of treaty and customary nature, amidst the sources of Community law while pointing to the specificities of the EU judicial system, the ECJ's methods of interpretation and the latter's main task to interpret and apply 'internal' primary and secondary EU law. Judge Rosas also demonstrates how the ECJ has developed a fairly open tradition of deference to the case-law of international courts and tribunals, notably the European Court of Human Rights and the International Court of Justice. In his vision, the ECJ should certainly contribute to both the observance and the development of international law, although in his view developing international law is primarily a task for the political bodies of the EU.

[43] N. Lavranos, *supra* n. 9.

Finally, *Pieter Jan Kuijper* thoroughly analyses the position of customary international law, decisions of international organisations (both organisations created by the EC and others) and techniques – other than direct effect – for ensuring respect for international rules in EU law. He concludes that the ECJ's case-law is at present extraordinarily open to customary international law and decisions of international organisations, without dodging the delicate issues of democratic legitimisation of the reception of these rules within the EU legal system.

The contributions in the second part of the book address the **consequences of 'europeanisation' for domestic law, international law and judicial protection in the EU**. *Johan Callewaert* analyses whether the 'europeanisation' of international law also affects the European Convention on Human Rights. He demonstrates that no unilateral 'europeanisation' of the Convention exists. Instead, through the willingness of both the ECJ and the European Court of Human Rights to take each other's respective case-law into account, a bilateral interplay between EU and Convention law exists. This results in a twofold process of 'conventionisation' of EU law and 'unionisation' of Convention law, though with different timings and intensities. He expresses the hope that in the end these processes may result in a truly harmonious overall architecture deserving to be called a 'europeanisation' of fundamental rights.

The two following contributions specifically study the status of 'europeanised' international law in specific domestic legal systems in Europe, with the interesting variation that not all European jurisdictions examined are EU Member States.

Astrid Epiney and Bernhard Hofstötter in collaboration with Markus Wyssling analyse the status of such law in Austria, Switzerland and Liechtenstein. The 'europeanisation' of international law appears to have reached different stages in these three countries, which is partly due to their different degree of integration with the EU: the first is an EU Member State since 1995, the second is only linked to the EU legal system through bilateral agreements, and the third is part of the European Economic Area with EU and (most) EFTA Member States. Nevertheless, the influence of EU law on international agreements is tangible in all these States. The 'pressure' of the common market and the far-reaching development of Community law make it impossible for non-EU Member States to conclude treaties disregarding the legal dynamics of the EU legal order.

For Hungary, which only joined the EU in 2004, the contribution of *Nóra Chronowski and Tímea Drinóczi* points to the learning curve of the domestic courts in terms of the triangular relationship between international law, EU law and national law, in a constitutional setting with a dualist tradition, as far as international law is concerned, and with constitutional provisions dealing with the status of EU and international law without fully clarifying it however.

Nikolaos Lavranos makes a case-study of yet another example of 'europeanisation' of international law, namely the implementation of UN Security Council sanctions through EU law. His timely contribution analyses the implications of the European Court of First Instance rulings in the *Yusuf/Kadi* cases and the *Bosphorus* judgment of the European Court of Human Rights for the availability of judicial review at the European level for private parties affected by UN sanctions. Last but not least, *Joost Pauwelyn* compares European and American attitudes to international law while bearing in mind the perceived threats to the unity of international law. He takes the view that the definition and pursuit of a European agenda or approach to international law does not threaten the unity of international law. Pauwelyn argues that Europe must offer its own, positive agenda on how to view and refine the international system, rather than negatively attacking the way other nations approach international law.

Part I
THE PHENOMENON OF EUROPEANISATION

Chapter 2
EUROPEANISATION BEYOND SUPREMACY

Rainer Wahl*

1. THE COMPLEXITY OF EUROPEANISATION AS A FUNDAMENTAL PROCESS

Since 1958 the most momentous developments within the legal systems of (at least) the western EU Member States have resulted from their membership in the European (Economic) Community, and nowadays in the European Union (EU).[1] Of course, each Member remains a State. However, in many respects it is more appropriate to characterise them as *Member States*. Their legal systems are no longer autonomous. Rather, the law in an EU Member State is pluralistic. The law effective in those States is not only national law but also a highly composite law fed by various sources.[2] This basic condition defines the starting position for nearly every area of law: no area of national law is left untouched.[3] Instead, it is now the norm that every field of law has been 'europeanised' in the sense that there exists a predominant Community law and a number of indirect ways of interference.[4]

---

* Dr. jur. (Heidelberg, Germany), Professor of Public and Administrative Law, Administrative Sciences and Constitutional History, Director of the Institute for Public Law, Faculty of Law, Albert-Ludwigs-Universität Freiburg, Germany. In remembrance of my colleague Konrad Hesse. I am particularly indebted to Claus Binder for the translation and helpful comments.

[1] See generally, on the character of nation States being Member States in the European Union, Ingolf Pernice, in Josef Isensee and Paul Kirchhof (eds.), *Handbuch des Staatsrechts*, Vol. VIII (Heidelberg, C. F. Müller Verlag 1995), para. 191 Rn. 20 et seq.

[2] See generally Jürgen Schwarze and Meinhard Hilf, *Europäisches Verwaltungsrecht im Werden* (Baden-Baden, Nomos Verlagsgesellschaft 1982); Jürgen Schwarze, *Europäisches Verwaltungsrecht*, 2nd edn. (Baden-Baden, Nomos Verlagsgesellschaft 2005) (1st edn. in two volumes, 1988).

[3] Such a statement contrasts sharply with the overall assessments up to the 1960s. Compare it with Ulrich Scheuner's well-known dictum on the German legal system: 'Administrative law is one of those legal subject matters, which is – compared to others – coined by the idiosyncrasies of a nation and a state in the most distinctive way. That is why its interconnections to other legal systems are relatively rare.' Ulrich Scheuner, 'Der Einfluss des französischen Verwaltungsrechts auf die deutsche Rechtsentwicklung', 15 *Die öffentliche Verwaltung (DÖV)* (1963), p. 714 et seq., at p. 714. See also Thomas von Danwitz, *Verwaltungsrechtliches System und europäische Integration* (Tübingen, Mohr Siebeck 1996), at p. 1. Jürgen Schwarze and Meinhard Hilf published pioneering works on this topic in the early 1980s (see *supra* n. 2).

[4] The literature on europeanisation as a fundamental process cannot be overlooked any longer. For some German references see, e.g., Rainer Wahl, 'Die zweite Phase des Öffentlichen Rechts', 38 *Der Staat* (1999) p. 495 et seq. and Rainer Wahl, 'Zwei Phasen des Öffentlichen Rechts', in Rainer Wahl,

J. Wouters, P.A. Nollkaemper, E. de Wet (eds.), The Europeanisation of International Law

These facts are well-known, however, they are usually interpreted quite narrowly, by focusing only on the supremacy of Community law. Indeed, this well-established concept is an important component of the process called europeanisation. Nevertheless, europeanisation is much more fundamental.

A blind spot of those who discuss matters of europeanisation is the international dimension. Normally, it is assumed that the European institutions build European law from scratch, influenced by legal conceptions that are realised within the Member States, as the individuals within the EU institutions themselves have national backgrounds. Nevertheless, international law quite often conceals itself behind European law. That is, the EU is itself quite often either bound by international agreements, and thereby passes those obligations on to its Member States, or is influenced by trends or discussions within the international realm. By passing on obligations or other matters of international law to its Member States, the international dimension is translated into a European version with its own rules. As a matter of quality, soft rules of international law become strict European law (and thereby acquire supremacy).

Another blind spot which stems from the focus on supremacy, centers around the interest on change within national legal systems, thereby distracting from the fact that the EU has a life of its own. The EU not only consists of an enormous body of legal rules directed towards EU Member States. Instead, the EU has developed into a legal system with its own autonomous methodology, conceptualisations, case-law techniques, etc.

These two examples demonstrate that europeanisation is a most complex process. In short, European law is fed by various sources, one source being the law 'above' the EU, i.e., international law. Further, European law is not only 'above' national law but amounts to its own legal entity with independent existence. Out of the wealth of possible issues that could be discussed under the topic of europeanisation this chapter will delve into these aforementioned issues in the following manner: it will start with some words on the international dimension (section 2). The chapter's main focus, however, will be on the momentum that has been gathered by the EU within the past decades (sections 3-7). En route, this chapter will talk about EU Member States as such, however, examples from Germany will be drawn upon from time to time when those examples can be generalised.[5]

Verfassungsstaat – Europäisierung – Internationalisierung (Frankfurt am Main, Suhrkamp Verlags 2003) p. 411 et seq.; Friedrich Schoch, 'Die Europäisierung des Verwaltungsprozessrechts', in *Festgabe 50 Jahre Bundesverwaltungsgericht* (Cologne, Carl Heymanns Verlag 2003) p. 507 et seq.; Th. von Danwitz, *supra* n. 3; Stefan Kadelbach, *Allgemeines Verwaltungsrecht unter europäischem Einfluss* (Tübingen, Mohr Siebeck 1999).

[5] Germany serves as quite a good example as it has over 60 years of experience with federalism, constitutionalism and supremacy in national context.

2. INTERNATIONAL LAW – EUROPEAN LAW – NATIONAL LAW: A THREE LAYER CAKE

International law paves its way into European and national law of EU Member States through multiple means.

One of the most important channels of interference is the EU's competence to enter into international agreements. Clearly, this is the case regarding all of the EU's external actions, especially when it comes to the terms of common commercial policy (cf. Article 131 et seq. TEC). The Community itself is bound by its international commitments. Additionally, it regularly passes these commitments on to its Member States by adopting regulations or directives. Henceforth, those commitments are not just regulated by soft rules of international law (which is still weak in terms of enforcement), but by hard and effective European norms. Such a transformation is, at least, important for all those EU Member States which follow the dualist model. But it also makes a difference for those who have a monist conception. European external actions become effective in the internal realm as soon as they are translated into Community legislation, with all the consequences of direct effect and supremacy. In the end, this process inevitably has a very strong impact on implementing international agreements.

Most notably, such a statement is true when EU Member States are themselves party to an international agreement alongside to the Community, e.g., in the case of the Aarhus Convention.[6] When ratifying such an international agreement, signatories usually have some kind of leeway. In most cases, international agreements do not provide for effective enforcement mechanisms, except perhaps for convention meetings where the parties might adopt new decisions. In this way every party is able to bypass compliance and international law-making therefore always bears the risk of being insufficient compared to national law-making. This scene changes as soon as the EU gets into designing Community legislation itself, to ratify its own commitments. By doing so, the EU is the actor who decides how and when to comply with the international agreement and, more importantly, blocks Member States' own self-dominated compliance activities.[7] Such a change in compliance regimes – i.e., from then on, Member States are bound directly (by regulations) or indirectly (by directives) with all the power of European law – is just one feature characteristic of the ongoing process called europeanisation.

[6] UNECE Convention on Access to Information, Public Participation in Decision-Making and Access to Justice in Environmental Matters, adopted on 25 June 1998.

[7] In the case of the Aarhus Convention the European Community set the pace and standard for compliance through own law-making activity: cf. Directive 2003/4/EC on public access to environmental information of 28 January 2003, Directive 2003/35/EC providing for public participation in respect of drawing up of certain plans relating to the environment of 26 May 2003, and Directive 2001/42/EC on the assessment of certain plans and programs on the environment of 27 June 2001; see also proposal for a directive on access to justice in environmental matters, (COM (2003) 624 final), and Regulation (EC) No. 1376/2006 on the application of the provisions of the Aarhus Convention on access to information, public participation in decision-making and access to justice in environmental matters to Community institutions and bodies.

We need to consider a second aspect within the international dimension: the rapid expansion of the body of international law. Such an expansion evolved up to the formation of distinct legal regimes like the global trading system formed by the WTO, the Agreement on Trade Related Aspects of Intellectual Property Rights (TRIPS), or the United Nations Framework Convention on Climate change with its Kyoto Protocol, etc. These regimes are part of a system of multi-level-governance.[8] For our purposes we talk about a three-level-system or, better, a three layer cake. For example, you will find trade related aspects of law on three levels: on the international level within the WTO, on the European level within the European Community, and on the national level within the legal system of every Member State. The law on each level is not separate but interwoven with the others and sticks to the others like the layers within a cake.

There are numerous examples fitting within the three-layer cake analogy. Telecommunications law, food and drug law, the law of intellectual property, and the laws to protect cultural assets are just some.[9] The problems, unique features, rules, and reciprocities within this three-layer-model should be the subject of ongoing research. The reciprocal relationship between the first (international) and the third (national, local) layer is particularly important. Clearly, it must be the first layer that sets definitions and standards, otherwise, local or national institutions are free to a have a life of their own. Thus, the first layer often not only generates general conditions or the framework (like a constitution), but provides detailed and packed information for specific problems or definitions. The Food and Agriculture Organization (FAO) and WTO Codex Alimentarius Commission that develop detailed international food standards are a good example of this phenomenon.

3. The transformation of an autonomous legal system to the legal system of an EU Member State

Let me switch from the international, external perspective, to a specific internal perspective of europeanisation. From an internal perspective, europeanisation encompasses not only individual fields of law but the legal system as a whole.[10] Europeanisation leads to a comprehensive encounter between different legal systems. This encounter takes place between Community law and German law directly and indirectly between the legal systems of the different Member States themselves. The fundamental process seizes not only the law 'in the books' but all dimensions

---

[8] The labels for this complex phenomenon are as manifold as the literature about it. The latter became unmanageable during the past decade.

[9] On the latter cf. Kerstin Odendahl, *Kulturgüterschutz – Entwicklung, Struktur und Dogmatik eines ebenenübergreifenden Normensystems* (Tübingen, Mohr Siebeck 2005).

[10] You will find an own genre of literature of the kind 'europeanisation of *xyz* law' in every legal system in Europe. As such this literature cannot be overlooked either. I, myself, have contributed to that genre by several articles; see, e.g., Rainer Wahl, 'Das deutsche Genehmigungs- und Umweltrecht unter Anpassungsdruck', in Klaus-Peter Dolde and Gesellschaft für Umweltrecht (eds.), *Umweltrecht im Wandel* (Berlin, Erich Schmidt Verlag 2001) p. 237 et seq.

of the law. Through the process of europeanisation a dialogue is initiated between the legal system as a whole, and the legal systems of the Community and of the other Member States. The encounter of two legal systems – an unknown concept so far – has a quality of its own. Like the law of the other EU Member States German law has entered a new – in my view, a second[11] – phase of development in the second half of the 20th century. During this period, Community law has not only increased objectively – in terms of both quality and quantity – but has also been perceived as being of utmost importance and has, therefore, increased in subjective terms. It is Community law's increasing pluralism that now characterises German law. Therefore, it is decisive for the new conception of German law that there is a regular and pervasive second actor, which could soon develop to be the first. I am certain that this description is true for the other EU Member States as well, despite the differences in length or number of phases of development.

To understand europeanisation as a fundamental process it is important to recall its different dimensions. One dimension, the supremacy of Community law, is crucial. We should recall, however, that it is not the only one. Certainly, supremacy demands utmost attention,[12] and this is no accident: the doctrine of supremacy of Community law itself is at the centre of interest to the European Court of Justice. Indeed, the Court developed the concept itself, a concept not agreed upon in the Treaty of Rome by the Member States.[13] With this doctrine the Court provided itself extensive competences and, so to speak, helped itself to power, thereby establishing its own impact. It is the doctrine of supremacy which is the cornerstone of the Court's judicial activism and the basis for the extensive change within the institutions of the European Community.

Despite the dominance of the Court's case-law on supremacy within the discourse on europeanisation, the consequences of EU membership for the Member States and their legal systems are much more complex. Membership itself provokes a comprehensive encounter between different legal systems. Such an encounter leads to manifold voluntary reception and learning processes. That is why membership is not only fed by concepts and ideas of Community law but also by eclectically chosen concepts derived from the Member States' own legal systems. Hence, there are various forces of adaptation beyond the formal concept of supremacy.[14] Those forces have strong impacts on the national legal systems, causing complex

---

[11] R. Wahl 1999, *supra* n. 4.

[12] See generally for the German literature Thomas Oppermann, *Europarecht*, 3rd edn. (Munich, Verlag C. H. Beck 2005) para. 6 IV 1; Bernhard Wegner, in Christian Callies and Mathias Ruffert (eds.), *Kommentar zu EU-Vertrag und EG-Vertrag*, 2nd edn. (Neuwied, Hermann Luchterhand Verlag 2002), Art. 220 EGV Rn. 22 et seq.; Eberhard Grabitz/Meinhard Hilf (eds.), *Das Recht der Europäischen Union* (Munich, Verlag C. H. Beck 2005), Art. 249 EGV Rn. 37 – 51.

[13] Its landmark decision is ECJ, Case 6/64 *Flaminio Costa* v. *ENEL* [1964] ECR English Special Edition 00585.

[14] The term 'adaptation' might be misleading. In case Community law addresses a specific field of law and demands for change, the rest of the law is not affected, at least in a formal sense. However, the implementation into national law leads to a sort of double-track law, which has its after-effects and consequential costs. Because of those implications one or the other national legal system might think of customizing its law at large. It is this what I mean by 'forces of adaptation'.

processes transforming the national legal systems into legal systems of Member States, which are not only deeply connected to Community law but are also deeply and permanently intertwined with each and every transformed national legal system.

In dealing with national legal problems, national legal experts almost surely realise that there are alternatives to their conceptualisations within the EU and within other Member States.[15] Alternatives which are not only theoretically interesting for their national law but which are practically relevant. Legal concepts that are realised within another Member State can have an impact on national legal development simply by virtue of the fact of the close relationship between two countries. If interest groups come across a more advantageous legal situation in another Member State than that which exists in their own state, they will frequently claim corresponding changes to their national law. The close interaction between economy and society generates pressure for legal adaptations on either side.[16]

An unprecedented rapprochement between the supranational law and the legal systems of the Member States is a consequence of the supremacy of Community law. The supreme law has taken control and operates on the present state of positive law within the Member States. From the perspective of German law, this process is a reiteration of the processes which occurred after 1949. In Germany, the intrastate or *internal* supremacy of the Federal Constitution (*Grundgesetz für die Bundesrepublik Deutschland*, 'the Constitution') has developed rapidly and in a distinctive way since it came into effect. This is a characteristic feature of the entire German legal system.[17] Since 1949 the Constitution has taken precedence over all laws: the Constitution and its interpretation have become important and binding measures for the validity of other laws. The supremacy of the Constitution was achieved step-by-step and, as a result, German law as a whole has become 'constitutionalised'. This process of 'constitutionalisation'[18] was a continuous and incremental one. The same is true for the *external* enforcement of Community law within German national law.[19] Both processes were rather tedious and met substantial internal resistance from the subordinate fields of law. Both times it was a struggle

[15] Lawyers who constantly experience that there are alternatives to their own legal concepts change their perspective from an introversive to an external one. This chapter will get into more details on this issue in the paragraph *infra* at n. 33.

[16] See generally for examples R. Wahl 1999, *supra* n. 4, at p. 505 et seq.

[17] Rainer Wahl, 'Der Vorrang der Verfassung', 20 *Der Staat* (1981) p. 485 et seq.; republished in Rainer Wahl, *Verfassungsstaat – Europäisierung – Internationalisierung* (Frankfurt am Main, Suhrkamp Verlag 2003) p. 121 et seq.

[18] See generally Gunnar Folke Schuppert and Christian Bumke, *Die Konsitutionalisierung der Rechtsordnung* (Baden-Baden, Nomos Verlagsgesellschaft 2000); Rainer Wahl, *Herausforderungen und Antworten: Das Öffentliche Recht der letzten fünf Jahrzehnte* (Berlin, Walter de Gruyter 2006) at p. 31 et seq., 35 et seq., and 97 et seq.

[19] Rainer Wahl, 'Erklären staatstheoretische Begriffe die Europäische Union?', 60 *Juristenzeitung (JZ)* (2005) p. 916, at p. 921. In that article I am differentiating between *internal* and *external* aspects of supremacy. *See also* Rainer Wahl, 'Konstitutionalisierung – Leitbegriff oder Allerweltsbegriff', in Carl-Eugen Eberle and Martin Ibler/Dieter Lorenz (eds.), *Festschrift für Winfried Brohm zum 70. Geburtstag* (Munich, Verlag C. H. Beck 2002), p. 191 et seq., at p. 197.

for the supremacy of one layer of law over another. The era that I refer to as the first phase of public law after 1949 was concerned with the supremacy of the Constitution with regard to the laws within Germany. It is the *acquis* of the German legal system that laws are coined by the Constitution.[20] Europeanisation focuses on another, external, supremacy. Furthermore, the supremacy of Community law is comprehensive; on its account all EC law, not only the EC Treaty itself, has supremacy over national law, including the Constitution. In this way, one can regard the supremacy of Community law as a federal process, the essence of which is that the entire law of the larger entity (i.e., the EC) has supremacy over the law of the smaller entities (i.e., the Member States).

4. Two perspectives on europeanisation

If we understand europeanisation as a fundamental process we have to investigate the issue in its full complexity. We cannot take into account the topic of supremacy of single norms or concepts of Community law only, as it is typically done. Separate from the international dimension,[21] we need to broaden the horizon in a twofold way.

First, Community law has long been more than an accumulation of legal norms. In terms of both the quantity and quality of its norms, Community law is a legal system shaped by many factors. These factors include, for example, a specific methodology, the conception of the role of judges and other legal actors, the different types of case-law, and the particular conception of justice. Together with the collection of norms, these factors form a legal system and, above all, a legal culture.

A second expansion is also necessary. If the topic is 'Europe and national law' then the prevalent *vertical* perspective – i.e., the relationship between the EU and, for example, German, French, or English law – is not only of interest. Rather, we have to consider a second *horizontal* perspective: i.e., the relationship of a Member State *vis-à-vis* other Member States. The EU not only constitutes a new legal system, but it also establishes a new relationship between the Member States regulated by laws. In other words, the EU initiates an encounter between the individual national legal systems. The legal systems of the individual Member States are not alien to one another anymore but highly intertwined, directly or indirectly. The elementary configuration within a supranational entity is mirrored by the individual legal systems. In short: the topic 'Europe and national law' centers the attention on the horizontal comparisons of the national systems.

Such a complex investigation necessarily implies that legal academics and practitioners discuss on a national, but also on a European basis. Such a discussion needs to consider the thoughts and appurtenances found within the whole body of European literature, which includes not only the Spanish, French, British, Dutch, Italian or German, but also the Slovenian, Portuguese, Swedish, Cypriot, etc. litera-

[20] R. Wahl 2006, *supra* n. 18, at p. 35 et seq.

[21] See *supra* section 2.

ture. One can imagine that such a challenge must be described as being colossal. In any case, European lawyers have to focus on a wider context than before, which is quite a great task and objective. This book is one piece and my contribution to this book is an even smaller piece of the jigsaw puzzle of such an objective. In my contribution I accept this challenge, however, I see my main task in describing this grand mission.[22]

5. Factors and dimensions of the encounter of Member States

5.1 The vertical dimension: the point of origin

The impact of EC law on national law has been one of the major playgrounds for academia and legal practice the last couple of decades. Within this ongoing discussion the concept of supremacy of Community law, both of primary and secondary EC norms, was and still is one of the major aspects of the vertical dimension. Since its creation by the European Court of Justice in 1962[23] the supremacy principle has ensured that national law becomes influenced by Community law, not all at once, but step-by step. Supremacy made its initial inroads in the range of economic law. Within that province it was accepted quite easily as it was one of the European (Economic) Community's major targets to operate a common or internal market. This goodwill towards supremacy made it much easier for the Court to implement its agenda on the four freedoms of the common/internal market. By doing so the Court was focused on European integration with a *negative* drive[24] as it was only interested in national laws that were in conflict with EC law.[25]

In the course of the process of European integration the European Community expanded into other sectors of society that are, in principle, independent but in fact connected to the economy, to a certain degree. The environment was just one of these sectors which came into the focus of the common/internal market and its laws. However, the negative drive that was chosen in the early days of the common market was quite ineffective in addressing the problems of environmental law. The challenge in that field was to create new and uniform laws. Therefore, directives and regulations europeanised environmental law to a similar extent as other sectors of law; with that, European integration developed a *positive* drive.[26] Of course,

[22] That is why my references are still mostly taken from the German literature.

[23] See *supra* n. 13.

[24] Categorized by Fritz W. Scharpf, *Regieren in Europa: effektiv und demokratisch?* (Frankfurt am Main, Campus-Verlag 1999) = *Governing in Europe: effective and democratic?* (Oxford, Oxford University Press 1999).

[25] The treaty freedoms had been the tools for such a 'negative integration' as they were set to break down national barriers to free movement of goods.

[26] For sure, European harmonisation was not the first 'positive' action as in the 60s and 70s various EC harmonisation directives had been adopted, e.g., in the areas of company law or of social policy. From a German perspective, environmental harmonisation, however, gives the better example as those directives asked for a change of basic dogmatic and systematic structures of German public law.

national jurists[27] did not easily accept this process. Positive integration turned out to need much more premises than its negative counterpart. To accept negative integration is much easier as only some aspects of one's own national law are erased. In contrast, positive integration not only erases national laws but implements different laws and new, perhaps unknown, structures whilst also asking national lawyers – who are accustomed to their own laws – to adopt even unwanted laws. It is not easy to overcome such resistance; all of us know that legal journals in every Member State are full of articles that respond to change by defending the established national rules. Those movements of opposition follow a recurrent pattern. The first pattern is indignation; indignation about European law-makers who try to implement new structures where one thinks that one's own legal system provides established and time-tested answers to problems. The second pattern is a long and cumbersome process of acclimatisation, a process which is dominated by the European Court of Justice and the national courts. These patterns are not only connected to past times, but are still relevant. One can see these patterns more clearly when European law-makers address subjects that are distant from economic issues and closely connected to cultural roots. Therefore, one of the best stages for indignation and lengthy acclimatisation will be law-making within the third pillar of the EU (Police and Judicial Cooperation in Criminal Matters, or PJCC).

5.2 The horizontal dimension: voluntary reception of legal concepts from Member States

The horizontal dimension has been discussed to a lesser extent within the literature. Such neglect, however, is not surprising, as the conventional legal tools, i.e., enforcement, compliance, and supremacy, are not apt to address the issue. To analyse this dimension we need to take into account its unique characteristics. Probably the best way to describe these characteristics would be to label the process of adaptation and reception as gentle, slow, passive, and voluntary. A direct effect of European integration is that the various actors (political, economic, legal, and so forth) constantly observe the legal systems of other Member States. By doing so, the body of acquired knowledge of the other systems increases perpetually, and not only within the legislating institutions. The actors are programmed to learn from the others. This should not astonish anybody, as the whole European project is based on horizontal activity and competition. Legal systems are not exempt from that process. Why should they be? The horizontal project itself tolerates no exceptions, therefore, legal systems and, most notably, their practical operation are a natural part of the 'European Contest'.[28] In the perspective of comparison and observation, the law in action is at the center of interest. The reasons are self-evident as there are

[27] The term 'jurist' within this article encompasses every legal profession without stating a reference to its importance; cf. *infra* n. 45.

[28] See generally on the concept of legal systems competing among each other Veith Mehde, *Wettbewerb zwischen Staaten – die rechtliche Bewältigung zwischenstaatlicher Konkurrenzsituationen im Mehrebenenbereich* (Baden-Baden, Nomos Verlagsgesellschaft 2005) at 507 et seq.

– at times large – differences in terms of the law in action in various Member States, even though uniform European directives govern it. An enquiry into the reasons is but one aspect of the horizontal dimension, the other aspect is the fact that those differences force law-makers to reconsider their practice. Influential groups within society often have a better argument for change merely because of the comparative perspective they take. In Germany, for example, arguments from the horizontal dimension were quite effective in the 1990s when legislation was forced in order to accelerate administrative proceedings within planning law and to shorten legal review for certain (extensive) enterprises.[29]

5.3 Problems in the aftermath of europeanisation

Europeanisation has different impacts. Of those, I will focus on one of the most important: the future viability of national legal systems, i.e., the capability of national legal systems to generate new legal concepts. Considering all the legal influences from the EU, which are large and inevitable both in quantity and quality, it cannot be assumed that all of the Member States' individual national legal systems will be able to continue to develop operative ideas.

To begin with, in a classical sense, law-making on the national level that claims to be autonomous is impossible within a multi-level system of governance,[30] which is dominated by supremacy of the higher level. That does not only apply to those laws which govern specific parts of society such as telecommunication, environment, and so forth, but also to those laws which address the whole, i.e., private law, the core of criminal law, procedural laws, and justice. The central question is: are the national legal systems of Member States capable of maintaining and (re)constructing their own legal concepts and systems even though they are embedded in another legal system that claims to have supremacy? To speak metaphorically: how is it possible to be viable in the horizontal arena, *vis-à-vis* other Member States, when each national legal system is under pressure from the vertical one (via directives, supremacy, direct effect)? In this context, viability means a status in which a Member State tries to construct its own consistent and coherent legal system. As such, viability is not only an homage to aesthetics but is very important for the survival and the internal quality of every single Member State's national legal system. Without it, the process of europeanisation will reach a point where the

[29] Cf. *supra* the paragraph at n. 16.

[30] The concept of multi-level-systems of governance was designed within the realm of political science. See generally Beate Kohler-Koch, 'Regieren im Mehr-Ebenen-System der EU', in Thomas König, Elmar Rieger and Hermann Schmitt (eds.), *Das europäische Mehrebenensystem* (Frankfurt am Main, Campus-Verlag 1996) p. 203 et seq.; Markus Jachtenfuchs and Beate Kohler-Koch, 'Regieren und Institutionenbildung', in Markus Jachtenfuchs and Beate Kohler-Koch (eds.), *Europäische Integration* (Opladen, Leske+Budrich 1996) p. 15 et seq. For its use within the legal arena see Martin Morlok, 'Grundfragen einer Verfassung auf europäischer Ebene', in Peter Häberle, Martin Morlok and Vassilios Skouris (eds.), *Staat und Verfassung in Europa* (Baden-Baden, Nomos Verlagsgesellschaft 2000) p. 73 et seq., at p. 88; for a detailed analysis see Franz C. Mayer, *Kompetenzüberschreitung und Letztentscheidung* (Munich, Verlag C. H. Beck 2000) at pp. 31-57.

national legal systems will at best be a conglomeration of laws effectuated by Europe or, at worst, a sort of 'rag-rug' of eclectic influences.[31]

The viability of the Member States' legal systems is not only a matter of survival and internal quality for themselves, but also for Community law. EC law is not as comprehensive as the law of the national legal systems. The EU is dependent on the existence, efficiency, and quality of its rich variety of Member States' national legal systems. Those are complete national systems or, at least, they were. Notwithstanding, each legal system (still) has its unique character. For example, in Germany, systematically composed codified law like the German code of civil law (*Bürgerliches Gesetzbuch*, BGB) dominates the scene,[32] whereas English law is case-law of its own kind. Nobody expects that Community law will try to govern these basic structures – structures which underpin these very legal systems – in the near future. Moreover, those ideas indoctrinate every national jurist in terms of the way they approach individual legal problems. The uniqueness of English law is not as much the content of specific rules or legal concepts but the way in which English lawyers deal with case-law and think within their categories. In contrast, the uniqueness of German law could be best described as a way of thinking in dogmatic categories, concepts, terms, definitions, and systems.

It would be a big drawback for the composition of the law of Europe if the viability of Europe's individual national legal systems became strongly derailed. Of course, no nation can keep all of its traditional concepts while integrating into Europe. Indeed, some concepts have already been lost. In individual cases this might undoubtedly hurt, but within the whole process we can surmount such loss, as change is the natural part of the enlargement of Europe. What this chapter focuses on is a different point: single reforms do not threaten long-term viability, but reforms made without an overarching strategy may just do that. It is in relation to this strategy that needs have so far not been satisfied.

---

[31] In this respect, European law-making receives bad reviews from nearly all legal fields in all legal systems. In Germany, e.g., academia and practitioners criticize European private law for being without a system, full of antagonisms, and imperfect. See generally Peter Hommelhoff, 'Zivilrecht unter dem Einfluss europäischer Rechtsangleichung', 192 *Archiv für civilistische Praxis (AcP)* (1992) p. 71 et seq.; Jürgen Basedow, 'Anforderungen an eine europäische Zivilrechtsdogmatik', in Reinhard Zimmermann, Rolf Knütel and Jens Peter Meincke (eds.), *Rechtsgeschichte und Privatrechtsdogmatik* (Heidelberg, C. F. Müller Verlag 1999), p. 79 et seq., at p. 82-84; Jürgen Basedow, 'Das BGB im künftigen europäischen Privatrecht – der hybride Kodex', 200 *AcP* (2000) p. 445 et seq.; Axel Flessner, 'Juristische Methode und europäisches Privatrecht', 57 *JZ* (2002), p. 14 et seq.; Gert Brandner, *Überschießende Umsetzung von Richtlinien* (place of publication, publisher 2003); Tobias Tröger, *Zum Systemdenken im europäischen Schuldvertragsrecht,* 11 *Zeitschrift für Europäisches Privatrecht (ZEuP)* (2003) p. 525 et seq.; Jens Koch, 'Die Einheit der nationalen Rechtsordnung und die europäische Privatrechtsangleichung', 61 *JZ* (2006) p. 277 et seq., with a detailed account on systematic flaws at p. 278 et seq. For a critique from the perspective of public law cf. R. Wahl 2001, *supra* n. 10.

[32] See *infra* n. 44.

6. The encounter of legal systems and its dimensions

6.1 Problems of comparing legal systems on the whole

Let me turn to the single dimensions and topics of the encounter. In the following, the most important issues out of the entire host of different dimensions that together shape a legal system, a legal culture, and a specific legal thought will be addressed. From my point of view there is no need to give a detailed description of every single issue, as I only want to define the setting. For this reason, every issue will only be covered briefly.

To begin with, let me reiterate the fundamentals of the discussion. A legal system is more than the sum of its laws. Hence, the process of European integration not only creates new legal sources and supreme positive law, but affects all dimensions of a legal system. Because of that all-embracing character, europeanisation is fundamental. Therefore, there is no doubt that we – being jurists in our times and being witnesses of an energetic lab of legal experiments – need to concentrate our whole attention on the ongoing process of construing EC law, its interconnection with national systems and the interaction between national systems themselves. In doing so, the basic structure of the process of europeanisation should come under scrutiny. This process could be characterised at best as an encounter of legal systems in which *all* elements of a (legal) system meet. As a technique, comparison unearths the latent dimensions of law. These dimensions include the methodology, the unique basic structures of a legal system, the specific disposition of case-law, the role of the legal actors, and the conception of justice.

As (most) national jurists in Europe experience European law via comparison,[33] their own legal system gets its characteristic shape and outline against the background of rules, legal institutes and legal thought of other legal systems. (European) jurists no longer define their own role as national players with a strong focus on their own legal system, but as European actors who constantly glance to their neighbours. It is this shift from an inward-looking to an outward-looking perspective which is new.[34] To 'seesaw the look on one's own legal system and on (all) the other legal systems'[35] has become the standard. Indeed, it should be noted that this is not only an academic standard but also a professional one. All jurists – academics, lawyers, judges, in-house counsels, etc. – subscribe to it.[36]

---

[33] See generally about that dialogue and its external perspective R. Wahl 2003, *supra* n. 4, p. 496, at p. 513 et seq.

[34] R. Wahl 1999, *supra* n. 4, at p. 515.

[35] An homage to and a slight modification of the dictum of Karl Engisch, *Logische Studien zur Gesetzesanwendung*, 3rd edn. (Heidelberg, Carl Winter Universitätsverlag 1963) at p. 15, which is well-known to every German jurist: 'Das Hin- und Herwandern des Blicks zwischen Norm und Sachverhalt'.

[36] R. Wahl 2003, *supra* n. 4.

6.2 The methodology

'You don't talk about methods but you have them' is a common preconception of German lawyers. In itself, this dictum is arrogant and diffuse. However, we can extract one true statement from it: as long as we are among our peers and act within a well-known legal community, we are able to afford silence to methodological questions because legal education and professional experience happens to be largely homogeneous. Due to their common background, lawyers within any given community are socialised and think in a similar way. However, the minute those lawyers cross the borders of their community and turn towards different legal traditions, everything changes. This happens to be the primary experience of those who perform cross-frontier action and comparison.

Let me give one example: German lawyers use methods of purposive interpretation of statutes quite extensively. Moreover, these arguments often show up in the guise of so-called objective interpretation. Teleological arguments are used as a matter of course and the everyday awareness of the problems of such a legal technique is underdeveloped. Other jurisdictions, however, are much more reserved in using purposive arguments. The reasons for this reservation are obvious: as long as the person who asks about the spirit and the purpose of the law is the same person as (s)he who answers, it is (s)he who is the master of the rule. The well-known German lawyer Johann Wolfgang von Goethe wrote about purposive interpretation in a quite distinctive way: it is the master's own spirit that the master puts inside his rules, therefore, lawyers just extract their own thoughts.[37] Apparently, the use of purposive interpretation runs a high risk of abuse; however, there is no true and single answer to the problem of statute interpretation. Hence, nobody should be surprised that every legal system tries to find his own solution, and that there are as many solutions as there are systems.

Furthermore, it is obvious that a continental lawyer and an English lawyer who want to talk about interpretation will not be on the same wavelength before having defined their topic: the first might want to talk about interpreting statutes whereas the second might want to talk about deciding cases.[38] Bearing that in mind let me adjust the dictum mentioned above: 'You don't talk about methods but you have one as the others have another'.

The problem, of course, is much more complex. Nobody can talk about the methodology of another legal system by just defining the topic. For such a conversation you need to comply with other crucial premises for which the basic know-

---

[37] Cf. Johann Wolfgang von Goethe, 'Zahme Xenien (II)', in *Werke, Gedichte und Versepen* (1st Vol., ed. by Walter Höllerer) (Frankfurt am Main, Insel Verlag 1986) at p. 190.

[38] See generally on interpretation in Europe Stefan Vogenauer, *Die Auslegung von Gesetzen in England und auf dem Kontinent*, 2 Vol. (Tübingen, Mohr Siebeck 2001), with detailed chapters on interpretation in Germany, at pp. 28-232, in France, at pp. 232-241, in the European Union, at pp. 344-429, and in England, at pp. 669-1253. In Germany, one of the standard works on the technique of interpreting statutes is Karl Larenz and Claus-Wilhelm Canaris, *Methodenlehre der Rechtswissenschaft*, 4th edn. (Berlin, Springer-Verlag 2005); see for a critical account Friedrich Müller and Ralph Christensen, *Juristische Methodik*, 7th edn. (Berlin, Duncker & Humblot 1997).

ledge about the structures of the other legal system is indispensable. Every single ambitious question you want to address towards your object implies that you already know the object – a simple hermeneutic insight, which applies to the law and to comparing legal systems as well as to other interpretive enterprises.

Talking about methodology within Community law[39] is another topic with its own complex implications. Just read the inspiring anthology on case-law in Europe that has been published in Germany in 2003.[40] You will be surprised by the way English, French, Italian, Spanish, Dutch, Belgian, and German jurists talk about the case-law of the European Court of Justice. Apparently, they all address the same topic, but do so in a very different manner. Every single one talks about the same subject with their (national) preconceptions and their personal experiences in mind. Thus it appears that an analysis of the methodology of the European Court of Justice is already quite complicated.[41] To approach this subject – i.e., the subject of a European methodology – in a satisfactory manner seems to require more than just one conference. Rather, it requires ongoing and concerted efforts by jurists of all Member States.

6.3 The significance of different dogmatic and systematic concepts, and of different legal literary genres

The whole forum widens if you try to analyse the basic internal structures of a legal system, i.e., the way in which national lawyers organise their legal materials. In Germany, jurists distinctively think within, and argue with, dogmatic and systematic concepts.[42] Those who fail to do so do not just sail close to the wind, but

---

[39] See generally S. Vogenauer, *supra* n. 38, at p. 344 et seq., esp. at p. 346 et seq. and p. 358 et seq. See also Christian Hillgruber, 'Grenzen der Rechtsfortbildung durch den EuGH – Hat Europarecht Methode?', in Thomas von Danwitz et al. (eds.), *Auf dem Weg zu einer europäischen Staatlichkeit* (Stuttgart, Richard Boorberg Verlag 1993) p. 31 et seq.; Thomas M. Möllers, *Die Rolle des Rechts im Rahmen der europäischen Integration – zur Notwendigkeit einer europäischen Gesetzgebungs- und Methodenlehre* (Tübingen, Mohr Siebeck 1999) at p. 47; Werner Schroeder, *Das Gemeinschaftsrechtssystem* (Tübingen, Mohr Siebeck 2002) at p. 209 et seq.; A. Flessner, *supra* n. 31; Martin Nettesheim, in E. Grabitz and M. Hilf, *supra* n. 12, Art. 4 EGV Rn. 55; Bernhard Wegener, in Chr. Callies and M. Ruffert, *supra* n. 12), Art. 220 EGV Rn. 11-15.

[40] Reiner Schulze and Ulrike Seif (eds.), *Richterrecht und Rechtsfortbildung in der Europäischen Rechtsgemeinschaft* (Tübingen, Mohr Siebeck 2003); the articles are in German, English, and French, every one comes along with a summary in English.

[41] See generally Albert Bleckmann, 'Zu den Auslegungsmethoden des Europäischen Gerichtshofs', 37 *NJW* (1982) p. 1177 et seq.; Jochen Anweiler, *Die Auslegungsmethoden des EuGH* (Frankfurt am Main, Peter Lang 1997); Mariele Dederichs, *Die Methodik des Gerichtshofes der Europäischen Gemeinschaft*, 39 *Europarecht (EuR)* (2000) p. 345 et seq.; Elke Scheibeler, *Begriffsbildung durch den Europäischen Gerichtshof – autonom oder durch Verweis auf die nationalen Rechtsordnungen?* (Berlin, Duncker & Humblot 2004); Thorsten Kingreen, in Chr. Callies and M. Ruffert, *supra* n. 12, Art. 6 EUV paras. 39 et seq.; Jürgen Schwarze, in Jürgen Schwarze (ed.), *EU-Kommentar* (Baden-Baden, Nomos Verlagsgesellschaft 2000) Art. 220 EGV paras. 37-30.

[42] See generally Winfried Brohm, 'Die Dogmatik des Verwaltungsrechts vor den Gegenwartsaufgaben der Verwaltung', 30 *Veröffentlichungen der Vereinigung der Deutschen Staatsrechtslehrer (VVDStRL)* (1972) p. 254 et seq.; Otto Bachof, 'Die Dogmatik vor den Gegenwartsaufgaben der

actually jump out of their boat (i.e., the legal community). Other jurisdictions operate differently and use other styles and techniques. In England, for example, you would not find the German style at all or, at least, hardly ever. The English have countervailing strategies, of course. They tend to address questions of methodology much more directly than the Germans do; perhaps this sensibility for questions about their legal methods is one of their strategies. Incidentally, such an insight provides one important reminder for those who take a comparative perspective: those who stop after having figured out that a certain rule or principle does not exist in another legal system almost always miss the point. Their ongoing task would be to search for functional equivalents that are institutions or models which address the same problem. The focus on dogmatic categories in Germany and the focus on methodological questions in other jurisdictions is just one example of such a discussion. It will be an important task for European jurists to take up the search for equivalents in the manner just described.

Whether German legal thought, with its pronounced dogmatic and systematic categories, will catch up with Europe and will establish itself within a European legal thought, is open and unclear. Those who are sceptical in this regard might speculate that the days of such an approach to German law are numbered. Nevertheless, dogmatic legal thought as such could be found elsewhere in Europe, just with another intensity as in Germany. I would therefore recommend keeping an eye on the ongoing process and to be wary of jumping to the conclusion that those who think in dogmatic categories, such as the Germans, belong to an endangered species.

6.4 The disposition of case-law

At first sight, case-law as a topic[43] is much easier to address than the structural questions I have raised above. One reason might be that continental legal systems and especially the German one have undergone a structural change. The legal culture of Germany is still shaped by codified law, not just by statutes but by the whole project we call 'codification'. Nevertheless, even that axiomatic channel has been

Verwaltung', 30 *VVDStRL* (1972) p. 212 et seq.; Eberhard Schmidt-Aßmann, *Das Allgemeine Verwaltungsrecht als Ordnungsidee*, 2nd edn. (Berlin, Springer-Verlag 2004); Christian Bumke, *Grundrechtsvorbehalt* (Baden-Baden, Nomos Verlagsgesellschaft 1998) at pp. 30-33; Christian Bumke, 'Die Entwicklung der verwaltungsrechtswissenschaftlichen Methodik in der Bundesrepublik Deutschland', in Eberhard Schmidt-Aßmann and Wolfgang Hoffmann-Riem (eds.), *Methoden der Verwaltungsrechtswissenschaft* (Baden-Baden, Nomos Verlagsgesellschaft 2004) p. 73 et seq.; Uwe Volkmann, 'Veränderung der Grundrechtsdogmatik', 60 *JZ* (2005) p. 261 et seq., at pp. 261-263.

43 See generally on German 'Richterrecht' (that is case-law from a German perspective) Jörn Ipsen, *Richterrecht und Verfassung* (Berlin, Duncker & Humblot 1975); Friedrich Müller, *Elemente einer Verfassungstheorie – Richterrecht*, Vol. 4 (Berlin, Duncker & Humblot 1986); Fritz Ossenbühl, *Richterrecht im demokratischen Rechtsstaat – Rede zur Eröffnung des akademischen Jahres 1987/88 in Bonn* (Bonn, Bouvier Verlag 1988); Katja Langenbucher, *Die Entwicklung und Auslegung von Richterrecht – eine methodologische Untersuchung zur richterlichen Rechtsfortbildung im deutschen Zivilrecht* (Munich, Verlag C. H. Beck 1996). See generally for a Swiss perspective Giovanni Biaggini, *Verfassung und Richterrecht – verfassungsrechtliche Grenzen der Rechtsfortbildung im Wege der bundesgerichtlichen Rechtsprechung* (Basle, Helbing und Lichtenhahn 1991).

disturbed, maybe unexpectedly but also inevitably, as we stumbled into an ongoing process which has placed a second layer of case-law onto our codifications.[44] Experts of their field often express their legal knowledge by citing the names of the parties of a case. That is not new as such, but what is new for our conception is that those cases are branded or labelled by their parties, and also that lawyers not only cite one case but a whole series of rulings by their names – behaviour that does not necessarily establish understanding. In any event, the development towards more case-law within codified legal systems might be a significant reason why so many are devoted to the convergence of legal systems within Europe.

The description of the facts might be correct so far, but it is submitted that the above conclusion is premature. I for one prefer to go into more profound research. One reason is that national courts do not argue in the same way when producing case-law. German, French, Spanish case-law, and so forth, differ from English or European case-law – case-law is not case-law. The German judge is a German jurist; he works within systematic and dogmatic categories even when he produces case-law. English judges handle their cases in a different way; they focus on the facts and try to decide similar cases alike. Such a focus characterises English judges. Indeed, the English start to become aware of the importance of the factual side of a case right from the start of their legal education. Students in their first semesters focus on exercises to differentiate cases; they are trained in a specific technique to analyse facts. You will not find comparable standards within the German curriculum. German jurists focus on abstract norms and use them rather than the facts as a basis for solving their cases. They compare cases too, but not so much the factual situation of their cases. Instead, they examine abstract norms derived from cases and compare those with the new case. For that operation they consult systematically annotated statute books in which all the abstract norms are detached from their factual setting. In the end, both German and English judges decide their case as case-law but in doing so they apply a completely different set of techniques. In this respect, it would be more productive to get into a detailed analysis of those case-law techniques – i.e., distinguishing techniques for precedents, types of mandatory or persuasive precedents, different doctrines of *stare decisis* – than to proclaim the great convergence.

6.5 Socialising the legal staff – education matters

The differences of every legal system within the EU are not only established, but are also strengthened by legal education. Studying law not only means that students

---

[44] Legal culture within Germany was coined by the great project of codifying the civil code in the late 19th century. The German code of civil law (BGB) of 1896/1900 was the pathfinder for that movement. With that code Germany claimed to have legislation with a systematized output and to have a legal practice that is dominated by legislation and its interpretation. To apply the law in such a codified system means to interpret statutes. There are other codifications within Germany apart from the BGB, e.g., the code of criminal law ('Strafgesetzbuch – StGB') and all the codes of procedure ('Zivilprozessordnung – ZPO, Strafprozessordnung – StPO, Verwaltungsgerichtsordnung – VwGO, Verwaltungsverfahrensgesetz – VwVfG').

of law study and consume a large body of positive law, but also that they grow into a whole body of thought, methodology, and culture. This process covers the accumulation of knowledge as much as the shaping of legal mentalities and emotions. In this respect, students of law become socialised in a very specific way, i.e., the way in which every legal system needs staff for administering everyday legal problems. Those needs are distinct for each Member State, as one tends to systemise legal information whereas the other chooses a pragmatic approach with a distinct focus on the facts of a case. Over the years students grow into their legal profession and will be equipped with a distinct way of dealing with issues of our society. Most importantly, that socialisation will be quite different in every Member State. Students do not become jurists, lawyers, judges, and so forth in general but, rather, become German, English, French, etc., jurists, lawyers, judges, and so forth.[45]

In any case, education matters. A characteristic feature of the differences between legal educations – and between every legal system – are the different styles of textbooks students use in class. The field of law where the differences are most obvious is EC law itself. The textbooks on Community law differ in a significant way switching from one Member State to the other. In Germany, those who write textbooks tend to systemise the whole field, whereas in England you will find case-books with their typical focus on case-materials. Of course, there are case-books in Germany as well, but compared to the textbooks with their dogmatic style they are backbenchers. In other words, education does not only matter, but style as well. In the end, these differences leave their mark on all students and, in doing so, on all legal practitioners and academics.

6.6 The different role of academia within legal practice and its reform

Those who cross legal boundaries will be quick to learn that the impact of academia and its literature on a legal system can be quite different from that in their own system. Moreover, not only the impact, but also the kind of legal literature in general differs a lot. One might say: if you think of a person being a jurist, you think of an attorney when you are in the States, of a judge when you are in England, and of a professor when you are in Germany.

However interesting this statement may be, in this context it should only act as an indicator for the existing difference of the role and self-conception of legal academia and legal writings. The simple question at issue is: where do you orientate yourself when you want to know what the law is? Do you consult case-materials? To what extent do you consult literature, and what sort of literature do you consult? This simple question is connected to a more analytical one: what does it mean if you ask 'what is the law'? A possible answer might be that the law is what

[45] One can see the differences just by referring to the abstract label of legal professions in the Member States. In Germany, students get educated to become jurists ('Juristen'), which is a term that encompasses every job within the legal arena, the so-called 'Einheitsjuristen'. You will not find a term with such a connotation in other legal systems. In England, for example, a lawyer is a solicitor or barrister whereas a judge is a judge. See also *supra* n. 27.

the judge says it is – with the effect that you have to shrug your shoulders when you are asked for the law that applies to a type of case that has not been decided yet. Presumably, almost everybody would call that answer too simple. There is a possibility for autonomous answers to the law before and beyond a judgment, the question is just to what degree.

6.7 Comparative law of a second generation

Let me stop highlighting the dimensions of legal systems one has to address and consider in order to talk about europeanisation, European legal systems, and Community law. Instead, let me connect the above to some general thoughts and observations which revolve around the necessity of a European strategy of comparison bearing all these dimensions in mind. In this context, it is important to acknowledge that the comparison of legal systems has its own great academic tradition beyond the process we call europeanisation. That is, the long lasting tradition of the discipline called comparative law. However, as we are aware of the fact that European integration, and moreover, internationalisation keep us moving, traditional comparative law would not be excluded from that process. Comparative law as such is right within a development towards a second generation of legal comparatists. In the following some issues that are connected to such an enterprise will be drawn upon.

From a comparative perspective, everybody wants to access law in action over law in the books. Such a claim is neither inventive nor new. However, in practice that cannot easily be realised, as it requires a focus on a comprehensive management of the methods of comparison. Such management needs to embrace the law with all its dimensions and relations. One could easily imagine the difficulties in addressing all the dimensions outlined above. The intricacy of the approach increases even more as soon as you turn to the law's relations to other systems of society. This aspect is generally being discussed under the topic of 'law in context'. One of the major interests in seeing law in context is to emphasise its cultural roots.[46] This chapter has already addressed some initial stages of this topic above, and right now an overall perspective will be taken: under a comparative and academic perspective, law needs to be revisited by a profound cultural analysis of its foundations.

6.8 Different perspectives on justice

Let me give one short example. One of the basic concerns of law is to assure justice. But what exactly do we expect from a law that provides justice? Do we expect *true decisions*, or do we expect a legal procedure that is open to every argument, accepting its outcome as just as long as the *process* itself was fair? Presumably, in Ger-

[46] See generally for a focus on the cultural dimension of the law Ulrich Haltern, Europarecht und das Politische, 2005, at 13 et seq. and 26 et seq.; Ulrich R. Haltern, *Europarecht – Dogmatik im Kontext* (Tübingen, Mohr Siebeck 2005) at pp. 6-13.

many most lawyers tend towards the first answer, for why should we struggle for our law[47] if not in respect of its correct content? The given response, of course, depends on the preconception(s) of its author. Across the English Channel, most lawyers tend towards the second choice. English lawyers value procedure over substance. Such an approach is connected to a deep-rooted doubt that humans who find themselves in a conflict situation are able to find *true* solutions, even if they delegate the ultimate decision to (governmental) judges. Instead, it is believed that the best solution for a conflict will be found by ensuring a fair setting in which everybody has the chance to speak up.[48]

Could there be a more distinctive difference between legal systems than having categorically different assumptions about how to ensure just decisions? It is obvious that the attitude towards justice has an impact throughout the whole system, regardless of which subject of law one chooses. Therefore, the 'rightness' of the judgments or of the legal proceedings is a decent example to demonstrate the problems of, and to postulate a broader horizon for, comparing legal systems. These questions are not only important for the law as such, but characterise a whole society. Hence, it is of the utmost importance to address the intellectual history of those (legal) systems being compared. In the foregoing, the reasons why the English system prefers the rightness of legal proceedings over those of its outcome have been spoken about. The roots of such an approach are to be found within English intellectual history and thought. Last, but not least, this is the reason that legal comparatists have one of the most difficult jobs within the legal arena while eliciting the law in its context.

Let me close these thoughts by citing a character out of the German literature: Michael Kohlhaas.[49] Certainly, Heinrich von Kleist drew a quite exaggerated character by making up his novel – a character that devotes his whole life on demanding justice for his own case. However, you will learn a lot about German legal consciousness just by studying Michael Kohlhaas, a character not to be found in English literature.

7. Mutual influences of national legal systems and of the European Community legal system

In the end, the spectrum of mutual influences of all (national) legal systems within Europe proves to be more comprehensive than the analysis of the – doubtlessly

---

[47] In allusion to Rudolf von Jhering, *Der Kampf ums Recht* (Vienna, Verlag Manz 1872). This standard work got translated into many languages: *Le combat pour le droit* (Vienna, Verlag Manz 1875); *La lotta pel diritto* (Milan, Ulrico Hoepli 1875); *The struggle for law* (Chicago, Callaghan 1879).

[48] See generally on the role of procedures Niklas Luhmann, *Legitimation durch Verfahren* (Neuwied, Hermann Luchterhand Verlag 1969). This pioneering work is available in French: *La légitimation par la procédure* (Sainte-Foy, Québec, Presses de l'Université Laval 2001).

[49] Heinrich von Kleist, *Michael Kohlhaas – aus einer alter Chronik* (Berlin, Realschulbuchhandlung 1810); English translations are available in *The Marquise of O and other stories* (London, Penguin Classics 1978) at pp. 114-213; and in *Selected writings* (Indianapolis, Hackett 2004) at pp. 209-280.

important – topic of supremacy could possibly unearth. Let me re-emphasise that European integration initiated a proactive encounter by which the national law of all Member States and EC law correlate to each other. During this encounter, it is not only positive law that interacts but, rather, everything that constitutes a legal system. All aforementioned topics – the methodology, the specific disposition of case-law, the specific role of legal actors and especially of legal academia, the basic assumptions about just judgments, and so forth – may be implemented into EC law in quite a different way than in each national system. The same is true for the horizontal relations between the national systems out of which new Community law develops.

In short, everything that constitutes law and legal thought is a matter of dialogue and encounter. Of course, this is a bold venture which implies that national jurists zoom in on an external perspective. Sensibility and curiosity are the key virtues with which to approach the differences between their own and other national legal systems. Nonetheless, you need distance from your subject. That is why a comparative perspective that tends to assess one legal system as being superior is flawed. Therefore, we need to implement a sort of *Leitmotif* for European jurists, who grew up in their national context. Such a legal ethos may be to adopt a dual perspective, that is, to be versed in one's own laws but to take into account – in a neutral way – the fact that there are other possible ways to address and to solve the same problem within a European context. For that purpose one needs to have a positive attitude towards difference and plurality.

Such a *Leitmotif* is not only conducive to a thirst for knowledge. The first generation of jurists within comparative law might have adhered to an encounter in which the cognitive interests had been of a theoretical and, to a lesser extent, an economic nature. Today, comparative law, at least within Europe, operates within a pragmatic environment as it serves the living law of Europe, that is, both national and Community law. Legal life in Europe essentially requires knowledge of other legal systems. Since we become increasingly well-informed about alternatives and differences we reconsider our own arguments, techniques, and styles and are much more open to reception. This has another implication, namely, that comparatists of the second generation focus on the enforcement of the rules, problems of compliance and the overall outcome. This is not, in itself, surprising as European (economic) players within the European market are interested in a uniform enforcement of Community law and not so much in uniform laws as an aesthetic category. Taking that perspective, again, comparatists do not have an easy task: you will only get decent information about compliance issues when you are able to ask for additional information like the length of administrative or judicial proceedings, the scope of judicial review, the ability of third parties to have standing and their affinity to resistance, and so forth. In short, you need to address the whole ensemble knowing that you will not find *one* solution.

Longing for the good old days – those days in which legal reform and thought were autonomous, and in which the whole legal system was designed by one's own national tradition and culture – is of no avail. Likewise, it would be a mistake to be anxious about europeanisation or to ward it off. One can only retain positive aspects of one's own legal culture or parts of it by taking an active role in framing the law within the laboratory provided by the EU. German (public) law offers much for that endeavour and one can already find some German concepts being realised through Brussels or Luxembourg.[50] The same is true for all the other legal systems within the EU. Everybody is a player; no one is a single player but a team-member.

8. Concluding remarks

To describe europeanisation as a concert of common (legal) traditions would best suit the process. The image of the concert involves different performers with their own character contributing to a common project but playing different instruments, different keys, and with different accents. I feel that europeanisation as such sets up a completely new generation of law. For Germany, I have described that process as being law in its second phase or generation. The first phase was characterised by the project of redrafting our legal system after 1949. That led to a law that is basically shaped by constitutional rights and concepts. Germany's law entered a second phase while becoming europeanised. As with other Member States, Germany cannot just go on in the same old way. Europeanisation has its own, new, and fundamental impact. Its central idea is change through comparison; that change covers every aspect of the law, the positive law itself up to central ideas of justice. In this way, europeanisation is all-embracing and radical. Only those who (want to) identify these effects, accepting the new situation, will be in a position to design the new order. In the future, Community law and national law will evolve around each other. National law would not be capable of achieving new solutions by existing on its own. National legal systems, however, are rich with their own traditions and concepts and therefore have a great opportunity to participate in that co-evolution.

---

50 German administrative law modeled – at least to a certain degree – the design of European case-law on the protection of legitimate expectations; cf. Hans Ragnemalm, 'Confiance légitime et délai raisonable – Quelques remarques sur le thème du retrait des actes administratifs en droit communautaire', in *Mélanges en hommage à Fernand Schockweiler* (Baden-Baden, Nomos Verlagsgesellschaft 1999) p. 511 et seq.

Chapter 3
THE EMERGENCE OF A EUROPEAN SYSTEM OF PUBLIC INTERNATIONAL LAW: THE EU AND ITS MEMBER STATES AS STRANGE SUBJECTS

Bruno de Witte*

1. INTRODUCTION

Is there a European system of public international law with distinctive features that differentiate the way in which international law develops and is practiced between European States from the way this is done in the rest of the world? There are many perspectives from which this question could be addressed. The main perspective chosen by the contributions to this volume is that of the relation between legal orders and dispute settlement. In this chapter, I propose a different but related perspective, which is that of the doctrine of *subjects of international law*.

The age-old subjects doctrine of international law has faced considerable uncertainties in recent decades,[1] but there is one element of apparent stability, which is that States on the one hand, and international organisations on the other, are the main (even if not the only) subjects of international law. In the standard account, *States* possess full capacity to act on the international plane, including through the conclusion of international treaties in all domains of their activity, whereas *international organisations* (the other main category of subjects) possess a limited capacity to act, as defined in their founding treaties, and only rarely conclude international treaties. The most common among such treaties are privileges and immunities agreements which the organisations conclude with the State that hosts them.

However, even this received textbook wisdom is shaky in the particular context of Europe today, where this neat picture is considerably more blurred in two related respects. First, there are 27 States with only a limited capacity to act on the international plane because of the European integration system in which they take part. Second, there are two closely intertwined international organisations, the

* Professor of European Union law, European University Institute, Florence.

[1] For recent critical accounts of the 'subject of subjects' in international law, see A. Clapham, *Human Rights Obligations of Non-State Actors* (Oxford, Oxford University Press 2006), chapter 2, and J. Klabbers, '(I Can't Get No) Recognition: Subjects Doctrine and the Emergence of Non-State Actors', in J. Petman and J. Klabbers (eds.), *Nordic Cosmopolitanism. Essays in International Law for Martti Koskenniemi* (Boston, M. Nijhoff 2003) pp. 351-369.

J. Wouters, P.A. Nollkaemper, E. de Wet (eds.), The Europeanisation of International Law

European Union and the European Community (hereafter, the EU and EC, respectively), that have become important actors of international relations and conclude international agreements on a wide range of subjects. These two interrelated phenomena will be examined in turn, in the following sections of this contribution.

2. The European Community and European Union as prominent subjects

The latter characteristic is well-known. It is readily acknowledged that there is, in Europe, a peculiar international organisation (the European Community) that remains unlike any other, despite attempts in other continents to establish regional organisations based on the EC model. In fact, this organisation is so peculiar that many Community lawyers have argued that it is not even an international organisation at all, but 'something else', a *sui generis* legal order. This *sui generis* qualification sits uneasily with the traditional doctrine of the subjects of international law and has therefore been largely ignored by international lawyers who continue to include the European Community (and *a fortiori* the European Union) within the category of international organisations, though only a few international lawyers have mounted a sustained argument as to why, despite all their special characteristics, the EC and EU are still to be considered as international organisations.[2] International legal practice also continues to deny the *sui generis* doctrine. There are many multilateral treaty provisions that use the terms 'international organisation' or 'regional international economic organisation' where it is clear from the context that the (only) organisation that is intended by that term is the European Community.[3]

The European Community has been an active treaty-maker for many years. It has been joined, more recently, by its sister organisation, the European Union. Thus, in the period between 1 January 2004 and 31 July 2006, the European Community signed 135 international agreements and the European Union 33 international agreements.[4] One agreement, the 'Schengen acquis' treaty with Switzerland, was signed by both the European Community and the European Union, thus providing a striking illustration of the fragmentation of the European Union's external relations caused by the 'pillar system' created by the Treaty of Maastricht.[5] The

---

[2] A very elaborate and compelling argument in this sense was presented by A. Pellet, 'Les fondements juridiques internationaux du droit communautaire', *Collected Courses of the Academy of European Law*, Vol. V, Book 2 (Dordrecht, Nijhoff 1994), pp. 193-271; see also, more briefly, P.-M. Dupuy, 'L'unité de l'ordre juridique international', *Hague Recueil,* Vol. 297 (2002), at pp. 438-450.

[3] See, for example, the Convention on Biological Diversity (1992), Art. 35; the UN Framework Convention on Climate Change (1992), Art. 20.

[4] These figures are based on the agreements database on the website of the Council of the European Union.

[5] The Commission had opposed the conclusion of this inter-pillar agreement, preferring the conclusion of two separate agreements with Switzerland on this matter, one by the EC and another by the EU. On this discussion, see C. Kaddous 'La place des Accords bilatéraux II dans l'ordre juridique de l'Union européenne', in C. Kaddous/M. Jametti Greiner (éd.), *Accords bilatéraux II Suisse-UE et autres Accords récents* (Genève/Bâle/Munich/Bruxelles/Paris, Helbing & Lichtenhahn, Bruylant, LGDJ 2006),

conspicuous treaty-making activity of the European Union may seem curious to those who still deny that the European Union possesses international legal personality; in fact, this practice undoubtedly shows that the European Union does have such international legal personality even though the text of the EU Treaty does not say so explicitly.[6] However, large numbers should not impress too much; EU agreements are often repetitive (i.e., they include identical agreements with several countries) and technical. Many of them deal, in fact, with the participation of third countries in EU-led crisis management operations.[7]

3. THE EU MEMBER STATES AS UNCOMMON SUBJECTS OF INTERNATIONAL LAW

The first mentioned specificity of Europe, in terms of the doctrine of subjects of international law, is not as widely acknowledged and will be the main focus of this contribution. It is a fact that 27 States on the European continent have accepted, more or less deliberately, to curtail their own capacity to act on the international plane in favour of, precisely, the European Community and European Union. This makes them States that are unlike any other from the point of view of international law. Member States of the EU have lost the capacity to conclude treaties with other States in some domains, such as trade in goods and fisheries, since these are now within the exclusive competence of the European Community. In other more numerous policy domains (trade in services, development cooperation, environment, immigration, crime, scientific cooperation, education, etc.), they share this capacity with the EC or the EU.[8] Even in those shared domains, the EC and EU often act on their own, and conclude international agreements without their Member States. This happens when the international agreement is closely related to an internal act which was previously adopted by the EC, in which case the European Community's com-

pp. 63-92, at 73-74. For a general analysis of inter-pillar fragmentation, see R. Wessel, 'Fragmentation in the Governance of EU External Relations: Legal Institutional Dilemmas and the New Constitution for Europe', in J.W. de Zwaan et al., *The European Union: An Ongoing Process of Integration – Liber Amicorum Alfred E. Kellermann* (The Hague, T.M.C. Asser Press 2004), pp. 123-140.

[6] For a thorough legal analysis of this relatively recent phenomenon, see G. de Kerchove and S. Marquardt, 'Les accords internationaux conclus par l'Union européenne', 50 *AFDI* (2004), pp. 803-825.

[7] See, on this phenomenon, V. Kronenberger, 'Common Foreign and Security Policy: International Law Aspects of the Association of Third States with the Common Positions of the Council of the European Union', in V. Kronenberger (ed.), *The European Union and the International Legal Order: Discord or Harmony?* (The Hague, T.M.C. Asser Press 2001), pp. 351-369; A. Sari, 'The Conclusion of International Agreements by the European Union in the Context of the ESDP', 57 *International and Comparative Law Quarterly* (2008), pp. 53-86.

[8] I will not attempt, here, to analyse the question of the distinction between exclusive and shared external powers of the EC, which is notoriously fraught with problems. See, among others, P. Eeckhout, *External Relations of the European Union – Legal and Constitutional Foundations* (Oxford, Oxford University Press, 2004), Chapters 2 to 4; M. Cremona, 'External Relations and External Competence: The Emergence of an Integrated Policy', in P. Craig and G. de Búrca (eds), *The Evolution of EU Law* (Oxford, Oxford University Press, 1999), pp. 137-175, at 152 et seq.

petence may become exclusive through pre-emption; this phenomenon is ill-defined and causes considerable headaches in the institutional practice of the EU. Often the legal services of the Commission and Council are genuinely puzzled as to whether a particular area of external relations comes within shared or exclusive competence and may ask the European Court of Justice (hereafter, ECJ) to decide it for them, as happened recently with the new Lugano Convention on recognition and enforcement of judgments.[9] In other cases, the Member States have preserved their legal capacity to conclude treaties with third States but find it convenient that the EC should not only negotiate but also sign and ratify on their behalf (an example of this are the readmission agreements that are currently being negotiated and concluded by the EC).[10] In many cases of shared competence, though, the Member States insist on being a formal party to the agreement alongside the EC. These are the famous 'mixed agreements'.[11]

It is often argued that most important EC agreements today take the form of mixed agreements; if that is the case, it could be said that the Member States have not abandoned the international scene to any major extent. It is certainly true that some major external agreements of the EC have been concluded as mixed agreements.[12] It is also true, however, that in quantitative terms the mixed agreements are far less numerous than the 'pure' EC agreements. In the period between 1 January 2004 and 31 July 2006, of the total number of 135 European Community agreements mentioned earlier, 33 were signed as mixed agreements. Thirty-three may seem like a high number, until one looks more closely at the list and finds that 26 of them are 'post-enlargement amendments', that is, amendments of existing mixed agreements that needed to be modified in order to accommodate the accession of the ten new Member States of the EU as of 1 May 2004. Thus, for example, a Protocol to the Partnership and Cooperation Agreement with Russia was signed on 27 April 2004 to take account of the pending enlargement of the European Union.[13]

---

[9] ECJ, *Opinion 1/03* of 7 February 2006. The new Lugano Convention, to be concluded with Iceland, Norway and Switzerland, was held by the ECJ to fall within the exclusive competence of the European Community, thus excluding the Member States of the EU from being separate contracting parties. This controversy is one illustration of the broader question of the external competence of the EC in matters of private international law, and of the respective role of the EC and its Member States in the Hague Conference on private international law. See generally M. Wilderspin and A.-M. Rouchaud-Joët, 'La compétence externe de la Communauté européenne en droit international privé', 93 *Revue critique de droit international privé* (2004), pp. 1-48; K. Boele-Woelki and R.H. van Ooik, 'Exclusieve externe bevoegdheden van de EG inzake het Internationaal Privaatrecht', *Nederlands tijdschrift voor Europees recht* (2006), pp. 194-201.

[10] The European Community has so far concluded readmission agreements, with Macao, Hong Kong, Sri Lanka, Albania, Russia, Macedonia, Serbia, Montenegro, Bosnia and Herzegovina, Ukraine and Moldova.

[11] For a synthesis of the legal issues explaining, and arising out of, mixity, see A. Rosas, 'The European Union and Mixed Agreements', in A. Dashwood and C. Hillion (eds.), *The General Law of E.C. External Relations* (London, Sweet & Maxwell, 2000) p. 200.

[12] For a list of mixed agreements up to 2000, see J. Helikoski, *Mixed Agreements as a Technique for Organizing the International Relations of the European Community and its Member States* (The Hague, Kluwer Law International 2001), Appendix 1.

[13] Naturally, enlargement normally does *not* require the amendment of existing 'pure' EC agreements; these are held to be automatically applicable to the European Community in its new size and composition.

So, in fact, only seven genuinely new mixed agreements were signed in this period: one each with the USA, Israel and Ukraine on satellite navigation systems, one with Switzerland on combating financial fraud, a partnership and cooperation agreement with Tadjikistan, the stabilisation and association agreement with Albania, and an amending protocol to the stabilisation and association agreement with Macedonia. The sample is too small to draw from them any firm conclusions, it could indicate that mixed agreements are an established phenomenon of the European Union's external relations, however, without their number 'steadily increasing'.[14]

It is worth remembering, in this regard, that when they participate in mixed agreements, the EU Member States do not act as entirely autonomous subjects of international law. They are subject to a general duty of cooperation, between themselves and with the EC, and this duty extends to the negotiation, ratification and application phases of those agreements. Thus, there is a collective management of the international legal relationship, in which the European Community is often the 'senior partner' and the Member States are little more than token contracting parties.[15] Take, for example, the Cotonou Agreement with the African, Caribbean and Pacific countries (otherwise known as the ACP countries). This is a mixed agreement, but the Member States do not act as genuinely separate contracting parties. The negotiation of the agreement was led by the European Commission, implementation of financial aid under the Agreement, even when coming from Member State budgets, is in hands of the Commission, and the decision to suspend the agreement (for instance, in the case of massive human rights violations in an ACP country) has been entrusted to the Council, which acts by qualified majority on behalf of both of the EU and of the Member States. The recently-concluded negotiations for a revision of the Cotonou Agreement[16] were similarly conducted by the Commission.

Not only the *making* of international treaties has been taken over, to some extent, by the EC and EU, but also the *application* of, and *compliance* with, international treaties by the Member States. Even in the case of mixed agreements, these 'downstream' matters of application and compliance by the Member States are to a large extent monitored by the EU institutions, including through infringement actions brought by the European Commission.[17] Furthermore, if the European Community adopts internal legislation, this may cause existing treaties concluded between its Member States and third States to become incompatible with the new internal Community rule, the Member States are then bound to try and discontinue the conflicting treaty rule, either by its unilateral denunciation or through negotiations with the third country.[18] This is another, less direct but practically important, way in

[14] As was stated in 2000 by Allan Rosas, *supra* n. 11, at 201.

[15] See P. Koutrakos, *EU International Relations Law* (Oxford, Hart Publishing 2006), at p. 137 et seq. for an analysis of this 'management of mixity'.

[16] The revised text of the Cotonou Agreement was published in OJ 2005, L 209/17.

[17] See, for example, the ECJ ruling in Case C-239/03 *Commission* v. *France*, judgment of 7 October 2004, with comment by P.J. Kuijper in 42 *CML Rev.* (2005), pp. 1491-1500. See, further, the chapter by C. Tietje in this volume.

[18] This obligation of the Member States is laid down in Article 307, 2nd para. EC and was elaborated in a number of ECJ judgments. See, for a comprehensive account, P. Koutrakos, *supra* n. 15, chapter 8.

which Member States' international action is curtailed by their membership of the EU.

There are two further, less visible, effects of EU membership on the international treaty practice of States. First, EC-EU membership has given rise to the phenomenon of *parallel agreements*, that is, agreements to which all the Member States are parties without the participation of any third States. These parallel agreements exist in a complementary relation to the activity of the European Union.[19] The most obvious and important example of such parallel agreements are the revision treaties, that is, the treaties through which the Member States from time to time amend the founding treaties of the European Union.[20] There are other, less prominent examples of parallel agreements. For the same 2004-2006 sample period mentioned above, the Council of Ministers database mentions eight such 'member-State-only' agreements: the Treaty on the Constitution of Europe signed in October 2004 (which, technically speaking, is a revision treaty), the agreements providing for the accession of ten new-coming Member States to the Rome Convention on contractual obligations and to the Convention on double taxation, an agreement on claims between Member States that may result from the participation in EU crisis management operations, two 'internal agreements' about the States' contribution to financial aid for ACP countries under the Cotonou Agreement, and two 'decisions of representatives' (that are, in fact, international agreements in simplified form)[21] on the privileges and immunities of the European Defence Agency and of Athena.[22]

The second indirect effect of EU membership is the virtual phenomenon of the *'absent' agreements:* Member States simply do not feel the need to conclude treaties among themselves that they might otherwise, in the absence of the European Union, would have wanted to conclude. This is such a banal fact that we tend to overlook it. Considering the vast amount of matters that are dealt with today by EU legislation, it is likely that, if the European Union did not exist, many of these matters would have been the object of bilateral or multilateral treaties between the

[19] On this phenomenon of parallel agreements, see B. De Witte, 'Chameleonic Member States: Differentiation by Means of Partial and Parallel Agreements', in B. De Witte, D. Hanf and E. Vos (eds.), *The Many Faces of Differentiation in EU Law* (Antwerpen, Intersentia 2001), pp. 231-267, at 246 et seq.

[20] For an analysis of these revision treaties from an international law perspective, see B. de Witte, 'Treaty Revision in the European Union: Constitutional Change through International Law', XXXV *NYIL* (The Hague, T.M.C. Asser Press 2004) pp. 51-84.

[21] The denomination 'Decisions of representatives of the member state governments' is a particular denomination of international treaties that was developed early on in the Community legal order, and is used to describe agreements in simplified form that do not seem to require, in the view of their authors, the approval of the national parliaments of the Member States, and may enter into force without ratification. See K. Lenaerts and P. Van Nuffel, *Constitutional Law of the European Union*, 2nd edn. (London, Sweet & Maxwell 2005), at pp. 39-40; B. de Witte, 'Chameleonic Member States: Differentiation by Means of Partial and Parallel International Agreements', in Bruno de Witte, Dominik Hanf and Ellen Vos, *The Many Faces of Differentiation in EU Law* (Antwerp, Oxford, New York, Intersentia, 2001), at pp. 251-255.

[22] Athena is the mechanism set up to manage the common costs of EU military operations.

States of Western and Central Europe. Instead, there has been a decline in the importance of international agreements between single States of the EU, which have become relatively rare except in some niche areas such as double taxation, cultural cooperation, maritime boundaries and trans-frontier administrative cooperation. The role of these *partial agreements* between EU Member States will be examined in the next section as a separate phenomenon characterising the evolution of the EU Member States towards becoming 'strange subjects' of international law.

4. Partial agreements between EU Member States: Instrument of neighbourly relations and of intra-EU flexibility

When the European Economic Community (hereafter, EEC) Treaty was concluded back in 1957, it was clear to all that the new Community institutions would not provide the exclusive framework for relations between the six Member States. The EEC Treaty terminated none of the existing bilateral or multilateral treaties between them. During the negotiation of the EEC Treaty, and in the period immediately afterwards, several partial agreements were concluded, also on matters related to those covered by the EEC Treaty; a prominent example is the Treaty establishing the Benelux Economic Union which was concluded on 3 February 1958, that is, only one month after the entry into force of the EEC Treaty. In anticipation of this, Article 233 EC (today, Article 306) stated – and still States today – that the EEC Treaty does not preclude 'the existence or completion of regional unions between Belgium and Luxembourg, or between Belgium, Luxembourg and the Netherlands ...'. Benelux cooperation was not the only form of international cooperation between small groups of States; for many years, the hegemonic position of the EC was not well established, and, as Helen Wallace notes, the history of relationships between European countries was also one 'of often vigorous regional groupings and intense special partnerships between neighbours.'[23] She adds that 'it is only quite recently that the argument for conceiving of the EU as all-encompassing in terms of both countries and of functional cooperation has gained momentum.'

There are indeed numerous examples of international agreements concluded between Member States of the EU ever since the 1950s, in areas such as tax law, environmental protection, defence, culture and education. The most prominent example of a partial agreement was the Schengen cooperation regime, composed of a first Agreement signed in 1985, and an implementing Convention adopted in 1990. Schengen cooperation was started at a time when a general consensus on abolishing the controls on persons at the intra-Community borders could not be reached (as it still cannot today, because of the position taken by the UK). The Schengen instruments were expressly presented as an interim arrangement in preparation of a final regime at the level of the European Community, rather than as a separate and

[23] H. Wallace, 'Flexibility: A Tool for Integration or a Restraint on Disintegration?', in K. Neunreither and A. Wiener (eds.), *European Integration after Amsterdam: Institutional Dynamics and Prospects for Democracy* (Oxford, Oxford University Press 2000) p. 175, at p. 176.

rival cooperation regime. The same reasons which justified the rule of Article 233 EEC Treaty, whereby the Benelux countries could adopt more advanced measures of integration, could be applied to Schengen.

So, by the mid-1990s, despite the much broader remit of EU activities since Maastricht, closer cooperation between smaller groups of countries outside the EU framework in matters of migration, border controls and police cooperation, became a prominent political reality, and was seen by some observers as a threat to the integrity of the European legal order. Indeed, the wish to avoid *inter se* agreements and to increase the incentives for making the EU framework predominant, was one of the strategic objectives pursued by those Member States pushing for a new intra-EU flexibility mechanism during the 1996-1997 IGC.[24] Yet, the establishment of a mechanism of enhanced cooperation by the Treaty of Amsterdam did not imply that international agreements between Member States *outside* the EU institutional framework would henceforth be outlawed. Indeed, such agreements continue to be concluded, as illustrated by the recent example of the Prüm Convention, concluded on 27 May 2005 between Belgium, Germany, Spain, France, Luxembourg, the Netherlands and Austria, for developing their cross-border cooperation in combating terrorism, cross-border crime and illegal migration.[25]

The fact that the Member States may, in principle, continue to conclude treaties between themselves, does not mean that they are entirely free to do so as and how they wish.[26] *Inter se* international agreements between two or more Member States of the EU are allowed, but only within the limits set by EU law obligations. In short, this means that such agreements may not be concluded in areas of exclusive EU competence (the same rule that prevents Member States from concluding treaties with third States also, and obviously, applies to their mutual relations), that they may not affect the normal operation of the EU institutional mechanisms (as a result of the duty of sincere cooperation), and they may not include any provisions that conflict with EU law or undermine existing EU policies. The practical importance of the principle of primacy of EU law over partial agreements between Member States was recently illustrated in a judgment of the ECJ that found the application of a Schengen Convention rule to be incompatible with the rights of free movement, which third country nationals who are family members of EU citizens derive from Community law.[27] The Court's finding was facilitated by the fact that Article 134 of the Schengen Convention contained an express conflict rule giving priority to Community law, but the ECJ would no doubt have

[24] H. Wallace, *supra* n. 23, at p. 188.

[25] The text of this Convention can be found in Council document 10900/05 of 7 July 2005.

[26] For a legal analysis of the admissibility of such agreements, see B. de Witte, 'Old-fashioned Flexibility: International Agreements between Member States of the European Union', in G. de Búrca and J. Scott (eds.), *Constitutional Change in the EU – From Uniformity to Flexibility?* (Oxford, Hart Publishing 2000) p. 31. See also the study by L.S. Rossi, *Le convenzioni fra gli Stati membri dell'Unione europea* (Milano, Giuffrè 2000).

[27] ECJ, Case C-503/03 *Commission* v. *Spain*, judgment of 31 January 2006, particularly the recitals 33 to 35.

come to the same conclusion with regard to a partial agreement not containing such an express primacy rule.

The priority of EC law (and EU law) over conflicting international agreements concluded between the Member States is an important cornerstone of the constitutional debate about the future of the European Union. Indeed, the idea of a vanguard or pioneer group of Member States arises regularly whenever the constitutional reform process of the EU is hampered by political reluctance, or failure to ratify a revision treaty, of one or more other States.[28] It became briefly prominent when the Intergovernmental Conference, at the Brussels European Council meeting of December 2003, failed to reach agreement on the text of a draft Constitutional Treaty. The French President immediately recalled the idea of a two-speed Europe, with a pioneer group of countries led by France and Germany. That pioneer group would set out to achieve the ambitious objectives of the draft Constitutional Treaty proposed by the Convention on the Future of the Union, in the absence of an agreement by all twenty-five national governments. This revival of the pioneer group idea did not last for long, though, since the European Council of June 2004 did eventually reach agreement on the text of the Constitutional Treaty. However, the prospect that the Constitutional Treaty would fail to enter into force, following the popular referenda in France and the Netherlands, renewed the interest in the possibility of setting up a 'core Europe' by means of a separate international agreement between those Member States that are willing and able to go ahead with the kind of reforms envisaged in the Constitutional Treaty.

Even though it now seems likely that the Lisbon Treaty will enter into force in 2009, the question of further revisions of the Treaty on European Union and the Treaty on the Functioning of the European Union will inevitably arise. It is easy to predict that many of their provisions will soon appear unsatisfactory or unduly constraining and that some countries will want to see those provisions revised, whereas others will resist further change. Given the rigid insistence, in the amended text of Article 48 EU Treaty, on an overall consensus by all 27 States on future changes of the Treaty, there may be acrimonious disagreements between the Member States, and plans for pioneer and vanguard groups of States may then be taken from the shelf again. In other words, the creation of a pioneer group of States, and the threat of these States to resort to separate break-away international treaties, may be a regular feature of the political and legal discourse about the future of European integration in the years to come. However, the formation of a true core group, adopting binding laws in a large range of crucial policy areas, is difficult to imagine because it would unavoidably affect the rights which the other Member States and their citizens have under current EU law, and thus fall foul of the principle that EU law prevails over international agreements concluded between its Member States.

---

[28] See B. de Witte, 'Future Paths of Flexibility: Enhanced Cooperation, Partial Agreements and Pioneer Groups', in J.W. de Zwaan et al., *The European Union: An Ongoing Process of Integration – Liber Amicorum Alfred E. Kellermann* (The Hague, T.M.C. Asser Press 2004), pp. 140-152.

In current practice, though, partial agreements between Member States are principally used for more mundane matters. They deal with subjects not yet absorbed within the scope of activities of the European Community or European Union, either because they are of concern only to two or three countries and not to the European Union as a whole (this is typically the case for agreements dealing with the protection of rivers or mountain ranges) or because their subject-matter lies outside Community law-making competence, as is the case with culture and education, and (more controversially) with bilateral tax treaties. These agreements may still be rather numerous,[29] but they no longer deal with vital matters of foreign policy.

One could even venture the view that on the *European* treaty-making scene (that is, treaty relations limited to the European continent) the EC and EU have become the dominant actors and the single Member States play only a secondary role. On the world scene (that is, for treaty relations involving non-European States), the situation is still quite different, with the Member States remaining at least as prominent as the EC and EU.

5. Fragmented sovereignty in Europe

In the preceding pages of this contribution, I have looked mainly at treaty law and treaty practice, but the special position of the EU Member States could also be illustrated by looking more broadly at State (and EC) practice, including the adoption of unilateral acts and statements, and the action taken in the framework of multilateral organisations. Also in those other areas of State practice, Member States are constrained in their freedom by the existence of European Community and European Union competences and concrete European norms. The nature of the constraint is, of course, different in the European Community context from the European Union context. With regard to CFSP, the Member States are subject to a duty to 'refrain from any action which is contrary to the interests of the Union or likely to impair its effectiveness as a cohesive force in international relations.'[30] With regard to EC external relations, the Member State duties are not as concisely defined but are more rigorous in practice, given the existence of the Community instruments to obtain Member State compliance (foremost, the infringement proceedings before the ECJ), which are not available to ensure compliance with European Union external action under the second and third pillar.

In view of this treaty and non-treaty practice, how could one characterise the place of EU Member States among the subjects of international law? There is a

[29] For example, of the 67 bilateral agreements concluded by France that were published in the *Journal Officiel* in 2004, 11 were concluded with fellow EU Member States. In 2003, 18 out of 72 were concluded with EU Member States (counting among them the new Member States that joined the EU only on 1 May 2004). The figures are calculated from the lists published in the *AFDI* (2003) and (2004).

[30] EU Treaty, Art. 11(2), second para.

long standing literature on the existence of 'not-full sovereign States'[31] in international law, which was recently revived by experiences of States, or parts of States, which became subject to international administration. Recently, there have been multiple examples of 'suspended', 'damaged' or 'residual' sovereignty.[32] Could the Member States of the EU also be fitted within this category of not entirely sovereign States, given the legal constraints on their external activities? After all, the capacity to enter into the full range of international relations continues to be listed among the main legal characteristics of a State,[33] and therefore States whose range of international relations is seriously curtailed could be considered to be not fully sovereign.

To call the Member States of the EU 'semi-sovereign' or at least 'not fully sovereign' States may seem a very heretic statement, and certainly not one that foreign affairs ministries of the Member States would be willing to endorse. However, there is no reason to pity these semi-sovereign States if one compares their effective space for political and legal maneuver with that of other European States, such as Norway, Switzerland or Albania (to name a few). Those other European States who are not members of the European Union may not have formally abandoned a share of their treaty-making power to an international organisation of which they are a member, but they have nevertheless been brought within the 'Eurosphere', within which their effective autonomy is seriously limited. EU Member States, from their side, have not entirely relinquished these fragments of their external sovereignty by allowing the EC/EU to develop its external role, but have rather 'pooled' these fragments of sovereignty within the institutional structure of the European Union, so as to enhance their joint capacity for effective international action. They have retained a partial but direct influence on the content of European Union policy-making through their participation in the Council of Ministers and all its working groups, and they have retained the ability to appear as co-signatories, with the EC, of a number of important mixed agreements. The constraints of EU membership are thus easily outweighed by the increased opportunities for external influence that this membership offers them. All Member State governments seem to agree on this point, though the governments of the smaller Member States might agree more readily than those of traditional international powers such as the United Kingdom and France. In legal terms, this could be described as a case of 'mixed sovereignty',

---

[31] I take this expression from L. Oppenheim, *International Law – A Treatise*, 8th edn. by H. Lauterpacht (London, Longman 1955), at p. 119.

[32] See the following accounts, among many others: B. Knoll, 'United Nations *Imperium*: Horizontal and Vertical Transfer of Effective Control and the Concept of Residual Sovereignty in "Internationalized Territories"', 7 *Austrian Review of International and European Law* (2002), pp. 3-52; C. Tomuschat, 'Yugoslavia's Damaged Sovereignty over the Province of Kosovo', in G. Kreijen (ed.), *State, Sovereignty, and International Governance* (Oxford, Oxford University Press 2002), p. 323; E. de Wet, 'The Direct Administration of Territories by the United Nations and its Member States in the Post Cold-War Era: Legal Bases and Implications for National Law', 8 *Max Planck Yearbook of United Nations Law* (2004), pp. 291-340.

[33] J. Crawford, *The Creation of States in International Law*, 2nd edn. (Oxford, Oxford University Press 2006) at p. 61.

in which sovereignty remains comprehensive but is manifested to the outside world in a non-unitary way, sometimes by the Member States, sometimes by the EC/EU, and sometimes by both acting together.[34]

The situation is not altogether satisfactory, though. From the point of view of *efficient problem-solving*, it is not always obvious that the lost capacity of action by the Member States is entirely compensated by the joint capacity of action through the EC/EU. This is due to the fact that (too) many external relations actions of the European Union remain subject to the unanimity rule, not only under the second and third pillar but also in first pillar (EC) matters where recourse to mixed agreements automatically means a reversion to unanimity as the mode of decision-making. It is also due, more generally, to the viscosity of EU decision-making procedures concerning external relations.

Problems also arise from a different perspective, namely that of the *constitutional quality* of foreign policy. The relative efficiency gain inherent in transferring treaty-making powers from the national to the European level (subject to the reservations made above) is often accompanied by a loss of transparency, democratic control and judicial review of respect for the rule of law and human rights. This is particularly so in second and third pillar matters, where both the European Parliament and the ECJ are by and large excluded.[35] The 'third pillar' agreements concluded between the European Union and the USA on extradition and mutual legal assistance provide a graphic illustration of this danger.[36] The replacement of the Member States by the European Union as an international law actor is therefore not neutral in terms of constitutional values.

Let us now shift back from the internal European perspective (of the relations between the EC/EU and its Member States) to the broader 'external' perspective of the evolution of the system of public international law. The first thing to note is that third States only half-heartedly accommodate the 'fragmented sovereignty' situation of Europe. Whereas the EC and EU are easily accepted by third countries as parties to bilateral treaties, they are less easily accepted as parties to multilateral agreements. Even where the door is opened for participation by the European Communities, this is often done in a circumlocutory, and almost hypocritical way, refer-

---

[34] For a reformulation of traditional sovereignty doctrine along these lines, see E. Cannizzaro, 'Fragmented Sovereignty? The European Union and its Member States in the International Arena', *Italian Yearbook of International Law*, Vol. XIII (Leiden, Brill Academic Publishers 2003), pp. 35-57, particularly at pp. 56-57. This description of the current state of Member States' sovereignty does not imply that they have lost the authority to withdraw entirely from the European Union and thus recover their fully-fledged sovereignty (or, at least as 'fully-fledged' as that of other countries). But such withdrawal has become politically very unattractive for them.

[35] R. Wessel, 'Good Governance and EU Foreign, Security and Defence Policy', in D. Curtin and R. Wessel (eds.), *Good Governance and the European Union* (Antwerpen, Intersentia 2005), pp. 215-251. For a broader perspective, dealing with both EC and EU external activities, see C. Lord, 'Accountable and Legitimate? The EU's International Role', in C. Hill and M. Smith (eds.), *International Relations and the European Union* (Oxford, Oxford University Press 2005) pp. 113-133.

[36] See the case-study by T. Georgopoulos, 'What Kind of Treaty-Making Power for the EU? Constitutional Problems Related to the Conclusion of the EU-US Agreements on Extradition and Mutual Legal Assistance', 30 *EL Rev.* (2005), pp. 190-208.

ring to the general category of 'regional economic international organisations' rather than to the EC directly. Take, as an illustrative example, the International Convention for the Protection of New Varieties of Plants of 1991. This Convention was opened for accession by any State and by 'any international organisation' but only if it has competence in respect of matters governed by the Convention, and if it has its own legislation on breeders' rights binding on all its Member States. In other words: if it is called the European Community![37] However, it must be conceded that this circumlocutory approach may have practical advantages. After all, there are interesting experiments of regional integration in other parts of the world that may lead, with time, to organisations that are legally similar to the EC and have an autonomous capacity to join multilateral international agreements. Moreover, another advantage is that, if the European Community disappears and is absorbed by the European Union (as the Lisbon Treaty proposes), the cost of adjusting the external obligations of the EC to this new State of play would be lower.[38]

A special problem is that of the accession of the European Community (or the European Union) to law-making multilateral organisations dealing with matters of its competence, without having obtained membership. This problem has often been noted and analysed in the legal literature. There are some cases in which the EC and EU act like 'black widows'[39] that devour long-established international organisations that stand in their way, as has happened in very different ways with the Western European Union and the Benelux Union.[40] Usually, within the world-wide organisations such as the United Nations Organization and the World Health Organization, life is made more difficult for the EC and EU both by other countries and, more deviously, by their own Member States.[41] It has been argued that the presence of the EC or EU in multilateral organisations may act as a 'catalyst for changing the State-centred structures

[37] This Convention was approved by the European Community only in 2005: OJ 2005, L 192/63 (with text of the Convention in annex).

[38] On this question, see B. Fassbender, 'Die Völkerrechtssubjektivität der Europäischen Union nach dem Entwurf des Verfassungsvertrages', 42 *Archiv des Völkerrechts* (2004), p. 28.

[39] I borrow the expression from Ramses Wessel: R. Wessel, 'The EU as a Black Widow: Devouring the WEU to Give Birth to a European Security and Defence Policy', in V. Kronenberger, *supra* n. 7, pp. 405-434.

[40] Of course, neither of these two organisations has actually disappeared, and both continue to serve a purpose, though a more modest one than prior to the development of EC/EU competences in their domain of activity. On the WEU's present role in relation to the EU, see E. Neframi, 'La politique étrangère et de sécurité commune et l'identité de l'Union européenne', *AFDI* (2004), pp. 826-860, at p. 856.

[41] See, among the numerous scholarly contributions: I. Govaere, J. Capiau and A. Vermeersch, 'In-Between Seats: The Participation of the European Union in International Organizations', 9 *EFA Rev.* (2004), pp. 155-187; E. Johansson-Nogues, 'The Fifteen and the Accession States in the UN General Assembly: What Future for European Foreign Policy in the Coming Together of the Old and New Europe?', 9 *EFA Rev.* (2004), pp. 67-92; L. Bini Smaghi, 'A Single Seat in the IMF?', 42 *Journal of Common Market Studies* (2004), pp. 229-248; J. Wouters, F. Hoffmeister and T. Ruys (eds.), *The United Nations and the European Union: An Ever Stronger Partnership* (The Hague, T.M.C. Asser Press 2006).

of the law of international organisations',[42] but more often than not the looming presence of this new actor provokes a conservative reflex among States who try to 'minimise the damage' caused by this unfamiliar legal phenomenon. Here again, the Member States of the EU are situated differently from other States: whereas the latter are free to try to keep the European Community 'out of the door' of a multilateral organisation, the EU Member States are under a duty of cooperation, which implies that they should facilitate accession of the Community where such accession would facilitate its tasks. A recent breakthrough in this regard is the decision to adapt the Statute of the Hague Conference on Private International Law so as to allow 'any regional economic international organisation' as a member, thus allowing the European Community to negotiate and conclude 'Hague' conventions directly rather than through the intermediary of its Member States.[43]

Not surprisingly, the European Community and European Union are more openly accommodated in the context of multilateral treaties that are limited to the European region, such as the numerous conventions concluded within the framework of the Council of Europe. In those conventions, the European Community often appears as one of the regular Parties alongside its Member States, and special arrangements are made for its participation in the management of the Convention. In fact, if the Council of Ministers of the EU is convinced by the Commission that participation of the EC to a new Council of Europe convention is necessary or useful, then the other members of the Council of Europe usually will not try to stop this from happening, since the EU group is clearly dominant in the Council of Europe. Things may be different when the EU seeks to join an existing Council of Europe Convention, as could be the case, soon, for the European Convention of Human Rights. In such cases, the existing non-EU parties of the Convention (such as Russia) have a considerable blockage power, since the agreement of most or all existing State parties is needed to allow EU accession.

Also, in the legal regime established by Council of Europe conventions, EU Member States are often treated differently from other States through the use of so-called *disconnection clauses*. These clauses provide that if the Council of Europe convention overlaps with EU legislation on the same subject, then EU law will prevail in the mutual relations between EU Member States. The disconnection clause was first introduced in the late 1980s when the Council of Europe adopted a Convention on Transfrontier Television almost at the same time as the European Community enacted its Directive on television without frontiers, and it has repeatedly been used since. As an example of this practice, one may refer to the Council of Europe Convention on the Prevention of Terrorism (concluded in Warsaw on 16 May 2005), whose Article 26(3), provides as follows:

---

[42] E.-U. Petersmann, 'International Activities of the European Union and Sovereignty of Member States', in E. Cannizzaro (ed.), *The European Union as an Actor in International Relations* (The Hague-London-Boston, Kluwer Law International 2002), pp. 321-345, at pp. 331-332.

[43] See Final Act of the Twentieth Session of the Hague Conference, 30 June 2005, and the Council Decision 2006/719 of 5 October 2006 on the accession of the European Community to the Hague Conference on Private International Law, OJ 2006, L 297. The European Community is a member of the Hague Conference since 3 April 2007.

> 'Parties which are members of the European Union shall, in their mutual relations, apply Community and European Union rules in so far as there are Community or European Union rules governing the particular subject concerned and applicable to the specific case, without prejudice to the object and purpose of the present Convention and without prejudice to its full application with other Parties.'

Through disconnection clauses, EU Member States become 'hyphened' parties to those Council of Europe conventions, since many of the rights and obligations contained in those conventions do not actually apply to their relations with other EU countries. The Council of Europe instrument is thus likely to become a marginal matter for them, much to the chagrin of the non-EU contracting parties.[44]

6. Conclusion

Textbooks of international law, especially those written by European authors and/or for European students, should perhaps give greater prominence, in their discussion of the age-old topic of 'subjects of international law', to the fact that the European Community and now also the European Union are something more than just any 'regional economic international organisation', and that the Member States of the EC and EU are no longer sovereign States to the same extent as other States in the world. This does not imply that the term 'sovereignty' is still an accurate description of the *political* position in which all other countries of the world find themselves – this is another debate which I do not wish to enter into here. But in *legal* terms, the freedom of action of EU Member States is – for as long as they remain members – limited in more numerous and meaningful ways than that of other States. This phenomenon may disturb the calm waters of international law doctrine, but is on the whole beneficial for the European countries involved and for their citizens. The pooling of their sovereignty in the external domain allows them, most of the time, to act more efficiently in the pursuit of their common interest on the world scene, and it leads them, arguably, to the development of a common European conception of international law.[45] Whether this common action and this common conception is also to the benefit of mankind as a whole is quite another

[44] For a discussion of these disconnection clauses and similar devices aiming at preserving the integrity of pre-existing or future EU law against conflicting international obligations, see J. Klabbers, 'Safeguarding the Organizational *Acquis*: the EU's External Practice', *International Organizations Law Review* (2007), pp. 57-89. The misgivings which the frequent use of disconnection clauses has provoked from the side of other Council of Europe Member States are noted in the report by Jean-Claude Juncker, *Council of Europe – European Union: "A Sole Ambition for the European Continent"*, Report to the attention of the Heads of State or Government of the Member States of the Council of Europe, 11 April 2006, at pp. 14-15.

[45] On the latter point, see R. Gosalbo Bono, 'Some Reflections on the CFSP Legal Order', 43 *CML Rev.* (2006), pp. 337-394, at 379 et seq. For an analysis emphasizing the particular configuration of the European Union as a global actor with distinct characteristics from the sum of its member states, see M. Cremona, 'The Union as a Global Actor: Roles, Models and Identity', 41 *CML Rev.* (2004), pp. 553-573.

matter, although some authors argue that the European Community and European Union, perhaps because of their own cooperative origins, tend to be less inspired by power politics than some of its Member States used to be in the past.[46] One element which distinguishes the EC/EU's foreign policy is that it seeks to promote regional cooperation and integration in other parts of the world, following its own model so to speak.[47] In doing so, it aims also at turning these other States into 'strange subjects' of international law.

---

[46] For some elements that allow to assess this claim, see A. Linklater, 'A European Civilising Process', in *International Relations and the European Union, supra* n. 35, pp. 367-387, particularly at pp. 382-385.

[47] N. Alecu de Flers and E. Regelsberger, 'The EU and Inter-Regional Cooperation', in *International Relations and the European Union, supra* n. 35, pp. 317-342; K.E. Smith, *European Union Foreign Policy in a Changing World* (Cambridge, Polity Press 2003), chapter 4.

Chapter 4
THE STATUS OF INTERNATIONAL LAW IN THE EUROPEAN LEGAL ORDER: THE CASE OF INTERNATIONAL TREATIES AND NON-BINDING INTERNATIONAL INSTRUMENTS

Christian Tietje*

1. INTRODUCTION

The European Community (EC) is a contracting party to numerous bilateral and multilateral treaties. Moreover, it is actively engaged in numerous international organisations and institutions of different legal character. Today the EC is therefore an important actor in the international community. It is obvious that its significant international role not only shapes the international system, but also has repercussions on the internal legal order of the Community. In other words, the more the EC is legally and/or politically involved in international structures, the more incidences of legal and political interdependence occur.[1] Prime examples of this are international treaties to which the EC is a contracting party. These will be the main focus of this chapter. However, it is not only interesting to analyse international commitments which are binding on the EC, but also international instruments which are *prima facie* not binding on the EC. As will be demonstrated, the latter are not only increasingly important in the international system, but are also of growing significance to the legal order of the EC.

This chapter is structured as follows: The first part will briefly outline the (more or less undisputed) legal framework concerning the relationship of international treaties to which the EC is a contracting party, and Community law. The second part will deal with some aspects of the well-known and problematic issue of the special relationship between WTO law and EC law. In the next part, the important issue of so-called mixed agreements and related aspects concerning infringement procedures (Article 226 EC Treaty) and responsibility under public international law and EC law will be discussed. Finally, some aspects of the rela-

* Dr. jur., LL.M. (Michigan), Professor of Public Law, European Law and International Economic Law, Director of the Institute for Economic Law, and Director of the Transnational Economic Law Research Center (TELC), Faculty of Law, Martin-Luther-University Halle-Wittenberg, Germany.

[1] See C. Walter, *Die Folgen der Globalisierung für die Europäische Verfassungsdiskussion* [Consequences of Globalisation on the Debate on a European Constitution], Deutsches Verwaltungsblatt (2000) pp. 1-13.

J. Wouters, P.A. Nollkaemper, E. de Wet (eds.), The Europeanisation of International Law

tionship between international instruments which are not binding on the EC and Community law will be briefly highlighted, and some overall conclusions will be drawn.

2. The general framework

The general framework concerning the relationship between international treaties to which the EC is a contracting party and Community law is governed by Articles 281 and 300(7) EC Treaty. Article 281 EC Treaty provides the EC with international legal personality, and thus the ability to become a party to an international agreement governed by international law as defined in the Vienna Convention on the Law of Treaties[2] and the Vienna Convention on the Law of Treaties between States and International Organisations or between International Organisations.[3]

Even though the legal personality of the EC under international law does not cause any problems as such, one obviously has to bear in mind that the capacity of the EC to conclude international treaties is restricted to those areas in which the EC has been granted the respective competences by its Member States. The principle that an international organisation may only conclude agreements in those areas in which it is competent to act is well recognised in public international law,[4] and is therefore not unique to the EC. It inherently implies that one cannot strictly distinguish between the internal law governing the relationship of the respective organisation and its Member States on the one hand, and public international law on the other. This is all the more important in the case of the EC. As the EC Treaty – as it is well-known – established a new legal order of a distinctive character which can be characterised today as being of a constitutional nature, its internal complexity and its specific features with regard to the relationship of the Community to its Member States must always be taken into account. The principle of public international law according to which the internal constitutional order of a state is irrelevant from a perspective of international law[5] is therefore not entirely applicable – at least not at first glance.

Once the EC has concluded an international agreement its legal effects are twofold, and in this regard one has to start the analysis by drawing a distinction between the perspective of public international law and the EC perspective. From the point of view of public international law, the EC is bound by the treaty, notwithstanding possible problems which might occur regarding the internal legal structure of the Community. This is without question if the treaty at issue was concluded entirely by the EC, without the direct participation of the Member States.[6]

[2] 1155 *UNTS* 331, No. 18232.

[3] Not yet in force, reprinted in *ILM* 25 (1986), p. 543.

[4] H.G. Schermers and N.M. Blokker, *International Institutional Law*, 4th edn. (Boston, Mass. et al., Nijhoff 2003) § 1748.

[5] See also G. Dahm, J. Delbrück, and R. Wolfrum, *Völkerrecht* [Public International Law], Bd. I/1, 2nd edn. (Berlin, Walter de Gruyter 1989) p. 102 et seq. and 123 p. et seq.

[6] See P. Eeckhout, *External Relations of the European Union – Legal and Constitutional Foundations* (Oxford et al., Oxford University Press 2004) p. 276 et seq.

The more problematic case of so-called mixed agreements will be dealt with in the latter part of this chapter.

The general rule of international law as codified in the common Articles 46 of the aforementioned Vienna Conventions, according to which a contracting party to an international agreement may not rely on its national laws in order to justify a treaty violation, indicates, from an international law perspective, a hierarchy of norms. This means that international treaty law prevails over both primary and secondary EC law.[7] It also means that the European Court of Justice (ECJ) – from an international law perspective – does not have the power to void a treaty that is in conflict with EC law. The Court may only declare invalid the act of an institution of the EC by which a treaty was concluded. This only affects the internal validity of the respective action, not the binding effect of the treaty from the perspective of public international law. It seems that the Court has recognised this principle, even though the wording of its decision regarding the illegality under EC law of the treaty on cooperation in competition law matters with the United States has raised some doubts.[8]

Traditionally, international law does not regulate the question of the legal status of an international agreement within the internal legal order of a contracting party.[9] This principle also applies to the EC. It is therefore up to Community law to determine how an international agreement gains legal relevance in EC law, and which hierarchical status it will have. The ECJ decided on this question in its famous *Haegeman* judgment, and held that from the entry into force of the respective treaty, its provisions form an integral part of Community law.[10] The far-reaching effects of this decision are of course only evident if one takes into account the general principle of *Costa* v. *ENEL* regarding the supremacy of EC law in general.[11] Resulting from a joint reading of *Costa* v. *ENEL* and *Haegeman*, provisions of an international agreement which have been concluded by the EC have, by virtue of EC law, supremacy over the internal law of the EC Member States.

However, the status of an international treaty as an integral part of Community law does not say anything about its hierarchical status within the sources of EC law. As regards the EC Treaty itself, that is to say primary EC law, Article 300(1), (5), (6) and (7) clearly indicate that – from the perspective of EC law – the

[7] A. Peters, 'The Position of International Law Within the European Community Legal Order', 40 *GYIL* (1997) at p. 36.

[8] Case C-327/91 *France* v. *Commission* [1994] ECR I-3641, in which the Court in the operative part held: 'Declares void the act whereby the Commission of the European Communities sought to conclude the Agreement with the United States of America regarding the application of the competition laws of the European Communities and the United States, which was signed and entered into force on 23 September 1991'; different however Case C-360/93 *Parlament* v. *Council* [1996] ECR I-1195; Case 207/96 *Commission* v. *Italy* [1997] ECR I-6869; see also H. Keller, *Rezeption des Völkerrechts* [The Reception of International Law] (Berlin et al., Springer 2003) pp. 258 and 560.

[9] G. Dahm et al., *supra* n. 5, at p.106.

[10] ECJ, Case 181/73 *Haegeman* v. *Belgium* [1974] ECR 449 para. 5.

[11] ECJ, Case 6/64 *Costa* v. *ENEL* [1964] ECR 1151.

EC treaty has priority over international treaty law.[12] Moreover, Article 300(7) EC Treaty provides that treaties concluded by the Community 'shall be binding on the institutions of the Community.' Consequently, the ECJ explicitly referred to 'the primacy of international agreements concluded by the Community over provisions of secondary Community legislation.'[13] In sum, within the sources of EC law, the hierarchical status of an international agreement concluded by the Community is between primary and secondary law. There is only one exception to this general principle. According to two recent judgments of the Court of First Instance, the UN Charter prevails over any EC law not only from the perspective of public international law (see Article 103 UN Charter) but also as a principle of EC law, if the EC – which is not a member of the UNO – took over the functions of its Member States within the UN legal system.[14]

Both the well-established case-law of the ECJ on international agreements being an integral part of Community law, and the recognised hierarchical status of international treaties within the sources of EC law have inspired many scholars to the opinion that the relationship of EC law and international treaties is of a monist nature.[15] It is certainly true that EC law does not follow a classical dualist model. However, it is doubtful whether one can really speak of a monist approach of EC law towards international treaties. Without going into too much detail, three arguments against a monist model shall be highlighted. First, the monist/dualist doctrine has historically been developed on the grounds of state sovereignty. It is more than questionable whether the concept of 'sovereignty' can be applied to the EC and to a framework which not only deals with the relationship between sources of law from two different origins, but with three legal regimes: international law, EC law and internal law of the Member States. Second, from a theoretical point of view it is, at the very least, difficult to explain how the ECJ may void the internal legal effects of an international agreement concluded in violation of EC law. If EC law followed a monist model, it would be doubtful whether one could draw a distinction between the legal effects of a treaty from the perspective of international law on the one hand, and EC law on the other. Third, and most important, if one were to follow the monist approach, which would mean that no transformation of international law into Community law would occur, it would be hard to explain why provisions of an international treaty should have priority over the internal laws of those Member States which follow a dualist model.[16] Taking these arguments into account, we reach the conclusion that the relationship of EC law to international treaty law may not be explained according to the classical doctrine of

---

[12] A. Peters 1997, *supra* n. 7, at p. 38 et seq. with further references.

[13] Case C-61/94 *Commission* v. *Germany* [1996] ECR I-3989 para. 52.

[14] CFI, Judgments of 21 September 2005, Case T-306/01 *Ahmed Ali Yusuf und Al Barakaat International Foundation* v. *Council and Commission* and Case T-315/01 *Yassin Abdullah Kadi* v. *Council and Commission*.

[15] See P.J. Kuijper, 'Direct effect, implementation, compensation for damages, or none of this?', 42 *CMLR* (2005), p. 1314.

[16] For these and other arguments see A. Peters 1997, *supra* n. 7, at p. 28 et seq.

monism and dualism. It is far more appropriate to speak of the 'communitarisation' of international law, as has already been suggested in the legal literature some years ago.[17]

Two more aspects concerning EC law and international treaties shall be mentioned briefly. First, according to well-established case-law of the ECJ, individuals may directly rely on provisions of an agreement to which the EC is a contracting party, if the conditions for 'direct effect' or 'direct applicability'[18] are fulfilled. In this regard, the ECJ applies a two-pronged test. First it asks whether, as a matter of principle, the respective international agreement is of such a nature that it might create directly effective rights and obligations for individuals. If this is answered affirmatively, the Court goes on to ask whether the provision in question is 'legally perfect' so as to directly create individual rights.[19] It is important to note that this two-pronged test was developed by the Court in preliminary rulings (Article 234 EC Treaty). Thus the ECJ only dealt with the possibility of invoking provisions of an international treaty before the judge of a Member State. This is one aspect which has to be borne in mind while discussing why the Court seems to take, at least concerning the results, a different approach in annulment procedures (Article 230 EC Treaty), notably with regard to WTO law.[20]

Second, the Court also made it clear in its more recent case-law that because international treaty law is an integral part of Community law, there is an obligation under EC law for national courts 'when called upon to apply national rules' related to a respective international agreement 'to do so, as far as possible, in the light of the wording and purpose' of the applicable provisions of this agreement.[21] This principle of interpretation in conformity with international law also applies to secondary EC law. The Court explicitly held that

> 'the primacy of international agreements concluded by the Community over provisions of secondary Community legislation means that such provisions must, so far as is possible, be interpreted in a manner that is consistent with those agreements.'[22]

3. WTO LAW AND EC LAW

Thus far, more or less undisputed aspects of the relationship between international agreements and EC law have been discussed. More controversial issues arise when one looks at different types of international agreements to which the Community is

[17] A. Peters 1997, *supra* n. 7, at p. 34 *et seq.*

[18] On the problems of confusing terminology in this regard see Peters 1997, *supra* n. 7, at p. 42.

[19] See ECJ, Case 12/86 *Demirel* v. *Stadt Schwäbisch Gmünd* [1987] ECR 3719, para. 14; ECJ, Case C-162/96 *Racke* v. *Hauptzollamt Mainz* [1998] ECR I-3655, para. 31; ECJ, Case C-300/98 *Christian Dior* [2000] ECR I-11307, para. 42.

[20] For this important aspect see also H. Keller 2003, *supra* n. 8, at p. 561 et seq.; A. Peters 1997, *supra* n. 7, at p. 50 et seq.

[21] ECJ, Case C-53/96 *Hermès* [1998] ECR I-3603, para. 28.

[22] ECJ, Case C-61/94 *supra* n. 13, *Commission* v. *Germany*, at para. 52.

a contracting party, and also the different subject-matters regulated by these treaties.

The most prominent controversial topic is of course the relationship between WTO and Community law. I will not go into the details of this discussion, on which so much has been written on already. Rather, I will touch upon only a few aspects.

First, it is important to recall that the ECJ in its well-established case-law denies direct effect as a possibility of individuals to refer to WTO law before national courts or the courts of the Community.[23] Moreover, the ECJ also held that '... having regard to their nature and structure, the WTO agreements are not in principle among the rules in the light of which the Court is to review the legality of measures adopted by the Community institutions.'[24] However, the Court – at least on paper – recognises that its *Fediol*[25] and *Nakajima*[26] case-law still applies, and that, with regard to WTO law, there is also the aforementioned obligation of interpreting Member State law and secondary EC law in conformity with the WTO agreements.[27] Moreover, the ECJ seems also to apply WTO law to questions of legality concerning measures of harmonisation of Member State law, namely according to Article 95 EC Treaty. In the case of *Netherlands* v. *Parliament and Council*,[28] concerning the biotechnology directive, the Netherlands argued, *inter alia*, that the Directive violated the Agreement on Trade-Related Aspects of Intellectual Property Rights (TRIPS) and imposed obligations on Member States that would lead to a breach of the Member States' TRIPS obligations. The Court – of course – did not touch upon the legality of the Directive directly with regard to TRIPS, but it did make a substantial assessment of the question on whether the Directive imposed obligations on Member States which would force the Member States to violate TRIPS. According to this judgment, the EC cannot enact legislation imposing obligations on Member States which are contrary to the Member States' obligations under WTO law. This is of particular relevance with regard to Article 95 EC Treaty, since the high standard of protection required under Article 95(3) EC Treaty inherently stands in possible conflict with the Agreement on Technical Barriers to Trade (TBT) and the Agreement on the Application of Sanitary and Phytosanitary Measures (SPS). Even though there are no Member State competences in the areas of TBT and SPS, the Member States are bound to the TBT and the SPS agreement under international law. Thus any Directive with obli-

---

[23] See only ECJ, Case C-53/96, *supra* n. 21, *Hermès*; ECJ, Case C-76/00 P *Petrotub and Republica* v. *Council* [2004] ECR I-79; ECJ, Case C-93/02 P *Biret International* v. *Council* [2003] ECR I-10497; ECJ, Case C-377/02 *Léon Van Parys* [2005] ECR I-1465.

[24] Also well-established case-law, most recently ECJ, Case C-377/02, *supra* n. 23, *Léon Van Parys*, at para. 39, with further references.

[25] ECJ, Case 70/87 *Fediol* [1989] ECR 1781.

[26] ECJ, Case 69/89 *Nakajima* [1991] ECR I-2069.

[27] Also ECJ, Case C-377/02 *supra* n. 23 *Léon Van Parys*, at para. 40, with further references.

[28] ECJ, Case C-377/98 *Netherlands* v. *Parliament and Council* ('Biotechnology Directive') [2001] ECR I-7079.

gations for Member States which would force them to violate the TBT or the SPS agreement could be illegal under Community law.

It is important to emphasise that the aforementioned exceptions to the denial of direct effect strongly indicate that the importance of the direct effect of WTO law is often exaggerated.[29] Thus, without analysing and criticising the respective case-law of the ECJ from all possible angles, the focus here will only be on a few aspects. In this regard it seems to be useful to make a comparison between the case-law of the ECJ concerning WTO law and other international agreements.

The areas in which the most far-reaching case-law of the ECJ concerning the direct effect of provisions of international treaties exists are the fields of free trade agreements and agreements of association. In fact it was the Agreement of Association between the European Economic Community (EEC) and Greece of 9 July 1961 that gave rise to the famous statement by the Court that international treaties are an integral part of Community law.[30] The other important judgment, *Kupferberg*,[31] concerned the free trade agreement between the EEC and the Portuguese Republic of 22 July 1972. In both cases the Member States had, in their written and oral submissions, strongly opposed any legal relevance of the agreements within the Community legal order. However, the Court did not follow the Member States' opposition, and laid the ground for a case-law that gives far-reaching effect to international agreements.[32] The most striking aspect of the *Kupferberg* judgment is that the three main arguments of the opposing Member States – institutional balance between the Community organs, lack of reciprocity, and the existence of an autonomous dispute settlement procedure within the respective treaty – were strongly rejected by the Court, but are applied in more or less the same manner today in order to deny the direct applicability of WTO law.[33]

Three different responses are possible if one draws this comparison between *Kupferberg* and the case-law on WTO law. First, one could simply argue that the Court's reasoning in *Portugal* v. *Council*,[34] *Hermès*,[35] *Christian Dior*[36] and other cases is not convincing and may be criticised harshly. Even though there are strong arguments in favour of this approach, it does not bring us any further; the Court has made it clear that it will not revise its case-law on WTO law in the near future. Second, one could try to reconcile *Kupferberg* with the Court's case-law on WTO law by arguing that *Kupferberg* is simply no longer good case-law, and that it ought to be revised. Pieter Jan Kuijper has made this argu-

[29] P.J. Kuijper, 'From Initiating Proceedings to Ensuring Implementation: The Links with the Community Legal Order', Paper presented at the conference 'The WTO at 10: The Role of the Dispute Settlement System', Stresa 11-13 March 2005, 15 (on file with the author).

[30] ECJ, Case 181/73 *supra* n. 10, *Haegeman*, 449.

[31] ECJ, Case 104/81 *Kupferberg* [1982] ECR 3641.

[32] For a detailed analysis see H. Keller 2003, *supra* n. 8, at p. 500 et seq.

[33] See ECJ, Case C-149/96 *Portugal* v. *Council* [1999] ECR I-8395.

[34] ECJ, Case C-149/96 *supra* n. 33, *Portugal* v. *Council.*

[35] ECJ, Case C-53/96 *supra* n. 21, *Hermès.*

[36] ECJ, Case C-300/98 *supra* n. 19, *Christian Dior.*

ment recently.[37] I respectfully disagree, at least in part. I do not see any indication in the case-law of the Court – beyond the issue of WTO law – that *Kupferberg* has ceased to be good case-law. On the contrary, looking at a judgment like that in the recent case of *Simutenkov*,[38] it becomes evident that the Court continues to build upon its *Kupferberg* case-law. Whilst Pieter Jan Kuijper has argued that, from the perspective of today's complexity of international relations, *Kupferberg* has too much of a one-sided positive attitude towards international law, it seems more appropriate to ask what the difference is exactly between WTO law on the one hand, and increasing case-law of the ECJ on the far-reaching effects of international agreements in the Community legal order on the other.

One possible explanation for the diverse case-law of the Court in cases such as *Wählergruppe Gemeinsam Zajedno*,[39] *Gloszczuk*,[40] and *Simutenkov*,[41] on the one hand, and cases such as *Léon Van Parys*[42] concerning WTO law on the other, is to argue that WTO law is not of the same legally perfect character or integrative nature as the association and free trade agreements dealt with by the Court in other cases. This line of reasoning could be based on the lengthy arguments of the Court in its different WTO judgments concerning the importance of diplomatic negotiations within the Dispute Settlement Understanding of the WTO (DSU). It has some persuasive force if one looks at the classic association and free trade agreement cases. These cases more or less dealt with bilateral agreements that established a close relationship between the Community and the respective states on the European continent with the direct or at least indirect perspective of EC membership. Thus one could argue that a higher degree of integration was established between the Community and the respective states compared to the multilateral framework of world trade law. However, the persuasiveness of this line of reasoning started to erode with the *Kziber* judgment.[43] In this case the Court granted direct applicability to provisions of the association agreement with Morocco, which is not based on any perspective of EC membership. Moreover, even though it was very doubtful whether the classic prerequisites for direct applicability in this case really were present, the Court directly applied principles of Community law to the interpretation of the agreement.[44] The case-law of the Court with regard to agreements that only govern a loose relationship of the Community with third states has recently reached its apex in *Simutenkov*.[45] According to this judg-

---

[37] P.J. Kuijper 2005, *supra* n. 15, 42 *CMLR* (2005), at 1317 et seq.

[38] ECJ, Case C-265/03 *Simutenkov* v. *Ministerio de Educación y Cultura and Real Federación Española de Fútbol* [2005] ECR I-2579.

[39] ECJ, Case 171/01 *Wahlergruppe 'Gemeinsam Zajedno/Birlikte Alternative und Grüne GewerkschafterInnen/UG'* v. *Bundesminister für Wirtschaft und Arbeit and Others* [2003] ECR I-4301.

[40] ECJ, Case C-63/99 *The Queen* v. *Secretary of State for the Home Department, ex parte Wieslaw Gloszczuk and Elzbieta Gloszczuk* [2001] ECR I-6369.

[41] ECJ, Case C-265/03 *supra* n. 38.

[42] ECJ, Case C-377/02 *supra* n. 23.

[43] ECJ, Case C-18/90 *Office national de l'emploi* v. *Bahia Kziber* [1991] ECR I-199.

[44] See also H. Keller 2003, *supra* n. 8, at p. 508 et seq.

[45] ECJ, Case C-265/03 *supra* n. 38.

ment, in which the Court granted direct applicability to a provision of the EU-Russia partnership agreement[46] and interpreted this provision by explicit reference to fundamental freedoms of EC law, all partnership agreements of the Community carry the potential of direct applicability. The most prominent example in this regard is the Contonou agreement,[47] which contains a provision that is nearly identical to the one at issue in *Simutenkov*.[48] It is obvious that the nature of these agreements is not as integrative as that of the aforementioned association and free trade agreements. On the contrary, one could make a strong argument that the WTO legal order is far more integrative and of a higher legal density than the partnership agreements of the EC.[49]

Thus, it is not convincing to argue on the basis of the specific legal nature and political rationale of international agreements in order to explain the different approaches of the ECJ. Rather, an analysis of the case-law of the Court indicates there might be another reason. Upon closer inspection of the respective international agreements in question, one sees certain structural differences. The association, free trade and partnership agreements dealt with by the ECJ so far are part of a political and economic framework which could be characterised as being of an asymmetric nature. Even though it would probably be going too far to characterise the respective agreements as being 'unequal treaties',[50] their specific feature is a certain asymmetry to the advantage of the Community.[51] The Community is the politically and economically more powerful contracting party in association, free trade and partnership agreements and it is legally and politically in a position to dominate the framing of these agreements and their operation.[52] This is different with regard to the WTO legal order. Even though the Community is a powerful economic actor within the world trading system, it is not in a position of dominance. Rather, it can only pursue its own interests by way of a multilateral compromise. Thus the position of the EC within the world trading system is of a symmetric multilateral nature.[53]

---

[46] OJ 1997, L 327/1.

[47] Partnership agreement between the members of the African, Caribbean and Pacific Group of States of the one part, and the European Community and its Member States, of the other part, signed in Cotonou on 23 June 2000, OJ L 317/3 of 15/12/2000.

[48] For details see K.A. Schuilenburg, 'The ECJ Simutenkov Case: Is Same Level not Offside after All?', Policy Papers on Transnational Economic Law No. 13, April 2005, available at <http://www.jura.uni-halle.de/telc/policy_papers.html>.

[49] See, e.g., *United States – Sections 301-310 of the Trade Act of 1974*, Report of the Panel of 22 December 1999, WT/DS152/R, para. 7.73 et seq.

[50] For the notion of unequal treaties in public international law see, e.g., G. Dahm, J. Delbrück, and R. Wolfrum, *Völkerrecht* [Public International Law], Bd. I/3, 2nd edn. (Berlin et al., Walter de Gruyter 2002) p. 538.

[51] Similar already A. von Bogdandy, 'Der rechtliche Rahmen der Zugangsregeln' [The Legal Regime for Market Access], in E. Grabitz, A. v. Bogdandy, and M. Nettesheim (eds.), *Europäisches Außenwirtschaftsrecht* [EC Foreign Trade Law] (München, C.H. Beck 1994) p. 70.

[52] H. Keller 2003, *supra* n. 8, at p. 516 et seq.

[53] See also Case C-149/96 *Portugal* v. *Council* [1999] ECR I-8395, para. 42: 'As regards, more particularly, the application of the WTO agreements in the Community legal order, it must be noted that, according to its preamble, the agreement establishing the WTO, including the annexes, is still

In sum, instead of proposing a complete revision of *Kupferberg*, one should realise there currently is not a single approach of Community law towards international agreements. Instead, the relationship between EC law and international treaties depends on the position of the EC within the respective international legal framework, and its ability to preserve or pursue its own interests. The Court seemed to have had this in mind in *Portugal* v. *Council*. Regardless of whether this approach is convincing or not, it at least means that one should openly admit that political and not primarily legal considerations are at stake. However, the Court in *Portugal* v. *Council* and its other WTO decisions tries to give the impression that its reasoning is purely legalistic. It would have been more honest to admit that, in the end, *Portugal* v. *Council* is nothing more than the application of the political-questions-doctrine. The remaining question would thus be whether applying the political-questions-doctrine is permissible under Article 220 EC Treaty.

4. Mixed agreements, infringement procedures and related aspects of responsibility under public international law and EC law

Specific problems occur in the case of so-called mixed agreements, and with regard to infringement procedures (Article 226 EC Treaty). Moreover, it is interesting to take a closer look at the consequences that arise from the international responsibility of the EC.

A first aspect deserving attention concerns the case-law of the ECJ which rules that a Member State may be held liable for a violation of WTO/GATT law within the procedural settings of an infringement procedure (Article 226 EC Treaty).[54] This case-law is of course not undisputed.[55] I will not review all of the numerous arguments that have been put forward criticising the possible contraction between *Portugal* v. *Council* on the one hand and *Commission* v. *Germany*[56] on the other. It is merely worth mentioning that the Court's case-law could be coherent if one were to follow the aforementioned general rationale explaining the different attitudes of the Court towards international agreements. However, one should note that the main problem with the Court's case-law in this regard is not so much the general attitude towards WTO law, but rather a systemic problem within the legal framework of the Common Commercial Policy. The EC's Common Com-

---

founded, like GATT 1947, on the principle of negotiations with a view to "entering into reciprocal and mutually advantageous arrangements" and is thus distinguished, from the viewpoint of the Community, from the agreements concluded between the Community and non-member countries which introduce a certain asymmetry of obligations, or create special relations of integration with the Community, such as the agreement which the Court was required to interpret in Kupferberg.'

[54] ECJ, Case C-61/94 *supra* n. 13, *Commission* v. *Germany*.

[55] For critical assessments see, e.g., G. Berrisch and H.-G. Kamann, 'WTO-Recht im Gemeinschaftsrecht – (k)eine Kehrwende des EuGH' [WTO Law and EC Law – (no) Changes in the Case-Law of the ECJ] *EWS* (2000) p. 89 et seq.; M. Bronckers, *The black hole for EC Member States*, 42 *CMLR* (2005) p. 1342 et seq.

[56] ECJ, Case C-61/94 *supra* n. 13, *Commission* v. *Germany*.

mercial Policy is dominated by the principle of majority voting (Article 133(4) EC Treaty). Thus, according to the current case-law of the Court, a Member State which was overruled in the Council does not have the possibility of challenging the majority position within the Council before the Court. This is due to the fact that primary EC law does not contain a large number of rules concerning trade with third countries, and WTO law is not applicable. This leads to a severe lack of minority protection, which is an essential element of the rule of law.[57]

A related issue which may be more important to consider concerns the question of how so-called mixed agreements are treated by the Court, and what effects they have on the general distribution of competences between the Community and its Member States. From the perspective of Community law, it was already discussed and disputed in *Haegeman II*[58] and *Demirel*[59] whether the Court has jurisdiction with regard to parts of a mixed agreement which are not covered by a respective competence of the Community.[60] The Court circumvented this problem in these cases and only came back to it in *Hermès* and *Christian Dior*. In *Christian Dior* the Court held that even though Member States remain free to make an autonomous decision on the legal status of parts of an international agreement that do not fall within the competence of the Community, in a situation

> 'where a provision … can apply both to situations falling within the scope of national law and to situations falling within that of Community law … the Court has jurisdiction to interpret it in order to forestall future differences of interpretation.'[61]

In recent judgments like *Schieving-Nijstad*[62] and *Anheuser-Busch*[63] the Court has clearly demonstrated that its competence to interpret provisions of mixed agreements is almost unlimited. Taking the specific procedural aspects of Article 234 EC Treaty and the general obligation under EC law of interpreting national law in conformity with obligations under international treaties together, it becomes evident that Member States retain very little truly autonomous competence once a mixed agreement has been concluded.

Moreover, the Court has recently extended its far-reaching case-law on mixed agreements to infringement procedures (Article 226 EC Treaty). In its judgment in *Commission* v. *France* of 7 October 2004, the Court held that in mixed agreements which

---

[57] G. Berrisch, and H.-G. Kaman, *supra* n. 55, at p. 89 et seq.

[58] ECJ, Case 181/73 *supra* n. 10, *Haegeman* 460; also ECJ, Case 87/75 *Bresciani* [1976] ECR 129.

[59] ECJ, Case 12/86, *supra* n. 19.

[60] For details see also H. Keller 2003, *supra* n. 8, at p. 563 et seq.

[61] ECJ, Joined Cases C-300/98 and C-392/98 *Parfums Christian Dior SA* [2000] ECR I-11307, para. 35 and 41 et seq.

[62] ECJ, Case C-89/99 *V.O.F. Schieving-Nijstad and others* v. *Robert Groeneveld* [2001] ECR I-5851.

[63] ECJ, Case C-245/02 *Anheuser-Busch* v. *Budjovický Budvar* [2004] ECR I-10989.

> 'create rights and obligations in a field covered in large measure by Community legislation, there is a Community interest in compliance by both the Community and its Member States with the commitments entered into under those instruments.'[64]

Moreover, the Court emphasised that the fact that the specific measures at issue 'have not yet been the subject of Community legislation is not capable of calling that finding into question.'[65] Even though it is unclear what the Court means by 'covered in large measure by Community legislation', it is evident that there are far-reaching obligations under EC law on Member States to comply with all parts of mixed agreements, regardless of the actual distribution of competences. Thus, one may speak of a diffusion of the specific characteristics of mixed agreements.

It is interesting to compare the recent case-law of the Court on mixed agreements with some aspects of state responsibility of the EC and its Member States under WTO law. In recent WTO dispute settlement procedures the question arose whether the EC is responsible under international law for measures taken by its Member States in cases of decentralised implementation of EC law. It is important to remember in this regard that in most areas of EC law the Community does not have a competence to regulate the administrative structure and procedure for implementation of Community law. Thus, in a typical situation it is within the competence of the Member States to regulate the administrative implementation of EC law. Moreover, it is also common in Community law for an EC directive or regulation to explicitly grant regulatory competences to Member States in certain areas. The WTO Panels in *Commercial Vessels* (2005) and *Geographical Indications* (2005) had to deal with those situations. In both cases the Community declared in a similar manner that it is 'full[y] responsible under international law' for the measures of its Member States,[66] and that in case of a decentralised implementation of EC law the Member States 'act de facto as organs of the Community, for which the Community would be responsible under WTO law and international law in general.'[67] It becomes clear from these two examples that the EC is responsible under WTO law also for measures of Member States, even though the EC Treaty does not grant the Community a competence in the respective area. Thus, at least in the case of those mixed international agreements with regard to which the EC has not declared a division of competences at the time of ratification, the full responsibility of the Community renders meaningless the remaining competences of Member States under EC law. It is only consequential to bring EC law and public international law in line by making non-fulfilment of obligations of Member States

---

[64] ECJ, Case C-239/03 *Commission* v. *France*[2004] ECR I-9325, para. 29 et seq.

[65] Ibid.

[66] *European Communities – Measures Affecting Trade in Commercial Vessels*, Panel Report of 22 April 2005, WT/DS301/R, para. 7.32.

[67] *European Communities – Protection of Trademarks and Geographical Indications for Agricultural Products and Foodstuffs*, Complaint by Australia, Panel Report of 15 March 2005, WT/DS290/R, para. 7.148.

under a mixed agreement subject to an infringement procedure according to Article 226 EC Treaty.

The aforementioned legal aspects have been further highlighted in the very recent WTO case 'EC – Selected Customs Matters'.[68] Moreover, it is also important to realise that the full responsibility of the Community under WTO law could lead to an obligation of the Community to enact EC legislation in areas in which a general EC competence is given. The most prominent example in this regard is Article 95 EC Treaty in conjunction with, as held by the Panel in *EC – Sardines*, 'the ongoing obligation ... to reassess ... existing technical regulations in light of the adoption of new international standards or the revision of existing international standards' according to Article 2.4. TBT Agreement.[69]

5. Non-binding international instruments

So far only international agreements which are binding on the Community have been analysed. In order to draw a complete picture of the relationship between EC law and codified international law, some words have to be said concerning non-binding international instruments. The most prominent example in this regard is of course the European Convention on Human Rights (ECHR). Even though numerous attempts have been made to argue that the EC is directly bound by the ECHR,[70] the ECJ has not yet given a conclusive answer to the exact legal status of the ECHR within Community Law. However, it is interesting to note that even though the ECHR does not seem to be an integral part of Community law, the Court makes every attempt to bring EC law in conformity with the ECHR. This is yet another indication that the notion of 'direct effect' should not be exaggerated.

There are yet further examples that the Court is willing to interpret and apply Community law in conformity with international standards, even though they are not directly binding on the Community. In the area of fundamental freedoms and human rights, the Court has, for example, made references to the European Social Charter,[71] ILO Conventions,[72] and the International Covenant on Civil and Political Rights.[73] Moreover, the Court takes into account international agree-

[68] *European Communities – Selected Customs Matters*, Panel Report of 16 June 2006, WT/DS315/R; Appellate Body, Report of 13 November 2006 WT/DS315/AB/R. Both, the Panel and the Appellate Body Report were published only after the manuscript of this paper had been finalised. Thus, no further analysis of this important case is given here.

[69] *European Communities – Trade Description of Sardines*, Panel Report of 29 May 2002, WT/DS231/R, para. 7.78; confirmed by the Appellate Body, Report of 26 September 2002, WT/DS231/AB/R, para. 199 et seq.

[70] For details on the discussion see, e.g., H. Keller 2003, *supra* n. 8, at p. 547 et seq.

[71] See, e.g., ECJ, Case 149/77 *Defrenne* [1978] ECR 1365 (1379); Case 24/86 *Blaizot* [1998] ECR 379 (403).

[72] See, e.g., Case 149/77, *supra* n. 71, *Defrenne*; ECJ, Case C-41/90 *Höfner* [1991] ECR I-1979; Case C-158/91 *Levy* [1993] ECR I-4287; ECJ, Case C-197/96 *Commission* v. *France*, [1997] ECR I-1489; ECJ, Case 207/96 *Commission* v. *Italy*, [1997] ECR I-6869.

[73] ECJ, Case 374/87 *Orkem* [1989] ECR 3283 (3350 et seq.); ECJ, Case C-249/96 *Grant* v. *South-West Trains Ltd*, [1998] ECR I-621 (650).

ments by which Member States, but not the Community, are bound. In these cases, of which the case on the German prohibition on night work in bakeries[74] is an example, international agreements not binding on the Community usually serve to show that a specific Member State measure is not in violation of EC law.

In sum, the Court usually tries to interpret and apply Community law in full conformity with international standards, even though the EC might not be bound in strict legal terms to the international agreement in question.[75] From the perspective of EC law, this evidences the existence of a general constitutional principle of a positive attitude and 'friendliness' of Community law towards international law. Form the perspective of international law, the mentioned case-law of the Court is further evidence of the fact that the border between 'binding' and 'non-binding' international instruments is diminishing.[76]

6. Conclusions

By way of conclusion it is, first of all, important to emphasize that only some aspects of the relationship of EC law to international treaty law have been dealt with in this chapter. Specifically, the whole issue of the possibility for individuals to obtain damages for breach of international treaty obligations on the grounds of unlawful or lawful acts of Member States' governments or EC organs has not been discussed.[77] Moreover, a lot more could be said concerning the procedural differences between preliminary rulings (Article 234 EC Treaty) and annulment procedures (Article 230 EC Treaty), and the different ways international treaty obligations are treated within these procedures by the ECJ.

However, the few issues that have been analysed clearly indicate the complexity of the relationship between EC law and international treaty law. Two aspects seem to be most important. First, international law, namely international agreements to which the EC is a contracting party, has far-reaching effects on Community law and therefore also on the national law of Member States. Therefore it is not sufficient to speak of restrictions on Member State sovereignty caused by Community law. Instead, the regulatory competences of Community law itself are also subject to respective international obligations. As this, of course, has repercussion for the Member States too, the complex structure within a multilayered system of governance becomes evident.

[74] ECJ, Case 155/80 *Oebel* [1981] ECR 1993 para. 12 et seq., referring to a respective ILO Convention.

[75] See also A. Peters 1997, *supra* n. 7, at p. 9 (72); H. Keller 2003, *supra* n. 8, at p. 520.

[76] For details on this 'erosion' of Art. 38 I ICJ-Status see C. Tietje, 'Recht ohne Rechtsquellen? Entstehung und Wandel von Völkerrechtsnormen im Interesse des Schutzes globaler Rechtsgüter im Spannungsverhältnis von Rechtssicherheit und Rechtsdynamik' [Law without Sources of Law? – Creation and Modification of Public International Law], 24 *Zeitschrift für Rechtssoziologie* (2003), pp. 27-42.

[77] For details on this issue see P.J. Kuijper 2005, *supra* n. 15, at p. 1314 (1330 et seq.).

Second, there is no one-sided and overall valid response of the ECJ to the indicated legal challenges within a complex multilayered system of governance. Instead, the Court seems to balance specific Community interests on the one hand, and a general 'friendliness' towards international law on the other. This, however, also indicates that the Court seems to hold the attitude that international law is still, at least in part, of a diplomatic-political character, and not of a comprehensive constitutional nature in the interest of the international community as a whole.[78]

[78] H. Keller 2003, *supra* n. 8, at p. 700 et seq.

Chapter 5
THE EUROPEAN COURT OF JUSTICE AND PUBLIC INTERNATIONAL LAW

Allan Rosas*

1. THE EU JUDICIAL SYSTEM

As is well-known, the European Union (EU) is a very special phenomenon in the international legal system.[1] While not being recognised as a State within the meaning of Article 4 of the Charter of the United Nations, it is not an intergovernmental organisation either. Intergovernmental organisations are not endowed with a concept of citizenship, do not possess legislative jurisdiction over a given territory and do not have their own currency or defence policy, prone to lead to a common defence.[2]

Further, the judicial system of the EU is of a *sui generis* character and does not easily fit into traditional international law or national law classifications. It consists of several instances, beginning as seen from the top, with the Court of Justice of the European Communities (ECJ), established in 1952. The ECJ was supplemented in 1988 by the Court of First Instance (CFI), which today has jurisdiction mainly over cases brought by private parties against decisions of EU institutions as well as cases brought by Member States against decisions of the European Commission and, in some cases, the Council. On points of law, the decisions of the CFI are subject to a right of appeal to the ECJ.

The Treaty of Nice (2001) introduced the possibility of a further extension of this institutional structure to specialised judicial panels (tribunals), the first of

* Doctor of Laws, Judge at the Court of Justice of the European Communities (since January 2002). Formerly Armfelt Professor of Law at the Åbo Akademi University (1981-1996) and Principal Legal Adviser (1995-2001) and Deputy Director-General (2001-2002) at the Legal Service of the European Commission.

[1] In the words of the ECJ, the Community is based on a new legal order and it possesses 'real powers stemming from the limitation of sovereignty or a transfer of powers from the States to the Community', ECJ, Case 6/64 *Flaminio Costa* v. *ENEL* [1964] ECR 585. See also ECJ, Case 26/62 *Van Gend en Loos* v. *Nederlandse Administratie der Belastingen* [1963] ECR 1, and generally, e.g., K. Lenaerts and P. Van Nuffel, *Constitutional Law of the European Union*, 2nd edn. (London, Sweet & Maxwell 2005).

[2] A. Rosas, 'International Dispute Settlement: EU Practices and Procedures', 46 *GYIL* (2003) p. 284 at pp. 285-286.

J. Wouters, P.A. Nollkaemper, E. de Wet (eds.), The Europeanisation of International Law

which was established in November 2004 to deal with EU civil service litigation.[3] Other such tribunals may be established in the future to deal with, *inter alia*, intellectual property law and/or competition law cases. Decisions of a specialised tribunal are subject to a right of appeal before the CFI.[4]

Moreover, one should not forget that the EU judicial system draws heavily upon the national courts of the 27 Member States. These courts apply EU law on a daily basis and are under Article 234 of the Treaty establishing the European Community (EC Treaty) empowered, and in the case of courts of last instance, obliged to request so-called preliminary rulings from the ECJ on questions of interpretation of EU law.[5] Secondary EU law may not be declared invalid by a national court but by the ECJ only.

Associated with the EU judicial system is the EFTA Court, with jurisdiction over matters belonging to the law of the European Economic Area ("EEA"), an integration regime of a less supranational character associating Iceland, Liechtenstein and Norway to the EU.[6]

The main tasks of the ECJ is to give legally binding preliminary rulings requested by national courts, to judge so-called infringement cases brought by the European Commission against individual Member States for alleged non-compliance with Community law[7] and to settle legal disputes between the EU political institutions (notably the European Parliament, the Council and the Commission) and between them and the Member States. These functions, and the possibility of private party-initiated litigation before the CFI,[8] and on appeal before the ECJ, underline the considerable differences which exist between the EU courts and more intergovernmental dispute settlement bodies such as the International Court of Justice (ICJ) or the World Trade Organisation (WTO) Appellate Body.

It needs to be added that EU law has its own internal hierarchical structure, which points to constitutional law rather than public international law.[9] Further, the main bulk of EU law regulates domains which are typically regulated in national

[3] Council Decision 2004/752/EC, Euratom, of 2 November 2004 establishing the European Union Civil Service Tribunal, OJ L 333, 9.11.2004, p. 7. The seven judges of the new Tribunal were elected in July 2005 and their term of office began on 1 October 2005. The constitution of the new Tribunal has been recorded by a decision of the President of the ECJ, which implies that staff cases come as from that decision before the Tribunal instead of the Court of First Instance, OJ L 325, 12.12.2005, p. 1.

[4] In this case, the decisions of the CFI are not subject to a right of appeal before the ECJ, but they may exceptionally be subject to review by the latter 'where there is a serious risk of the unity or consistency of Community law being affected', Art. 225, para. 2, of the Treaty establishing the European Community (EC Treaty) and Art. 62 of the Statute of the Court of Justice.

[5] See, however, Art. 68 EC Treaty and Art. 35 of the Treaty on European Union (EU Treaty), which depart somewhat from the system under Art. 234 EC Treaty.

[6] C. Baudenbacher et al. (eds.), *The EFTA Court: Ten Years On* (Oxford, Hart Publishing 2005).

[7] If the Member State concerned does not comply with a judgment of the ECJ, the European Commission may, under Art. 228 EC Treaty, bring the case before the Court, which, if it agrees with the Commission, may impose a lump sum or penalty payment on the Member State.

[8] This has recently been supplemented by the possibility of private-party litigation in personnel matters before the new Civil Service Tribunal.

[9] See, e.g., C. Timmermans, 'The Constitutionalization of the European Union', 21 *Yearbook of European Law* (2001-2002) p. 1; I. Pernice, 'Multilevel Constitutionalism in the European Union', 27 *European Law Review* (2002) p. 511; K. Lenaerts and P. Van Nuffel, *supra* n. 1.

(domestic) law, such as agriculture, environmental and consumer protection, taxation, social affairs, intellectual property, competition and state aid.[10]

I thus find it somewhat misleading to characterise the ECJ (or the CFI) as an international court and would agree with the current President of the ECJ, who has noted that 'the most accurate characterization of the ECJ is that of a very specific court performing both the functions of a supreme and a constitutional court.'[11]

It is true that in some cases, the ECJ has jurisdiction over disputes involving non-Member States. These are very special situations, however, relative to neighbouring countries such as the EEA States, Switzerland and Turkey. The non-Member State has in these limited circumstances accepted the jurisdiction of the ECJ instead of insisting on the setting up a new dispute settlement mechanism or using an existing international body such as the ICJ.[12]

2. Sources of law

The *basic Treaties* of the EU[13] are international treaties concluded by and between States. But their status and content, as interpreted by the ECJ, are quite different from what is normally found in international law contexts. The principle of supremacy (EU law prevails over the law of the Member States), combined with the principles of direct applicability and direct effect (considerable parts of EU law, including the basic Treaties, can be directly invoked by individuals before courts and authorities), is of fundamental importance. The Treaties also provide for legislative powers of the EU political institutions and set out the judicial system described above. These and other elements have led the ECJ to characterise them as a 'constitutional charter based on the rule of law'.[14]

The great bulk of EU *secondary legislation* (regulations and international agreements) becomes directly applicable by their adoption, in most cases by qualified majority, in the Member States, without national measures of implementation. While directives are addressed to the Member States, failure to implement them may under certain conditions give an individual a right to invoke their provisions before courts and public authorities.

---

[10] Of the almost 600 cases brought before the ECJ in 2007, the most common subject areas were environment and consumers (60), harmonisation of laws (60), taxation (48) and social policy (42). These figures do not cover the case-law of the CFI, where competition law, intellectual property law and staff cases (but see *supra*, at n. 3) are much more prominent categories.

[11] V. Skouris, 'The Position of the European Court of Justice in the EU Legal Order and its Relationship with National Constitutional Courts', 60 *ZöR* (2005) p. 323 at p. 327. Compare J. Allain, 'The European Court of Justice Is an International Court', 68 *Nordic JIL* (1999) p. 249.

[12] See, e.g., Art. 25, para. 2, of the Agreement establishing an association between the European Economic Community and Turkey of 1963 (OJ 1964, L 217). For further examples and details see A. Rosas, *supra* n. 2, at pp. 289-292.

[13] EC Treaty, Treaty establishing the European Atomic Energy Community and EU Treaty. There are also other sources of primary EU law, such as a number of Protocols and Accession Treaties.

[14] ECJ, Case 294/83 *Les Verts* v. *European Parliament* [1986] ECR 1365, para. 23; Opinion 1/91, *Draft Treaty on the establishment of a European Economic Area* [1991] ECR I-6102, para. 21.

In addition to the written primary and secondary law, the ECJ has recognised as an important source of law the *general principles of Community law*. In search for these principles, inspiration is sought from the national laws and legal traditions of the EU Member States and, especially in the field of fundamental rights, also from international human rights conventions binding upon the Member States, especially the European Convention on Human Rights (ECHR).[15] The general principles of Community law are an important component of a constitutional edifice and thus differ from the 'general principles of law recognised by civilised nations' mentioned in the Statute of the ICJ.[16]

The primary law of the EU will be modified if the Treaty of Lisbon amending the EU Treaty and the EC Treaty, signed in Lisbon on 13 December 2007, were to enter into force.[17] This treaty introduces a number of important modifications and additions to the EU and EC Treaties (the latter termed Treaty on the Functioning of the European Union) .The Treaty also provides for a Bill of Rights termed the Charter of Fundamental Rights of the Union, based on the Charter proclaimed by the three main EU political institutions in December 2000,[18] and provides for the accession of the EU to the ECHR.[19] It does not contain any radical changes to the organisational aspects of the EU judicial system as outlined above but provides for a broader scope of the jurisdiction of the EU courts to include more fully areas which have been dealt with previously in a more intergovernmental context, including matters of penal law. At the time of writing, the fate of the new treaty is an open question, in view of the on-going ratification process, but there is a clear possibility that it will enter into force at the beginning of 2009.

3. International agreements

That the EU, as a subject of international law, is bound both by the agreements it has concluded[20] and general (customary) international law has been recognis-

---

[15] The concept of general principles of Community law is to be found in Art. 6, para. 2, EU Treaty (in the context of fundamental rights), while Art. 288, para. 2, EC Treaty refers to the 'general principles common to the laws of the Member States' (in the context of the non-contractual liability of the European Community).

[16] Art. 38, para. 1, of the Statute of the ICJ. This is not to say that the principles envisaged in this provision could not play a role in an emerging constitutionalisation of the world legal order, see A. Rosas, 'State Sovereignty and Human Rights: towards a Global Constitutional Project', XLIII *Political Studies* (1995) p. 61.

[17] OJ C 306, 17.12.2007, p. 1. See also the abortive Treaty establishing a Constitution for Europe, OJ C 310, 16.12.2004, p. 1.

[18] This Charter was first prepared by a separate Convention and proclaimed as a legally non-binding instrument by the European Parliament, the Council and the Commission on 7 December 2000, OJ C 364, 18.12.2000, p. 1. The Convention preparing the Treaty establishing a Constitution for Europe proposed its integration into the Constitution as its Part II while the Intergovernmental Conference adopting the text of the Treaty of Lisbon decided to keep the text of the Charter separate from the EU Treaty but to give it the same legal status as the Treaty (Art. 6 of the EU Treaty as modified).

[19] Art. 6, para. 2, of the Treaty of Lisbon of 2007. See also Art. 17 of Protocol No. 14 to the European Convention on Human Rights, amending Art. 59 of the Convention (not yet in force).

[20] Most international agreements are still concluded in the name of one or both of the Communities but some agreements are made in the name of the EU under Art. 24 of the EU Treaty, see A. Rosas,

ed by the EU courts. Public international law is an integral part of the EU legal order.[21]

As far as treaties (agreements) are concerned, the EU approach is basically a *monistic* one: the treaties concluded by the Council become, *ipso facto*, part of EU law, without any need for further measures of transposition or incorporation. The decision by the Council to conclude the agreement thus makes it directly applicable.[22] Among roughly one thousand international agreements to which the EU (mostly in the name of the Community) is a party, multilateral conventions as well as bilateral agreements are to be found .

Some of the agreements have been concluded as so called mixed agreements, meaning that not only the Community but also the EU Member States are contracting parties. Mixed agreements raise difficult questions as to the scope of Community competence and the jurisdiction of the EU courts, as distinct from national competence (to the extent that these two aspects can be separated in a given agreement).[23]

Provisions of international agreements which are sufficiently clear, precise and unconditional may have direct effect, thereby establishing rights that individuals may invoke before courts and authorities. This is often the case with respect to non-discrimination clauses contained in bilateral agreements concluded with countries with which the EU maintains close relations, including association agreements concluded with candidate countries.[24] If a provision is of a general programmatic

---

supra n. 2, at pp. 285, 287-288, 307-308. The Treaty of Lisbon of 2007 abolishes the European Community as a separate legal person.

[21] C. Timmermans, 'The EU and Public International Law', 4 *EFA Rev.* (1999) p. 181; K. Lenaerts and E. De Smijter, 'The European Union as an Actor under International Law', 19 *Yearbook of European Law* (1999-2000) p. 122 at pp. 122-126; A. Rosas, *supra* n. 2, at p. 287.

[22] While earlier practice saw the conclusion of international agreements by way of regulation, subsequent practice is to use the instrument of decision, to underline that no act of transposition is needed to provide for direct applicability. But implementing measures may be needed if the agreement itself leaves open questions which require regulation in order to ensure full compliance. See also P. Eckhout, *External Relations Law of the European Union: Legal and Constitutional Foundations* (Oxford, Oxford University Press 2004) at pp. 176, 277-278.

[23] On the competence of the ECJ with respect to mixed agreements see, e.g., ECJ, Case C-239/03 *Commission of the European Communities* v. *French Republic* [2004] ECR I-9325, paras. 22-31, where the Court held that also questions which have not yet been the subject of specific Community legislation may fall within the jurisdiction of the Court if the provisions of the mixed agreement in question 'concern a field in large measure covered by Community law' (para. 31). In ECJ, Case C-459/03 *Commission of the European Communities* v. *Ireland* [2006] ECR I-4635, it was held that Ireland, in instigating arbitration proceedings against the United Kingdom concerning matters which are regulated by the UN Convention on the Law of the Sea (to which both the Community and its Member States are parties), had violated Art. 292 EC, which provides for the exclusive jurisdiction of the EU courts in disputes concerning the interpretation and application of Community law. On mixed agreements in general see notably J. Heliskoski, *Mixed Agreements as a Technique for Organizing the International Relations of the European Community and its Member States* (The Hague, Kluwer Law International 2001); A. Rosas, 'The European Union and Mixed Agreements', in A. Dashwood and C. Hillion (eds.), *The General Law of E.C. External Relations* (London, Sweet & Maxwell 2000) p. 200.

[24] There is an extensive case-law on the direct effect of international agreements. For a recent example, see ECJ, Case C-265/03 *Igor Simutenko* v. *Ministerio de Educaión y Cultura, Real Federación*

character, or conditional upon further measures being taken, it may lack such direct effect.[25]

With respect to the WTO agreements, the ECJ has taken a systemic approach, considering that these agreements, *in toto*, are devoid of direct effect. The main reason for this stand, criticised in part of the literature,[26] seems to be that the WTO agreements themselves, notably the Dispute Settlement Understanding, provide for several alternative forms of implementation, including not only direct implementation but also negotiated settlement, compensation and toleration of trade sanctions (suspension of concessions) in particular.[27] While compensation and suspension of concessions are 'temporary measures' which are not to be 'preferred' to full implementation, the Court seems to have considered that this preference for direct implementation is not a justiciable issue.[28]

It should be underlined that the case-law of the ECJ on the WTO agreements does not constitute a departure from monism.[29] While these agreements are devoid of direct effect, meaning that they cannot be invoked directly by private parties or by Member States to challenge the validity of Community legislation, they do possess direct applicability, meaning, *inter alia*, that they are part of the Community legal order and that EU law should be interpreted in the light of their provisions.[30] Applying the principle of consistent interpretation may, of course, in some instances lead to the same or a similar result as would direct effect.

It should also be noted that the ECJ rulings on the WTO agreements do not imply that multilateral agreements, in general, would be devoid of direct effect.[31] The Court has indeed recognised the direct effect of provisions of the Yaounde/ Lomé agreements concluded with the African, Caribbean and Pacific (ACP) coun-

---

Española de Fútbol [2005] ECR I-2579, which concerns the 1994 Partnership Agreement concluded with the Russian Federation. In ECJ, Case C-192/89 *S. Z. Sevince* v. *Staatssecretaris van Justitie* [1990] ECR I-3461, para. 24, the ECJ implicitly admitted the possibility of the direct effect not only of rights but also of obligations contained in international agreements.

[25] For instance, in ECJ, Case C-1/96 *The Queen* v. *Minister of Agriculture, Fisheries and Food, ex parte Compassion in World Farming Ltd* [1998] ECR I-1251, paras. 30-37, the Court of Justice held that a Council of Europe Convention, European Convention No. 87 for the Protection of Animals Kept for Farming Purposes, lacked direct effect. In ECJ, Case C-377/98 *Kingdom of the Netherlands* v. *European Parliament and Council of the European Union* [2001] ECR I-7079, para. 54, the Court, without making a definitive ruling itself, cited the contention of the Council that the 1992 Convention of Biological Diversity contains provisions which do not have direct effect. See also ECJ, Case C-189/ 01 *H. Jippes, Afdeling Groningen van de Nederlandse Vereniging tot Bescherming van Dieren and Afdeling Assen en omstreken van de Nederlandse Vereniging tot Bescherming van Dieren* v. *Minister van Landbouw, Natuurbeheer en Visserij* [2001] ECR I-5689, para. 74.

[26] For an overview see, e.g., P. Eckhout, *supra* n. 22, at pp. 292-299, 314.

[27] The most recent judgment to this effect is ECJ, Case C-377/02 *Léon Van Parys* v. *Belgisch Interventie- en Restitutiebureau (BIRB)* [2005] ECR I-1465.

[28] A. Rosas, Case law annotation on 'Case C-149/96, Portugal v. Council, judgment of the Full Court of 23 November 1999', 37 *CML Rev.* (2000) p. 797 at p. 809.

[29] A. Rosas, *supra* n. 28, at p. 811.

[30] For a recent example, see ECJ, Case C-245/02 *Anheuser-Busch* v. *Budejovický Budvar, národní podnik* [2004] ECR I-10989, which concerns the interpretation of the Agreement on Trade-Related Aspects of Intellectual Property Rights (TRIPS). See also P. Eckhout, *supra* n. 22, at pp. 314-316.

[31] A. Rosas, *supra* n. 28, at p. 813.

tries as well as of the Montreal Convention for the Unification of Certain Rules for International Carriage by Air.[32]

The ECJ has referred to the 'primacy of international agreements concluded by the Community over provisions of secondary Community legislation.' While the Court has added that this primacy means that such provisions 'must, so far as is possible, be interpreted' in a manner that is consistent with those agreements,[33] this formulation first appeared in a case concerning an agreement which did not have direct effect[34] and therefore does not exclude the possibility of questioning the legality of EU secondary legislation if found in contravention of an international agreement having direct effect. In fact, the Court has examined the question of the validity of a directive or a regulation in view of an international agreement binding on the Community.[35]

On the other hand, if the agreement has been concluded in violation of primary law, the decision to conclude it may be challenged before the ECJ. There are some cases where the Court has annulled such a decision on the basis of lack of competence of the organ concluding the agreement or a legal error in the choice of legal basis.[36] As a violation of internal rules for the conclusion of international

---

[32] ECJ, Case 87/75 *Conceria Daniele Bresciani* v. *Amministrazione Italiana delle Finanze* [1976] ECR 129, paras. 15-26 (Yaounde Convention of 1963); ECJ, Case C-469/93 *Amministrazione delle Finanze dello Stato* v. *Chiquita Italia SpA* [1995] ECR I-4533, paras. 30-37, 57 (Fourth Lomé Convention); ECJ, Case C-344/04 *The Queen on the application of: International Air Transport Association, European Low Fares Airline Association* v. *Department for Transport* [2006] ECR I-403, para. 39 (Montreal Convention). The question as to whether the UN Convention on the Law of the Sea has direct effect is raised in Case C-308/06 *The Queen on the application of International Association of Independent Tanker Owners (Intertanko) et al.* v. *Secretary of State for Transport*, pending at the time of writing (Opinion of Advocate General Juliane Kokott of 20 November 2007, judgment of 8 June 2008).

[33] ECJ, Case C-61/94 *Commission of the European Communities* v. *Federal Republic of Germany* [1996] ECR I-3989, para. 52; ECJ, Case C-341/95 *Gianni Bettati* v. *Safety Hi-Tech Srl.* [1998] ECR I-4355, para. 20; ECJ, Case C-286/02 *Bellio F.lliSrl* v. *Prefettura di Treviso* [2004] ECR I-3465, para. 33. See also ECJ, Case 142/88 *Hoesch AG and Germany* v. *Bergroth BmbH* [1989] ECR 3413, para. 30, and ECJ, Case C-179/98 *Kingdom of Spain* v. *Commission of the European Communities* [1999] ECR I-1251, para. 11 (argument of the Spanish Government).

[34] ECJ, Case C-61/94, *supra* n. 33, *Commission* v. *Germany*, concerned a dairy agreement concluded in 1980 within the framework of the Tokyo Round of negotiations of GATT, the predecessor to the WTO.

[35] In ECJ, Case C-1/96, *supra* n. 25, *Compassion in World Farming*, at issue was European Convention No. 87 for the Protection of Animals Kept for Farming Purposes and a Recommendation accompanying it (but the Court concluded that the validity of the directive was not affected, as the Convention was not found to be precise enough and the Recommendation was considered as not containing legally binding obligations). ECJ, Case C-377/98, *supra* n. 25, *the Netherlands* v. *Parliament and Council*, concerned the Convention on Biological Diversity (but the Court ruled that there was no conflict between the Convention and a Community directive). In ECJ, Case C-344/04, *supra* n. 32, *IATA,* paras. 34-48, the Court examined the validity of a regulation in the light of the Montreal Convention for the Unification of Certain Rules for International Carriage by Air (but concluded that there was no inconsistency between the two). In the last-mentioned Case, the Court noted that international agreements 'prevail over provisions of secondary Community legislation' (para. 35).

[36] ECJ, Cases C-327/91 *French Republic* v. *Commission of the European Communities* [1994] ECR I-3641 (agreement signed by the Commission and the United States Government); C-122/95 *Federal Republic of Germany* v. *Council of the European Union* [1998] ECR I-973 (Framework Agree-

agreements does not automatically lead to the termination of the agreement,[37] the latter may remain in force for the time being. Unless the error can be rectified, the Community may later have to withdraw from the agreement.

Thus, the following EU hierarchy of norms would emerge: 1) the basic Treaties and other primary law, including the general principles of Community law; 2) international agreements and 3) secondary legislation, notably regulations and directives.[38]

Two judgments of the CFI of 21 September 2005 suggest that this hierarchy would not apply to the UN Charter, in view of its Article 103, according to which the obligations of the Member States under the Charter shall prevail over their obligations under any other international agreement. According to the CFI, the EU Member States are obliged to leave unapplied any provision of Community law, including primary law or a general principle of law, that raises any impediment to the performance of their obligations under the Charter. The Court further held that the Community, by virtue of the EC Treaty, is bound by the obligations under the Charter in the same way as its Member States.[39] As these cases are pending on appeal before the ECJ,[40] the only thing that can be said here is that the Advocate General of the ECJ, in Opinions of 16 and 23 January 2008, has recommended that the Court annul the judgments of the CFI.

Finally, it should be noted that international agreements or arrangements may also be used as 'soft law' by the EU courts. This can arise notably in cases where the Member States but not the Community are contracting parties to the agreement in question, such as is the case, for instance, with respect to most Council of Europe conventions, UN Specialised Agency conventions and human rights conventions.[41] It can also be a question of an instrument accompanying a conven-

---

ment on Bananas concluded with four Latin American countries); C-281/01 *Commission of the European Communities* v. *Council of the European Union* [2002] ECR I-12049 (Energy Star Agreement concluded with the United States); C-211/01 *Commission of the European Communities* v. *Council of the European Union* [2003] ECR I-8913 (road transport agreements concluded with Bulgaria and Hungary); C-94/03 *Commission of the European Communities* v. *Council of the European Union*, judgment of 10 January 2006, n.y.r. (Rotterdam Convention relating to the prior informed consent procedure); C-317 and C-318/04 *European Parliament* v. *Council of the European Union and Commission of the European Communities* [2006] ECR I-4721

[37] See Arts. 27 and 46 of the Vienna Convention on the Law of Treaties of 1969. According to Art. 46, a State may not invoke violations of its internal law as grounds for invalidating its consent to be bound unless the violation is manifest and concerns a rule of internal law of fundamental importance. See also A. Aust, *Modern Treaty Law and Practice* (Cambridge, Cambridge University Press 2000) at pp. 252-253, who notes that '[g]iven the complexity of internal EC rules, if the EC enters into a treaty in breach of those rules any internal irregularity is most unlikely to be manifest' (at p. 253).

[38] In the third category, one can distinguish between legislation adopted by the Parliament and/or the Council, and implementing rules adopted by the Commission on the basis of Art. 202 EC.

[39] CFI, Case T-306/01 *Ahmed Ali Yusuf and Al Barakaat International Foundation* v. *Council of the European Union and Commission of the European Communities* [2005] ECR II-3533, paras. 231-251; CFI, Case T-315/01 *Yassin Abdullah Kadi* v. *Council of the European Union and Commission of the European Communities* [2005] ECR II-3649, paras. 181-208.

[40] ECJ, Cases C-402/05 P and C-415/05 P.

[41] Concerning Council of Europe Conventions to which the Community is not a party see, e.g., ECJ, Joined Cases C-320/94 et al., *Reti Televisive Italiane SpA* et al. [1996] ECR I-6471, para. 33; ECJ,

tion to which the Community is a party which in itself is not considered as legally binding.[42]

4. General international law

As far as *general (customary) international law* is concerned, the ECJ has recognised its binding force as a source of EU law. This has been done in the context of treaty law and the law of the sea, in particular.[43] Thus, for instance, the ECJ has stated that the Community 'must respect international law in the exercise of its powers' and that account must be taken in this context of the 1958 Geneva law of the sea conventions, 'in so far as they codify general rules recognised by international custom', and their successor of 1982, as 'many of its provisions are considered to express the current state of customary international maritime law.'[44]

Case C-11/95 *Commission of the European Communities* v. *Kingdom of Belgium* [1996] ECR I-4115, para. 24; ECJ, Case C-245/01 *RTL Television GmbH* v. *Niedersächsische Landesmedienanstalt für privaten Rundfunk* [2003] ECR I-12489, paras. 63 and 72; ECJ, Case C-89/04 *Mediakabel BV* v. *Commissariaat voor de Media* [2005] ECR I-4891, para. 41, in which reference is made to European Convention No. 132 on Transfrontier Television of 1989. Compare ECJ, Case C-222/94 *Commission of the European Communities* v. *United Kingdom of Great Britain and Northern Ireland* [1996] ECR I-4025, paras. 43-50, where the Court concluded that, on a certain question, the Community legislature had chosen to regulate television services 'in a way which differs from the path followed by the Convention'. See also on the interpretative value of World Customs Organisation classification opinions and explanatory notes ECJ, Case C-206/03 *Commissioners of Customs & Excise* v. *SmithKline Beecham plc*, Order of the Court of 19 January 2005, n.y.r., paras. 24-25. The status of International Maritime Organization (IMO) conventions in EU law has been raised in Case C-308/06, *supra* n. 32, *Intertanko*, judgment of 8 June 2008. As is well-known, the ECJ uses international human rights conventions as guidelines for applying fundamental rights as general principles of Community law, see, e.g., A. Rosas, 'The European Union and International Human Rights Instruments', in V. Kronenberger (ed.), *The European Union and the International Legal Order: Discord or Harmony?* (The Hague, T.M.C. Asser Press 2001) p. 53 and *infra*, n. 63.

[42] See, e.g., ECJ, Case C-162/97 *Criminal Proceedings against Gunnar Nilsson, Per Olov Hagelgren and Solweig Arrborn* [1998] ECR I-7477, para. 49, where the Court noted that the Recommendation concerning Cattle adopted by the Standing Committee of European Convention No. 87 for the Protection of Animals Kept for Farming Purposes, while it does not contain legally binding obligations for the Community, 'is an act adopted on the basis of a convention approved by the Community, and as such may be of use in interpreting the provisions of the convention'.

[43] P.J. Kuijper, 'From Dyestuffs to Kosovo Wine: From Avoidance to Acceptance by the European Community Courts of Customary International Law as Limit to Community Action', in I.F. Dekker and H.H.G. Post (eds.), *On the Foundations and Sources of Public International Law* (The Hague, T.M.C. Asser Press 2003) p. 151; A. Rosas, 'With a Little Help from My Friends: International Case-Law as a Source of Reference for the EU Courts', 5 *The Global Community YILJ* 2005 (2006) p. 203 at pp. 217-229. See also the literature mentioned *supra* n. 21.

[44] ECJ, Case C-286/90 *Anklagemyndigheden* v. *Peter Michael Poulsen and Diva Navigation Corp.* [1992] ECR I-6048, paras. 9-11. See also ECJ, Case C-405/92 *Établissements Armand Mondiet SA* v. *Armement Islais SARL.* [1993] ECR I-6133, paras. 13-14; ECJ, Case C-37/00 *Herbert Weber* v. *Universal Ogden Services Ltd.* [2002] ECR I-2013, para. 34, and A. Rosas, 'EU ja kansainvälinen merioikeus' ['The EU and the International Law of the Sea'], in T. Koivurova (ed.), *Kansainvälistyvä oikeus. Juhlakirja professori Kari Hakapää* (Lapin yliopiston oikeustieteellisiä julkaisuja C 41, Rovaniemi 2005), p. 419 at pp. 427-432.

The Court has also admitted the right of an individual to challenge the validity of Community legislation suspending a Community agreement which has direct effect on the basis that such suspension arguably violates customary international law (as codified in Article 62(1) of the Vienna Convention on the Law of Treaties of 1969) relating to the suspension of agreements.[45] The ECJ has also had an opportunity to consider whether, in the context of State succession in respect of treaties, the principle of the continuity of treaties was, at a given moment, a customary rule of international law.[46] The CFI has held that Article 18 of the Vienna Convention codifies the principle of good faith as a rule of customary international law, binding upon the Community.[47]

In a case concerning movement certificates issued by authorities of the northern part of Cyprus, calling itself 'The Turkish Republic of Northern Cyprus', the ECJ held that administrative cooperation with these authorities is excluded, as it is a question of 'an entity […] which is recognized neither by the Community nor by the Member States', who only recognise the Republic of Cyprus, and that the Community has no right to interfere in the internal affairs of this latter State. Parallels drawn by the Commission with the status of Namibia and an Advisory Opinion of the International Court of Justice in this regard were rejected by the ECJ.[48]

While the EU Courts do not seem to have made explicit pronouncements to this effect, their case-law appears to be based on the idea that customary international law, too, is directly applicable in the EU legal order (which is not to say that it would have direct effect), in accordance with a monistic approach. No specific hierarchy seems to have been established by the courts between treaty law and customary law. Thus, one can surmise that they are, in principle, at the same hierarchical level.

An exception may have to be made for peremptory norms of public international law (*jus cogens*). In the two CFI judgments of September 2005 mentioned above, the Court of First Instance, while considering that the resolutions of the UN Security Council fall, in principle, outside the ambit of the Court's judicial review (as UN Charter obligations prevail over other international obligations), held that an exception had to be made for *jus cogens*, 'understood as a body of higher rules of public international law binding on all subjects of international law […] and from which no derogation is possible.'[49] As was noted above, these two cases are at the time of writing pending before the ECJ.

---

[45] ECJ, Case C-162/96 *A. Racke GmdH & Co.* v. *Hauptzollamt Mainz* [1998] ECR I-3655, paras. 45-61. See also P.J. Kuijper, 'The Court and the Tribunal of the EC and the Vienna Convention on the Law of Treaties 1969', 25 *Legal Issues of European Integration* (1998), pp. 1-23.

[46] ECJ, Case C-216/01 *Budejovický Budvar, národní podnik* v. *Rudol Ammersin GmbH* [2003] ECR I-13617, para. 154.

[47] CFI, Case T-115/94 *Opel Austria GmbH* v. *Council of the European Union* [1997] ECR II-39, para. 90.

[48] ECJ, Case C-432/92 *The Queen* v. *Minister of Agriculture, Fisheries and Food, ex parte S.P. Anastasiou (Pissouri) Ltd and others* [1994] ECR I-3087, paras. 34-35, 40, 47, 49.

[49] CFI, Case T-306/01, *supra* n. 39, *Yusuf*, para. 277.

5. Methods of interpretation

With respect to the interpretation of Community law in general, it is commonplace to assert that the EU courts follow a 'teleological' method of interpretation, drawing upon the general objective of European integration and the more specific objectives of EU primary and secondary law. This is supposed to be done not primarily in the sense of the subjective intentions of the authors of the Treaties and the Community legislator but rather as the 'objective' goals of integration and measures for its development and implementation.

It is true that the EU courts have not given preponderance to a purely textual interpretation. With respect to the basic Treaties, that would have been difficult already because of the absence or scarcity of *travaux préparatoires*, the general indeterminate nature of many of the provisions of the Treaties as well as the fact that they leave some important questions open.

The method of interpretation of the EU courts seems to have become more textual, especially with the development of secondary legislation.[50] They often refer to a combination of textual (literal), contextual (systemic) and teleological interpretations. The text of a legal provision provides the starting point. If the text is not clear, for instance if the language versions (there are now more than 20 official languages) differ, it is necessary to place the provision 'in its context' and to interpret it in relation to its 'spirit and purpose'.[51] The often quite extensive preambular parts of regulations and directives help to establish the objectives and context of a particular piece of legislation.

As a supplementary means of interpretation, the EU courts may also resort to the *travaux préparatoires*. Recent studies seem to indicate that there is an increasing use of preparatory works to shed further light on the text of a provision of secondary legislation and its context.[52]

The situation is at least partly different as far as international agreements concluded by the Community are concerned.[53] As instruments governed by international law, they are in principle subject to the customary rules of treaty interpretation expressed in Articles 31 and 32 of the Vienna Convention on the Law of Treaties. The ECJ sometimes refers expressly to Article 31[54] and has recently stated

---

[50] A. Rosas, 'Tolknings- och tillämpningsproblem i mötet mellan nordisk och internationell juridisk metod' ['Nordic Law Facing International Legal Methodology: Problems of Interpretation and Application'], *Forhandlingerne ved Det 37. nordiske Juristmøde i Reykjavik 18. – 20. august 2005*, Bind I (Den islandske Styrelse, Reykjavik 2005), p. 319 at pp. 335-337.

[51] The quotations are from ECJ, Case C-257/00, *Nani Givane and Others* v. *Secretary of State for the Home Department* [2003] ECR I-345, para. 38.

[52] S. Schønberg and K. Frick, 'Finishing, Refining, Polishing: On the Use of Travaux Préparatoires as an Aid in the Interpretation of Community Legislation', 28 *European Law Review* (2003) p. 149.

[53] P. Eckhout, *supra* n. 22, at pp. 256-270. See also P.J. Kuijper, *supra* n. 45, at pp. 2-11.

[54] Opinion 1/91, *supra* n. 14, *EEA Agreement*, para. 14; ECJ, Case C-312/91 *Metalsa* [1993] ECR I-3751, para. 12; ECJ, Case C-416/96 *Nour Eddline El-Yassini* v. *Secretary of State for Home Department* [1999] ECR I-1209, para. 47; ECJ, Case C-268/99 *Aldona Malgorzata Jany and Others* v. *Staatssecretaris van Justitie* [2001] ECR I-8615, para. 35; ECJ, Case C-344/04, *supra* n. 32, *IATA*, para. 40.

that this provision expresses general customary international law on the subject.[55] In some cases involving the interpretation of association agreements or other bilateral agreements of close cooperation concluded with neighbouring countries, the reference to Article 31 has underlined that an international agreement is to be interpreted 'not solely by reference to the terms in which it is worded but also in the light of its objectives.'[56] In the *Polydor* line of case-law, this has implied the denial of a Community law interpretation of a provision of an international agreement, even if the wording of the latter is identical to a Community provision.[57]

For the EU courts, their own case-law is of considerable importance. The objective of the uniform application of EU law and the principle of legal certainty are thought to require a great deal of consistency over time. With the quantitative development of the case-law (the total number of cases completed, in most cases by a judgment, by the three EU courts per year is nowadays more than 1000[58]), its relative importance has increased. This does not mean that the ECJ cannot, in carefully considered situations, revise its earlier case-law.[59] The CFI will normally uphold the ECJ case-law but may exceptionally attempt to develop it on some point.[60]

The ECJ relies on its own case-law and will normally not refer explicitly to CFI judgments, although such references are not completely unknown.[61] There is an increasing number of cases in which the ECJ has referred to judgments of the EFTA Court.[62] The latter Court is a 'sister' or 'cousin', whose case-law on the EEA

[55] ECJ, Case C-344/04, *supra* n. 32, *IATA*, para. 40.

[56] The quotation is from ECJ, Case C-416/96, *supra* n. 54, *El-Yassini*, para. 47. See also P.J. Kuijper, *supra* n. 45, at pp. 2-4.

[57] ECJ, Case 270/80 *Polydor Limited and RSO Records Inc.* v. *Harlequin Record Shops Limited and Simons Records Limited* [1982] ECR 329. On subsequent case-law, see P. Eckhout, *supra* n. 22, at pp. 258-269.

[58] Court of Justice of the European Communities, *Annual Report 2006* (Luxembourg 2007).

[59] Perhaps the most well-known case is ECJ, Cases C-267 and ECJ, C-268/91 *Criminal Proceedings against Keck and Mithouard* [1993] ECR I-6097, in which the Court held that, 'contrary to what has previously been decided', national provisions restricting or prohibiting certain selling arrangements do not necessarily affect trade between the Member States to such an extent that they are caught by Art. 28 EC on free movement of goods (para. 16 of the judgment).

[60] Compare CFI, Case T-177/01 *Jégo-Quéré et Cie SA* v. *Commission* [2002] ECR II-2365 with ECJ, Case C-50/00 *Unión de Pequeños Agricultores* [2002] ECR I-6677.

[61] An example of a reference to CFI case-law is to be found in the judgment in ECJ, Case C-160/03 *Kingdom of Spain* v. *Eurojust* [2005] ECR I-2077, para. 35. See also A. Rosas, *supra* n. 43, p. 207.

[62] See, e.g., the judgment of 11 March 1997, ECJ, Case C-13/95 *Ayse Süzen* v. *Zehnacker Gebäudereinigung GmbH Krankenhausservice* [1997] ECR I-1259, para. 10 (citing the advisory opinion of 19 December 1996 in ECJ, Case E-2/96 *Ulstein and Røiseng*); judgment of the Court of Justice of 15 June 1999, ECJ, Case C-140/97 *Walter Rechberger, Renate Greindl, Hermann Hofmeister and Others* v. *Republik Österreich* [1999] ECR I-3499, para. 39 (citing the judgment of 10 December 1998 in Case E-9/94 *Sveinbjörnsdottir*); judgment of the Court of Justice of 9 September 2003, ECJ, Case C-236/01 *Monsanto Agricoltura Italia SpA and Others* v. *Presidenza del Consiglio dei Ministri and Others* [2003] ECR I-8105, para. 106 (citing the judgment of 5 April 2001 in ECJ, Case E-3/00 *EFTA Surveillance Authority* v. *Norway*); judgment of 23 September 2003, ECJ, Case C-192/01 *Commission of the European Communities* v. *Kingdom of Denmark* [2003] ECR I-9693, paras. 47-53 (citing the same judgment); ECJ, Case C-286/02, *supra* n. 33, *Bellio*, para. 34 (citing the judgment of 12 December 2003 in ECJ, Case E-1/03 *EFTA Surveillance Authority* v. *Iceland*). See also C. Baudenbacher, 'The EFTA Court Ten Years On', in C. Baudenbacher, *supra* n. 6, p. 13 at pp. 35-48.

Agreement can be of interest for the interpretation of an identical provision in Community law.

Despite the fact that the Community is not a contracting party to the ECHR, since the mid-1990s the ECJ has referred fairly frequently to the case-law of the European Court of Human Rights to back up a certain interpretation of the Convention.[63] Its provisions and the case-law accompanying them are then used as a source of inspiration for the determination of fundamental rights as general principles of Community law. The Court has observed that, in situations where it has interpreted the European Convention in a certain manner, while subsequently the Strasbourg Court has arrived at a different interpretation, 'regard must be had to the case-law of the European Court of Human Rights subsequent to' the earlier case-law of the ECJ.[64]

The ECJ has also referred to judgments from the ICJ on points of customary international law despite the fact that the Community cannot be a party before that Court.[65] More recently, the ECJ for the first time referred to decisions of the WTO Appellate Body on the interpretation of provisions of a WTO agreement (in this case, the TRIPS).[66] There seem to be no references so far to the case-law of the International Tribunal for the Law of the Sea but such references cannot be excluded, as the Community is a contracting party to the Law of the Sea Convention.[67]

The ECJ is, of course, not directly bound by such 'external' case-law in the strict meaning of the term. However, the ECJ seems to give special relevance to the case-law of international courts and tribunals if the court or tribunal in question constitutes a generally accepted adjudicatory body set up to interpret rules of in-

[63] A. Rosas, 'Fundamental Rights in the Luxembourg and Strasbourg Courts', in C. Baudenbacher, *supra* n. 6, p. 163 at pp. 168-171.

[64] ECJ, Case C-94/00 *Roquette Frères* [2002] ECR I-9011, para. 29.

[65] See, e.g. ECJ, Cases C-286/90, *supra* n. 44, *Poulsen*, para. 10; C-405/92, *supra* n. 44, *Mondiet*, paras. 13-14; C-432/92, *supra* n. 48, *Anastasiou*, para. 35; CFI, T-115/94, *supra* n. 47, *Opel Austria*, para. 90; ECJ, C-162/96, *supra* n. 45, *Racke*, para. 50; ECJ, C-37/00, *supra* n. 44, *Weber*, para. 34; CFI, T-306/01, *supra* n. 39, *Yusuf*, paras. 233-234 and CFI, T-315/01, *supra* n. 39, *Kadi*, paras. 183-184 (the two latter judgment on appeal, pending before the ECJ as Cases C-402/05 P and 415/05 P). See also A. Rosas, *supra* n. 43, pp. 222-226 and A. Rosas, 'The European Court of Justice in Context: Forms and Patterns of Judicial Dialogue', 2 *European Journal of Legal Studies* (on-line <http//www.ejls.eu/> 2007) at p. 10.

[66] ECJ, Case C-245/02, *supra* n. 30, *Anheuser-Busch*, para. 49 (reference to the Report of the Appellate Body of 18 September 2000 in Canada – Term of Patent Protection (AB-2000-7), WT/DS170/AB/R) and 67 (reference to the Report of the Appellate Body of 2 January 2002 in United States – Section 211 of the Omnibus Appropriations Act (AB-2001-7), WT/DS176/AB/R). See also A. Rosas, *supra* n. 65, at p. 11.

[67] While it is true that the Community has not accepted the jurisdiction of the Hamburg Tribunal under Art. 287 of the Convention, the Community may do so on an *ad hoc* basis, as has, in fact, been done in the Case concerning the Conservation and Sustainable Exploitation of Swordfish Stock in the South-Eastern Pacific Ocean (Chile/European Community), List of Cases No. 7, see Order 2000/3 of the International Tribunal for the Law of the Sea of 20 December 2000 and Order 2005/01 of 29 December 2005. By the latter Order, the time-limits for the proceedings have been suspended until 1 January 2008 but the case is still pending before the Tribunal. See also A. Rosas, *supra* n. 2, p. 301. See also A. Rosas, *supra* n. 65, at p. 11.

ternational law that have a special significance for the EU legal order. This is done either because they constitute general customary international law (ICJ), are contained in a treaty used as a source of inspiration or guideline by the ECJ in determining the general principles of Community law (the European Court of Human Rights) or appear in an international agreement directly binding on the Community (the WTO dispute settlement system).

There are, of course, situations where the EU courts have to proceed to an interpretation of a rule of international law even if there is no guidance, or no clear guidance, from the case-law of international courts and tribunals. Examples from ECJ case-law include the application of Article 8 of the ECHR (privacy) to business premises,[68] the principle of the continuity of treaties in the context of State succession[69] and the scope of the concept of liability in the Montreal Convention for the Unification of Certain Rules for International Carriage by Air.[70]

6. Summary and conclusions

While public international law and international agreements binding on the EU constitute an important source of law for the EU courts, the courts' main task is to interpret and apply 'internal' primary and secondary EU law, notably the founding Treaties, the general principles of Community law as well as regulations and directives. There are some special cases in which the ECJ has jurisdiction over disputes between the EU and neighbouring countries. Outside this very particular framework, the EU courts cannot settle disputes between the EU and third countries. Such disputes have to be submitted to international dispute settlement mechanisms such as the WTO system, the International Tribunal for the Law of the Sea or *ad hoc* arbitration.

The EU courts may be called upon to interpret and apply international agreements or customary international law binding on the EU, but in this case they approach the international norm much in the same way as national courts do. The specific status of the norm is then determined by EU law, as general international law does not oblige States or the EU to apply, in a domestic law context, the principles of supremacy, direct applicability (monism) or direct effect.

By adopting the principles of direct applicability and direct effect, the EU courts have demonstrated an 'open' attitude towards public international law. This phenomenon seems to have increased over the years. In the early days of European integration, the ECJ was perhaps more concerned about the autonomy and uniqueness of the Community legal order and less keen to seek inspiration from outside. But it may also be that the increasing role of public international law in the Court's case-law is simply due to the increasingly important role of the EU in international cooperation and rule-making.

---

[68] Joined Cases 46/87 and 227/88 *Hoechst AG* v. *Commission of the European Communities* [1989] ECR 2859, paras. 17-18. Cf. Case C-94/00, *Roquette Fréres*, *supra* n. 64, para. 29.

[69] ECJ, Case C-206/01, *Budejovickiý Budvar*, *supra* n. 46, paras. 149-167.

[70] ECJ, Case C-344/04, *IATA*, *supra* n. 32, paras. 41-48.

While not all agreements concluded by the EU fulfil the conditions for direct effect, the principle of consistent interpretation implies that all agreements binding on the EU, and general customary international law, are of legal relevance in the interpretation and application of EU internal legislation. The importance of this factor is highlighted by the principle of the primacy of international agreements over secondary legislation. In this way, the EU courts contribute to the observance by the EU of its international commitments.

As the EU courts do not see themselves as public international law dispute settlement mechanisms, it is understandable that they have not attempted to assert any central role in the development of public international law as such. They have rather manifested deference to the case-law of international courts and tribunals, notably the ECHR and the ICJ. While the decisions of these courts and tribunals are not formally binding on the EU courts, the practice of the latter seems to be based on the idea that it makes sense to take this 'external' case-law fully into account. The EU courts will not necessarily be in a position to 'know better' than the bodies specifically set up to interpret and apply public international law. Following this international case-law will also diminish the risk of the EU being found in violation of its international obligations or contributing to a further fragmentation of public international law.[71]

This is not to say that the role of the EU courts would be limited to a mere registration of what other courts have decided. Like national courts, they might sometimes be called upon to 'take public international law into their own hands', in particular if international case-law is lacking or is conflicting. All courts, whether international, regional or national, have a role to play in a continuing judicial dialogue.[72] But national courts, including the EU courts, should show restraint in developing new concepts or interpretations which could be seen as 'judge-made' public international law. The EU should certainly contribute to not only the observance but also the development of public international law.[73] However, developing public international law is in my view primarily a task for the political bodies of the EU, notably the Commission and the Council.

---

[71] On the discussion on the fragmentation of international law and the proliferation of international courts and tribunals see, e.g., the journal *The Law & Practice of International Courts and Tribunals* (since 2002) and the Project on International Courts and Tribunals (PICT), <www.pict-pcti-org>. PICT-related publications include Symposium Issue on 'Proliferation of International Tribunals: Piecing Together the Puzzle', 31 *New York University Journal of International Law and Politics* (1999); P. Sands et al., *Manual on International Courts and Tribunals* (London, Butterworths 1999); Y. Shany, *The Competing Jurisdictions of International Courts and Tribunals* (Oxford, Oxford University Press 2003). In 2002, the International Law Commission set up a Study Group on the Fragmentation of International Law, Report of the Study Group, 1 August 2004, UN Doc. A/CN.4/L.628. See also R. Higgins, 'The ICJ, the ECJ and the Integrity of International Law', 52 *ICLQ* (2003) p. 1, and A. Rosas, *supra* n. 43

[72] A. Rosas, *supra* n. 65.

[73] According to Art. 2, para. 5, of the EU Treaty, as amended by the Treaty of Lisbon of 2007 (not in force, see *supra* n. 17), the EU shall contribute, *inter alia*, to the 'strict observance and the development of international law'.

Chapter 6
CUSTOMARY INTERNATIONAL LAW, DECISIONS OF INTERNATIONAL ORGANISATIONS AND OTHER TECHNIQUES FOR ENSURING RESPECT FOR INTERNATIONAL LEGAL RULES IN EUROPEAN COMMUNITY LAW

Pieter Jan Kuijper*

1. INTRODUCTON

This contribution will look at the reception of customary international law and decisions of international organisations in European Community (EC) law.[1] Unlike many constitutions of EC Member States, the Treaty Establishing the European Community (EC Treaty) does not contain any provision on the relationship between Community law and general international law.[2] Moreover, only since the Treaty of Amsterdam has a provision on decisions of international organisations set up by an agreement to which the EC is a party and the way in which they should be adopted (Article 300(2), second subparagraph)[3] been part of the EC Treaty. Earlier, a very specific rule on amendments of international agreements by a body set up by the agreement had already been introduced at Maastricht (Article 228(4), later Article 300(4)).[4]

Given the relative absence of rules concerning the adoption and reception of general international law and decisions of international organisations, most of the law in this domain is judge-made, and therefore raises delicate issues of democratic legitimization of the reception of these rules within the Community legal

* Prof. Dr. Pieter Jan Kuijper is Professor of the Law of International Organisations, University of Amsterdam. Previously he was Director for External Relations in the Legal Service of the European Commission.

[1] This contribution is concerned only with Community law and not with the law of the European Union.

[2] Examples of such provisions are: Art. 25 *Grundgesetz* (Germany), Art. 9(1) *Bundes-Verfassungsgesetz* (Austria): Art. 10(1) *Costituzione* (Italia).

[3] See Art. 2, point 56(b) Treaty of Amsterdam, at that moment restricted to decisions of a body constituted on the basis of an agreement concluded on the basis of Art. 238, later by Art. 2, point 46(b) of the Treaty of Nice extended to decisions of a body set up by any agreement.

[4] See Art. G.80 Treaty of Maastricht.

J. Wouters, P.A. Nollkaemper, E. de Wet (eds.), The Europeanisation of International Law

system as well as questions of balancing such issues of legitimization against the interest of the international legal order.[5]

In addition, there are two other legal techniques that may be used to ensure respect by the Community of rules of international law. One of these consists of private parties claiming damages for breaches of international law that have caused them commercial or other losses, a technique that is also available in states. The other one is a typical Community remedy: the use of infringement cases by the Commission against Member States, if the latter engage the Community's international responsibility by their actions.

2. Customary international law and Community law[6]

First of all it is interesting to note that, even in Member States which have a dualist approach to the reception of treaty law in their national legal orders, such as Austria, Germany and Italy, general international law is considered to be part of the law of the land and, to a certain extent, its supremacy is being recognised.[7] In what follows we will see that this must have had some influence on the case-law of the European Court of Justice (ECJ) in this domain.

There are three strands in this case-law that can be distinguished. Namely cases concerning jurisdiction, cases where customary international law is used as a rule of interpretation and cases where customary law is called in aid to set aside a rule of Community law (direct effect cases).

2.1 How far does the arm of Community law and of the Community institutions, in particular the ECJ, reach?

This type of case goes back very far, since it is the kind of case with which nearly every judge is confronted: 'how far does my competence, or the competence of other (State/Community) authorities go?' The initial reaction of a judge or a court in such a situation is to look at the rules of national/Community law which deter-

[5] On such issues of legitimization with respect to direct effect see John H. Jackson, 'Status of Treaties in Domestic Legal Systems: A Policy Analysis', 86 *AJIL* (1992), pp. 310-346. These questions do apply *a fortiori* to customary international law and to decisions of international organisations.

[6] See, *inter alia,* Jan Wouters and Dries Van Eeckhoutte, 'Enforment of Customary International Law through European Community Law', in J.M. Prinssen and A. Schrauwen (eds.), *Direct Effect, Rethinking a Classic of EC Legal Doctrine* (Groningen, Europa Law Publishing 2002) pp. 183-234 and Pieter Jan Kuijper, 'From Dyestuffs to Kosovo Wine: from avoidance to acceptance by the Community Courts of customary international law as limit to Community action', in Ige F. Dekker and Harry H.G. Post (eds.), *On the Foundations and Sources of International Law: Essays in Memory of Herman Meijers* (The Hague, T.M.C. Asser Press 2003) pp. 251-271.

[7] See, on Art. 25 of the German Grundgesetz: Hans D.Jarass and Bodo Pieroth, *Grundgesetz* [The Constitution], 7th edn. (München, Beck 2004) p. 650 et seq.; on Art. 9(1) of the Austrian Bundes-Verfassungsgesetz, Walter Berka, *Lehrbuch des Verfassungsrecht* [Manual of (Austrian) Constitutional Law] (Wien-New York, Springer 2005) pp. 67-68 and on Art. 10(1) Italian Costituzione, G.U. Rescigno, *Corso di Diritto Publico* [Course of Public Law], 8th edn. (Bologna, Zanichelli 2004) pp. 114-115.

mine the competence. It is only after some time or after further reflection that a court will recognise that norms extraneous to the legal system in which it functions, such as international law, may set certain limits on its jurisdiction, the authority of the other institutions in the system, or even on the application of the rules of the system themselves.

This is perfectly illustrated by the development of the treatment of jurisdictional questions by the Community Courts in the various cases concerning the extent of the Community's jurisdiction in international competition cases. These cases can still best be characterised as an evolution 'from avoidance to acceptance of customary international law as limit to Community action.' At the same time one can also characterise that evolution as one 'from avoidance to acceptance of the effects doctrine' in international competition law. This was linked to the strong aversion that practitioners of international law in a number of Member States had developed against the excessive application of the effects doctrine by the US antitrust authorities and courts and, in direct connection to that, against the extreme view of jurisdiction derived by many from the Permanent Court of International Justice (PCIJ) judgment in the old *Lotus* case,[8] namely that in this field international law allowed anything that it did not prohibit.

The ECJ, and later the Court of First Instance (CFI), slowly evolved its views between 1973 and 2003. In the *Dyestuffs* case[9] the Court was presented with all the arguments of international law it could have wished for by both parties and by its Advocate General, Mayras, who advised that the Court accept a moderate effects doctrine.[10] Nevertheless the Court followed a new thesis, developed by the Commission in its pleadings, namely that the parent companies (outside the Community) and their subsidiaries (inside the Community) had acted as one concern and that the parent companies thus had acted constructively inside the territorial jurisdiction of the Community.[11] No need, therefore, to have recourse to the effects doctrine at all, and the Court indeed does not devote a single word to it or to international law. This so-called 'unity-of-the-concern' approach is further developed and refined by the Court in the so-called *Penicillin* cases,[12] but still without reference to international law.

In the *Woodpulp* cases[13] the ECJ was once more confronted squarely with the question of whether or not to take an international law approach to jurisdiction and to accept a moderate effects doctrine within that framework. This time the

---

[8] See *The Case of the SS 'Lotus'* (*France* v. *Turkey*), Judgment No. 9 (PCIJ, Series A, No. 10, 1927).

[9] ECJ, Case 48/69 *Imperial Chemical Industries Ltd.* v. *Commission of the European Communities* [1972] ECR 619.

[10] Ibid., Opinion AG Mayras, [1972] ECR 669, in particular at pp. 699-704.

[11] Ibid., n. 9, see points 136-141 of the judgment.

[12] ECJ, Cases 6/73 and 7/73 *Istituto Chemioterapico Italiano S.p.A. and Commercial Solvents Corporation* v. *Commission of the European Communities* [1974] ECR 223, at points 36-41.

[13] ECJ, Joined Cases C-89/85, C-104/85, C-114/85, C-116/85, C-117/85, C-125/85, C-126/85, C-127/85, C-128/85 and C-129/85 *A. Ahlström Osakeyhtiö and others* v. *Commission of the European Communities* [1988] ECR 99.

Court made a clear distinction between the Community law limits to jurisdictional authority in the field of anti-trust on the basis of the relevant treaty article (Article 85, now Article 81 EC Treaty) and the international law limits to jurisdiction. There is a link between the two in the reasoning of the Court, since what is decisive under Article 85 EC Treaty, namely that competition in the common market is affected by company behaviour, can be brought about by actions from outside the territorial jurisdiction of the Community. The Court in this case could not rely on the unity-of-the-concern approach since the woodpulp companies had no subsidiaries, and sometimes did not even have agents in the common market. Rather, they made their price offers directly by long-distance communications to their buyers in the Community. This was sufficient for the Court to decide that the woodpulp companies had engaged in competition in the Community for the purpose of Article 85,[14] as well as constructively acted within the territory of the Community for the purpose of the international law of jurisdiction. The Court arrived at the latter conclusion because it held the view that what was decisive in this respect was not the *formation* of the anti-competitive agreement, decision or concerted practice, but rather its implementation which, through long distance communication, took place on the territory of the Community, in line with the universally recognised territoriality principle in international law.[15]

Most recently in the *Gencor platinum* case, a merger case, the CFI, just like the ECJ in the *Woodpulp* case, made a clear distinction between the assessment of the territorial scope of the Merger Regulation[16] and the compatibility of the contested decision disallowing the merger with public international law.[17]

The CFI simply posits that application of the Merger Regulation to a merger outside the Community is justified under public international law when it is foreseeable that the proposed concentration will have an immediate (direct) and substantial effect in the Community. This amounts to a limited effects doctrine subject to the three criteria of direct and substantial effect and foreseeability.

It would seem that only now, did the CFI feel safe to say openly that which the ECJ had already said 'en sourdine' in Woodpulp, namely that a moderate effects doctrine – one that requires that the negative economic effects are not too remote and can be foreseen – is in conformity with international law. This has come after many years of developments in US anti-trust and export control cases, doctrinal

---

[14] Ibid., at points 12-14 of the judgment.

[15] Ibid., at points 16-18 of the judgment. This is very much like the so-called objective territoriality principle which is in many ways identical to the effects principle, see for example the English case of *DPP* v. *Stonehouse* [1978] AC 55. Also note the special treatment of the KEA, the US federation of paper and kraft producers, which did not act constructively in the Community because it merely co-ordinated action between paper and pulp producers on the North-American continent. The Court found a way to exclude KEA substantively from the case, because otherwise it would have had to apply the effects doctrine to bring it under its jurisdiction, which it did not want to do.

[16] CFI, Case T-102/96 *Gencor Ltd* v. *Commission of the European Communities* [1999] ECR II-753, at points 78-88.

[17] Ibid., at points 89-111.

discussions and the formulation of the Third Restatement of the Foreign Relations Law of the US,[18] which had espoused a mitigated effects doctrine.

In the case before it, the CFI decided that the effect of the merger was immediate because it could be foreseen that the combination of the two companies' operations (Lonrho and Gencor) with respect to platinum and rhodium would give rise with certainty to a dominant duopoly as soon as the Russian stocks were exhausted. In such a situation the structure of the market in these two metals would be changed in such a way as to make abuses of the combined dominance not only possible but even rational.[19]

In addition, the effect was substantial, since the dominant duopoly would hold up to 65 per cent of the market in platinum and rhodium in Western Europe. Moreover, it did not matter in this respect that the Community was not affected more than the rest of the world market. This could not be a reason for the Community not to exercise its jurisdiction over the merger, since the merger did not affect competition within the common market any the less for it.[20] According to the CFI, its arguments on the direct and substantial nature of the effect of the merger also demonstrated the foreseeability of the effect. Therefore, according to the CFI, the application of the Merger Regulation to the proposed merger was consistent with public international law. Once again, the CFI did not elaborate on where these criteria came from in this conclusion. As stated earlier, they are most likely derived from judgments of other national courts, doctrinal discussions and the Third US Restatement.

The Community courts have also had to rule on private law jurisdiction cases. It is interesting to note how the Court in these cases shifts ground a bit and is no longer obsessed by public law notions of 'extra-territoriality', but has recourse to private international law notions of jurisdiction, such as 'sufficient connection' with the Community (in German: *Anknüpfungslehre*).

In its first case of this nature, the well-known '*pace-makers* case' in relation to World championships cycling,[21] the ECJ took the position that the contract between the cyclist and his pace-maker, even if concluded outside the Community, clearly had sufficient connections with the Community to be covered by Community law and the freedom to provide services.

Similarly, a contract between a Community development organisation and one of its employees which covered work to be done in Africa, having been concluded in Paris, had sufficient connections with the EC to be covered by Community social security.[22]

---

[18] See, *inter alia*, ILA Report of the 64th Conference held at Broadbeach, Queensland, Australia 1990, Report of the Committee on Legal Aspects of Extra-territorial Jurisdiction, at pp. 312-330; American Law Institute, *Restatement of the Law (Third) Foreign Relations Law of the US* (St. Paul, American Law Institute Publishers1987) § 402 et seq.; Karl M. Meessen (ed.), *International Law of Export Controls* Jurisdictional Issues (London etc., Graham & Trotman 1992).

[19] CFI Case T-102/96, *supra* n. 16, *Gencor* v. *Commission*, at points 93-95.

[20] Ibid., points 96-98.

[21] ECJ, Case 36/74 *B.N.O. Walrave and L.J.N. Koch* v. *Association Union cycliste internationale, Koninklijke Nederlandsche Wielren Unie et Federación Española Ciclismo* [1974] ECR 1405.

[22] ECJ, Case 237/83 *SARL Prodest* v. *Caisse Primaire d'Assurance Maladie de Paris* [1984] ECR 3153.

Finally, in the so-called *Oil Platforms* case, the question arose whether Article 5(1) of the Brussels Convention of 1968 on Jurisdiction and the Enforcement of Judgments in Civil and Commercial Matters (since then replaced by Article 5(1) of Regulation 44/2001, the so-called Brussels Regulation) to labour contracts performed on an oil platform on the continental shelf. On the basis of Articles 2 and 3 of the Geneva Convention of 1958 on the Continental shelf as well as the ICJ Judgment in the *North Sea Continental shelf* cases, the ECJ arrived at the conclusion that international (customary) law, and thus Community law, accepted that the rights exercised by states on the continental shelf exist *ipso facto*, as the continental shelf in a natural prolongation of a state's land territory and need not to be claimed.[23]

2.2 International law as a rule of interpretation

First of all, customary rules of international law on treaty interpretation are used widely by the Community courts in order to interpret international agreements concluded by the Community and even – from time to time – the EC Treaty itself.

This calls for a few remarks. First of all, neither the Community nor the Union is a party to either of the two Vienna Conventions on the Law of Treaties (1969 and 1986).[24] Therefore, when the Community courts have recourse to the treaty interpretation rules of Articles 31 and 32 of both Conventions, they do so under the guise of customary international law.

Second, in its recourse to the rules of treaty interpretation the Court places great emphasis on the context and the object and purpose. This is very important for the Court in order to maintain important differences in interpretation of comparable, or even identical, provisions in the EC Treaty and, in particular, in free trade agreements concluded with third countries. This enables the Court to come to very nuanced results. The provisions on the free movement of goods in the EC Treaty imply an exhaustion approach to intellectual property in the light of the context, object and purpose of the EC Treaty,[25] but not in the light of the same criteria when interpreting the same provision in a free-trade agreement with one of the Community's neighbouring States.[26] On the other hand, provisions relating to the prohibition of tax discrimination need to be interpreted in the same way and be given direct effect both within the Community context and in a free-trade agreement with one of the neighbouring States.[27]

Perhaps the most important application of international law as a rule of interpretation occurs when a rule of customary international law (or a rule of treaty

---

[23] See ECJ, Case C-37/00 *Herbert Weber* v. *Universal Ogden Services Ltd.* [2002] ECR I-02013, at points 32-34.

[24] Vienna Convention on the Law of Treaties (1969) and Vienna Convention on the Law of Treaties between International Organisations and between States and International Organisations (1986).

[25] ECJ, Case 15/74 *Centrafarm BV et Adriaan de Peijper* v. *Sterling Drug Inc.* [1974] ECR 1147.

[26] ECJ, Case 270/80 *Polydor Limited and RSO Records Inc.* v. *Harlequin Records Shops Limited and Simons Records Limited* [1982] ECR 329.

[27] ECJ, Case 104/81 *Hauptzollamt Mainz* v. *C.A. Kupferberg & Cie KG a.A.* [1982] ECR 3641.

law) is used as a means of interpretation of Community secondary legislation. In such cases the Community courts have recourse to rules of international law in the interpretation of rules of Community law with a view to avoiding placing the Community in a position of international responsibility. This is the technique of harmonious or consistent interpretation in international law, which in the United States goes by the name of the 'Charming Betsy' doctrine.[28]

The classical example in Community law is the case of *Poulsen and Diva Navigation*.[29] In that case the Court interpreted a Community regulation, which had been adopted with a view to implementing the Convention for the Protection of North-Atlantic Salmon, in light of that Convention and the customary rules of the law of the sea. The customary rules of the law of the sea were largely derived at the time from the old Law of the Sea Conventions of 1958, to which the Community could not become a party, and the new UN Convention on the Laws of the Sea (UNCLOS), which had not yet entered into force for the Community. In this way the Court came to the conclusion that a formerly Danish, but now Panamanian, fishing vessel with an illegal cargo of salmon caught on the high seas on board could be apprehended by Danish authorities only on the basis of its jurisdiction over internal waters (and not in the territorial sea or the Exclusive Economic Zone or on the basis of the – largely Danish – nationality of the vessel's crew).[30] The Court left the question of whether that jurisdiction could be excluded on the basis of the doctrine of distress – incorrectly, it is submitted – to the national courts as a question of fact.[31]

This case and cases such as those interpreting Community (or even Member State) law in the light of the WTO Agreements[32] show that European Community law is open to the influence of international law, even in situations where there is no wish on the part of the Community courts to grant direct effect. It is an international-law-friendly approach to Community law which reverberates inside the national legal systems of the Member States, since most of these cases are concerned with the interpretation of Community law in response to preliminary questions of courts of the Member States (Article 234 of the EC Treaty).

---

[28] See *Murray* v. *Schooner Charming Betsy*, 6 US (2 Cranch) 64 (1804).

[29] ECJ, Case C-286/90 *Anklagemyndigheden* v. *Peter Michael Poulsen and Diva Navigation Corp.* [1990] ECR I-6019.

[30] See ibid., points 12-29.

[31] See ibid., points 35-39. This is incorrect because the continued existence of the doctrine of distress as a customary rule excluding jurisdiction over vessels which have put into port because of distress is a question of law and not of fact, whilst the question whether its conditions have been fulfilled is indeed a question of fact.

[32] See ECJ, Case C-53/96 *Hermès International (a partnership limited by shares)* v. *FHT Marketing Choice BV* [1998] ECR I-3603; ECJ, Joined Cases C-300/98 and C-392/98 *Parfums Christian Dior SA* v. *TUK Consultancy BV and Assco Gerüste GmbH and Rob van Dijk* v. *Wilhelm Layher GmbH & Co. KG and Layher BV* [2001] ECR I-11307; and, Case C-89/99 *Schieving-Nijstad vof and Others* v. *Robert Groeneveld* [2001] ECR I-5851.

2.3 Customary international law as a possible reason for the invalidity of Community law

Whether the great openness of Community law to customary international law goes as far as a willingness to leave conflicting rules of Community law unapplied (thus granting direct effect to rules of customary international law) is not certain. In two much discussed cases, *Racke*[33] and *Opel Austria*,[34] the Community courts seem in principle to be open to rely on customary international law in order to quash conflicting rules of Community law. However, in practice, in both cases the Court ultimately baulks at drawing the consequences or takes evasive action by, *inter alia*, adding additional requirements, shifting the ground for its decision, or granting a large measure of discretion to the Community authorities.

As far as additional requirements are concerned, it is interesting to note that in both cases the Community courts attach almost more importance to the fact that the companies concerned could rely on directly enforceable treaty rights (in both cases, zero tariffs)[35] than on the direct effect of the rules of customary international law being invoked. This was perhaps not without reason, since the (customary) rule of the law of treaties that was being invoked in *Opel Austria*, namely the obligation not to defeat the object and purpose of an agreement between the date of signature and that of ratification,[36] was an obligation incumbent on the Community and arguably not so clear in its consequences as to allow individuals to invoke it before the Court. Moreover, the customary rule invoked in *Racke*, namely the *clausula rebus sic stantibus* and its improper application by the Community *vis-à-vis* the former Yugoslavia[37] at the beginning of the civil war, was an even more unsuitable rule to be invoked by a private individual or company, given its highly contested and controversial origins and its character as a rule that is supposed to protect the sovereignty of states. It is, therefore, perhaps better to speak of direct effect given to treaty provisions colored by a directly applied rule of customary law than of direct effect being granted to a rule of customary international law as such.

In *Opel Austria* the CFI solved its dilemma by shifting from the good faith of the Community in the period between signature and the entry into force to the principle of legitimate expectations of the economic operators which, it claimed, was the Community law equivalent of the international law principle of good faith of the signatory state. In other words, it shifted from a (customary) rule of treaty law to a general principle of Community law, so that in the end its decision was no longer grounded in the customary law principles originally invoked by the applicant, *Opel Austria*.

---

[33] ECJ, Case C-162/96 *A. Racke GmbH & Co.* v. *Hauptzollamt Mainz* [1998] ECR I-3655.

[34] CFI, Case T-115/94 *Opel Austria GmbH* v. *Council of the European Union* [1997] ECR II-39.

[35] In *Opel Austria* as a consequence of the EEA Agreement entering into force for Austria and in *Racke* as a consequence of a tariff quota for wine in the Cooperation agreement EC-Yugoslavia.

[36] Art. 18 of the Vienna Convention on the Law of Treaties (1969).

[37] Ibid., Art. 62.

In *Racke*, the ECJ in the end decided to draw very broad boundaries for the test of whether or not customary international law had been breached by the Community. In light of the controversial and 'political' character of the *rebus sic stantibus* rule in international law, the Court's decision that the standard to be applied was one of 'manifest errors of assessment' – which, the Court found, had not been transgressed by the Community institutions – was probably justified.[38]

2.4 Some concluding remarks on customary international law and Community law

First of all a word on sources and authorities: where and how do the Community courts '*find*' customary international law and on the basis of which authority do they accept it as customary international law?

The Community courts find customary international law primarily in international conventions to which the Community is not a party. In this respect the Community courts are quite in line with modern trends in customary international law. It has often been remarked by authors in this field that modern customary international law is often a consequence of large scale international conferences that result in a codification.[39] The cases mentioned above are uniformly illustrative of that trend. Nearly all rules 'found' by the Community courts come from these large codifying conferences: the conferences of Vienna on the law of treaties and the old and new Law of the Sea conferences.

The Community courts accept these sources as authoritative of customary international law largely on the basis of judgments of the International Court of Justice (ICJ), an interesting example of deference among international courts.[40] It is submitted that the Community courts would have much more difficulty recognising and applying customary international law if these sources and authorities were not readily at hand. This is well illustrated by the Court's one encounter with a possible 19th century rule of customary international law, namely the rule on distress as exclusionary rule for the exercise of port state authority over foreign ships in the *Poulsen* case.[41] Referring this aspect back to the national courts as a question of fact was not only incorrect, as already suggested above, but possibly also evasive

[38] Note also the subtle distinction the Court made between the *rebus sic stantibus* rule itself (Art. 62 Vienna Convention), which it considered to be part of customary international law, and the procedural rules to be applied (Art. 65 Vienna Convention) which it found not to be customary international law, except that clear advance notice had to be given – a criterion that the Community satisfied.

[39] See, *inter alia*, G.J.H. Van Hoof, *Rethinking the Sources of International Law* (Deventer, Kluwer 1983) p. 109 et seq.

[40] See, *inter alia*, references in the Court's case-law to PCIJ case-law (the *Chorzow Factory* case (*Germany* v. *Polish Republic*) Judgment No. 13 (PCIJ Series A, No. 17, 1928, at p. 30) for the principle of good faith as customary international law in the *Opel Austria* case, *supra* n. 34, at point 90 and to a large number of ICJ cases in order to show that the Convention on the Law of the Sea 1958 and the UNCLOS 1984 are or have become customary international law on many points in the *Poulsen* case, *supra* n. 29, point 10.

[41] See ECJ, Case C-286/90, *supra* n. 29, *Poulsen and Diva Navigation*, at point 35 et seq.

action, since the ECJ had no convenient authoritative source for this rule except the doctrine largely rooted in 19th century Admiralty cases.[42]

There is very little of this 'old-fashioned' customary law left and verifying its true existence on the basis of the classical elements of customary international law, namely consistent practice of states and *opinio iuris*, is an arduous and complicated task for which courts generally are not well-equipped, the European Community courts being no exception.

This may well be one of the reasons why courts in the EC are generally wary of setting aside rules of national law because of a conflict with rules of customary international law. This is a fairly general trend, even in those Member States which have a monist system and are generally very open to international law, such as France, Belgium, the Netherlands and Spain, but also in Member States that are dualist for treaties, but nevertheless follow a more or less monist trend with respect to general (including customary) international law, such as Germany, Austria and the United Kingdom.

From the perspective of democratic legitimacy, where it concerns the internal (direct) effect of international agreements, one can argue that if a parliament collaborates in the adoption of an agreement, it has presumably done so 'en connaissance de cause' and hence must accept that the agreement possibly sets aside national or Community norms, because in principle it should have known that the adopted treaty norms might conflict with earlier legislation. However, in the case of customary international law, a parliament obviously cannot be said to have adopted or collaborated in the adoption of an international norm that may set aside a national or Community norm. This may also be a contributing factor to the lack of enthusiasm of the highest courts, both in the Community and its Member States, for direct effect of customary international law.

3. Decisions of international organisations and Community law

In discussing decisions of international organisations and their position within European Union Community law, it is useful to make a distinction between decisions of organisations which have been founded by the European Community pursuant to its own Treaty, mostly the so-called Associations, and decisions of organisations of which the Community is simply one of the members, or even in which it is merely an observer.

---

[42] For a discussion of distress in the light of doctrine based on national Admiralty cases, see D.P. O'Connell, *International Law*, Vol. II, 1st edn., pp. 685-687. He quotes, *inter alia*, Lord Stowell in *The Eleanor*: '... the danger must be such as to cause apprehension in the mind of an honest and firm man ...'.

3.1 Decisions of international organisations founded by the European Community

It is well-known that, according to Article 310 of the EC Treaty, the Community may conclude with one or more states or international organisations, agreements establishing an association involving reciprocal rights and obligations, common action and special procedures. The Court has added to these criteria of Article 310, that such agreements often involve participation in part of the Community system.[43]

Such association agreements have been concluded for various purposes, from nearly complete participation in the EC internal market for the European Economic Area (EEA) countries, over so-called pre-accession associations (the associations with Greece, Turkey, Malta and Cyprus, as well as the more recent Europe agreements with the countries of Central Europe), to development associations, such as the multilateral one with the African, Caribbean and Pacific countries and the bilateral ones with the Mediterranean countries. One feature that all these different associations have in common is that they have a number of institutions, one of which, the Association Council (the institution at the ministerial level), is often bestowed with considerable decision-making power. The decisions taken by the Association Council are binding on the parties.[44]

There are no differences between a normal Community agreement with a third State concluded pursuant to Article 300 EC Treaty and association agreements concluded pursuant to Article 310. According to the ECJ the association agreements are, just as other agreements concluded by the Community, an integral part of the Community legal order.[45] As a consequence the Court has taken the view that the decisions taken by the institutions of the Association, which are supposed to give effect to the Association, in the same way as the Agreement itself, also form an integral part of the Community legal system.[46]

Hence there can be no doubt that the Court has the power to interpret such decisions adopted by the authorities established by the Agreement and entrusted with responsibility for its implementation.[47]

As to the possibility of granting direct effect to provisions of decisions of the Association Council, the Court also treats the association agreements and the decisions based upon it in the same way. Since provisions of association agreements can have direct effect, according to the Court, when they fulfil the necessary requirements for that,[48] the decisions of association councils can similarly have direct effect.[49]

---

[43] ECJ, Case 181/73 *R. & V. Haegeman* v. *Belgian State* [1974] ECR 449; ECJ, Case 12/86 *Meryem Demirel* v. *Stadt Schwäbisch Gmünd* [1987] ECR 3719.

[44] See for instance the EC-Turkey Association Agreement, Art. 22(1), OJCE N° C 113 of 24/12/1973, p. 1.

[45] ECJ, Case 30/88 *Hellenic Republic* v. *Commission of the European Communities* [1989] ECR 3711, at point 12.

[46] Ibid., at point 13.

[47] ECJ, Case 181/73, *supra* n. 43, *Haegeman*.

[48] ECJ, Case 12/86, *supra* n. 43, *Demirel*, at point 14.

[49] ECJ, Case C-192/89 *S. Z. Sevince* v. *Staatssecretaris van Justitie* [1990] ECR I-3461.

They may have such effect as from the moment they enter into force, even if they have not been published. If no date of entry into force has been foreseen, it is assumed to be from the date of their adoption.[50]

In short, the Community Courts have been very liberal in opening up the Community legal order to the decisions of Association Councils and in granting them direct effect. There can be no doubt that the interpretation of certain terms borrowed from Community law in such decisions must be different from that given in Community law itself. Nevertheless this open attitude to these decisions has been of great practical value, for instance to Turkish workers in the Community in acquiring rights in the employment sphere as well as consequential rights of residence, and in overcoming discrimination in this field and in the related field of social security.[51]

3.2 Decisions of other international organisations

The status of (binding) decisions of other international organisations within Community law has not been clarified to the same extent as that of decisions of Association Councils. One must assume that if the organisation is one of which the Community is a full member and the provisions of the treaty establishing the organisation are considered capable of having direct effect, the (binding) decisions of the organs of that organisation are an integral part of Community law and may themselves also have direct effect.[52] This would imply that the decisions of the General Council and the Ministerial Conference of the WTO, though part of Community law and subject to the Court's interpretation, would not be capable of having direct effect, as the ECJ has ruled that the WTO Agreement itself is not capable of having such direct effect.[53]

Other international organisations that the Community is a fully-fledged member of, are the Food and Agricultural Organisation (FAO) and the Codex Alimentarius Commission. The FAO is not an organisation equipped with the capacity to make binding decisions, but the Codex Alimentarius Commission, which is a semi-independent organisation supported by the FAO and World Health Organisation (WHO), takes decisions which, if not by themselves, at any rate through

[50] ECJ, Case C-277/94 *Z. Taflan-Met, S. Altun-Baser, E. Andal-Bugdayci* v. *Bestuur van de Sociale Verzekeringsbank and O. Akol v Bestuur van de Nieuwe Algemene Bedrijfsvereniging* [1996] ECR I-4085, at points 17-21.

[51] See, *inter alia*, ECJ, Case C-192/89, *supra* n. 49, *Sevince* and Case C-277/94, *supra* n. 50, *Taflan-Met*, and many others in respect of Turkish Workers. It is interesting to note that comparable rights have been granted to Moroccan workers in the Community on the basis of the non-discrimination provision of the EC-Morocco Agreement (Art. 40) and its successor Euro-Mediterranean agreement with Morocco (Art. 64), see ECJ, Case C-18/90 *Office national de l'emploi* v. *Bahia Kziber* [1991] ECR I-199, Case C-416/96, *El-Yassini* [1999] ECR I-1209, and Case C-97/05 *Mohamed Gattousi* v. *Stadt Rüsselsheim,* [2006] ECR I-11917.

[52] See analogy with ECJ, Case 30/88, *supra* n. 45, *Commission* v. *Greece* and ECJ, Case C-192/89, *supra* n. 49, *Sevince.*

[53] ECJ, Case C-149/96 *Portuguese Republic* v. *Council of the European Union* [1999] ECR I-8395, at points 41-47.

reception via the WTO Agreement on the Application of Sanitary and Phytosanitary Measures (the SPS Agreement), can have considerable legal consequences for the presumption of legality of Community sanitary and phytosanitary measures.[54] It is not easy to predict, on this basis, what the Court's view would be on decisions of the Codex Alimentarius – possibly that they become part of Community law, but it is unlikely that they could have direct effect, since they have their effect on Community law primarily through the operation of one of the WTO agreements.

The WHO is capable of taking decisions that (in the end)[55] may have binding effect for its Members. In particular the International Health Regulations (IHR) have this character; they have been recently renewed with active participation of the Community which, however, remains an observer, and not a Member, of the Organisation. Hence the Community Member States, all of them also Members of the WHO, will be bound by these new IHR in the first place. On the other hand it remains a fact that the Member States have transferred part of their powers relating to the IHR, in particular in the field of the import and export of goods, to the Community and the Community therefore needs to be bound by them as well. In such a situation there is no alternative but to adopt the IHR as a quasi-treaty by following the procedure of Article 300 EC Treaty. This approach to decisions of international organisations, of which the Community is not a member, was already accepted by the Court in its Opinion 1/75,[56] when it approved the participation of the EC in the so-called Understanding on a Local Cost Standard in the field of export credits which was about to be adopted by a Resolution of the OECD Council.[57]

In situations like these, such as the Local Cost Standard, the decisions of the international organisations concerned (of which the Community is formally not a member) should undoubtedly be regarded as an integral part of Community law, since the Community has participated in their negotiation within the international organisation concerned and the Council has used the approval procedure of Article 300(2), first subparagraph to adopt them.[58]

There are situations where binding resolutions of an organisation, of which the Community is not a member, are carried out by the Union/Community. Here, the actual status in Community or Union law of the binding resolutions in question remains rather murky. This is, of course, the case for Security Council resolutions

---

[54] See Art. 3(2) SPS Agreement 'Sanitary or phytosanitary measures which conform to international standards, guidelines or recommendations shall be deemed to be necessary to protect human, animal or plant life or health, and presumed to be consistent with the relevant provisions of this Agreement and of GATT 1994.'

[55] There is an objection procedure, see Art. 22 Constitution of the WHO.

[56] Opinion 1/75 of 11 November 1975, [1975] ECR 1355.

[57] See ibid., at p. 1360. The OECD Resolution was, however, not fully binding under international law. Nevertheless it was later converted into Community law by a Council decision.

[58] In the case of the OECD local cost standard, the so-called 'Arrangement on the application of certain Guidelines in the field of officially supported export credits' was first incorporated in Community law by Council Decision of 4 April 1978, the latest version can be found attached to Decision of the Council 2001/76/EC, OJ2001, L 32/1. In the case of the IHR, the EC did not conclude them as a kind of quasi-treaty, but the Commission issued a communication on the IHR on a coordinated implementation of the IHR by the Community and the Member States, Doc. COM (2006) 552 final.

ordering the UN Members to take economic sanctions. It is not the intention to go here into an in-depth analysis of the status and implementation of Security Council resolutions in Community law; that has been done elsewhere.[59] It should suffice here to say that the Community regulations which have been adopted on the basis of Article 301 EC Treaty (or on the basis of Article 133 before the entry into force of Maastricht) in order to implement certain Security Council resolutions have repeatedly been interpreted by the ECJ in the light of the detailed provisions of these Security Council resolutions.

This was the case, for instance, in the *Bosphorus* case,[60] where the Court invoked the terms of the Security Council Resolutions on the sanctions against Yugoslavia, in particular Security Council Resolution 820 (1993),[61] in order to bolster the extensive interpretation of the impoundment of aircraft in Article 8 of EC Council Regulation 990/93. This was done so as to affect the aircraft in which a majority or controlling interest was held by a person, undertaking in, or operating from the Federal Republic of Yugoslavia without it being necessary for such person to have actual control or use of the aircraft (which in this case was leased to a Turkish company).

It was equally the case in the *Ebony Maritime* case,[62] where the Court ruled that the sanction of forfeiture of the cargo by any ship that had attempted to break the UN sanctions against Yugoslavia was in line with paragraph 25 of SC Resolution 820 (1993) and that the Italian version of the text of the Community implementing the Regulation, which omitted this sanction for vessels, rested on a material error.

To the extent that the text of such resolutions guides the Court in its interpretation of Community law, it may be said that these resolutions have become part of the Community legal order, or at the very least are considered relevant context for the interpretation of Community law. There are no indications, however, that the Court would be ready to grant direct effect to Security Council resolutions and to leave provisions of the Community implementing regulations unapplied for reasons of non-conformity with the Security Council resolutions. To the contrary, the CFI, seems to have taken the view that Security Council resolutions should not have direct effect in Community law.[63]

Although the judgment in question is still subject to appeal, it would seem that this is a logical approach to take (i.e., to put the emphasis rather on the interpretation of Community law in light of the Security Council resolutions which that law is supposed to implement, rather than on overruling it), given that Article 301 EC

---

[59] See chapter 10 by Nikolaos Lavranos in this volume.

[60] ECJ, Case C-84/95, *Bosphorus Hava Yollari Turizm ve Ticaret AS* v. *Minister for Transport, Energy and Communications and others* [1996] ECR I-3953, at points 13-15.

[61] S/RES/820 (1993), 17 April 1993.

[62] See ECJ, Case C-177/95 *Ebony Maritime SA and Loten Navigation Co. Ltd* v. *Prefetto della Provincia di Brindisi and others* [1997] ECR I-1111, at point 31.

[63] See CFI, Case T-315/01 *Yassin Abdullah Kadi* v. *Council of the European Union and Commission of the European Communities* [2005] ECR II-3649 at point 213, in the meantime appealed under No C-402/05P, *Yassin Abdul Kadi* v. *Council and Commission*.

Treaty seems implicitly to take a somewhat dualist approach to Security Council resolutions. Moreover, there is a legitimacy problem in granting direct effect, since the Community is not a party to the UN Charter and the democratically legitimized European Parliament has never had a chance to express itself on it.

3.3 Some final remarks on decisions of international organisations

As a matter of fact there is a general problem of the legitimacy of binding decisions of international organisations. Theoretically, this has been solved by Article 300(2), second subparagraph, as modified by the Nice Treaty. Initially this provision, inserted at Amsterdam,[64] reflected and codified the practice followed by the Community institutions in respect of binding decisions of Association Councils. Namely, a decision defining the position of the Community in respect of such an Association Council decision *before* the decision was taken. In Nice it was rather thoughtlessly extended to Community positions to be taken in respect of binding decisions of all international organisations (whether or not the Community is a member of these organisations).[65] This extension in no way took account of the fact that in its self-created Association Councils, the Community was very much the master of the preparation of the decisions to be taken. The Commission could hence foresee fairly precisely when such decisions were to be taken, so that it could prepare a proposal for the Council to take a position on them in due time before their adoption by the Association Council. The drafters at Nice did not sufficiently consider that such would not be the case in other international organisations, especially in respect of those organisations (still the vast majority) of which the Community is not a member.

However, even organisations of which the Community *is* a member (and an important one at that) have organs with negotiating and decision-making methods which do not permit the Community institutions to take a position on the decision before it is adopted, e.g., Fisheries Organisations and the WTO.[66] The only way open to the Community institutions in such a situation is to follow the same

---

[64] Art. 2(56)(b) of the Treaty of Amsterdam, by which, *inter alia*, the 2nd alinea of Art. 228(2) was introduced.

[65] See Art. 2(46)(b) of the Treaty of Nice. Even if the Community sometimes is in a position to express itself on a decision of an organ of an organisation of which it is not a Member, this is a quite remarkable omission.

[66] In the WTO Council or Ministerial Conferences typically negotiations on a decision relating to trade negotiations continue until the last minute before its adoption, unless they are well-prepared in advance such as waiver decisions and accessions. In addition, decisions relating to trade negotiations, unlike decisions on waivers and accession, normally do not have (final) legal effects. A waiver is granted and accession is effective simultaneously with the decision concerned. However, decisions on trade negotiations, which will normally consist of amendments to the WTO agreements and (new) schedules of concessions and commitments will only have legal effects once the text of the amendments is ratified by the WTO Members pursuant to Article X of the WTO Agreement and once the new schedules – which in the GATT tradition were concluded as separate agreements – are ratified. Their approval in the form of a WTO decision is equivalent to the (collective) initialling of a treaty text, if fixes their final, agreed terms, but does not (yet) have legal effects.

approach as they would follow in an organisation of which the Community is not a member. That is, to treat the decision in question as a quasi-treaty (traité en forme simplifiée) and use the directives for negotiation under Article 300(1) EC Treaty as the way in which the position of the Community *vis-à-vis* the decision is determined. Later on the decision will be approved (or not) by a treaty-adoption procedure or by implementation (transformation) into Community law. This has happened in situations such as the implementation of the OECD local cost standard, the implementation of Security Council Resolutions, and presumably the future implementation of the Doha Round decisions, much as the implementation of the Uruguay Round by legislative package.[67]

These specific problems with the adoption of decisions of international organisations are being recalled here in order to highlight the problems with respect to their position in Community law. They also warn us that the very open-minded and direct-effect-friendly approach of the Community Courts to decisions of Association Councils may not necessarily apply in the same way to decisions with legal effects of other international organisations.

4. A typical Community approach to ensure conformity with international law: the infringement procedure

An important weapon for ensuring Member States' compliance with international law is the infringement procedure. The Court has declared that, since Community agreements according to Article 300(6) EC Treaty bind not only the Community but also the Member States, the latter fulfil an obligation *vis-à-vis* the Community when they obey and implement such an agreement. This is also true for the Community parts of so-called mixed agreements.[68] Further, there is no reason to assume (though Article 300(6) EC Treaty mentions only international agreements concluded by the Community) that decisions of international organisations which bind the Community or rules of customary international law binding on the Community are any different in this respect. Both are just as much as integral part of Community law as an agreement concluded by the Community.

Hence they can be enforced as Community law through the infringement procedure.

In practice this has remained a rather exceptional occurrence (one would hope because the Member States breach Community obligations under international

---

[67] See OJ 1994, L 349, p. 1 et seq.

[68] Mixed agreements are agreements which are concluded by the Community and the Member States together, because they contain competences that are shared as between Community and Member States or exclusive Community competences and Member State competences. For a typology of mixed agreements, see Allan Rosas, 'Mixed Union, Mixed Agreements', in Martti Koskenniemi (ed.), *International Law Aspects of the European Union* (The Hague, Kluwer Law International 1998) pp. 125-148. See also Joni Heliskoski, *Mixed Agreements as a Technique for Organizing the International Relations of the European Community and its Member States* (The Hague, Kluwer Law International 2001).

law rather seldomly). On one occasion Germany was condemned for a breach of the Community dairy legislation as well as of the GATT International Dairy Agreement (now defunct).[69] On another, Ireland was found wanting because it had not ratified the Paris Convention, which it was obliged to do under the EEA Agreement.[70] More recently, France succumbed in a case brought by the Commission because it had not carried out its obligations to limit sweet water and sediment effluents into the Etang de Berre under the Protocol concerning the protection of the Mediterranean against pollution from effluents from land.[71]

The latter two cases are of special interest, since they concern mixed agreements in areas where the density of Community law is not particularly great (namely, intellectual property, in particular copyright, and pollution of the sea by effluents from land) and the subject-matter of the international agreement was not (fully) covered by Community law. However, the Court ruled that it did not matter that the specific treaty obligation that had been infringed by the Member State in question was not covered by Community law. The Court was of the view that in such a situation, as long as Community law 'largely' covered a specific domain, there is a 'Community interest' in the international agreement being obeyed. Presumably this is the case because, in mixed agreements where there is no clear demarcation between Community competence and Member State competence, in the Court's view Community and Member States are equally responsible under international law for any breach of such agreement.[72] Hence the Community has a legitimate interest in preventing a Member State from breaching *its* international obligations, since such a breach may lead to co-responsibility of the Community for a Member State's breach of its own obligations.

It is obvious that, compared to states, the Community offers an interesting additional guarantee that the Member States, as constituent parts of the Community, will obey and implement not only international agreements, but also customary international law and decisions of international organisations that bind the Community or the Community and its Member States: namely, the infringement procedure. This situation may be compared to the responsibility of federal states for the acts of their constituent states. However, some federal states do not offer the same guarantees offered by the Community infringement procedure, i.e., the internationally unlawful act of its constituent states may not be sanctioned as easily and directly as the Community infringement system.[73] On the other hand, thus far the Commission has not used the infringement procedure against Member States in a systematic manner in order to prevent breaches of international legal rules by the

[69] ECJ, Case C-61/94 *Commission of the European Communities* v. *Federal Republic of Germany* [1996] ECR I-3989.

[70] ECJ, Case 13/00 *Commission of the European Communities* v. *Ireland* [2002] ECR I-2943.

[71] ECJ, Case C-239/03 *Commission of the European Communities* v. *French Republic* [2004] ECR I-09325.

[72] ECJ, Case C-316/91 *European Parliament* v. *Council of the European Union* [1994] ECR I-625, at points 29-33.

[73] See Ivan Bernier, *International Legal Aspects of Federalism* (Hawden Conn., Archon Books 1973) passim.

Community. It is unlikely ever to get that far, but it is a useful 'emergency brake' in specific situations.

5. Damages for private parties for breach of international legal rules by the Community

A final yardstick for determining the position of international law in the Community legal system is the possibility to obtain damages for breach of international legal rules by the Community.

In principle there is no reason why the standing case-law of the ECJ concerning compensation for non-contractual damages (Article 288 EC Treaty) would not apply to breach by Community authorities of international legal rules and injury caused thereby. The normal criteria that would apply are the following:[74]

1) There needs to be injury;
2) This injury has to be brought about by an act attributable to a Community institution (causality);
3) This act needs to be contrary to a norm that is intended to protect individuals (*Schutznorm)*; and,
4) It needs to be a serious breach of such norm (qualified breach).[75]

In the case of alleged breach of rules of international law, the third criteria is of particular importance and will normally be linked to the direct effect of the norm in question.[76] This is so because such direct effect irrefutably demonstrates its capability of protecting individuals under international law.

This is the approach the Court has taken in cases of alleged damages for breach of WTO rules. However, such cases obviously met with a negative result, since it is by now standing Court doctrine that the WTO can have no such direct effect.[77] It must be assumed that, therefore, given the Court's reluctance/hesitation to grant direct effect to rules of customary international law, the breach of customary international law by Community institutions will normally not give rise to the award of extra-contractual damages to individuals. The same is likely to be true of the breach of decisions of international organisations, unless they are provisions of

[74] According to Art. 288 EC Treaty these criteria are common to the law of the Member States.

[75] These conditions are summed up in, *inter alia*, ECJ, Case C-352/98P *Laboratoires pharmaceutiques Bergaderm SA and Jean-Jacques Goupil* v. *Commission of the European Communities* [2000] ECR I -5291, at points 42-45. Note that a qualified breach of the norm is necessary only where the Community institution in question disposes of a wide margin of discretion, which must have been evidently misused.

[76] It is worthwhile to point out that in internal EC law the notion that a norm is a 'Schutznorm' does not necessarily entail the requirement that it has direct effect in EC law, while the Court does read this requirement into the equation, when it concerns a treaty norm that is supposed to protect individuals.

[77] See ECJ, Case C-149/96, *supra* n. 53, *Portugal* v. *Council.*

decisions by Association Councils for which such direct effect has clearly been recognised.[78]

So far, however, there have been no awards of damages at all, whether for breach of rules of international agreements, decisions of international organisations, or rules of customary international law. In principle, however, the possibility remains open in the case of self-executing rules of international law.

In light of the negative approach taken by the Community courts to damages in compensation for alleged breach of the WTO agreements, there have been attempts to obtain damages under a 'Community liability without fault' approach. For the WTO this has been rejected by the CFI, since the notion of liability without fault in Community law (as in the law of the Member States which know this concept outside the area of ultra hazardous activities),[79] *inter alia*, rests on the idea that one is forced to accept burdens in the public interest which go beyond the normal risks an economic operator has to accept and, according to the CFI, the damages caused by retaliatory measures taken with WTO authorisation, fall within the normal risks operators must accept within international trade.[80] The final word on this issue needs to be said by the ECJ.[81]

Everything considered, one may say that claims of damages for breach of international legal rules by Community institutions could be a useful additional tool to stimulate the conformity of the Community with its international obligations, but that thus far in practice not few results have been achieved in this way.

6. Summing up

Briefly recapitulating the above, it is clear that the Community legal system is quite open to customary international law and to decisions of international organisations. However, it is also necessary to make some provisos here. Direct effect of customary international law is a possibility for the Community Courts, but on closer scrutiny, is far from easily granted. As to decisions of international organisations, they are treated very generously by the Community courts when they are in reality decisions of Association Councils (which are largely controlled by the Community). Whether binding decisions of other international organisations will be treated in the same way, now that the new version of Article 300(2), second subparagraph EC Treaty has entered into force remains to be seen, especially since that for some international organisations ill-suited procedure has as yet hardly been applied to other decisions than those of Association Councils.

---

[78] Note, however, that many such decisions are executed by national authorities.

[79] In French law and in the Member States influenced by French administrative law, this is called the principle of the 'égalité devant les charges publiques'. In German law it is the doctrine of the 'Sonderopfer'. Both notions are based on the idea that a person or limited class of persons is forced by the authorities to shoulder a disproportionate burden for the common good.

[80] CFI, Case T-69/00 *Fabbrica italiana accumulatori motocarri Montecchio SpA (FIAMM) and Fabbrica italiana accumulatori motocarri Montecchio Technologies, Inc. (FIAMM Technologies)* v. *Council of the European Union and Commission of the European Communities* [2005] ECR II-5393.

[81] An appeal is pending under No. C-120/06P, *FIAMM et al.* v. *Council and Commission.*

Alternative ways of ensuring conformity of the EC, such as action for damages for breach of international law rules and the use of the infringement procedure by the Commission provide interesting possibilities, but remain relatively ineffective (e.g., damages) or are as yet insufficiently exploited (e.g., infringement procedures).

Part II
CONSEQUENCES OF EUROPEANISATION FOR DOMESTIC LAW, INTERNATIONAL LAW AND JUDICIAL PROTECTION IN THE EU

Chapter 7
'UNIONISATION' AND 'CONVENTIONISATION' OF FUNDAMENTAL RIGHTS IN EUROPE: THE INTERPLAY BETWEEN UNION AND CONVENTION LAW AND ITS IMPACT ON THE DOMESTIC LEGAL SYSTEMS OF THE MEMBER STATES

Johan Callewaert*

The present chapter endeavours to address the question of whether the 'europeanisation' of public international law, which is in progress as a consequence of the increased influence of European Union (EU) law in this area, also affects the European Convention on Human Rights ('the Convention' or ECHR). It will do so by showing, in the first part, that what is taking place is in fact not so much a unilateral Europeanisation of the Convention but, rather, a kind of bilateral interplay between the EU and Convention law,[1] thereby producing a twofold process of 'conventionisation' of Union law and 'unionisation' of Convention law, though with different timings and intensities. In the second part, the consequences of the process for the domestic legal systems of the EU Member States will be addressed. In both parts, matters will be considered from a judicial and a legislative perspective.

1. 'Unionisation' and 'Conventionisation' of fundamental rights

Dealing with the Convention in the wider context of the europeanisation of public international law requires that the question of the status of the Convention in international law is first briefly addressed. The Convention is itself already a form of europeanisation of international law, meant to represent, as the Preamble to the Convention states, 'the first steps' undertaken by 'the governments of European countries which are like-minded and have a common heritage of political traditions, ideals, freedom and the rule of law, … for the collective enforcement of

* Dr. iur. Johan Callewaert, Deputy Grand Chamber Registrar, European Court of Human Rights, Strasbourg; Lecturer at the German Postgraduate School for Administrative Studies, Speyer. Any views expressed are personal. The chapter has been updated as at 15 April 2008.

[1] The notion of 'Convention law' will be used here as encompassing both the Convention itself and the case-law of the ECHR.

J. Wouters, P.A. Nollkaemper, E. de Wet (eds.), The Europeanisation of International Law

certain of the rights stated in the Universal Declaration' of Human Rights of 10 December 1948. However, it is clear that, used in the present context, the notion of 'europeanisation' has a different meaning and, in relation to the Convention, refers to the impact of EU law[2] on the Convention considered as part of international law. Consequently, the notion of 'unionisation' – rather than 'europeanisation' – will be used below to refer to this impact.

The Convention, for its part, can rightly be considered as belonging to public international law, but not without some restrictions. The European Court of Human Rights (ECtHR) has consistently held that the Convention must be interpreted in the light of the rules of interpretation set out in the Vienna Convention on the Law of Treaties, among which Article 31(3)(c) provides that account is to be taken of any relevant rules of international law applicable to the relations between the parties. According to the Court, the principles underlying the Convention cannot be interpreted and applied in a vacuum. On the contrary, the Convention should, so far as possible, be interpreted in harmony with other rules of international law of which it forms part, bearing in mind, however, its special character as a human rights treaty, which in a few instances has proven capable of justifying some departures from classic international law.[3]

1.1 'Conventionisation' of Union law

The 'conventionisation' of Union law has been taking place via two different channels: the 'general principles of Community law' and the EU Charter on fundamental rights.

1.1.1 *The judicial level: the 'general principles of Community law'*

The first moves in the relationship between Union and Convention law were seen on the jurisprudential level, with steps taken by the European Court of Justice (ECJ) towards gradually introducing into Union law a judicial control of respect for fundamental rights. This was done in response to the criticism by some Constitutional Courts, notably those of Germany and Italy, of the fact that Union law was claiming supremacy over the legal systems of the Member States without ensuring its own compliance with fundamental rights.[4]

---

[2] For the sake of convenience, the notions of 'EU law' or 'Union law' will be used in this chapter as referring to either Union or Community law, as the case may be.

[3] One of the most prominent of these departures relates to the question of the severability of invalid parts of declarations made by contracting States under former Arts. 25 and 46 of the Convention; on this, see ECtHR, *Belilos* v. *Switzerland*, judgment of 29.4.1988 and ECtHR, *Loizidou* v. *Turkey* (preliminary objections), judgment of 23.3.1995. See also ECtHR, *Loizidou* v. *Turkey* (merits) judgment of 18.12.1996; ECtHR, *Bankovic and others* v. *Belgium and 16 other Contracting States*, judgment of 12.12.2001 (dec.) [GC] , para. 57; ECtHR, *Al-Adsani* v. *United Kingdom*, judgment of 21.11.2001 [GC], para. 55.

[4] See Italian Constitutional Court 27.12.1973, *Frontini*, 183/1973, Foro italiano, 1974, I, 314; German Constitutional Court 29.5.1974 ('*Solange I*'), BVerfGE 37, 271.

The main stages of this evolution largely coincide with the developments characterising the role of the Convention in the Luxembourg case-law. The ECJ indeed gradually moved from mere implicit[5] to explicit references to the Convention,[6] albeit most often not to the Convention *as such* but rather to the so-called 'general principles of Community law', one source of which is provided by the Convention.[7] Even though the ECJ now sometimes omits the reference to the 'general principles of Community law',[8] these principles still form the legal basis upon which, according to Article 6(2) TEU,[9] compliance with fundamental rights is to be ensured under Union law.[10]

In other words – and to sum up more than three decades of jurisprudential evolution – it can be said that over the years an ever greater amount of Union law has been reviewed by the ECJ in the light of the Convention. As such, this already represents a kind of 'conventionisation' of Union law. An important test, however, is whether on such occasions the ECJ also relies on the Strasbourg interpretation of the Convention provisions referred to, as their adaptation to a Union law context could mean that the Convention is being 'unionised'. This also touches on the reasons why, despite early proposals to this effect,[11] the EU has still not acceded to the Convention.

It is indeed not the least of paradoxes characterising this area that, although the ECJ has over the years demonstrated an ever greater readiness to take on board

---

[5] See ECJ, Case 4/73 *Nold, Kohlen- und Baustoffgroßhandlung* v. *Commission of the European Communities* [1974] ECR 419.

[6] The Convention's provisions were first explicitly referred to in ECJ, Case 36/75 *Rutili* v. *Ministre de l'intérieur* [1975] ECR 1219.

[7] See, among many others, ECJ, Case C-94/00 *Roquette Frères SA* v. *Directeur général de la concurrence, de la consommation et de la répression des fraudes, and Commission of the European Communities* [2002] ECR I-09011, para. 23: 'According to settled case-law, fundamental rights form an integral part of the general principles of law observance of which the Court ensures. For that purpose, the Court draws inspiration from the constitutional traditions common to the Member States and from the guidelines supplied by international treaties for the protection of human rights on which the Member States have collaborated or to which they are signatories. The ECHR has special significance in that respect.' See V. Skouris, 'La protection des droits fondamentaux dans la jurisprudence de la Cour de justice: les étapes d'une consolidation progressive' in J. Iliopoulos-Strangas and H. Bauer (eds.), 'The New European Union' (Athens-Berlin-Brussels, Sakkoulas/Berliner Wissenschafts-Verlag/Bruylant, 2006) p. 87 et seq.

[8] For instance in ECJ, Case C-185/95 *Baustahlgewebe GmbH* v. *Commission of the European Communities* [1998] ECR I-08417; ECJ, Case C-273/99 P & C-274/99 P *Bernard Connolly* v. *Commission of the European Communities* [2001] ECR I-01575 & [2001] ECR I-01611.

[9] 'The Union shall respect fundamental rights, as guaranteed by the European Convention for the Protection of Human Rights and Fundamental Freedoms signed in Rome on 4 November 1950 and as they result from the constitutional traditions common to the Member States, as general principles of Community law.'

[10] See, among many others, ECJ, Opinion 2/94 [1996] ECR I-01759, para. 33; ECJ, Case C-112/00 *Eugen Schmidberger, Internationale Transporte und Planzüge* v. *Republik Österreich* [2003] ECR I-05659, para. 71; ECJ, Case C-36/02 *Omega Spielhallen- und Automatenaufstellungs-GmbH* v. *Oberbürgermeisterin der Bundesstadt Bonn* [2004] ECR I-09609, para. 33; ECJ, Case C-540/03 *European Parliament* v. *Council of the European Union* [2006] ECR I-05769, paras. 35-36.

[11] See, *inter alia*, the European Commission Memorandum of 4 April 1979 (OJ C 127, 21.5.1979).

the Strasbourg case-law, there have always been hesitations on the part of Union law experts with regard to whether accession by the EU to the Convention – meaning a *general* acceptance by the EU of the Convention legal standards, including those resulting from the Strasbourg case-law – is compatible with the very nature of the EU legal system. In this context, questions were raised as to whether the Convention was really adapted to the EU reality, which at that time pursued mainly economic purposes. These questions included whether acceding to the Convention would not jeopardise the supremacy and autonomy of the EU legal order which, along with the direct effect of Union law, the ECJ had established at a very early stage,[12] including over 'national' fundamental rights,[13] making it one of the cornerstones of the EU legal system. Further, what of the exclusive competence of the ECJ to interpret Union law if the Strasbourg Court were to have a say in Union law matters?[14] In fact, many of the hesitations thus expressed came down to questioning whether the Convention rights were really adapted to the specific nature of the EU legal system.[15] Hence the insistence, in the relevant legal texts, on the fact that the Convention was not to be applied *as such* in Union law but only as a source of inspiration in identifying the 'general principles of Community law'. In this way, the ECJ was given, at least in theory, some interpretational leeway.

In practice, however, the ECJ has hardly made use of this leeway, as demonstrated by the very limited number of jurisprudential conflicts between Strasbourg

[12] ECJ, Case 6/64 *Flaminio Costa* v. *ENEL,* ECR English Special Edition 00585.

[13] ECJ, Case 11/70 *Internationale Handelsgesellschaft mbH* v. *Einfuhr- und Vorratsstelle für Getreide und Futtermittel* [1970] ECR 01125; ECJ, Case 48/71 *Commission of the European Communities* v. *Italian Republic* [1972] ECR 00529; ECJ, Case C-285/98 *Tanja Kreil* v. *Bundesrepublik Deutschland* [2000] ECR I-00069.

[14] On this, see among many others F. Benoit-Rohmer, 'L'adhésion de l'Union à la Convention européenne des droits de l'homme', 12 *Rev. univ. dr. h.* (2000) p. 57 ; G. Cohen-Jonathan, 'L'adhésion de l'Union européenne à la Convention européenne des droits de l'homme', in *Quelle justice pour l'Europe?* (Brussels, Bruylant 2004) p. 59; O. De Schutter, 'L'adhésion des Communautés européennes à la Convention européenne des Droits de l'Homme', *Courrier hebdomadaire du CRISP* (Brussels, CRISP 1994); A. Verstichel, 'European Union Accession to the European Convention on Human Rights', in P. Lemmens and W. Vandenhole (eds.), *Protocol No. 14 and the Reform of the European Court of Human Rights* (Antwerp/Oxford, Intersentia, 2005) p. 123 et seq.; S. Winkler, *Der Beitritt der Europäischen Gemeinschaften zur EMRK* (Baden-Baden, Nomos 2000). A great number of these questions were addressed by Working Group II of the EU-Convention on the Future of Europe (see, *inter alia*, the auditions of MM. Schoo, Piris and Petite (WG II, Working Document 13, 5.9.2002) and the final report of the Working Group (CONV 354/02, WG II 16, 22.10.2002).

[15] Remaining hesitations on this point seem to be reflected in Protocol No. 32 to the EU-Constitutional Treaty relating to Art. I-9 para. 2 of the Constitution which, in its Art. 1, refers to the need to preserve 'the specific characteristics of the Union and Union law'. Furthermore, a 'Declaration on Article I-9 para. 2' with the following wording was annexed to the Final Act of the Intergovernmental Conference which adopted the Constitutional Treaty: 'The Conference agrees that the Union's accession to the European Convention on the Protection of Human Rights and Fundamental Freedoms should be arranged in such a way as to preserve the specific features of Union law. In this connection, the Conference notes the existence of a regular dialogue between the Court of Justice of the European Union and the European Court of Human Rights; such dialogue could be reinforced when the Union accedes to that Convention.'

and Luxembourg.[16] The main conflicts have concerned the notion of 'home' within the meaning of Article 8 of the Convention[17] and the right to reply to the opinion of the Advocate General in proceedings before the ECJ.[18] Even so, the relevance of these examples can be questioned. The former can be explained by the fact that there was no Strasbourg determination on whether the notion of 'home' encompassed commercial premises at the time when the ECJ was first confronted with that question. In later cases, the ECJ conformed to the Strasbourg case-law on this point.[19] As to the latter, it can be argued that it does not represent a real conflict, since the ECJ did not formally depart from the Strasbourg criteria but simply made its own different assessment of the role of its Advocate Generals in the Luxembourg procedure.[20]

Yet it would appear that jurisprudential conflicts may occur more frequently in areas not open to review by the Strasbourg Court, as a consequence of the EU not being a contracting party to the Convention. As acts of the EC, determinations on the merits by the Community Courts cannot be challenged before the Strasbourg Court.[21] The privilege against self-incrimination, especially in competition law litigation, is a good example of such a 'hidden conflict', the main divergence in the respective approaches relating to the kind of information and/or evidence covered by the privilege.

---

[16] See A. Busch, *Die Bedeutung der Europäischen Menschenrechtskonvention für den Grundrechtsschutz in der Europäischen Union – Grundrechtskontrolle des EGMR über das Recht der EU* [The Importance of the European Convention on Human Rights for the Protection of Fundamental Rights in the European Union – Review of EU Law by the European Court of Human Rights] (Baden-Baden, Nomos 2003) at p. 128 et seq.; K. Lenaerts and M. Desomer, 'Het E.V.R.M. en de Europese Unie' [The European Convention on Human Rights and the European Union], in P. Lemmens (ed.), *Uitdagingen door en voor het EVRM* [Challenges by and for the European Convention on Human Rights] (Mechelen, Kluwer 2005) at p. 177 (187 et seq.); D. Spielmann, 'Human Rights Case Law in the Strasbourg and Luxembourg Courts: Conflicts, Inconsistencies and Complementarities', in Ph. Alston (ed.), *The EU and Human Rights*, (Oxford, Oxford University Press 1999) at p. 757 et seq.; M. Wathelet and S. Van Raepenbusch, « La protection des droits fondamentaux au sein de l'Union européenne après le Traité de Nice », in *Avancées et confins actuels des droits de l'homme aux niveaux international, européen et national – Mélanges offerts à S. Marcus Helmons* (Bruxelles, Bruylant 2003) at p. 345 et seq.

[17] Compare ECJ, Case 46/87 & 227/88 *Hoechst AG* v. *Commission of the European Communities* [1989] ECR 02859 with ECtHR, *Niemitz* v. *Germany*, judgment of 16.12.1992 and ECtHR, *Société Colas Est and Others* v. *France*, judgment of 16.4.2002.

[18] Compare ECJ, Case C-17/98 (Order) *Emesa Sugar (Free Zone) NV* v. *Aruba* [2000] ECR I-00675 and ECJ, C-432/04 *Commission of the European Communities* v. *Édith Cresson* [2006] ECR I-06387, paras. 49-52 with ECtHR, *Vermeulen* v. *Belgium*, judgment of 20.2.1996 and ECtHR, *Kress* v. *France*, judgment of 7.6.2001.

[19] See ECJ, Case C-94/00, *supra* n. 7, *Roquette Frères SA*. On this, see J. Mischo, 'Hoechst, Colas, Roquette: illustration d'une convergence', in N. Colneric, D. Edward, J-P Puissochet, D. Ruiz-Jarabo Colomer (eds.), *Une communauté de droit* (Festschrift für G.C. Rodriguez Iglesias) (Berlin, Berliner Wissenschafts-Verlag 2003) p. 137.

[20] See J. Callewaert, 'Note on ECJ 4.2.2000', *European Human Rights Cases* (Maastricht, Sdu Uitgevers 2000) p. 213; K. Lenaerts and M. Desomer, *supra* n. 17, p. 201 et seq.

[21] 'Acts of the EC as such cannot be challenged before the Court because the EC is not a Contracting Party' (ECtHR, *Matthews* v. *United Kingdom*, judgment of 18.2.1999 [GC], para. 32).

According to the Community Courts, a right to silence can be recognised only to the extent that the undertaking concerned – through its representatives – would otherwise be compelled to provide answers which may involve an admission relating to an infringement which it is incumbent upon the Commission to prove. The mere fact of being obliged to answer purely factual questions put by the Commission and to comply with its requests for the production of documents already in existence could not constitute a breach of the principle of respect for the rights of defence or impair the right to fair legal process, which offered, in the specific field of competition law, protection equivalent to that guaranteed by Article 6 of the Convention. There was indeed nothing to prevent the addressee of a request for information from showing, whether later during the administrative procedure or in proceedings before the Community Courts, when exercising his rights of defence, that the facts set out in his replies or the documents produced by him had a different meaning from that ascribed to them by the Commission.[22]

By contrast, the European Court of Human Rights ruled that the right not to incriminate oneself cannot reasonably be confined to statements of admission of wrongdoing or to remarks which are directly incriminating. Testimony obtained under compulsion which appears on its face to be of a non-incriminating nature – such as exculpatory remarks or mere information on questions of fact – might later be deployed in criminal proceedings in support of the prosecution case, for example to contradict or cast doubt upon other statements of the accused or evidence given by him during the trial or to otherwise undermine his credibility. Where the credibility of an accused had to be assessed by a jury the use of such testimony might be especially harmful. What was of the essence in this context was the use to which evidence obtained under compulsion was put in the course of the criminal trial.[23]

However that may be, it remains the case that on the whole the ECJ has been following the Strasbourg case-law ever more closely, and referring to it ever more frequently.[24] In so doing, it in fact prepared the ground for Article 52(3) of the

---

[22] See, e.g., CFI, T-112/98 *Mannesmannröhren-Werke AG* v. *Commission of the European Communities* [2001] ECR II-00729, paras. 66-67, 77-78; CFI, T-236/01 et seq. *Tokai Carbon Co. Ltd and Others* v. *Commission of the European Communities* [2004] ECR II-01181, paras. 402-406.

[23] ECtHR, *Saunders* v. *United Kingdom* [GC], judgment of 17.12.1996, paras. 70-73. See also *J.B.* v. *Switzerland*, 31827/96, para. 66; ECtHR *Jalloh* v. *Germany*, judgment of 11.7.2006 [GC], 54810/00, paras. 100 et seq. On this, see Johan Callewaert, 'The Privilege against Self-Incrimination in European law – An Illustration of the Impact of the Plurality of Courts and Legal Sources on the Protection of Fundamental Rights in Europe', ERA-Forum 4/2004, Academy of European Law Trier, p. 488.

[24] See, among many others, ECJ, C-74/95 & C-129/95 *Criminal proceedings against X* [1996] ECR I-06609; ECJ, Case C-368/95 *Vereinigte Familiapress Zeitungsverlags- und vertriebs GmbH* v. *Heinrich Bauer Verlag* [1997] ECR I-03689; ECJ, Case C-185/95, *supra* n. 8, *Baustahlgewebe GmbH*; ECJ, Case C-7/98 *Dieter Krombach* v. *André Bamberski* [2000] ECR I-01935; CFI, T-112/98, *supra* n. 22, *Mannesmannröhren-Werke AG*; ECJ, Case C-274/99, *supra* n. 8, *Connolly*; ECJ, Case C-60/00 *Mary Carpenter* v. *Secretary of State for the Home Department* [2002] ECR I-06279; ECJ, Case C-276/01 *Joachim Steffensen* [2003] ECR I-03735; ECJ, Case C-465/00, C-138/01 & C-139/01 *Rechnungshof (C-465/00)* v. *Österreichischer Rundfunk and Others and Christa Neukomm (C-138/01) and Joseph Lauermann (C-139/01)* v. *Österreichischer Rundfunk* [2003] ECR I-04989; ECJ, Case

EU Charter on fundamental rights[25] which drops any reference to the 'general principles of Community law' and provides, in substance, that the rights borrowed from the Convention are to be given *the same meaning and scope*, it being understood that Union law can offer a more extensive protection.[26] This in turn facilitated the conclusion first reached by the Convention on the future of Europe and now laid down in Article 6(2) TEU as amended by the Lisbon Treaty,[27] according to which the EU should also accede to the Convention, since the EU is adhering to the same set of rights as its Member States. Prior to that conclusion, a number of eminent experts had been heard, a large majority of whom had expressed the view that accession to the Convention would not endanger the 'autonomy' of Union law.[28]

Thus, it appears that for as long as there have been relations between the Convention and the EC/EU, the question has remained as to whether – to use the terminology of this paper – the Convention had to be somehow 'unionised' or whether it was rather for Union law to be 'conventionised'. It in fact all came down to whether or not the Convention could be applied *unchanged* in a Union law context. The answers given by the ECJ were in the affirmative, demonstrating a clear willingness on the part of the ECJ to contribute to ensuring harmony between the Luxembourg and Strasbourg case-law.[29]

C-109/01 *Secretary of State for the Home Department* v. *Hacene Akrich* [2003] ECR I-09607; ECJ, Case C-117/01 *K.B.* v. *National Health Service Pensions Agency and Secretary of State for Health* [2004] ECR I-00541; ECJ, Case C-71/02 *Herbert Karner Industrie-Auktionen GmbH* v. *Troostwijk GmbH* [2004] ECR I-03025; ECJ, Case C-482/01 & C-493/01 *Georgios Orfanopoulos and Others (C-482/01) and Raffaele Oliveri (C-493/01)* v. *Land Baden-Württemberg* [2004] ECR I-05257; ECJ, Case C-105/03 *Criminal proceedings against Maria Pupino* [2005] ECR I-05285; ECJ, Case C-540/03, *supra* n. 10, *Parliament* v. *Council*.

[25] OJ 2007, C 303/13.

[26] See 1.1.2 *infra*.

[27] OJ 2007, C 306/13.

[28] 'L'adhésion à la CEDH n'est pas en général en conflit avec l'autonomie du droit communautaire. La totalité des normes de droit communautaire (à la seule exception de celles figurant à la CEDH) continueront d'être adoptées par les institutions de la Communauté et mises en oeuvre par sa propre administration et/ou par l'administration des Etats membres; en outre, leur application et leur interprétation continueront d'être assurées par les juridictions nationales et par la Cour de justice, comme le prévoit le traité actuel. Toutefois, dans le domaine couvert par la CEDH, l'adhésion à celle-ci représentera une limitation de l'autonomie du droit communautaire. Pour ce qui concerne plus particulièrement la Cour, celle-ci perdra en substance son monopole de statuer définitivement sur la validité d'un acte de droit communautaire lorsque la violation d'un droit garanti par la CEDH sera en cause. Cette éventualité ne constitue pas, à mon avis, quelque chose de choquant. Le même phénomène s'est produit avec les Cours Constitutionnelles ou les Cours Suprêmes des Etats membres pour ce qui concerne le contrôle de constitutionnalité ou de légalité des actes de droit interne' (V. Skouris, Hearing by Working Group II, 17.9.2002, Working Document 19, 20.9.2002, p. 6). See also CONV 223/02, WG II 8, 31.7.2002; CONV 295/02, WG II 10, 26.9.2002 ; WG II, Working Document 13, 5.9.2002.

[29] See L. Garlicki, 'The Relationship between the European Court of Justice and the European Court of Human Rights: the Strasbourg Perspective', in J. Iliopoulos-Strangas and H. Bauer (eds.), *The New European Union* (Athens-Berlin-Brussels, Sakkoulas/Berliner Wissenschafts-Verlag/Bruylant, 2006) p. 113 et seq.; A. Rosas, 'Fundamental Rights in the Luxembourg and Strasbourg Courts', in C. Baudenbacher, P. Tresselt and T. Orlygsson (eds.), *The EFTA Court – Ten Years On* (Oxford-Portland, Hart Publishing 2005) p. 163 et seq.; F. Tulkens and J. Callewaert, 'La Cour de justice, la Cour européenne des droits de l'homme et la protection des droits fondamentaux', in M. Dony and E. Bribosia

To some extent, this development might also be the result of the good understanding which has long been prevailing in the relationship between the two Supreme European Courts and has been fostered, *inter alia,* by regular contacts. Once or twice a year, sizeable delegations of each Court have been meeting in Strasbourg or Luxembourg to exchange information on jurisprudential and procedural developments and discuss matters of common interest, with the exception of pending cases. Against the background of the difficulties recently encountered by the EU Constitutional Treaty – thus indirectly by the Charter as well – there might be something of an increased awareness among judges of both Courts that a large part of the responsibility for ensuring legal certainty in the European fundamental rights landscape is now resting on their own shoulders.

An outstanding illustration of this state of mind may be found in the opinion recently delivered by Advocate General Tizzano in the case of *Spain* v. *United Kingdom,*[30] which deals with the consequences of the *Matthews* judgment given by the Strasbourg Court.[31]

1.1.2 *The legislative level: the EU Charter of Fundamental Rights*

The jurisprudential developments described above were confirmed and taken one step further on the legislative level, through the EU Charter of Fundamental Rights. In this respect, it is quite significant to note that the Charter, as the most comprehensive legislative initiative taken to date by the EU in the field of fundamental rights, at the same time creates the closest link so far between Convention and Union law: about half of the 50 substantial rights contained in the Charter are borrowed from the Convention[32] and/or the Strasbourg case-law.[33]

This fact, and the Charter's relationship with the Convention more generally, turned out to be one of the major challenges confronting the drafters of the Charter. The crucial question was how to preserve the autonomy of the EU legal system while avoiding the creation of new and different European standards which, if not harmonised with those of the Convention, could cause confusion and disrupt legal certainty. After numerous sessions and lengthy discussions devoted to that question,[34] a satisfactory solution was found which is laid down in Article 52(3) of the Charter, according to which

---

(eds.), *L'avenir du système juridictionnel de l'Union européenne* (Brussels, Editions de l'Université de Bruxellles 2002) p. 177 et seq.

[30] ECJ, Case C-145/04 *Kingdom of Spain* v. *United Kingdom of Great Britain and Northern Ireland* [2006] ECR 0000, n.y.r.

[31] See 2.2 *infra.*

[32] Arts. 2, 4 to 7, 9, 10 para. 1, 11 para. 1, 12 para. 1, 14, 17, 19 para. 1, 21, 45, 47 to 50.

[33] Arts. 1, 3, 8, 11 para. 2, 13, 19 para. 2, 22 to 26 and 37.

[34] See G. Braibant, *La Charte des droits fondamentaux de l'Union européenne* (Paris, Seuil 2001) p. 261 et seq.; M. Borowsky, 'Article 52', in J. Meyer (ed.), *Kommentar zur Charta der Grundrechte der Europäischen Union* [Commentary on the EU Charter of Fundamental Rights] (Baden-Baden, Nomos 2003) Art. 52, No. 8 et seq.

> 'Insofar as [the] Charter contains rights which correspond to rights guaranteed by the Convention for the Protection of Human Rights and Fundamental Freedoms, the meaning and scope of those rights shall be the same as those laid down by the said Convention. This provision shall not prevent Union law providing more extensive protection.'

This provision contains two different rules. The first one guarantees under Union law the same minimum standard of protection as under the Convention, the reference to the latter being understood, according to the Explanations to that provision, as including the Strasbourg case-law.[35] By virtue of the second rule, the EU is entitled to provide a more extensive protection. This is already being achieved by the Charter itself in respect of, for example, the right to marry and to found a family (Article 9), the safeguard against discrimination (Art. 21), the right to an effective remedy (Article 47(1)) as well as to legal aid (Article 47(3)). Unlike lower standards, higher standards are no challenge to the requisite harmony between the Convention and the Charter. For, in line with the principle of subsidiarity underlying the Strasbourg system,[36] the Convention itself, in its Article 53, allows its standards to be surpassed 'under the laws of any High Contracting Party or under any other agreement to which it is a Party.' What is decisive for the harmonious relationship between the two instruments is the fact that, via the Charter, Union law adopts the Convention standards as its own minimum standards, thereby building upon them when further developing its own standards, just as national legal systems do.

Thus, the first sentence of Article 52(3) of the Charter appears as another example of 'conventionisation' of Union law. By doing away with the 'general principles of Community law' referred to in Article 6(2) TEU[37] and providing for an identical 'meaning and scope' of the rights borrowed from the Convention, once legally binding the Charter will in effect achieve an indirect adoption of these rights by the EU legal system.[38] The Explanations to Article 52(3) are not entirely accurate as regards the rights which can be considered to 'correspond' to those guaran-

[35] 'The reference to the ECHR covers both the Convention and the Protocols to it. The meaning and the scope of the guaranteed rights are determined not only by the text of those instruments, but also by the case-law of the European Court of Human Rights and by the Court of Justice of the European Union. The last sentence of the paragraph is designed to allow the Union to guarantee more extensive protection. In any event, the level of protection afforded by the Charter may never be lower than that guaranteed by the ECHR' (Explanations to Art. 52 of the Charter, Declaration concerning the Explanations relating to the Charter of Fundamental Rights, OJ 2004, C 310/456).

[36] See J. Callewaert, 'La subsidiarité dans l'Europe des droits de l'homme: la dimension substantielle', in Marc Verdussen (ed.), *L'Europe de la subsidiarité* (Brussels, Bruylant 2000) p. 13 et seq.; H. Petzold, 'The Convention and the Principle of Subsidiarity', in R. Macdonald, F. Matscher, H. Petzold (eds.), *The European System for the Protection of Human Rights* (Dordrecht, Nijhoff 1993) p. 41 et seq.

[37] See however Art. 6 para. 3 EU as amended by the Lisbon Treaty.

[38] See J. Callewaert, 'Die EMRK und die EU-Grundrechtecharta – Bestandsaufnahme einer Harmonisierung auf halbem Weg', *Europäische Grundrechte-Zeitschrift* [The European Convention on Human Rights and the EU Charter of Fundamental Rights – Stocktaking on a Harmonization at Halfway] (Kehl, Engel 2003) p. 198.

teed by the Convention.[39] Nonetheless, one can be reasonably optimistic that, as the former President of the ECJ Mr Rodriguez Iglesias put it, by providing valuable guidance on the way in which the Charter is to be interpreted, Article 52(3), along with Article 53 and the reference to the Strasbourg case-law in the Preamble to the Charter, 'should make it possible for the case-law of the European Court of Human Rights to continue to be taken fully into account in the Community sphere', thus ensuring that 'rather than competing with each other and creating a schism in the protection of fundamental rights in Europe, the Convention and the Charter should serve to enrich one another.'[40]

The Charter, for its part, cannot be said to have had no legal effect since its adoption as a solemn political declaration at the Nice Summit on 7 December 2000. Already, at quite an early stage, it was referred to by the Court of First Instance[41] and the Advocate Generals of the ECJ as a source of inspiration, with Advocates General Tizzano[42] and Léger expressing some of the most elaborate opinions on the subject. According to the latter, the nature of the rights laid down in the Charter

---

[39] Declaration concerning the explanations relating to the Charter of Fundamental Rights, OJEU 16.12.2004, C 310/424 (456 et seq.); see J. Callewaert, 'Les rapports entre la Charte et la Convention européenne des droits de l'homme', in W. Heusel (ed.), *The Charter of Fundamental Rights and Constitutional Development in the EU* (Cologne, Bundesanzeiger 2002) p. 129 et seq.

[40] G.C. Rodriguez Iglesias, address at the Solemn hearing of the European Court of Human Rights on the occasion of the opening of the judicial year, 31 January 2002, European Court of Human Rights, Strasbourg, Annual Report 2003. On the relationship between the Convention and the Charter, see also S. Alber and U. Widmaier, 'Die EU-Charta der Grundrechte und ihre Auswirkungen auf die Rechtsprechung – Zu den Beziehungen zwischen EuGH und EGMR' [The EU Charter of Fundamental Rights and its Impact on the Case-Law – The Relationship between the European Court of Justice and the European Court of Human Rights], *Europäische Grundrechte-Zeitschrift* (2000), p. 497 et seq.; M. Fischbach, 'Le Conseil de l'Europe et la Charte des droits fondamentaux de l'Union européenne', *Rev. univ. dr. h.* (2000), p. 7 et seq.; H.C. Krüger and J. Polakiewicz, 'Proposals for a Coherent Human Rights Protection System in Europe / The European Convention on Human Rights and the EU Charter of Fundamental Rights', *Human Rights Law Journal* (2001) p. 1 et seq.; O. Le Bot, 'Charte de l'Union européenne et Convention de sauvegarde des droits de l'homme: la coexistence de deux catalogues de droits fondamentaux', *Rev. trim. dr. h.* (2003) p. 781 et seq.; C.L. Rozakis, 'The extension of European human rights protection under a Constitution for Europe and the new institutional balances', in G. Dimitrakopoulos and G. Kremlis (eds.), *A new constitutional settlement for the European people* (Athens-Brussels, Sakkoulas/Berliner Wissenschafts-Verlag/Bruylant 2004) p. 69 et seq.; V. Skouris, 'Introducing a binding Bill of Human Rights for the European Union – Can three parallel systems of protection of fundamental rights coexist harmoniously?', in *Verfassung im Diskurs der Welt – Liber amicorum für Peter Häberle* (Tübingen, Mohr Siebeck 2004) p. 261 et seq.

[41] CFI, T-54/99 *max.mobil Telekommunikation Service GmbH* v. *Commission of the European Communities* [2002] ECR II-00313; CFI, T-377/00 et seq. *Philip Morris International, Inc and Others* v. *Commission of the European Communities* [2003] ECR II-00001: 'Although [the Charter] does not have legally binding force, it does show the importance of the rights it sets out in the Community legal order' at para. 122.

[42] 'In proceedings concerned with the nature and scope of a fundamental right, the relevant statements of the Charter cannot be ignored; in particular, we cannot ignore its clear purpose of serving, where its provisions so allow, as a substantive point of reference for all those involved – Member States, institutions, natural and legal persons – in the Community context' (Opinion in ECJ, Case C-173/99 *The Queen* v. *Secretary of State for Trade and Industry, ex parte Broadcasting, Entertainment, Cinematographic and Theatre Union (BECTU case)* [2001] ECR I-04881, para. 28).

of Fundamental Rights precluded it from being regarded as a mere list of purely moral principles without any consequences. Where rights, freedoms and principles were described, as in the Charter, as needing to occupy the highest level of reference values within all the Member States, it would be inexplicable not to take from it the elements which make it possible to distinguish fundamental rights from other rights.[43]

While the ECJ itself has long been avoiding any explicit reference to the Charter in its judgments, it seems to have departed from this approach in a Grand Chamber judgment recently delivered in the case of *European Parliament* v. *Council* which dealt with the compatibility with fundamental rights of Directive 2003/86/EC on the right to family reunification.[44] Under the heading 'The rules of law in whose light the Directive's legality may be reviewed', after a reminder of the established case-law concerning the role and the sources of fundamental rights under Community law, it noted that:

> 'The Charter was solemnly proclaimed by the Parliament, the Council and the Commission in Nice on 7 December 2000. While the Charter is not a legally binding instrument, the Community legislature did, however, acknowledge its importance by stating, in the second recital in the preamble to the Directive, that the Directive observes the principles recognised not only by Article 8 of the ECHR but also in the Charter. Furthermore, the principal aim of the Charter, as is apparent from its preamble, is to reaffirm "rights as they result, in particular, from the constitutional traditions and international obligations common to the Member States, the Treaty on European Union, the Community Treaties, the [ECHR], the Social Charters adopted by the Community and by the Council of Europe and the case-law of the Court … and of the European Court of Human Rights".'[45]

This judgment seems to acknowledge that even before its 'entry into force' by virtue of Article 6(1) EU as amended by the Lisbon Treaty, the Charter already has some legal status in the current EU legal system. In particular, the reference to the fact that the 'principal aim' of the Charter is to 'reaffirm' fundamental rights 'as they result' from a number of legal sources which are already in existence, might be seen as an indication that, in the ECJ's view, some of these rights already have some binding effect.

However that may be, any kind of consistency between Convention and Union law is to be much welcomed, both from a theoretical and a practical point of view. From a theoretical point of view, it entails the acknowledgment of an essential feature of fundamental rights. Namely, that because of their fundamental nature, their substance should in principle not be allowed to vary depending only on the legal system in which they are applied. But also in practical terms is the kind of

[43] Advocate General Léger, opinion in the case of ECJ, Case C-353/99 P *Council of the European Union* v. *Heidi Hautala* [2001] ECR I-09565, paras. 80-83.

[44] ECJ Case C-540/03, *supra* n. 10, *Parliament* v. *Council*.

[45] Ibid., para. 38.

'conventionisation' of Union law which we are witnessing of high importance. For, as has been repeatedly stated by the Strasbourg Court – and subject to the effects of the presumption of equivalence within the meaning of the *Bosphorus* case-law[46] – national authorities remain bound in principle to comply with the Convention when applying Union law.[47] Thus, without a basic level of harmony between Union and Convention law, they might find themselves in a fairly difficult position.[48]

1.2 'Unionisation' of Convention Law

'Unionisation' of Convention law, for its part, has also made itself felt on both the judicial and legislative level, though with unequal results.

1.2.1 *The judicial level*

1.2.1.1 The *Bosphorus* case-law

The most significant form of 'unionisation' of Convention Law so far might have been accomplished by the Strasbourg Court itself, in the landmark judgment given in the case of *Bosphorus* v. *Ireland.*[49] In *Bosphorus*, the Court had to rule on whether a Member State could be held responsible under the Convention for the application by its courts of an EC Regulation.

The case concerned the impounding by the Irish authorities of an aircraft which had been leased by the applicant company from a Yugoslavian airline. The Irish authorities had acted in pursuance of EC Council Regulation 990/93 which, in turn, had implemented the UN sanctions regime against the Federal Republic of Yugoslavia. In a preliminary ruling delivered on 30 July 1996, the ECJ had found, *inter alia*, that the consequences of the impounding for the applicant company were not disproportionate and therefore did not amount to a breach of the latter's property rights.

The Strasbourg Court found itself confronted with two seemingly conflicting principles. It noted that, on the one hand, the Convention did not prohibit contracting parties from transferring sovereign power to an international (including a supranational) organisation in order to pursue cooperation in certain fields of activity. In that connection, it also stressed the growing importance of international cooperation and the resulting need to secure the proper functioning of international organisations. Even as the holder of transferred sovereign power, such an organisation was not itself to be held responsible under the Convention for proceedings before, or decisions of, its organs as long as it was not a contracting party itself. On the

[46] See 1.2.1.1 *infra*.

[47] See ECtHR, *Cantoni* v. *France*, judgment of 15.11.1996; ECtHR *Matthews* v. *United Kingdom*, judgment of 18.2.1999 [GC]; ECtHR, *Bosphorus Hava Yolları Turizm ve Ticaret Anonim Şirketi* v. *Ireland* [GC], judgment of 30.6.2005 (see also 1.2.1.1 *infra*).

[48] See 1.2 and 2. *infra*.

[49] ECtHR, *supra* n. 47, *Bosphorus*, paras. 155-157.

other hand, a contracting party was responsible under Article 1 of the Convention for all acts and omissions of its organs, regardless of whether the act or omission in question was a consequence of domestic law or of the necessity to comply with international legal obligations. Article 1 made no distinction as to the type of rule or measure concerned and did not exclude any part of a contracting party's 'jurisdiction' from scrutiny under the Convention. Absolving contracting States completely from their Convention responsibility in the areas covered by such a transfer of sovereign power would be incompatible with the purpose and object of the Convention, as its guarantees could be limited or excluded at will, thereby depriving it of its peremptory character and undermining the practical and effective nature of its safeguards. Consequently, the State retained Convention liability in respect of treaty commitments subsequent to the entry into force of the Convention.[50]

The Court reconciled these positions by ruling that State action taken in compliance with legal obligations flowing from the State's membership of an international organisation was justified, as long as the relevant organisation was considered to protect fundamental rights in a manner which could be considered at least equivalent to that for which the Convention provided. 'Equivalent' meant 'comparable', as any requirement that the organisation's protection be 'identical' could run counter to the interest of international cooperation pursued. If such equivalent protection was considered to be provided by the organisation, the presumption would be that a State had not departed from the requirements of the Convention when it did no more than implement legal obligations flowing from its membership of the organisation. However, any such presumption could be rebutted if, in the circumstances of a particular case, it was considered that the protection of Convention rights was manifestly deficient. In such cases, the interest of international cooperation would be outweighed by the Convention's role as a 'constitutional instrument of European public order' in the field of human rights. Furthermore, a State would be fully responsible under the Convention for all acts falling outside its strict international legal obligations.[51]

The question then arose whether the fundamental rights protection under Community law was equivalent to that ensured under the Convention. After an in-depth review of the substantive and procedural guarantees provided by Community law to that effect, the Court answered in the affirmative. It noted, *inter alia*, that respect for fundamental rights had become 'a condition of the legality of Community acts' and that in carrying out this assessment the ECJ referred extensively to the Convention provisions and to the Strasbourg Court's case-law.[52] The Charter of Fundamental Rights of the European Union was also mentioned in this connection. Although it was not fully binding, it was substantially inspired by the Convention and recognised the latter as establishing the minimum human rights standards, the Court said.[53]

[50] Ibid., paras. 152-154.
[51] Ibid., paras. 156-157.
[52] Ibid., para. 159.
[53] Idem.

In sum, the Court held that the protection of fundamental rights under EC law could be considered to be, and to have been at the relevant time, 'equivalent' to that of the Convention system. Consequently, the presumption arose that Ireland had not departed from the requirements of the Convention when it implemented legal obligations flowing from its membership of the EC. In the absence of any indication of a dysfunction of the mechanisms of control of the observance of Convention rights in the instant case, the presumption of Convention compliance by the respondent State had not been rebutted. It followed that there had been no violation of Article 1 of Protocol No. 1.

The presumption of conformity of Community law has lead some academics[54] to raise the question of whether the *Bosphorus* approach was a kind of adaptation to the Convention system of the 'Solange II' theory developed some time ago by the German Constitutional Court.[55] Even though *Bosphorus* and *Solange* both utilise a presumption of conformity, a major difference between the two lies in the fact that under the former the presumption can be rebutted on a case-by-case basis, whereas the *Solange* approach requires proof of structural or large-scale shortcomings in the protection of fundamental rights under Community law be adduced in order for the presumption to be rebutted.[56] According to the former President of the German Constitutional Court, this is very unlikely and will therefore most probably remain a fairly theoretical eventuality.[57] This is why, unlike complaints to the German Constitutional Court and to the former European Commission on Human Rights,[58] individual applications to the Strasbourg Court alleging a breach of fundamental rights resulting from compliance with Community law in a specific case are not inadmissible *ratione materiae* and thus not barred from being examined on the merits.[59]

If we now turn to the notion of 'manifest deficiency', which is the criterion for rebutting the presumption of equivalence established in *Bosphorus*, it might be

---

[54] See J.-P. Jacqué, 'L'arrêt Bosphorus, une jurisprudence 'Solange II' de la Cour européenne des droits de l'homme?', 41 *Rev. trim. dr. eur.* (2005) p. 756 ; F. Schorkopf, 'The European Court of Human Rights' judgment in the case of Bosphorus Hava Yollari Turizm v. Ireland', *German law journal* (2005) p. 1255.

[55] BVerfGE 73, 339 (378-381); BVerfGE 102, 147.

[56] 'Sonach sind auch nach der Entscheidung des Senats in BVerfGE 89, 155 Verfassungsbeschwerden und Vorlagen von Gerichten von vornherein unzulässig, wenn ihre Begründung nicht darlegt, dass die europäische Rechtsentwicklung einschließlich der Rechtsprechung des Europäischen Gerichtshofs nach Ergehen der Solange II-Entscheidung (BVerfGE 73, 339 <378 bis 381>) unter den erforderlichen Grundrechtsstandard abgesunken sei. Deshalb muss die Begründung der Vorlage eines nationalen Gerichts oder einer Verfassungsbeschwerde, die eine Verletzung in Grundrechten des Grundgesetzes durch sekundäres Gemeinschaftsrecht geltend macht, im Einzelnen darlegen, dass der jeweils als unabdingbar gebotene Grundrechtsschutz generell nicht gewährleistet ist. Dies erfordert eine Gegenüberstellung des Grundrechtsschutzes auf nationaler und auf Gemeinschaftsebene in der Art und Weise, wie das Bundesverfassungsgericht sie in BVerfGE 73, 339 (378 bis 381) geleistet hat' (BVerfGE, 102, 164).

[57] J. Limbach, 'Die Kooperation der Gerichte in der zukünftigen europäischen Grundrechtsarchitektur', 27 *Europäische Grundrechte-Zeitschrift* (2000) p. 417 et seq.

[58] See European Commission of Human Rights 9.2.1990 (dec.), *M. & Co* v. *Germany*, 13258/87, Decisions and Reports 64, p. 138.

[59] ECtHR, *supra* n. 47, *Bosphorus*, para. 137.

seen as – and has indeed been criticized for – fixing a fairly low standard to be complied with by Community law, to the effect that in practice the Strasbourg Court might have given away a substantial part of its competence to review the implementation of Community law by domestic authorities.[60] This is also the opinion expressed by Judge Rozakis and his colleagues in their concurring opinion to the *Bosphorus* judgment:

> 'In spite of its relatively undefined nature, the criterion 'manifestly deficient' appears to establish a relatively low threshold, which is in marked contrast to the supervision generally carried out under the European Convention on Human Rights.'[61]

Yet if this had been the Court's intention, one wonders why it did not follow the *Solange* approach by not allowing a case-by-case review of Community law protection. Quite apart from the paradox which arises out of seeing the Strasbourg Court offer Community law latitude which, through the case-law of the ECJ and the Charter, it has consistently been seeking to forego.

Actually, it has not yet been clarified whether in this context 'manifest' means only 'clear', 'obvious' or also 'serious' and/or 'gross'. Every gross violation of the Convention is certainly manifest, but not every manifest violation is a gross one. According to another concurring opinion to the judgment, that of Judge Ress, the protection of a Convention right would be manifestly deficient if, in deciding the key question in a case, the ECJ were to depart from the interpretation or the application of the Convention or the Protocols that had already been the subject of well-established ECtHR case-law.

Be that as it may, the notion of 'manifest deficiency' can be expected to play a minor role in practice, given the ECJ's commitment to follow closely the Strasbourg case-law when applying fundamental rights in general and the Convention in particular. An increased role of the Charter in the ECJ case-law[62] would only reinforce this prediction, as the Charter fixes the Convention standards as EU minimum standards.

In any event, the *Bosphorus* judgment makes several important contributions. In addition to confirming the indispensable role of inter-state cooperation within the framework of international organisations,[63] the judgment acknowledges the legitimacy of the EU integration project and its specificity, including in respect of its implications for the protection of fundamental rights, to the effect that 'equivalent' – i.e., 'unionised' – standards are acceptable from a Convention perspective.

---

[60] See the chapter by N. Lavranos in this volume. See also C. Costello, 'The Bosphorus Ruling of the European Court of Human Rights: Fundamental Rights and Blurred Boundaries in Europe', *Human rights law review* (2006) p. 87 et seq.

[61] Para. 4 of the opinion.

[62] See ECJ, Case C-540/03, *supra* n. 45, *Parliament* v. *Council*; see 1.1.2 *supra*.

[63] See already ECtHR, *Waite and Kennedy* v. *Germany* [GC], judgment 18.2.1999, para. 63.

1.2.1.2 The impact of the ECJ case-law

In the last couple of years, the ECJ case-law has had a limited but nonetheless increasing impact on the Strasbourg case-law. A striking example in this respect is the case of *Pellegrin* v. *France*[64] where, in order to re-determine the scope of Article 6(1) of the Convention in respect of public service litigation, the Court borrowed a new criterion from EC-legislation: the notion of 'public service' within the meaning of former Article 48(4) (now Article 39(4)) TEC, as interpreted by the ECJ[65] and the European Commission.[66] The Court ruled that in the future only disputes involving members of the 'public service' so defined would be excluded from the scope of Article 6(1). That is, disputes which were raised by public servants whose duties typified the specific activities of the public service in so far as the latter was acting as the depositary of public authority responsible for protecting the general interests of the State or other public authorities. The Court said that it would, in practice, ascertain in each case whether an applicant's post entailed direct or indirect participation in the exercise of powers conferred by public law and duties designed to safeguard the general interests of the State or of other public authorities. Yet, in making this finding the Court proceeds in an autonomous way and does not rely on, or consider itself bound by, the relevant ECJ case-law.[67]

In the case of *Stec and Others*, the Strasbourg Court had to rule on whether or not a British law which linked the cut-off date for the benefit of a reduced earnings allowance to pension age, which for women was lower than for men, amounted to sex-based discrimination prohibited by Article 14 of the Convention taken in conjunction with Article 1 of Protocol No. 1.[68] At an earlier stage of the proceedings in the case, the ECJ had given a preliminary ruling acknowledging the compatibility of the impugned regulations with Council Directive 79/7/EEC of 19 December 1978 on the gradual implementation of the principle of equal treatment for men and women in matters of social security.[69] The Strasbourg Court, for its part, found no violation of the invoked provisions. In reaching that conclusion, it relied, *inter alia*, on the ECJ ruling in the following terms:

> '[The Court] finds it significant that, in the present applicants' case, the ECJ found that since [the reduced earnings allowance (REA)] was intended to com-

---

[64] ECtHR, *Pellegrin* v. *France*, judgment of 8.12.1999 [GC]. Meanwhile, however, this judgment was overturned in ECtHR, *Vilho Eskelinen and Others* v. *Finland*, judgment of 19.4.2007 [GC].

[65] ECJ, Case C-149/79 *Commission of the European Communities* v. *Kingdom of Belgium* [1980] ECR 03881; ECJ, Case C-473/93 *Commission of the European Communities* v. *Grand Duchy of Luxembourg* [1996] ECR I-03207.

[66] Communication from the Commission of the European Communities, OJEC No. C 72 of 18.3.1988.

[67] See, e.g., ECtHR, *Kajanen and Tuomaala* v. *Finland*, judgment of 19.10.2000 (dec.); ECtHR, *Mickovski* v. *Macedonia*, judgment of 10.11.2005 (dec.).

[68] ECtHR, *Stec and Others* v. *United Kingdom*, judgment of 12.4.2006 [GC].

[69] ECJ, Case C-196/98 *Regina Virginia Hepple* v. *Adjudication Officer and Adjudication Officer* v. *Anna Stec* [2000] ECR I-03701.

pensate people of working age for loss of earning capacity due to an accident at work or occupational disease, it was necessary, in order to preserve coherence with the old-age pension scheme, to link the age-limits … . While it is true that Article 7(1)(a) of the Directive provides an express exception to the general prohibition on discrimination in social security …, the ECJ was called upon, in deciding whether the case fell within the Article 7 exception, to make a judgment as to whether the discrimination in the REA scheme arising from the link to differential pensionable age was objectively necessary in order to ensure consistency with the pension scheme. In reaching a conclusion on this issue which, while not determinative of the issue under Article 14 of the Convention, is nonetheless of central importance, particular regard should be had to the strong persuasive value of the ECJ's finding on this point.'[70]

Finally, one should also mention that the Charter has had some impact on the Strasbourg case-law. In its judgment in the case of *Christine Goodwin*, in which it overturned its case-law on Article 12 of the Convention and adopted a more protective approach to the right to marry of transsexuals, the Strasbourg Court referred, *inter alia*, to Article 9 of the Charter, thus becoming – quite ironically – the first of the Supreme European Courts to explicitly rely on the Charter.[71]

1.2.2 *The legislative level*

A first example of legislative 'unionisation' of Convention standards can be seen in Protocol 12 to the Convention which imposes a general ban on discrimination. The adoption of Protocol 12 on 4 November 2000 was clearly accelerated by a similar provision being prepared in the context of the work on the Charter.[72] Once the Charter will have 'entered into force' under the Lisbon Treaty, more such examples of Convention standards being raised under the influence of Union law could be expected.

Another form of legislative 'unionisation' of Convention standards can be observed in more specific areas, as a consequence of increased legislative activity on the part of the EU in areas relevant to fundamental rights. The Convention imposes a *minimum* rather than a *uniform* standard, thus accepting that its own protection may be replaced by a more extensive one.[73] Therefore, any such 'unionisation' raising or at least maintaining Convention standards does not, in principle, run counter to the latter.

A recent example of Convention standards being raised by EU legislation is provided by Directive 2004/58 of 29 April 2004 on the right of citizens of the Union and their family members to move and reside freely within the territory of

[70] ECtHR *supra* n. 69, *Stec and Others*, para. 58.

[71] ECtHR, *Christine Goodwin* v. *United Kingdom* [GC], judgment of 11.7.2002, para. 100. See also the reference to this judgment in ECJ, Case C-117/01, *supra* n. 24, *K.B.* concerning the entitlement of a transsexual partner to a survivor's pension.

[72] Art. 21 of the Charter (Art. II-81 of the Constitutional Treaty).

[73] Art. 53 of the Convention.

the Member States. Articles 15 and 28 to 31 of this Directive lay down a number of important procedural safeguards against expulsion which cannot be vindicated under the Convention, its Article 6 not being applicable to expulsion procedures.[74] A similar rise in standards is being achieved by Directive 2003/4 of 28 January 2003 on public access to environmental information, when compared with the requirements flowing from Articles 8 and 10 of the Convention in this respect.[75]

At the same time, some doubts remain as to the standard-raising impact of some other recent legislative initiatives, such as Directive 2002/8 of 27 January 2003 to improve access to justice in cross-border disputes by establishing minimum common rules relating to legal aid for such disputes and the Commission Proposal of 28 April 2004 for a Framework Decision on certain procedural rights in criminal proceedings.[76]

The latter even raises some serious concerns related to the question of whether, in its present form, it is not going to put at risk legal certainty and, ultimately, the goal which is said to be pursued: that of 'enhanc[ing] the rights of all suspects and defendants generally'.[77] For, despite the stated intention of the drafters of the Framework Decision to ensure compliance with the Convention,[78] there is an obvious lack of harmony between its provisions and those of the Convention. This stems from a fair amount of ambiguity as regards the level of the Framework Decision standards as compared with those of the Convention and its legal terminology.

As regards the standards, it is fairly unclear whether the Framework Decision is intended to merely reflect or to raise Convention standards. On the one hand, it is stated in the Preamble to the Framework Decision that 'the provisions of [the] Framework Decision do not impose obligations on Member States that go further than the Convention, but merely set out common ways of complying with Article 6 of the Convention.'[79] On the other hand, the Framework Decision is said to aim at

[74] See ECtHR, *Maaouia* v. *France* [GC], judgment of 5.10.2000.

[75] See ECtHR, *Guerra and Others* v. *Italy*, judgment of 19.2.1998; ECtHR, *Roche* v. *United Kingdom* [GC], judgment of 19.10.2005.

[76] COM(2004) 328 final. On this, see J. Callewaert, 'EU Law on Criminal Justice from a Strasbourg Perspective', ERA-Forum 4/2005, Academy of European law (Trier, Academy of European Law 2005) pp. 536 at 539 et seq. Meanwhile, the proposal was adopted by the European Commission and submitted to the Council of the EU, where it underwent substantial changes (see, for the last version, DROIPEN 56, 10287/07, 5.6.2007). However, on 12-13 June 2007, the Council concluded that no agreement could be attained on this file (Doc. 10699/07, 13.9.2007). Art. 82 of the future Treaty on the Functioning of the European Union, for its part, provides for the possibility to establish minimum rules concerning, *inter alia*, the rights of individuals in criminal procedure.

[77] See Explanatory Memorandum, para. 7.

[78] Ibid., para. 9: 'The intention here is not to duplicate what is in the ECHR, but rather to promote compliance at a consistent standard'; Preamble to the Draft Framework-Decision, 20th recital: 'This Framework Decision aims to strengthen the fundamental rights and principles recognised by Article 6 of the Treaty on European Union and reflected by the Charter of Fundamental Rights of the European Union and in particular its Articles 47 to 50. It cannot lead to divergent judicial interpretations of the relevant provisions of the Convention since the reference to fundamental rights in Article 6 EU Treaty is necessarily contingent on their interpretation in the European Court of Human Rights case-law.'

[79] Preamble, 12th recital. In the same sense: 'The intention here is not to duplicate what is in the ECHR, but rather to promote compliance at a consistent standard. This can be done by orchestrating

'[enhancing] the rights of all suspects and defendants generally',[80] it being left open whether this is to be achieved only via better compliance with existing rights or also with the help of new rights to be agreed on by Member States.

Be that as it may, it is clear that, if compared with the Convention, the Framework Decision lays down some new, additional rights, such as the right to the recording of proceedings (Article 9), to consular assistance (Article 13) or to the so-called 'Letter of Rights' (Article 14). While they might represent a welcome contribution to raising fundamental rights standards in Europe, such provisions cannot possibly be said, in the present state of the case-law, to merely 'set out common ways of complying with Article 6 of the Convention'.

Of greater concern, however, are another set of provisions whose relationship with the Convention is even less clear since their wording make it uncertain whether they are meant to depart from the Convention and, if so, in what way. This is, for instance, the case with the right to 'legal advice' laid down in Article 2 which will no doubt raise the question whether it is identical to the right to 'legal assistance' set forth in Article 6 of the Convention, as 'legal assistance' would appear to be broader a notion than 'legal advice'.[81] If the intention of the Framework Decision is to refer to Convention rights, it is probably not very helpful to depart from the Convention terminology, as different wordings in legal texts are normally intended to mean different things.

Other provisions of the Framework Decision do not differ from the Convention in terms of their terminology, but are drafted in a way which raises similar questions as to their relationship to the Convention. This applies, for instance, to Articles 6 (right to free interpretation) and 7 (right to free translation of relevant documents) which both set forth a number of rights 'in order to safeguard the fairness of the proceedings'. Both these articles leave open the question of whether, in this context, the formula 'in order to' means – in line with the Strasbourg case-law – 'to the extent necessary to' or – departing from the Strasbourg case-law – 'as a means of' safeguarding the fairness of proceedings.

These problems are quite redolent of those encountered with the EU Charter of Fundamental Rights, which borrowed a large amount of Convention rights but used different terminology to identify them.[82] Fortunately, as mentioned above, a solution could be found through the so-called horizontal provisions at the end of the Charter, especially Article 52(3). It would be very helpful if the Framework

agreement between the Member States on a Union wide approach to a "fair trial"' (Explanatory Memorandum, para. 9); '… the Commission's aim is to render more efficient and visible the practical operation of ECHR rights with this proposal so that everyone in the criminal justice system is more aware of them, not only defendants but alos police officers, lawyers, translators and interpreters and all other actors in the criminal justice system. This should lead to better compliance with the ECHR' (Explanatory Memorandum, para. 22).

[80] Explanatory Memorandum, paras. 7-8.

[81] The representatives of the Commission at a hearing before the European Union Committee of the House of Lords were of a different opinion; see House of Lords, European Union Committee, 'Procedural Rights in Criminal Proceedings', Report with Evidence, 7 February 2005, paras. 111-114.

[82] See 1.1.2 *supra*.

Decision contained a similar provision which would clarify and thus put on a firm and reliable basis its relationship with the Convention by clearly identifying those provisions which are meant to surpass Convention standards and those which are not. This applies to all EU legislative initiatives in areas relevant to fundamental rights.[83]

At the end of the day, regardless of whether or not such partial initiatives raise the Convention standards, one thing is clear: they certainly raise the level of complexity of legislation on fundamental rights to be applied by judges. While they may be legitimate in terms of their expected positive impact on European integration, the fact remains that most of them end up in new texts, with new and different wordings, categories and standards, in addition to varying scopes, while older legal instruments already regulating the same matter, such as the Convention, remain in force. The result is an inflation of legal instruments, confronting domestic courts with an ever-greater legal complexity and making it increasingly difficult to handle them in a consistent way. If not kept under close control in order to prevent confusion and relativism, developments of that kind might fairly soon turn out to be detrimental to the very rights which they are meant to promote.

2. Impact on the legal systems of the Member States

Just as the interplay between Union and Convention law itself, its impact on the legal systems of the Member States can be observed on both the judicial and the legislative level.

2.1 The judicial level

Being on the front line of the application of the law, national courts play a central role in European protection of fundamental rights. Depending on the nature of the case, they may have to simultaneously take into account up to three different sources: their own national law, the Convention and Union law. While they are commonly called 'Community courts of ordinary jurisdiction', they could in fact equally be called 'Convention courts of ordinary jurisdiction', for under the Convention it is an essential admissibility requirement that any complaint to the Strasbourg Court first be duly raised before the national courts of the respondent State.[84] The domestic courts' response to the developments described above will be looked at from this twofold perspective.

---

[83] Further texts are being prepared by the European Commission; see COM(2005) 696 on conflicts of jurisdiction and the principle of *ne bis in idem* and COM(2006) 174 on the presumption of innocence.

[84] Art. 35 para. 1 of the Convention.

Another interesting development regarding the interplay of Union and Convention Law at the domestic level is the fact that in two cases the Strasbourg Court has found a violation of the Convention on account of non-compliance of domestic courts with Union Law.

In the case of *Dangeville* v. *France*,[98] the Court found a violation of Article 1 of Protocol No. 1 to the Convention, which protects property rights, for breach of a Community directive. The applicant company, a firm of insurance brokers which was liable for value-added tax (VAT) on its commercial activity, was denied the benefit of the Sixth EC Directive granting an exemption from VAT. The Court first held that the applicant company's claim was based on a Community norm that was perfectly clear, precise and directly applicable. Long-standing jurisprudential principles, such as those relied on by the domestic courts, could not by themselves justify a failure to comply with the present requirements of European law. The applicant company's claim against the State constituted an asset and therefore amounted to a 'possession' within the meaning of Article 1 of Protocol No. 1 to the Convention. No reasons could be found justifying on general-interest grounds the administrative courts' refusal to give effect to a directly applicable provision of Community Law or the legislature's failure to bring the domestic law into line with a Community directive.[99]

In the case of *Aristimuño Mendizabal* v. *France*, the applicant, a Spanish national, complained, *inter alia*, under Article 8 of the Convention about the fact that it had taken 14 years for the French authorities to grant her a residence permit, in breach of both domestic and Community Law. The Strasbourg Court ruled that, given the EU citizenship of the applicant, the notion of 'law' within the meaning of Article 8 had to be construed in the light of Community Law, especially its provisions relating to the entry and residence of EU citizens. The Court concluded that the impugned period of 14 years was excessive both under domestic and Community Law and therefore amounted to a breach of Article 8.[100]

2.1.2 *Domestic courts as 'Convention courts of ordinary jurisdiction'*

More than 50 years after the entry into force of the Convention,[101] the application of the Convention at the domestic level still leaves much to be desired. This is illustrated, *inter alia,* by the fact that some 60 to 65 per cent of all violations found in cases examined on the merits are structural or systemic violations occurring in so-called repetitive cases, i.e., cases identical to previous ones in which the Court has already made clear determinations. In an attempt to improve the situation, over the last couple of years the Committee of Ministers of the Council of Europe has adopted, partly as a complement to Protocol No. 14 to the Convention, a series of specific instruments designed to reinforce the role of national authorities in the

[98] ECtHR, *S.A. Dangeville* v. *France*, judgment of 16.4.2002.

[99] ECtHR, *supra* n. 98, *Dangeville*, paras. 47-48, 56-57.

[100] ECtHR, *Aristimuño Mendizabal* v. *France*, judgment of 17.1.2006.

[101] On 3 September 1953.

implementation of the Convention.[102] The Explanatory Report to Protocol No. 14, for its part, states:

> 'In accordance with the principle of subsidiarity, the rights and freedoms enshrined in the Convention must be protected first and foremost at national level. Indeed this is where such protection is most effective. The responsibility of national authorities in this area must be reaffirmed and the capacity of national legal systems to prevent and redress violations must be reinforced. States have a duty to monitor the conformity of their legislation and administrative practice with the requirements of the Convention and the Court's case-law.'[103]

Yet it seems that the increasing impact of Union law on domestic legislation might make things even more complicated by causing some domestic courts to 'forget' about the Convention where it should be applied. This was illustrated by the case of *Koua Poirrez* v. *France*, which raises many questions, not least concerning the application of the Convention *ex officio.*[104]

The applicant in this case, a national of Ivory Coast, was physically disabled and had been adopted as an adult by a French citizen, although he did not thereby acquire French nationality. He applied for an adult disability allowance, but the French courts turned down his application on the ground of his Ivory Coast nationality. The French court hearing his appeal decided to ask the Court of Justice of the European Communities for a preliminary ruling on the compatibility of the relevant French law with Community law, on the basis that the applicant was a direct descendant of a citizen of the European Union. The Court of Justice found that Community law did not apply to the facts of the case: although the applicant's adoptive father was indeed a national of a Member State of the European Communities, he did not qualify as a migrant worker, since he had always lived and worked in France. On the strength of this Luxemburg judgment, all of the French courts which successively dealt with the appeal rejected the applicant's request for a disability allowance. He then applied to the Strasbourg Court which, in a judgment of 30 September 2003, i.e., more than 13 years after he had originally applied, found

[102] Recommendation No. R (2000) 2 on the re-examination or reopening of certain cases at domestic level following judgments of the European Court of Human Rights; Recommendation Rec(2002)13 on the publication and dissemination in the member states of the text of the European Convention on Human Rights and of the case-law of the European Court of Human Rights; Recommendation Rec(2004)4 on the European Convention on Human Rights in university education and professional training; Recommendation Rec(2004)5 on the verification of the compatibility of draft laws, existing laws and administrative practice with the standards laid down by the European Convention on Human Rights; Recommendation Rec(2004)6 on the improvement of domestic remedies; Resolution Res(2002)58 on the publication and dissemination of the case-law of the European Court of Human Rights; Resolution Res(2002)59 concerning the practice in respect of friendly settlements; Resolution Res(2004)3 on judgments revealing an underlying systemic problem.

[103] Protocol No. 14 to the Convention, opened for signature on 13 May 2004, Explanatory Report, para. 15.

[104] ECtHR, *Koua Poirrez* v. *France*, judgment of 30.9.2003. See J. Callewaert, 'Paris, Luxembourg, Strasbourg: trios juges, une discrimination – L'interaction entre les ordres juridiques national, communautaire et conventionnel à l'épreuve de la pratique', 16 *Rev. trim. dr. h.* (2005) p. 159 et seq.

that the applicant had been the victim of discrimination based on nationality, in breach of Article 14 of the Convention taken together with Article 1 of Protocol No. 1.

The case illustrates very well the complementarity of the three legal systems involved, and also the complexity of their interplay. French law contained an element of discrimination which Community law was powerless to remedy, because it did not apply in the particular case; accordingly it was only in Strasbourg that the situation could finally be remedied. At the same time, while it is true that the ECJ had no option but to rule that Community law was not applicable to the facts of the case, it would not have taken much for Community law to apply and for the ECJ to be required to rule on whether French law contained an element of discrimination that was contrary to Community law. It would have sufficed if, for example, the applicant's adoptive father had been a German or Italian rather than a French national.

The said complexity may be at the root of the quite astonishing fact that in this case, the domestic courts inquired of their own motion about the effects of Community law – which in the event was inapplicable – but failed to consider the impact of the Convention, which not only was applicable but, moreover, had been violated. If the domestic courts had applied the Convention of their own motion, the applicant might not have had to wait for more than 13 years before receiving his allowances.

Yet, some relief might be provided in this respect by the increased reliance of the ECJ on the Convention and its case-law,[105] in the same way as the Strasbourg Court is now increasingly reminding domestic courts of the need to comply with Union Law.[106] To this extent, a kind of cautious integration seems to be taking place between the case-law of the two European Courts which, in addition to producing the complexity already mentioned, may serve the more commendable purpose of fostering legal harmony.

2.2 The legislative level

On the legislative level, one of the main challenges confronting the national authorities as a consequence of the 'conventionisation' referred to above is the execution of Strasbourg judgments where participation of the EU as such is required. For, pending the accession of the EU to the Convention, the EU can neither be a party to proceedings before the Strasbourg Court nor be bound by judgments delivered by the latter. This leaves the Member States alone with the duty to execute the Strasbourg Court's judgments, even when this requires action by the EU for the purpose of amending Union Law.

A vivid illustration of this problem has been provided by the *Matthews* case.[107] This case concerned a British citizen residing in Gibraltar who challenged

---

[105] See 1.1.1 *supra*.

[106] See 2.1.1 *supra*.

[107] ECtHR, *supra* n. 21, *Matthews* v. *United Kingdom*

before the Strasbourg Court the exclusion of Gibraltar from European Parliament elections, as provided for by the Act Concerning the Election of the Representatives of the European Parliament by Direct Universal Suffrage of 20 September 1976. On 18 February 1999, the Strasbourg Court ruled that by failing to organise such elections in Gibraltar, the United Kingdom had infringed Article 3 of Protocol No. 1 to the Convention. In an attempt to execute the judgment, the United Kingdom in 2002 proposed an amendment to the 1976 Act. However, strong opposition by Spain blocked the adoption of the proposal, which caused the United Kingdom to enact the European Parliament (Representation) Act 2003 enabling the inhabitants of Gibraltar to participate in the said elections. Spain reacted by initiating proceedings before the ECJ under Article 227 EC, claiming that the United Kingdom had breached Community law.[108]

In his opinion on the case, Advocate General Tizzano states, *inter alia*, that for the purpose of executing the *Matthews* judgment, the United Kingdom was entitled to pass national legislation without a formal amendment being made to the above-mentioned 1976 Act. This was beyond doubt, having regard to the privileged position accorded to the protection of fundamental rights by the Community legal order. Both the Community and its Member States were required to respect fundamental rights on a primary basis. Measures which were incompatible with observance of those rights were therefore not acceptable in the Community legal order.[109] In its judgment, the ECJ basically followed the same approach, considering that in the light of the *Matthews* judgment, the United Kingdom '[could] not be criticized' for adopting the impugned legislation.[110]

Thus, where the EU legislature is prevented from amending Union law, it would appear to fall to its national counterpart to bring domestic legislation in line with fundamental rights as they result, *inter alia*, from the Strasbourg case-law. This is a remarkable attempt to break by judicial means the double deadlock resulting from the failing membership of the EU in the Convention system and the failure of a Member State to contribute to necessary amendments to Union Law. It remains to be seen whether this approach can work in cases where the EU legislation to be amended applies in all Member States rather than in only one, as in the *Matthews* case.

3. Concluding remarks

At the end of this overview, at least two conclusions can be drawn. First, fundamental rights today are an essential part of each of the legal systems co-existing on the European continent, providing a large part of their legitimacy. It is therefore no surprise to see the EU seek to expand the role of fundamental rights within its own

---

[108] ECJ, C-145/04, *supra* n. 30, *Spain* v. *United Kingdom*.

[109] Opinion delivered in the case of ECJ, C-145/04, *Spain* v. *United Kingdom*, *supra* n. 30, paras. 118 and 121.

[110] ECJ, C-145/04, *supra* n. 30, *Spain v. United Kingdom*, para. 95.

legal system. Nor is it a surprise to see, as a consequence, fundamental rights being caught up in the larger process of entanglement which increasingly characterises the relationship between the different co-existing legal systems in Europe. The result is an increasing complexity, producing an enhanced sensitivity in this area. This development is to be kept under control. For the more 'versions' of fundamental rights emerge, and the more varied their contents become, the more they lose their fundamental character, the less fundamental they become, and the more their univocal meaning is likely to be eroded by a kind of relativism which their many different versions tend to spread and uphold.

Secondly, the process is still going on, sometimes even producing sudden and rapid changes. On the judicial level developments are quite satisfactory, with both European Supreme Courts shaping up their respective case-law so as to take account, where appropriate, of the case-law and position of the other. Inasmuch as this represents a gradual – albeit still cautious – cross-system integration of European case-law, the process is also benefiting the domestic courts, as it contributes to harmonising some of the many different – and sometimes differing – legal sources to be taken into account by domestic courts.

On the legislative level, the picture to a large extent is a positive one too. The plan to draw up a specific binding EU catalogue of fundamental rights, combined with accession by the EU to the Convention, finds itself finally upheld in the Lisbon Treaty, after it had to be put on ice following the French and Dutch 'no' to the EU Constitutional Treaty. It will be of great help in putting fundamental rights in Europe on a coherent and therefore solid and lasting basis, by placing those rights which are protected by Union law in the same kind of relationship with the Convention as national fundamental rights. Meanwhile the ECJ has embarked on giving the Charter an increased impact. It is to be hoped that accession by the EU to the Convention will soon follow the entry into force of the Lisbon Treaty as the non-membership of the EU in the Convention mechanism is creating problems, especially with regard to the execution of Strasbourg judgments. While the ECJ appears to be willing to help solve the problem, it is clear that a lasting solution would require more than just a judge-made fix, however commendable its intentions. As for the other more limited legislative initiatives currently undertaken within the EU in respect of some specific fundamental rights, some of them remain a cause of concern from the viewpoint of legal certainty.

In the light of the above, it seems a fair to note, by way of conclusion that most developments are going in the right direction. If this trend is confirmed, the on-going 'unionisation' and 'conventionisation' process might well be capable of effectively fulfilling what should be its very purpose, the 'Europeanisation' of fundamental rights.[111]

---

[111] See 'Justice constitutionnelle, justice ordinaire, justice supranationale: à qui revient la protection des droits fondamentaux en Europe?', *Annuaire international de justice constitutionnelle*, Vol. 20, (Paris/Aix-Marseille, Economica/P.U.A.M., 2004); I. Verougstraete, 'De verhouding tussen het EVRM en de EU' in G.J.M. Corstens, W.J.M. Davids and M.I. Veldt-Foglia (ed.), *Europeanisering van het Nederlands Recht – opstellen aangeboden aan W.E. Haak* (Deventer, Kluwer 2004) p. 10 et seq.

Chapter 8
THE STATUS OF 'EUROPEANISED' INTERNATIONAL LAW IN AUSTRIA, SWITZERLAND AND LIECHTENSTEIN

Astrid Epiney and Bernhard Hofstötter in collaboration with Markus Wyssling*

1. INTRODUCTION

The European Community (EC), very often together with its Member States,[1] is a party to a multitude of international agreements in various fields. According to the European Court of Justice (ECJ) these treaties form an 'integral part of the Community legal system.'[2] The interpretation and application of those treaties is, thus, not only a matter of international law or each Member State's domestic constitutional law but also an issue of European Community law. In other words, as far as their legal effects in the Member States are concerned, those treaties are different from any treaty that a Member State has concluded independently of the EC. The following contribution explores this issue – based on the framework of Community law (section 2) – for one Member State in particular (Austria) and analyses how Community law standards are applied (and respected) in Austrian Law (section 3).

The relationship between international law and European Community law also embraces another aspect: in many international agreements, the EC succeeds in integrating sometimes very large parts of European Community law, otherwise known as the *acquis communautaire*. In such agreements, international law serves as a medium to introduce parts of the *acquis communautaire* into international agreements. As a consequence, Community law has to be applied between the EC and the third State, and very often within the third State itself. Nevertheless, such treaties are 'regular' international agreements even if their contents are heavily inspired by EC law. As far as the interpretation and the legal effects of those treaties are

* Astrid Epiney, Dr. jur., Professor for European Law, Public International Law and Public Law at the University of Fribourg (Switzerland), Managing Director of the Institute for European Law, Vice-President of the University, Beauregard 11, CH-1700 Fribourg; Bernhard Hofstötter, Dr. iur., LL. M., European Ombudsman, Lecturer at the Institute for European, University of Fribourg (Switzerland); Markus Wyssling, lic. Iur, lawyer, assistant and doctoral candidate at the Institute for European, University of Fribourg (Switzerland).

[1] So-called 'Mixed Agreements'.

[2] ECJ, Case 181/73 *Haegemann* para. 2/6; ECJ, Case 104/81 *Kupferberg* [1982] ECR 3641 para. 13; ECJ, Case 12/86 *Demirel* [1987] ECR 3641 para. 7; ECJ, Case C-192/89 *Sevince* [1990] ECR I-3461 para. 8.

J. Wouters, P.A. Nollkaemper, E. de Wet (eds.), The Europeanisation of International Law

concerned, they give rise to a number of problems, such as the risk of fragmentation of the case-law in the polities involved. For this reason this chapter aims to take a closer look at two of those arrangements in two different States: the legal effects of the European Economic Area Agreement (EEA Agreement) in Liechtenstein and the 'bilateral agreements' between the European Community (and partly the EU Member States) and Switzerland (section 4).

2. Legal effects of international agreements in European Community law

International agreements concluded by the EC – and, as the case may be, the EU Member States – entail a number of legal effects. This being so, the effects in the international legal order (section 2.1) are to be distinguished from those in the Community legal order (section 2.2). Mixed agreements,[3] especially, raise a series of problems that are worth paying particular attention to.

2.1 The international legal order

Following their entry into force, international agreements are binding for the parties (*pacta sunt servanda*).[4] The binding effect will in principle embrace all the agreement's provisions as a whole.[5] In the case of federally or supranationally

[3] On the notion of mixed agreements in general cf. D. O'Keeffe and H.G. Schermers (eds.), *Mixed Agreements* (Antwerp etc., Kluwer Law and Taxation Publ. 1983); K.D. Stein, *Der gemischte Vertrag im Recht der Außenbeziehungen der Europäischen Wirtschaftsgemeinschaft* [The mixed agreement in the law of external relations of the European Economic Community] (Berlin, Duncker & Humblot 1986); J. Heliskoski, *Mixed Agreements as a technique for organizing the international relations of the European Community and its Member States* (The Hague, Kluwer Law International 2001); A. Bleckmann, *Europarecht* [European Law] (Köln, C. Heymann 1997) at p. 513; A. Rosas, 'Mixed Union – Mixed Agreements', in M. Koskienniemi (ed.), *International Law Aspects of the European Union* (The Hague, Kluwer Law International 1998) at p. 125 et seq.; N.A. Neuwahl, 'Joint Participation in international treaties and the exercise of power by the EEC and its Member States: Mixed Agreements', 28 *CMLR* (1991) p. 717 et seq.

[4] The binding effect of international law is a consequence of international law principles cf. Art. 26 of the Vienna Convention on the Law of Treaties, and not only of Art. 300(7) EC Treaty, which refers to the Community legal system. On this problem cf. W. Heintschel von Heinegg, 'EG im Verhältnis zu internationalen Organisationen und Einrichtungen' [The EC *vis-à-vis* international organizations and institutions], in H.-W. Rengeling (ed.), *Handbuch zum deutschen und europäischen Umweltrecht* [Handbook of German and European environmental law] (Köln, C. Heymanns 2003) para. 22 No. 35.

[5] P.E. Holzer, *Die Ermittlung der innerstaatlichen Anwendbarkeit völkerrechtlicher Vertragsbestimmungen* [Determining the domestic applicability of treaty law] (Zurich, Schulthess Polygraphischer Verlag 1998) at p. 15 et seq.; W. Heintschel von Heinegg, *supra* n. 4, at para. 22 No. 38; L. Granvik, 'Incomplete Mixed Environmental Agreements or the Community and the Principle of Bindingness', in M. Koskienniemi (ed.), *International Law Aspects of the European Union* (The Hague, Kluwer Law International 1998) p. 255 at p. 262. However, the parties other than the EC and the EU Member States cannot pray in aid Article 300(7) EC Treaty. See A. Oehmichen, *Die unmittelbare Anwendbarkeit der völkerrechtlichen Verträge der EG* [The direct applicability of international agreements concluded by the EC] (Frankfurt am Main, Berlin etc., P. Lang 1992) at p. 104 et seq. and M. Björklund, 'Responsibility in the EC for Mixed Agreements – Should Non-Member Parties care?', 70 *Nordic JIL* (2001) at p. 373 et seq.

organised entities the binding effect extends to the hierarchically superior level (i.e., the federal State or EC) even if it is domestically not competent to conclude, partially or entirely, an analogous agreement. In relation to mixed agreements it follows that the Community as well as the EU Member States are bound by the entire agreement, independently of the internal allocation of competences, which in principle cannot be relied on against third parties.[6] This principle, of course, applies only as long as the wording or the object and purpose of the agreement do not clearly indicate the contrary.[7] In other words, according to international law the EC and the EU Member States are equally responsible for the performance of the entire treaty, unless the parties have explicitly agreed on a different approach taking recourse to a 'commitment clause' which explicitly signals to the other contracting States the respective areas of competence and responsibility of the EC and the EU Member States.[8] In this latter case, mixed agreements will be binding on the parties only to the limited extent of the clause.

2.2 The Community legal order

Based on Article 300(7) EC Treaty[9] the ECJ has consistently stressed that international agreements concluded by the EC form an 'integral part'[10] of the Community

[6] In his opinion in Case C-316/91 Advocate General Jacobs states that the Community, as well as the EU Member States, are bound by a mixed agreement, unless the agreement provides to the contrary. AG Jacobs, Case C-316/91 *European Parliament* v. *Commission* [1994] ECR 625. See also W. Heintschel von Heinegg, *supra* n. 4, at para. 22 No. 38.

[7] Cf. as well Arts. 27 and 46 of the Vienna Convention on the Law of Treaties.

[8] A. Oehmichen, *supra* n. 5 at p. 101; J, Ukrow, 'Art. 281', in C. Calliess and M. Ruffert (eds.), *Kommentar zum EU-Vertrag und EG-Vertrag* [Commentary on the EU and the EC Treaty] (Neuwied etc., Luchterhand 2002) No. 17. Contra C. Pitschas, *Die völkerrechtliche Verantwortlichkeit der Europäischen Gemeinschaft und ihrer Mitgliedstaaten* [The International Responsibility of the EC and its Member States] (Berlin, Duncker & Humblot 2001) at p. 240 et seq., who takes the view that the EC, as well as the EU Member States, regardless of the lack of a 'commitment clause' will only be bound to those provisions coming under their explicit sphere of competence. For, in so far as the conclusion of a treaty serves to bridge a split of competences, the latter would also have to be taken into consideration in relation to third parties. However, it is apparent that this approach does not give heed to the pertinent rules of the Vienna Convention on the Law of Treaties (VCLT), which proceed on the assumption that internal 'difficulties' in principle cannot put into question the binding effects of an international agreement on the parties to a treaty. Cf. Arts. 27 and 46 VCLT. It is not to be concealed that 'commitment clauses' may give rise to intricate legal issues, since they are often phrased in unclear terms. Cf. for this matter in detail M. Björklund, *supra* n. 5, at p. 376 et seq., who addresses the significance of Arts. 27 and 46 VCLT in this context.

[9] Whereupon agreements concluded by the Community are binding for the institutions of the Community and the Member States.

[10] ECJ, Case 181/73, *supra* n. 2, *Haegemann* para. 2/6; ECJ, Case 104/81, *supra* n. 2, *Kupferberg* para. 13; ECJ, Case 12/86, *supra* n. 2, *Demirel* para. 7; ECJ, Case C-192/89, *supra* n. 2 *Sevince* para. 8. Cf. A. Epiney, 'Zur Stellung des Völkerrechts in der EU. Zugleich Besprechung von EuGH, EuZW 1998, 572 – Hèrmes und EuGH, EuZW 1998, 694 – Racke' [On the position of international law in the EU. At the same time case note on ECJ, Hèrmes and ECJ, Racke], *Europäische Zeitschrift für Wirtschaftsrecht* (1999), pp. 5-6; A. Ott, *GATT und WTO im Gemeinschaftsrecht* [GATT and WTO in the Community legal order] (Köln, C. Heymann 1997) p. 68 et seq.; S. Hobe and P. Müller-Sartori, 'Rechtsfragen der Einbindung der EG/EU in das Völkerrecht' [Legal issues of the integration of EC and EU in the international legal order], *Juristische Schulung* (2002) pp. 8-12.

legal system and are of a 'Community nature'.[11] This characterisation implies that the provisions form part of positive EC law. However, such agreements are not to be classified as Community law but rather as international law, as upon entry into force on the international level, international agreements become an integral part of the Community legal system[12] and require no further measures of transposition. This suggests that the content of these provisions is not subject to change and that they retain their legal nature as instruments of international law.[13] Moreover, the principles of interpretation of international agreements support this approach: provisions in treaties that are the same as those in Community law are not necessarily to be interpreted in the same way, rather, their interpretation has to comply with international law standards.[14]

Nevertheless, the treaties form part of the Community legal order as far as they gain validity in the Community. Even though they do not lose their international law-character which not least finds expression in the applicability of the ordinary methods of treaty interpretation codified in Articles 31 et seq. Vienna Convention on the Law of Treaties, they are binding on the EU Member States and the EU institutions just like other acts of Community law. This also implies the applicability of the principle of supremacy of Community law to such international norms.[15] To this extent international agreements binding on the EC simply form part of Community law.

The question of direct effect – that is, the ability of individuals to invoke provisions of a treaty[16] – is to be answered by applying these principles.[17] The fact that treaties form part of the Community legal system implies that treaty provisions are capable of having direct effect, since provisions of Community law can be

[11] See ECJ, Case 104/81, *supra* n. 2, *Kupferberg* para. 14.

[12] Cf. ECJ, Case 181/73, *supra* n. 2, *Haegemann* para. 11/16; ECJ, Case 12/86, *supra* n. 2, *Demirel* para. 7; ECJ, Case C-192/89, *supra* n. 2, *Sevince* para. 8.

[13] See also C. Tomuschat, 'Art. 300', in H. Groeben and J. Schwarze (eds.), *Kommentar zum EU-/EG-Vertrag* [Commentary on the EU/EC Treaty], 6th edn. (Baden-Baden, Nomos 2003) No. 67; C. Eberle, *Die EG als Partei internationaler Umweltschutzübereinkommen* [The EC as a party to international environmental agreements] (Heidelberg, Doctoral Dissertation – University of Heidelberg, 2001) p. 224 et seq.; see also A. Peters, 'The Position of International Law within the European Community Legal Order', 70 *GYIL* (1997) p. 9 at p. 28 et seq.; see also A. Epiney, *supra* n. 10, at pp. 5-6.

[14] ECJ, Case 270/80 *Polydor* [1982] ECR 329 para. 18 et seq. For a more detailed analysis with further references see A. Epiney and A. Felder, 'Europäischer Wirtschaftsraum und Europäische Gemeinschaft: Parallelen und Divergenzen in Rechtsordnung und Auslegung' [European Economic Area and European Community: Convergences and Divergences in legal order and interpretation], *Zeitschrift für Vergleichende Rechtswissenschaft* (2001) at p. 425 et seq.

[15] See A. Epiney, *supra* n. 10, at pp. 5-6; see also W. Heintschel von Heinegg, *supra* n. 4, para. 22 No. 36.

[16] Incidentally, one has to point out that international agreements may, in principle, be directly applicable – without necessarily conferring individual rights – as long as the obligations therein are sufficiently precise and clear. Cf. e.g., ECJ, Case 17/81 *Pabst und Richarz KG* [1982] ECR 1331 para. 27.

[17] From the point of view of international law, the question whether and in how far provisions of an agreement are directly effective, depends on the interpretation of the particular treaty and the constitutional law of the State concerned. Cf. P.E. Holzer, *supra* n. 5, p. 36 et seq.; C. Eberle, *supra* n. 13, p. 232 et seq.

directly effective.[18] Treaty law, however, applies as such and does not lose its international character. Therefore, the question of the circumstances under which a provision is directly effective cannot simply be answered in the abstract by automatically referring to the Community law principles that have been developed for that purpose. Rather, the specifics of each particular treaty need to be taken into account.[19]

Mixed agreements pose particular problems. They contain (at least *a priori*) provisions that fall within the competence of the Community, as well as provisions that fall within the competence of the Member States. This raises the question of whether the entire treaty or only those components that fall within the competence of the Community are to be regarded as an integral part of the Community legal system. The more convincing arguments plead for the latter option. According to the principles of division of competences between the Community and the Member States, Community law effects cannot be assumed for those provisions of international agreements that fall within the competence of the Member States. Otherwise, the division of competences provided by primary Community law could be modified by concluding mixed agreements.[20] It is, however, the Member States' task to decide what effects treaties, as far as they relate to their competence, can display in the domestic forum. Thus, the treaty provisions falling within Member States' competence do not share the special character of Community law and their effects are determined according to the principles of domestic (constitutional) law.

It cannot be overlooked that this differentiated approach will encounter certain practical difficulties. In fact, it will not always be clear which provisions (still) fall within the competence of the Community and which do not (anymore).[21]

[18] See also W. Heintschel von Heinegg, *supra* n. 4, para. 22 No. 36.

[19] Cf. A. Epiney, *supra* n. 10, at pp. 5-6, with further indications. For details G. Bebr, 'Gemeinschaftsabkommen und ihre mögliche unmittelbare Wirksamkeit' [Treaties concluded by the EC and their potential direct effect], *EuR* (1983), p. 128 et seq.; C. Tomuschat, *supra* n. 13, at para. 70 et seq.; E.U. Petersmann, 'Auswärtige Gewalt, Völkerrechtspraxis und Völkerrechtsbindungen' [External power, international law practice and international law bonds], *ZaöRV* (1975) p. 261 at p. 270; C. Eberle, *supra* n. 17, at p. 234 et seq. Cf. also W. Heintschel von Heinegg, *supra* n. 4, para. 22 No. 35. Jurisdiction: ECJ, Case 12/86, *supra* n. 2, *Demirel* para. 14; ECJ, Case C-192/89, *supra* n. 2, *Sevince* para. 15; ECJ, Case C-432/92 *Anastasiou* [1994] ECR I-3087 para. 23; ECJ, Case C-162/96 *Racke* v. *Hauptzollamt Mainz* [1998] ECR I-3655 para. 31; ECJ, Case C-262/96 *Sema Sürül* v. *Bundesanstalt für Arbeit* [1999] ECR I-2685 para. 74.

[20] See also C. Tomuschat, 'Art. 228', in H. Groeben and J. Schwarze (eds.), *Kommentar zum EU-/EG-Vertrag* [Commentary on the EU/EC Treaty] (Baden-Baden, Nomos 2003) para. 88; A. Ott, *supra* n. 10, at p. 212 et seq.; S. Hobe and P. Müller-Sartori, *supra* n. 10, at pp. 8-12; H.G. Schermers, 'International Organizations as Members of other International Organisations', in B. von Rudolf, et al. (eds.), *Völkerrecht als Rechtsordnung, internationale Gerichtsbarkeit, Menschenrechte* [International law as a legal order, settlement of international disputes by judicial means, human rights] (Berlin, Springer-Verlag 1983) p. 831 et seq.; K. Schmalenbach, 'Art. 300 EGV', in C. Calliess and M. Ruffert, *Kommentar zu EU-Vertrag und EG-Vertrag*, 2nd edn. (Neuwied, Hermann Luchterhand Verlag 2002) Art. 300 EGV para. 69; W. Heintschel von Heinegg, *supra* n. 4, para. 22 No. 38; *contra* K.D. Stein, *supra* n. 3, p. 134 and p. 187; H. Krück, 'Völkerrechtliche Verträge im Recht der Europäischen Gemeinschaften' [International agreements in the law of the European Communities], 70 *Beiträge zum ausländischen öffentlichen Recht und Völkerrecht* (1977), p. 102 et seq.

[21] Cf. D. Thieme, 'European Community External Relations in the Field of the Environment', 10 *EELR* (2001), pp. 252-254.

In any event, one cannot object the view expounded above by arguing that the ECJ would normally qualify mixed agreements *in toto* and without differentiating between spheres of competence as an integral part of the Community legal system.[22] On the one hand, in exercising its jurisdiction to interpret provisions of mixed agreements, the ECJ reviews whether they come within the sphere of competence of the Community.[23] On the other hand, this does not necessarily include a statement regarding the precise legal effects of mixed agreements. Furthermore, it has to be pointed out that the Community will also be competent to conclude treaties in cases of competence which is shared with the Member States at the time of conclusion of an international agreement. However, the Community is not competent to conclude provisions of mixed agreements, which do not fall within its (shared) competence.

International agreements concluded by the Community take precedence over secondary Community law. This follows from Article 300(7) EC Treaty according to which agreements are binding, *inter alia*, on the institutions. Under certain circumstances Article 300(6) EC Treaty provides for the possibility to obtain the opinion of the ECJ as to whether an envisaged international agreement is compatible with the provisions of the EC. If compatibility is denied, the agreement may enter into force only in accordance with the procedure for amendment of the EC. This implies the supremacy of primary Community law over international agreements.[24] However, this hierarchy of norms is to be interpreted in line with the principle of *pacta sunt servanda*. Consequently, if an agreement is incompatible with primary Community law, it may be disregarded only to the extent that this is consonant with the international commitments in issue.[25] Faced with ambiguous provisions of secondary Community law, the priority of international law implies giving preference as far as possible to an interpretation which renders the provisions of secondary Community law consistent with treaty rules.[26] From a dogmatic point of view, the obligation to interpret in conformity with international law amounts to yet another facet of the doctrine of conform interpretation. Over and above that, as a result of the principle of the supremacy of Community law, domestic authori-

---

[22] Cf. ECJ, Case 181/73, *supra* n. 2, *Haegemann* para. 11/16. Critical towards *Haegemann* and the following judgments P. Gasparon, 'The Transposition of the Principle of Member State Liability into the Context of External Relations', 10 *EJIL* (1999), p. 605 at p. 610. Whether questions for a preliminary ruling concerning mixed agreements are admissible cf. J. Heliskoski, 'The Jurisdiction of the European Court of Justice to Give Preliminary Rulings on the Interpretation of Mixed Agreements', 69 *Nordic JIL* (2000), p. 395.

[23] Cf. e.g., ECJ, Case C-53/96 *Hermès* [1998] ECR I-3603.

[24] See also S. Hobe and P. Müller-Sartori, *supra* n. 10, at pp. 8-12.

[25] We will not address this problem further. Cf. for more details and further indications A. Epiney, *supra* n. 10, at pp. 5-8.

[26] ECJ, Case C-61/94 *Commission* v. *Germany* [1996] ECR I-3989 para. 52; confirmed in ECJ, Case C-179/97 *Kingdom of Spain* v. *Commission* [1999] ECR 1251 para. 11; on the former judgment cf. T. Heukels, 'Von richtlinienkonformer zur völkerrechtskonformen Auslegung im EG-Recht: internationale Dimensionen einer normhierarchiegerechten Interpretationsmaxime' [From an interpretation in conformity with directives to an interpretation in conformity with international law: International dimensions of an interpretative maxim paying due regard to normative hierarchies], 3 *Zeitschrift für europarechtliche Studien* (1999), p. 313 at p. 319 et seq.

ties are obliged to interpret and apply domestic law in accordance with treaties of the Community and therefore in conformity with Community law.[27] The principle of interpretation in conformity with international law is *a fortiori* valid especially for secondary Community law implementing treaties concluded by the Community.[28]

3. 'Europeanised' international agreements in Austria

With regard to the reception in Austria of international agreements concluded by the EC, or jointly by the EC and the EU Member States, the following analysis will dwell on three relevant questions. First, procedures applicable to the conclusion and ratification of treaties pursuant to the Austrian Constitution will be scrutinised for possible elements of europeanisation. This will require a short exposition of the pertinent general rules foreseen by Austrian constitutional law in order to pinpoint the specifics for international agreements concluded by the EC, or jointly with the EU Member States. Second, the implementation of international agreements in a federal State, such as Austria, customarily poses problems as to the competences of the various national actors on the State and sub-State level. This, in turn, holds equally true for agreements concluded by the EC, and has received specific attention by the Austrian legislature. Third, select examples of the recent case-law of the Austrian supreme courts will shed some light on the implementation of 'europeanised' international agreements by the national judiciary. The focus of the discussion will be on the question of whether or not Austrian courts tend to accept the legal consequences associated with treaties in the Community legal order, in particular the doctrines of direct applicability and direct effect.

3.1 'Europeanisation' of rules pertaining to the involvement of Austrian actors in the conclusion/ratification of international agreements?

Pursuant to Article 9(1) of the Austrian Constitution[29] general rules of international law are automatically incorporated into Austrian federal law. Whereas the controversy as to the rank of such incorporated international law in the domestic legal order has not yet been definitively settled[30] and it is equally debated whether or not

[27] See P. Manin, 'A propos de l'accord instituant l'Organisation mondiale du commerce et de l'accord sur les marches publics: la question de l'invocabilité des accords internationaux conclus par la Communauté Européenne, *RTDE* (1997) p. 399 at p. 412 et seq.

[28] ECJ, Case C-341/95 *Gianni Bettati* v. *Safety Hi-Tech Srl* [1998] ECR I-4355 para. 19 et seq.; ECJ, Case C-284/95 *Safety Hi-Tech Srl* v. *S. & T. Srl.* [1998] ECR I-4301 para. 21 et seq.

[29] Austrian Constitution (Bundes-Verfassungsgesetz (B-VG)), (Austrian) Official Gazette (BGBl.) Nr. 1/1930, as most recently amended by Official Gazette I Nr. 2005/121.

[30] For the different approaches advocated in scholarly writing cf. R. Walter and H. Mayer, *Grundriss des österreichischen Bundesverfassungsrechts* [An introduction to federal Austrian constitutional law] (Vienna, Manz 2000) p. 102 et seq.; B. Simma, 'Das Völkergewohnheitsrecht' [Custom], in H. Neuhold, et al. (eds.), *Österreichisches Handbuch des Völkerrechts* [Austrian Handbook of International Law], Vol. 1 (Vienna, Manz 2004) p. 44; for the widespread view that international law incorporated by

this provision extends to general principles of international law,[31] it is generally recognised that it covers (at least) customary international law. It is equally uncontested that it does not apply to treaties since the issue of the transformation of treaties is governed by separate rules laid down in the Constitution.[32] According to Article 65 of the Constitution, treaties are concluded by the Federal President. In line with pertinent rules of public international law,[33] Austrian constitutional law builds on the seminal distinction between simple and composite procedures of concluding treaties. In the former case, the signature of a competent organ will give rise to the binding force of a treaty. In principle, the Federal President will be the organ competent for signature pursuant to Article 65 of the Constitution. However, in conformity with Article 66(2) of the Constitution, the Federal President has delegated the conclusion of certain categories of treaties to the Federal Government or competent ministers.[34] This delegation may only relate to treaties not falling under Article 50 of the Constitution, that is, treaties of a political character and treaties supplementing or amending statutory law which require prior approval of the National Council and, as the case may be, the Federal Council.[35] By means of this provision Austrian constitutional law accommodates the composite procedure of concluding international agreements. Only once treaties covered by Article 50 of the Constitution have been approved by parliament can they be ratified by the Federal President (Article 50 of the Constitution). This right of the Federal President presupposes a prior request to this end by the Federal Government (Article 67(1) of the Constitution). The President is under no duty to ratify a treaty, but only his ratification in conjunction with the exchange or deposit of the documents of ratification will give rise to the conclusion of a treaty.[36] Upon the subsequent publication of a treaty – as a rule in the Austrian Official Gazette – the treaty will become valid and effective within the national legal order.

---

means of Art. 9 takes a place in between national constitutional law and (simple) statutory law (so-called *'Mezzanintheorie'*) see Th. Öhlinger, *Verfassungsrecht* [Constitutional Law] (Vienna, WUV Universitätsverlag 2005) p. 77.

[31] In the affirmative: Th. Öhlinger, *supra* n. 30, at p. 76; undecided: R. Walter and H. Mayer, *supra* n. 30, at p. 102; *contra*: B. Simma, *supra* n. 30, at p. 43 et seq., and H. Hausmaninger, *The Austrian Legal System* (Vienna, Manz 2003), p. 28.

[32] R. Walter and H. Mayer, *supra* n. 30, at p. 102; Th. Öhlinger, *supra* n. 30, at p. 76 et seq.

[33] Cf. Art. 11 VCLT; on this article see – instead of many – M. Fitzmaurice, 'The practical working of the law of treaties', in M. Evans (ed.), *International Law* (Oxford, Oxford University Press 2006), p. 191 et seq.

[34] Decision of 31 December 1920, Austrian Official Gazette 1921/49; see also K. Zemanek, 'Völkervertragsrecht' [Treaties], in H. Neuhold, et al. (eds.), *Österreichisches Handbuch des Völkerrechts* [Austrian Handbook of international law], Vol. 1 (Vienna, Manz 2004).

[35] R. Walter and H. Mayer, *supra* n. 30, at p. 106. The National Council is the first chamber of the Austrian parliament, with supreme legislative powers vested in this body. By contrast, the Federal Council as the second chamber of parliament may at best exercise a suspensive veto, but has no power to permanently oppose a legislative proposal. In light of these imbalances it is fitting to speak of an imperfect bicameral system. Cf. L. Prakke, 'The Republic of Austria', in L. Prakke and C. Kortmann (eds.), *Constitutional Law of 15 EU Member States* (Deventer, Kluwer 2004), p. 34 et seq.

[36] R. Walter and H. Mayer, *supra* n. 30, at p. 107.

Austria's accession to the European Union in 1995 saw a new section introduced into the Austrian Constitution (Articles 23a-23f, entitled 'European Union'),[37] setting out the rules necessary to give shape to Austrian participation in the decision-making of the European Union. The primary aim of this section is therefore to facilitate the functioning of the pertinent provisions of EU constitutional law by means of national constitutional law.[38] In more concrete terms, the said section addresses Austria's participation in the EU institutions, such as the *modus operandi* of elections of the Austrian Members of the European Parliament, as well as the participation of the Austrian Parliament and – to the extent their sphere of interest is touched upon – of the Austrian *Länder* in legislative projects of the European Union. With regard to the participation of the Austrian parliament, Article 23e(1) of the Constitution[39] obliges the competent member of the Federal Government to inform and consult the National and the Federal Councils about all projects *('alle Vorhaben')* in the framework of the European Union without delay. If the (legislative) projects need to be implemented by federal statutory law, or otherwise relate closely to the adoption of a directly applicable legal act impinging on a competence held by the Federal State, the opinion expressed by the National Council is binding. Deviations will only be possible in the light of compelling reasons of foreign and integration policy and only after a fresh consultation of the National Council (Article 23e(2) of the Constitution). The question is thus how far treaties to be concluded by the EC may be taken to fall under the category of 'all projects' of the European Union, thereby necessitating the involvement of the Austrian Parliament. Given the implicit allusion of Article 23e(1) of the Constitution to directives and regulations it seems clear that it is first and foremost concerned with secondary Community law.[40] At the same time there is no compelling reason for excluding parliamentary involvement in case of the envisaged conclusion of treaties. Finding in favour of subsuming international agreements under the 'all projects'-rule is further corroborated by the central role taken by the Council of the European Union in the adoption of treaties, either in issuing a mandate to the European Commission to negotiate, or in finally concluding treaties on behalf of the EC.[41] In obliging *ministers* to consult with the national parliament, Article 23e of the Constitution takes the central law-making function of the Council as its point of departure,[42] and consequently must also be applicable in the case of treaties. Assuming, as is done in this chapter, the applicability of Article 23e of the Constitution to treaties concluded by the EC, a feature of 'europeanisation' of the procedures applicable to the conclusion of treaties may be discerned here. To be sure, there is no comparable provision in the case of the conclusion of international agreements by

[37] Austrian Constitution, as amended by (Austrian) Official Gazette Nr. 1994/1013.

[38] Th. Öhlinger, *supra* n. 30, at p. 97.

[39] Austrian Constitution, as amended by (Austrian) Official Gazette I Nr. 2001/121.

[40] Th. Öhlinger, *supra* n. 30, at p. 100 et seq.

[41] Cf. K. Lenaerts and P. van Nuffel, *Constitutional Law of the European Union* (London, Sweet & Maxwell 2005), p. 410.

[42] Th. Öhlinger, *supra* n. 30, at p. 100.

the Republic of Austria alone. On the other hand, this should not come as too much of a surprise since in the case of international agreements concluded by Austria the Parliament will almost inevitably – within the confines of Article 50 of the Constitution – have a say in the ratification process. In order to confer democratic legitimacy in the national polity the participation of parliament *qua* mandatory consultation with binding effects thus intends to bridge the gap resulting from the absence of a tangible influence of national parliaments at the European level.[43]

Now, for which kinds of international agreements will the said provisions of the Constitution be of relevance? The aforementioned dichotomy between international agreements concluded by the EC alone and mixed agreements contains the key to an answer. As far as mixed agreements have a political character, or supplement or amend statutory law, the principles flowing from Article 50 of the Constitution will apply. Ratification by Parliament is thus required. This applies to the agreement in its totality, even though only some of its provisions may be of the requisite character.[44] In the less frequent case of international agreements concluded by the EC alone, the institutional involvement of the Austrian Parliament via the competent minister exercising voting rights on behalf of Austria is the consequence of the view represented here.

3.2 Implementation of international agreements within Austria's federal structure

The approach taken by the Austrian Constitution to the reception of international law in the national legal order may adequately be termed 'moderately' monistic, in principle giving primacy to international law.[45] It is 'moderate' in as much as na-

[43] It is both with regard to the mandatory information and the consultation of parliament with binding effect that Austrian constitutional law goes way beyond the Protocol on the Role of National Parliaments in the European Union (OJ 1997, C 340/113) attached to the Treaty of Amsterdam, which merely provides that Commission proposals 'shall be made available in good time so that the government of each Member State may ensure that its own national parliament receives them as appropriate'. Thus, the protocol confers no autonomous right of information on national parliaments. Art. 2 of a homonymous Protocol (OJ 2004, C 310/204) annexed to the Treaty establishing a Constitution for Europe slightly upgrades the precarious role of national parliaments by affording a self-standing right of information relating to legislative proposals. This right, in turn, lies at the heart of national parliaments' envisaged role as watchdogs of the principle of subsidiarity (Art. I-11(3), 2nd subparagraph) whose ramifications are spelled out in a modified Protocol on the application of the principles of subsidiarity and proportionality (OJ 2004, C 310/207) annexed to the constitutional treaty.

[44] R. Walter and H. Mayer, *supra* n. 30, at p. 105 et seq.; Th. Öhlinger and M. Potacs, *Gemeinschaftsrecht und staatliches Recht – Die Anwendung des Gemeinschaftsrechts im innerstaatlichen Bereich* [Community law and domestic law – The application of Community law within the state] (Vienna, Orac 2006), p. 13; cf. also Th. Öhlinger, *Verfassungsfragen einer Mitgliedschaft zur Europäischen Union* [Constitutional issues of Membership in the European Union] (Vienna/New York, Springer 1999), p. 192.

[45] R. Walter and H. Mayer, *supra* n. 30, at p. 101; Th. Öhlinger, *supra* n. 30, at p. 75 et seq.; cf. also F. Ermacora and W. Hummer, 'Völkerrecht, Recht der Europäischen Union und Landesrecht' [International law, law of the European Union and domestic law] in H. Neuhold, et al., *Österreichisches Handbuch des Völkerrechts* [Austrian Handbook of international law], Vol. 1 (Vienna, Manz 2004); but see W.

tional law conflicting with international law will not be invalidated as such, but rather may give rise to international responsibility.[46] As a matter of principle, international law will be incorporated by means of 'general transformation'. Thus, by the mere publication of the pertinent instrument of international law in the Austrian Official Gazette the agreement is henceforth part of the law of the land in force and applicable. This process is also referred to as 'adoption' which appears to be more appropriate, as it emphasizes the fact that it is a treaty and not national law which provides the source of validity.[47] Thus, the 'transformed' treaty provisions retain their international law character.[48] On the other hand, recourse to 'special transformation' – i.e., the adoption of a national statute prescribing the behaviour mandated by the international instrument – may be had if the National Council so decides (Article 50(2) of the Constitution; so-called *Erfüllungsvorbehalt*). This will particularly be the case when non-self-executing treaties are ratified. Whereas a radical monist may tend to ascribe a dualistic character to the Austrian system, for a 'moderate' monist the need for transformation as such in a monistic system does not amount to a *contradictio in se*, accepting that more often than not international law obligations are addressed to the State and thus require transformation in order to have legal effects also for individuals.[49] At the same time it is to be conceded that the monism/dualism debate is of fairly limited relevance for the interpretation of pertinent Austrian constitutional law.[50] Of far greater relevance is the question of which entity is under an obligation to transpose or implement international law in a federal State.

From Article 16(4) of the Constitution it can be inferred that the competence to implement corresponds to the general allocation of competences between the federal State and the *Länder*. Thus, the *Länder* are fully competent to implement international agreements whose contents touch upon their autonomous scope of action. At the same time, Article 16(4) of the Constitution provides for a devolution of this competence to the federal State if one of the *Länder* fails to fulfil its obligations in due time. Article 23d(5) provides for a 'europeanisation' of this rule, transferring its main thrust to the question of the implementation of legal acts adopted in the framework of European integration. However, here the devolution is subject to the additional requirement of the ECJ having found a breach of an obligation to implement, translating in practical terms into a condemning judgment within the framework of the infringement procedure (Article 226 *et seq.* of the EC Treaty).[51] It is exactly this elevated threshold for triggering devolution which necessitates a

---

Wormuth, *Die Bedeutung des Europarechts für die Entwicklung des Völkerrechts* [The significance of European law for the development of international law] (Frankfurt, Peter Lang 2004), p. 129 et seq., who – erroneously – attributes the hallmarks of an 'explicitly dualistic' approach to the Austrian system.

[46] F. Ermacora and W. Hummer, *supra* n. 45, at p. 112.

[47] K. Zemanek, *supra* n. 34, at p. 61.

[48] F. Ermacora and W. Hummer, *supra* n. 45, at p. 115.

[49] Cf. Th. Öhlinger, *supra* n. 30, at p. 76.

[50] Ibid.

[51] Ibid., at p. 90.

delimitation between Article 16(4) and Article 23d(5) of the Austrian Constitution. There is little doubt that agreements concluded by the EC alone need to be qualified as legal acts adopted in the framework of European integration, to which Article 23d(5) of the Constitution refers. Consequently, the devolution to the federal State of implementing competences pertaining to the *Länder* will be dependent on a prior finding of a violation by the ECJ. The answer is less clear-cut with regard to mixed agreements, owing to their double nature of legal acts adopted in the framework of European integration (Article 23d(5) of the Constitution) and 'ordinary' treaties from the viewpoint of Article 16(4) of the Constitution. Again, an approach differentiating between Community and national competences is well advised. In so far as the content of a mixed agreement is covered by Community competence the additional requirement of a prior ECJ-involvement under Article 23d(5) of the Constitution will be applicable. Conversely, as far as national competences are concerned, Article 16(4) applies.[52] Needless to say, striking the balance between these two provisions will entail similar interpretative difficulties, as will answering the question of which provisions of a mixed agreement form an integral part of the Community legal order.[53]

3.3 'Europeanised' international agreements in the case-law of Austrian supreme courts

Since Austria's accession to the European Union on 1 January 1995 sufficient time has passed to allow Austrian courts to develop case-law against the background of the precepts flowing from European Community law. Taking a look at the case-law of Austrian supreme courts[54] relating to international commitments of the EC since accession, cases in connection with the association agreement between the EEC and Turkey abound. As a comprehensive overview is clearly beyond the scope of this short survey,[55] the following analysis will be highly selective inasmuch as it focuses on jurisprudential choices of Austrian supreme courts which could put into doubt the Community law features of international agreements concluded either by the EC alone or in conjunction with EU Member States. Two areas of potential shortcomings in Austrian supreme courts' approaches to international agreements

---

[52] Th. Öhlinger, *supra* n. 44, at p. 193.

[53] See *supra* 2.2.

[54] In the given context, the term 'supreme court' is to be understood as referring to organisational courts of last instance only. This notion is thus different from the concept of functional courts of last instance which the ECJ favours in connection with the duty to refer pursuant to Art. 234(3) of the EC Treaty. Cf. ECJ, Case C-99/00 *Lyckeskog* [2002] ECR I-4839 para. 15. With regard to the Austrian legal system, the Constitutional Court *(Verfassungsgerichtshof)*, the Administrative Court *(Verwaltungsgerichtshof)*, and the Supreme Court *(Oberster Gerichtshof)* form the *trias* of courts whose case-law is at issue here.

[55] For a meticulous study on the implementation of European Community law by Austrian courts which extends to the implementation of international agreements forming part of the Community legal order see B. Bapuly and G. Kohlegger, *Die Implementierung des EG-Rechts in Österreich – Die Gerichtsbarkeit* [The implementation of EC law in Austria – the judiciary] (Vienna, Manz 2003).

can broadly be distinguished. The first category relates to the actual taking into account by Austrian supreme courts of international agreements which are applicable *ratione temporis, ratione materiae* and *ratione loci.* Put bluntly, do Austrian supreme courts apply the doctrines of direct applicability and direct effect also to 'europeanised' international agreements? This category may be termed as procedural compliance/non-compliance. Conversely, the second category is concerned with the question of substantive non-compliance. That is, how far do Austrian supreme courts honour the contents of the rights and obligations derived from 'europeanised' international agreements?

3.3.1 *Direct applicability and direct effect*

From a conceptual point of view, there is little difference between the potential legal effects of international agreements concluded by the EC and treaties concluded by Austria. In both instances direct application and direct effect may in principle attach to treaty provisions. Within the Austrian constitutional system, international agreements concluded by Austria will in general be directly applicable, as long as their provisions are self-executing in the sense of defining the addressee and the contents of a norm to such an extent that it may be applied by the competent national authorities without there being a need for further implementing measures.[56] In line with the already mentioned doctrine of 'transformation', however, only upon its (general) transformation or adoption in conformity with national constitutional law may a provision of an international agreement in principle be invoked before a national court. In essence, this requirement is not different from the monism underlying the effects of treaties concluded by the EC which form an integral part of the Community legal order right from the time they enter into force.[57] Thus, from the point of view of Austrian constitutional law the application of 'europeanised' international agreements is not an altogether novel problem. This is somewhat confirmed by the case-law of Austrian courts. Numerous judgments rendered by, *inter alia,* the Administrative Court demonstrate that Austrian supreme courts are at ease with applying international agreements forming an integral part of the Community legal order as part of the law of the land. This finding is corroborated rather than weakened by the fact that the direct applicability of, for instance, the association agreement with Turkey is not expressly discussed but rather presumed. This holds equally true for legal acts derived from 'Europeanised' international agreements, such as decisions of an Association Council established pursuant to an association agreement.[58] As a consequence, Austrian supreme courts show no hesitation in

[56] F. Ermacora and W. Hummer, *supra* n. 45, at p. 117; K. Zemanek, *supra* n. 34, at p. 61. As will be noted, these criteria come close to the notion of direct effect in the Community legal order. There, the test is whether, 'regard being had to its wording and the purpose and nature of the agreement itself, the provision contains a clear and precise obligation which is not subject, in its implementation or effects, to the adoption of any subsequent measure'. See ECJ, Case 12/86, *supra* n. 2, *Demirel* para. 14.

[57] Th. Öhlinger and M. Potacs, *supra* n. 44, at p. 74; cf. also K. Lenaerts and P. van Nuffel, *supra* n. 41, at p. 739 et seq.

[58] See for instance Administrative Court, judgment of 4 December 1996, 95/21/0897, and judgment of 23 July 1998, 95/18/0763.

implicitly acknowledging the direct effect of treaty provisions that grant rights to individuals in a sufficiently precise and unconditional manner.[59] On the other hand, there are occasional instances where courts omit to refer to applicable 'europeanised' agreements, not necessarily to the applicant's detriment, however. Hence, in a case of wage discrimination of a Bulgarian chemist working in Austria due to the non-recognition of periods of service in Bulgaria, the Supreme Court failed to apply the Europe Agreement with Bulgaria. Instead of applying the pertinent prohibition of discrimination contained in Article 38 of the Europe Agreement, by way of analogy to the EC Treaty the Supreme Court relied on a general principle of equal treatment as an expression of material justice.[60]

By way of conclusion, the case-law of Austrian supreme courts is not free from mistakes, but equally shows no signs of a general lack of implementation of 'europeanised' international agreements. Two problematic constellations remain, however. The first one concerns the obligation to apply international agreements *ex officio*. The other one relates to the potential retroactive effect of treaties to facts having materialized before Austria's accession to the European Union. Both of these issues will be examined in turn.

3.3.1.1 *Ex officio* application of international agreements

Are national courts under an obligation to apply international agreements *proprio motu*, if the relevant provisions have not been pleaded by the parties to proceedings? If one accepts that certain international agreements form an integral part of the Community legal order, the answer given must not be different from that with regard to other sources of Community law. The nuanced approach adopted by the ECJ in *Peterbroeck*[61] and *Van Schijndel*[62] is therefore of equal relevance when the implementation of international agreements is at stake. Thus, in principle there is no requirement for national courts to raise provisions of Community law of their own motion,[63] unless there is also a duty to raise points of *national* law *proprio motu*. The question becomes one of national procedural laws, albeit subject to the double proviso of equivalence and effectiveness.[64] Requiring, as a rule, that applicants substantiate the legal grounds for challenging individual legal acts,[65] Austrian law relies on the initiative of the parties as to raising points of law (so-called *Dispositionsmaxime*). In *Van Schijndel*, the Court dealt with civil law proceedings, eventually holding as follows:

---

[59] See for instance Administrative Court, judgment of 4 December 1996, 95/21/0897, and judgment of 19 February 1997, 96/21/1118.

[60] Supreme Court, judgment of 23 May 1996, 8 ObA 2105/96. For a more detailed discussion of this judgment see B. Bapuly and G. Kohlegger, *supra* n. 55, at p. 568 et seq.

[61] ECJ, Case C-312/93 *Peterbroeck* [1995] ECR I-4599.

[62] ECJ, Joined Cases C-430 and C-431/93 *Van Schijndel* [1995] ECR I-4705.

[63] Ibid., at para. 15.

[64] Cf. K. Lenaerts and D. Arts, *Procedural Law of the European Union* (London, Sweet & Maxwell 1999), 3-014.

[65] See for instance Art. 28(1) 4 of the Law on the Administrative Court.

> 'In the present case, the domestic law principle that in civil proceedings a court must or may raise points of its own motion is limited by its obligation to keep to the subject-matter of the dispute and to base its decision on the facts put before it.
>
> That limitation is justified by the principle that, in a civil suit, it is for the parties to take the initiative, the court being able to act of its own motion only in exceptional cases where the public interest requires its intervention. That principle reflects conceptions prevailing in most of the Member States as to the relations between the State and the individual; it safeguards the rights of the defence; and it ensures proper conduct of proceedings by, in particular, protecting them from the delays inherent in examination of new pleas.'[66]

A fortiori, this reasoning must also hold for administrative law proceedings where party initiative is usually more limited and the judge takes a more pro-active role in raising points of law on his own motion. In the light of more limited party initiative in the case of the Administrative Court,[67] a dominant stream in Austrian literature assumes a duty of the Administrative Court to raise points of law on its own motion, within the framework of the dispute set by the parties' submissions.[68] At the same time, Austrian supreme courts do not always live up to this standard, at least not if applied strictly. Thus, the Administrative Court has been criticized for restricting its legal analysis to those provisions relating to rights of residence of Decision No. 1/80 adopted by the Association Council under the association agreement between the EEC and Turkey which had been invoked by the applicant (and as a consequence denying a right of residence), without examining more favourable provisions which could eventually have led to a finding to the contrary.[69]

3.3.1.2 Retroactivity?

Austrian supreme courts are at times quick to discard the applicability of 'europeanised' international agreements to sets of facts which occurred before Austria's accession in 1995. A case in point is a judgment of the Administrative Court with regard to the Cooperation Agreement between the EEC and Tunesia.[70] Here the exclusion from Austrian territory of a Tunesian national for a period of five years, which had been ordered in July 1994, was in issue. The applicant challenging this decision was a student at an Austrian university and had been caught operating a taxi cab without having obtained the requisite permit. Upon his request to refer to the ECJ a preliminary question regarding his entitlement to work in Austria and related rights flowing from the cooperation agreement, the Administrative Court denied the necessity of a referral given the fact that the challenged deci-

---

[66] *Van Schijndel*, *supra* n. 62, at paras. 20-21.

[67] B. Bapuly and G. Kohlegger, *supra* n. 55, at p. 201.

[68] Ibid., at p. 201 with further references.

[69] Administrative Court, judgment of 4 December 1996, 95/21/0897, and the criticism voiced by B. Bapuly and G. Kohlegger, *supra* n. 55, at p. 201 et seq.

[70] Administrative Court, judgment of 9 November 1995, 95/18/0102.

sion dated from the time before Austria's accession. Appealing as this reasoning may appear at first sight, it is highly doubtful whether it is in conformity with the pertinent case-law of the ECJ, in particular from the point of view of legal certainty and legitimate expectations.[71] In *Saldanha* the Court held as follows:

> 'In view of the fact that the Act of Accession contains no specific conditions whatsoever with regard to the application of Article 6 of the Treaty, the latter provision must be regarded as being immediately applicable and binding on the Republic of Austria from the date of its accession, with the result that it applies to the future effects of situations arising prior to that new Member State's accession to the Communities. From the date of accession, therefore, nationals of another Member State can no longer be made subject to a procedural rule which discriminates on grounds of nationality, provided that such a rule comes within the scope ratione materiae of the EC Treaty.'[72]

Consequently, Community law may apply also to 'future effects' of factual situations having arisen prior to accession. It is conspicuous that in *Saldanha* the ECJ explicitly dispelled the view that Community law would not apply if the challenged decision issued by an Austrian court predated Austria's accession.[73] Dealing with non-discrimination in the labour law context, in the more recent *Pokrzeptowicz-Meyer* case the ECJ applied analogous reasoning, holding that the prohibition of discrimination as contained in the Europe Agreement with Poland applied from the entry into force of that agreement, *without any need to consider whether workers are employed under a contract of employment concluded before or after that entry into force*.[74] It would appear from these judgments that the 'future effects' doctrine as applied by the ECJ comes into play when a legal determination by a court of last instance is still pending, such as is the case when a supreme court has been called upon to adjudge in a particular case after the time of accession. The reasoning of Austrian supreme courts as to the non-applicability of Community law to facts predating accession is thus in need of refinement, whereas at the same time this problem is liable to gradually fade away as the date of accession becomes more and more remote in time.

3.3.2 *Substantive non-compliance*

The implementation of 'europeanised' international agreements by national courts requires interpretative choices which may eventually give rise to non-compliance with the substantive precepts of Community law. In this respect the implementation of international agreements is no different from applying other sources of Community law, such as regulations or directives, and indeed no differences in the compliance rate with international agreements on the one hand and other Community law

[71] B. Bapuly and G. Kohlegger, *supra* n. 55, at p. 349 et seq.
[72] ECJ, Case C-122/96 *Saldanha* [1997] ECR 1997, I-5325 at para. 14.
[73] Ibid., at paras. 12-14.
[74] ECJ, Case C-162/00 *Pokrzeptowicz-Meyer* [2002] ECR I-1049 at para. 56.

acts on the other hand could be found by the authors. Whereas in general the compliance rate of Austrian supreme courts is very high,[75] occasional problems remain, particularly in connection with violations of the duty to refer pursuant to Article 234(3) of the EC Treaty.[76]

4. Community law in international agreements with third States

When parts of Community law are integrated into international agreements between the EC and third States, the question arises how these agreements are applied and interpreted by the contracting States.[77] The fact that such agreements embody tailor-made modes of cooperation, remaining in general far below the threshold of full-fledged EU membership, and often reflect the outcome of subtle political bargaining tends to add substance to the legal analysis and at the same time makes it imperative to separately analyse the legal situation for each State concerned. In the following two different cases will be examined: First, the legal effects of some of the bilateral agreements of the European Community (partly in conjunction with the EU Member States) with Switzerland will be dealt with (section 4.1). Second, the legal effects of the EEA Agreement in Liechtenstein will briefly be dealt with ('section 4.2). This brevity is due to the fact that many questions of EEA law have by now received the attention of a host of contributions in legal writing. Moreover the European Free Trade Association (EFTA) Court already had the chance to clarify a great number of issues.[78] The differences between the legal situations in both countries warrant different approaches to evaluating legal phenomena in light of the sliding scale of 'europeanisation'. So, in the case of Switzerland the study will focus on the varying degrees of Switzerland's *rapprochement* with the Community legal order and their impact on the Swiss legal order, whereas with regard to Liechtenstein, given the more standardised and familiar approach of EEA law, the emphasis of the discussion will be placed on the effects of EEA law in the Liechtenstein legal order.

4.1. Bilateral agreements EU – Switzerland

Switzerland has concluded two 'packages' of bilateral and sectoral[79] agreements with the EC and the Member States respectively. The so-called 'bilateral I' agree-

[75] Cf. B. Bapuly and G. Kohlegger, *supra* n. 55, at p. 25 et seq.

[76] See for instance Administrative Court, judgment of 29 November 2000, 99/09/0103. In this judgment the Supreme Administrative Court 'autonomously' determined the required duration of integration of a sponsor into the labour market in order for rights of residence of his family members to be derivable. In light of the uncertainties left by the relevant provision of Decision No. 1/80 of the Council of Association under the association agreement between the EEC and Turkey, a reference to the ECJ would have been required.

[77] See *supra* 2.2.

[78] Cf. to both aspects the contributions and tables in C. Baudenbacher, P. Tresselt and T. Orlygsson (eds.), *The EFTA Court Ten Years On* (Oxford and Portland, Hart Publishing 2005).

[79] The expression 'bilateral agreements' is apparently only used in Switzerland and contrasts with the multilateral approach of the EEA. From a legal point of view, the expression is imprecise, to say the

ments entered into force in 2002. They consist of seven treaties, among the most important of which is the agreement on 'free movement of persons'.

The seven agreements form a 'package' insofar as they could only enter into force collectively and as the non-prolongation or cancellation of any single one would result in the concomitant cancellation of all the other agreements. Nevertheless, each agreement relates to different subject-matter, there being no framework or skeleton agreement whatsoever.

Contrary to the EEA Agreement, these treaties do not qualify as 'integration agreements' and therefore do not encompass a real involvement in the ongoing integration process of the EU Member States. In fact, as far as their form is concerned, they are 'classic' international law instruments. They are based on the principle of equivalence of legislation and standards, and provide for central bodies consisting of representatives of each party: joint committees deciding by unanimity. It is incumbent upon these committees, among other things, to ensure the correct application of the agreements, to settle interpretative differences between the parties and to modify certain parts of the treaties. In principle, no provisions of Community law are taken over. Nevertheless – and this is especially true of the agreement on free movement of persons[80] – the agreements are partially aiming at the participation in the relevant sections of the *acquis communautaire.*

Soon after concluding the 'bilateral I' agreements, the very same parties entered into negotiations for the 'bilateral II'[81] agreements. These eight treaties deal with the 'leftovers' of the 'bilateral I' agreements as well as with some new political concerns from both sides. In the present context the agreement on cooperation in the fields of justice, police, asylum and migration (Schengen/Dublin) is of major interest. It envisages the true integration of Switzerland into the corresponding parts of the *acquis communautaire*, including in principle the obligation to adopt its further developments.[82] The various 'bilateral II' agreements are not legally connected with each other, whereas they are (partially) linked from a political point of view.

In order to elicit the exact effect of the bilateral agreements, one has to distinguish between different categories of obligations contained therein. Depend-

least, because the agreements are partially multilateral (since the EU Member States are also involved). For this reason, the shorthand of 'sectoral agreements' is more adequate for its emphasis on the fact that these agreements only cover chosen policy areas. Nevertheless, we will use the terms 'bilateral I' agreements and 'bilateral II' agreements in the following, since they have become customary in Switzerland.

[80] For details see A. Epiney, 'Zur Bedeutung der Rechtsprechung des EuGH für Anwendung und Auslegung des Personenfreizügigkeitsabkommens' [On the relevance of the case-law of the ECJ for application and interpretation of the agreement on the free movement of persons], *Zeitschrift des Bernischen Juristenvereins* (2005), p. 1; A. Epiney, 'Das Abkommen über die Personenfreizügigkeit – Überblick und ausgewählte Aspekte' [The agreement on the free movement of persons – overview and selected aspects], in A. Achermann, et al. (eds.), *Jahrbuch für Migrationsrecht/Annuaire du droit de la migration 2004/2005* [Yearbook of migration law], (Bern, Stämpfli 2005) p. 45.

[81] Text and 'Message' of the bilateral II Agreements in: BBl. 2004, 5965 et seq.

[82] To a great extent the agreement is analogous to the association agreements with Norway and Island. Cf. A. Epiney, 'Schengen, Dublin und die Schweiz' [Schengen, Dublin, and Switzerland], *Aktuelle Juristische Praxis* (2002), p. 300 at p. 304 et seq.

ing on the manner and extent of the *rapprochement* to already existing provisions in the Community legal order, we distinguish as follows:

- An agreement can refer directly to Community law provisions, and Switzerland will then be obliged to ensure an according legal position. This technique is often used with reference to the at times fairly technical acts of secondary Community law. Annexes I and II of the agreement on the 'free movement of persons', for instance, contain a list of legal acts that Switzerland has to apply ('equivalence of legislation'). Annex 1 of the agreement on overland transport equally lists a number of technical provisions, whereas Switzerland has to apply provisions that are 'equivalent' to Community law provisions. Finally, the substantive law provisions in the Schengen/Dublin agreements basically refer to the *acquis communautaire*.
- Furthermore Switzerland's obligations can be mentioned in the agreement itself (or in the annexes respectively), whereas their content is largely or entirely based on the situation in EC law. Annex I of the 'agreement on free movement of persons', for instance, in part literally adopts Community law provisions or alludes to parallel obligations that can be found in Community law. Article 1(3) of the agreement on overland transport refers correspondingly to the principle of non-discrimination contained in Article 12 EC. A similar solution can be found in Article 6 of the agreement on certain aspects of government procurement which again contains the non-discrimination principle.
- Finally, the bilateral treaties can contain completely autonomous provisions that do not refer in any form to the *acquis communautaire*.

As far as the agreements – directly or indirectly – go back to the *acquis communautaire*, the complex question arises, whether and in how far those provisions are to be interpreted in parallel with the legal position in Community law. Since they are treaties, this question has to be answered based on international law principles of interpretation and separately for each agreement. In cases in which the aim of the agreement – i.e., to aspire to a parallel legal position – can clearly be detected, there is much to be said for a parallel interpretation, while the temporal frame of reference has to be specified.[83] The technique of implanting large and significant parts of the *acquis communautaire* entails complex problems of interpretation, since a parallel interpretation cannot be assumed for every aspect in advance. Consequently, the meaning of each provision has to be determined for each individual case, which brings about considerable legal uncertainty.

Legal protection in Switzerland – where, due to a monist understanding of international and domestic law, agreements are effective as such and certain rules are self-executing[84] – is disconnected from the Community judiciary as Swiss courts

[83] For a detailed comment concerning the agreement on free movement on persons compare A. Epiney, *supra* n. 80 ('Zur Bedeutung der Rechtsprechung ...'), at p. 1 et seq.

[84] Compare for example D. Wüger, *Anwenbarkeit und Jusitziablität völkerrechtlicher Normen im schweizerischen Recht* [Applicability and justiciability of international law norms in Swiss law] (Bern, Stämpfli 2005), passim.

have no access to the ECJ within the preliminary rulings procedure. The ensuing danger of differential case-law on the interpretation of the agreement by the ECJ on the one hand (which has to interpret the agreements as an integral part of the Community legal system) and Switzerland on the other hand, aggravates rather than remedies legal uncertainty. If the ECJ rules differently on a certain issue than Swiss courts, the question arises whether the latter are under an obligation to modify their case-law. This problem is closely associated with the question of the pertinence of the ECJ's case-law in instances in which the bilateral agreements refer to parts of the *acquis communautaire*. Some of these agreements contain (direct or indirect) obligations to take ECJ judgments into consideration that were rendered before the signing of the agreements. For instance, according to Article 16(2) of the agreement on free movement of persons, the rulings of the ECJ (rendered until the signature of the agreement) have to be taken into consideration while interpreting and applying the agreement as far as the latter refers to Community law notions. Furthermore, according to the Schengen association agreement a qualified deviation from case-law may lead to the cancellation of the agreements. In other treaties, however, there is no reference to the case-law of the ECJ, even though they frequently employ Community law terms. In any case the relevance of the case-law of the ECJ is largely undetermined and does not emerge clearly from the agreements. If mandatory recourse to the case-law is provided for, it is doubtful which judgments are precisely relevant and how the 'old' case-law is to be distinguished from the 'new' (that is to say, the case-law developed since signing the treaties). Even if no recourse to the case-law of the ECJ is provided for, a few arguments still speak in favour of such an option, since when referring to the *acquis communautaire* the agreements aim at constructing a parallel legal regime in relation to Switzerland. Thus, it will often be unclear whether and how far the case-law of the ECJ has to be taken into account in order to render a judgment in a particular case, and this again detracts from legal certainty.

The approach of the bilateral agreements, which is inspired by 'classic' international law implies that – unlike the EEA Agreement – they contain in principle static obligations and that the joint committees play an important role in settling disputes and further developing the treaties. Concerning the adoption of the *acquis communautaire*, this approach indicates that one has to refer to the actual state of Community law (including, as mentioned before, case-law) at the time of signing the treaty. In other words, when Community law is modified it is not automatically incorporated on the basis of the bilateral agreements. Nevertheless, the agreements aim to ensure a parallel legal position in Switzerland in relation to the EU, at least as far as they 'directly or indirectly' refer to the *acquis communautaire*. However, this aim cannot be achieved if the bilateral agreements cannot incorporate further developments of Community law. Therefore, as a rule the agreements contain specific provisions for the adoption of new Community law. Referring to legislation, one can basically distinguish between two 'mechanisms of adoption'.[85]

[85] Only mechanisms referred to in the agreements themselves are taken into account here. Apart from that, the agreements could of course be modified at any time which, however, implies going through the rather ponderous procedure of concluding a new treaty.

- Either the joint committee is competent to modify provisions (of the annexes as a rule), which is provided for in several bilateral agreements; or,
- the agreements establish the obligation in principle to adopt future developments of the relevant parts of the *acquis communautaire*. Whereas the adoption takes place in accordance with domestic law, the agreement will terminate automatically if new Community law remains unadopted. The Schengen and Dublin association utilises this model.

Analysing the manner in which Switzerland is directly or indirectly bound by the *acquis communautaire*, one can conclude as follows:

- The legal effects of the provisions contained in the bilateral agreements that take over Community law are largely unclear, especially the degree of dependence on corresponding interpretations used in Community law as well as the relevance of the case-law of the ECJ. These insecurities will be removed only on a limited scale by developing relevant general principles. In the end some legal uncertainty concerning the interpretation of various provisions will remain. In this respect it is telling that the Court for social insurance of the Canton of Zurich and the Federal Council (the Swiss Government) take opposite stances concerning the range of the freedom to provide services contained in the agreement on free movement of persons.[86] For the law abiding citizen this situation is awkward, as a large number of questions of interpretation – which could easily be answered in Community law – have to be answered on a case-by-case basis.
- Concerning legislation, Switzerland has to adopt those parts of Community law, as referred to by certain agreements. In cases in which the take-over of further developments of Community law is provided for in an agreement, apart from the legal obligation there will be considerable political and economical pressure to adopt new laws, even though Switzerland has not taken part in the decision-making process on the European plane.[87]

4.2 Legal effects of the EEA Agreement in Liechtenstein

The legal effects of the EEA Agreement in Liechtenstein have to be seen against the background of the general relationship between national and international law in Liechtenstein's legal system. Like Switzerland, Liechtenstein takes a monist approach to the relationship between international and national law. That is to say that, in line with doctrine, courts apply treaties automatically upon their entry into

---

[86] See Sozialversicherungsgericht des Kantons Zürich, judgment of 19 February 2004, IV.2003. 00221, E.6. A. Epiney, *supra* n. 80 ('Das Abkommen…') at p. 59 et seq.

[87] In the context of the Association of Schengen, Swiss representatives will be consulted when a corresponding project is elaborated. In a political perspective this involvement should not be underestimated.

force on the international level.[88] This principle is of a constitutional nature, though it is not expressly laid down in the Constitution but rather presupposed by several of its provisions. As far as the relationship between treaties and national law is concerned, treaties (at least those consented to by the Parliament) are in any case hierarchically situated above national legal acts.[89] Furthermore, some international agreements may have a constitutional character, such as the European Convention on Human Rights.

As far as the EEA Agreement is concerned, it has been concluded by reference to the 'ordinary' procedure.[90] The difference from other treaties lies in the legal effects of the EEA Agreement and 'secondary EEA law', which is of particular interest in the context of the present discussion. The Liechtenstein Constitutional Court ruled that the EEA Agreement has a constitutional character insofar as it modifies parts of the Constitution. Thus, the Agreement itself takes precedence over the Constitution. Although it is not clear if secondary law based on the EEA Agreement also has precedence over the Constitution, the Constitutional Court pleads in favour of such a position. The basis of this proposition is certainly the special character of the EEA Agreement which demands at least an 'in fact superiority' of EEA law in relation to national law.[91] Consequently, EEA law is in general considered as a sort of 'quasi-supranational law', so that in fact its characteristics are similar to those of European Community law.[92] This approach has in principle been confirmed by the EFTA Court. The president of this Court has summarised the position on key questions of the effects of EEA law as 'quasi-direct effect, quasi primacy and full State liability'.[93] So, according to practice and doctrine, EEA (primary and secondary) law can have direct effect. The question of whether a particular provision is capable of having direct effect has to be answered by applying the same principles as those in European Community law.[94] As far as other questions of interpretation of EEA law are concerned, practice in Liechtenstein – based on the

---

[88] Cf. with further references Stefan Becker, *Das Verhältnis zwischen Völkerrecht und Landesrecht nach Massgabe der Praxis des Staatsgerichtshofes des Fürstentums Liechtenstein* [The relationship between international and domestic law as interpreted by the State Court of the Principality of Liechtenstein] (Schann, GMG 2003) p. 107 et seq.

[89] Cf. with further references on this point S. Becker, *supra* n. 88, at p. 295 et seq.

[90] Cf. S. Becker, *supra* n. 88, at p. 133 et seq.

[91] Cf. Art. 97 et seq. EEA, cf. also Art. 7 EEA which rules that the system of secondary law has in fact to be applied also by EEA States. Cf. on this issue A. Epiney, *Der Stellenwert des europäischen Gemeinschaftsrechts in Integrationsverträgen* [The significance of European Community law in intergration agreements] (Bern, Stämpfli Verlag 1992) p. 90 et seq.

[92] Cf. on this issue with further references S. Becker, *supra* n. 88, at p. 201 et seq.

[93] Carl Baudenbacher, 'The EFTA Court Ten Years On', in C. Baudenbacher, P. Tresselt and T. Orlygsson (eds.), *supra* n. 78, at p. 13 (26).

[94] Provisions of treaties concluded by Liechtenstein outside the EEA context may have direct effect, provided they are sufficiently precise and concrete, and thus self-executing. On this cf. for instance, the first additional country report of the Principality of Liechtenstein of 3 June 1998 pursuant to Art. 19 of the 1984 Convention Against Torture and Other Cruel, Inhuman or Degrading Treatment or Punishment, para. 48, available online at <http://www.liechtenstein.li/pdf-fl-staat-aussenpolitik-cat2.pdf#search=%22Liechtenstein%20%22self-executing%22%22> (5 October 2006).

rulings of the EFTA Court[95] – generally interprets EEA law in parallel with European Community law.[96]

5. Conclusion

It can be seen that Austria's accession to the European Union in 1995 has brought about a moderate 'europeanisation' of rules of national constitutional law with regard to the conclusion, ratification and implementation of international agreements concluded by the EC alone or in conjunction with EU Member States. In general, Austrian supreme courts have lived up to the challenges posed by the implementation of 'europeanised' international agreements by giving effect to their provisions in disputes before them. The bilateral agreements between Switzerland and the EC (and the EU Member States respectively) aim, *inter alia*, at the participation of Switzerland in particular parts of the *acquis communautaire*, by resorting to instruments of international law. The bilateral treaties are, from a formal point of view, pure international law instruments and, in contrast to the EEA, have no integrationist character. Ultimately, however, large parts of the bilateral agreements entail a sort of 'partial integration' into the legal system of the Union. The further the material area of application of such partial integration without Member State status reaches, the more it meets the legal and political confines discussed. Therefore a continuation of the 'bilateral path' leads inevitably to the consideration of the advantages and disadvantages of EU membership. In Liechtenstein EEA law is capable of having direct effect. In order to detect whether a provision has this capability Community law principles are applied. As far as other interpretative questions of EEA law are concerned practice tends to proceed in parallel with European Community law.

To sum up, we can note that the 'europeanisation of international law' has reached different stages in the three countries in question. This is of course partly due to the different levels of integration into the Community legal order. Nevertheless, the influence of Community law on international agreements is tangible in all these States. Not only the 'pressure' of the common market but also the far-reaching development of Community law make it impossible for non-EU Member States to conclude treaties disregarding the legal dynamism of the Community legal order.

---

[95] Cf. on this issue the contributions in C. Baudenbacher, P. Tresselt and T. Orlygsson (eds.), *supra* n. 78.

[96] Cf. with further references on this point S. Becker, *supra* n. 88, at p. 373 et seq.

Chapter 9
A TRIANGULAR RELATIONSHIP BETWEEN PUBLIC INTERNATIONAL LAW, EC LAW AND NATIONAL LAW? THE CASE OF HUNGARY

Nóra Chronowski and Tímea Drinóczi*

1. Introduction

Determining the nature and manifestations of the triangular relationship between public international, Community and national law is a rather complicated undertaking. Since much has been written already on the relationship between international and Community law (or on the external relations of the Community),[1] the present contribution will focus on the interrelation of international and Community law from the viewpoint of national law, more specifically, Hungarian constitutional law.

Hungary makes for an interesting case-study for a variety of reasons. First of all, it displays several uncertainties in this area. A number of its constitutional provisions (in particular Articles 2/A and 7) give rise to uncertainty, as will be shown below. In addition, Hungarian courts and other authorities appear unwilling to apply international law in cases before them. Secondly, since 1 May 2004, Hungary has been a Member State of the European Union. Thus, its legal system has

* Respectively Associate Professor and Senior Lecturer, Faculty of Law, University of Pécs, Hungary.

[1] See for example, Koen Lenaerts and Piet van Nuffel and Robert Bray (eds.), *Constitutional law of the European Union* (London, Sweet & Maxwell 1999) pp. 550-564, 611-621; Robert Uerpmann-Wittzack, 'The Constitutional Role of Multilateral Treaty Systems', in Armin von Bogdandy and Jürgen Bast (eds.), *Principles of European Constitutional Law* (Oxford, Hart Publishing 2006) pp. 145-183; Balázs Péter, *Az Európai Unió külpolitikája és a magyar-EU kapcsolatok fejlődése* [Foreign Policy of the European Union and the development of Hungarian-EU relations] (Budapest KJK KERSZÖV 2002) pp. 27-111; Giuseppe Federico Mancini, *Democrazia e costituzionalismo nell' Unione europea* [Democracy and constitutionalism in the European Union] (Bologna, il Mulino 2004) pp. 347-365; Szalayné Sándor Erzsébet, *Az Európai Unió közjogi alapjai* [Public Law Basis of the European Union] (Budapest-Pécs, Dialóg Campus Kiadó 2003) pp. 219-220; Kecskés László, *EU-jog és jogharmonizáció* [EU law and law-harmonization] (Budapest, HVG-ORAC Kiadó 2005) pp. 421-424, 535-536; Jan Wouters and Dries Van Eeckhoutte, *Giving Effect to Customary International Law Through European Community Law*, Working paper No. 25, K.U. Leuven, Faculty of Law, Institute for International law 2002; Paola Goi, *The External Relations of the European Community: Legal aspects of the Relationships with Foreign States and International Organizations*, <www.apfpress.com/book2/pdf-files/6pdf> (4 July 2006); Alessandra Mignoli, *The EU's Powers of External Relations* <www.isi.it/pdf/articles/mignolli.pdf> (4 July 2006); Philipp Gasparon, '*The Transposition of the Principle of Member State Liability into the Context of External relations*', 10:3 *EJIL* (1999).

J. Wouters, P.A. Nollkaemper, E. de Wet (eds.), The Europeanisation of International Law

been undergoing important changes in recent years, expanding because of the application and implementation of the legal norms issued by EU institutions and also the international commitments undertaken by the Community. These commitments are binding on Hungary by virtue of Article 300 TEC and Article 26 TEU.

The main focus in this contribution is on how the Hungarian Constitution regulates the relationship between international, Community and national law. This question is important because it is the Constitution which determines the positions of national authorities (legislature, judiciary, etc.) towards these legal orders (section 2). Second, this contribution examines how this triangular relationship affects the Hungarian legal system at the legislative level (section 3). Finally, after discussing the legislature's approach towards the Europeanisation of international law, we will examine the practice of ordinary courts (section 4).

2. The Hungarian constitutional framework

In this section, the relationship between provisions of the Hungarian Constitution and both international and Community law will be examined.

2.1 International law in the Hungarian constitutional system

Article 7(1) of the Constitution provides that 'The legal system of the Republic of Hungary accepts the generally recognised principles of international law, and shall harmonise the country's domestic law with the obligations assumed under international law.' This provision, at first sight, adopts a dualist approach towards international law. It is not unambiguous, however, and can only be understood and interpreted together with the decisions of the Constitutional Court and the standpoints of legal scholars.

2.1.1 *'General principles of international law' and 'international obligations'*

In relation to the 'harmonisation' of domestic law, the question arising is which sources of international law should be taken into account when establishing Hungary's 'international obligations'. The main sources are international treaties and general principles of international law, which involve customary international law, *jus cogens* and general principles of law.[2] When States describe their alignment to international law on a constitutional level, they use, in most cases, the term 'general principles of international law' and regard international treaties and agreements as separate.[3] However, in light of the case-law of the Constitutional

[2] See in more detail, Bruhács, János, *Nemzetközi jog I. Általános rész* [International law, I. General Part] (Budapest-Pécs, Dialóg Campus Kiadó, 1998) pp. 79-82, Bokorné Szegő, Hanna, *Nemzetközi jog* [International law] (Budapest, Aula Kiadó 2003) pp. 33-43; Nguyen Quoc Dinh-Patrick Daillier-Allain Pellet- Péter Kovács, *Nemzetközi közjog* [International Public Law] (Budapest, Osiris Kiadó 2003) from pp. 71 and 162.

[3] Bokorné, *supra* n. 2, at p. 50.

Court,[4] the notion of 'general principles of international law', as it appears in the Constitution, should be taken to refer to customary international law and international *jus cogens*.[5]

2.1.2 *'Acceptance' and 'assurance of harmony' – general principles of international law*

'Assurance of harmony' indicates that the State should develop a domestic legal order in which international principles are recognised and international treaties having been entered into by the State prevail. According to the Constitutional Court, the fact that the enforcement of an obligation undertaken at the international level appears as a constitutional obligation[6] means that the Constitution and domestic law should be interpreted so as to make the principles of international law prevail. Thus, in order to make Article 7 prevail, the Constitution, international legal obligations and domestic law should be interpreted together and in view of their correlation with one another.[7] More precisely, this obligation of interpretation means that the provisions of the Constitution and domestic law should be construed so that the general principles of international law can prevail.[8] Despite the obligation of interpretation, in its decision 53/1993 (X.13), the Constitutional Court regarded it contradictory if harmonisation is intended to be achieved by the adjustment of international law to the conditions of domestic law.[9] The Constitutional Court made the obligation of interpretation one-sided because international law cannot be construed in terms of national law. To support its reasoning, the Constitutional Court stated that national law might be applied in so far as it is explicitly ordered by international law, and national law should not prevail over the explicit and cogent principles of international law with different content. On the other hand, the Court held that ignoring international law would conflict with Article 7(1) of the Constitution.[10]

Since generally recognised principles of international law qualify as part of domestic law, their application in domestic law requires an automatic or general

---

[4] But, since the Constitutional Court (CC) fails to use international legal terminology, it is difficult to construe from the resolution, what the Body denoted under the general principles of International law. See 53/1993 (X. 13.) AB határozat, (CC decision), ABH 1993, 323, 329.

[5] For a contrasting opinion see Bokorné, *supra* n. 2, at p. 50. In her opinion the constitutions, since they refer to general principles of International law, leave the question open if they denote customary international law, *jus cogent* or both.

[6] For a similar view in Italian legal literature see Gustavo Zagrebelsky, *Manuale di diritto Constituzionale I. Sistema delle fonti del diritto* [Handbook of constitutional law I. Legal source system] (UTET 1987) p. 120.

[7] 53/1993. (X. 13.) AB határozat, (CC decision), ABH 1993, 323, 327.

[8] In the case examined in the resolution according to Constitutional Court (CC) Art. 57(4) and Art. 7(1) of the Constitution should be interpreted in consideration with each other. 53/1993. (X. 13.) AB határozat, (CC decision), ABH 1993, 323, 327.

[9] In the case of the CC resolution referred to, e.g., in consideration with penalty. 53/1993. (X. 13.) AB határozat, (CC decision), ABH 1993. 323, 333.

[10] 53/1993. (X. 13.) AB határozat, (CC decision), ABH 1993, 323, 327.

adoption.[11] This is justified by the view represented in legal literature, according to which the generally recognised principles of international law cannot be transformed but only adopted.[12] Furthermore, a comparative analysis of more detailed provisions of a few European constitutions with Article 7(1) leads to a similar conclusion.[13]

Article 7(1) operates as a 'permanent transformer' of every present and future norm belonging to general principles of international law.[14] It also means that, by virtue of the explicit 'acceptance' clause in Article 7(1), certain rules of another legal order, namely those of international law, prevail simultaneously in a compulsory manner.[15]

The stronger the automatic application of international law in the domestic legal system, the more important it is that the Constitution includes guarantees which ensure that international law does not infringe upon the fundamental values of the Constitution.[16] In this respect, the Hungarian Constitution has a serious handicap, since it includes no material restriction at all. Based on the case-law of the Constitutional Court, the rule of law[17] and other basic values of the republic, such as

---

[11] Cf. Bragyova, András, 'A magyar jogrendszer és a nemzetközi jog kapcsolatának alkotmányos rendezése' [The constitutional organisation of the connection between the Hungarian legal system and International law] in Bragyova, András (ed.), *Nemzetközi jog az új Alkotmányban* [International law in the new Constitution] (Budapest, Közgazdasági és Jogi Könyvkiadó MTA Állam- és Jogtudományi Intézete 1997) p. 16. G. Zagrebelsky, *supra* n. 8, at p. 120.

[12] Bodnár, László, 'A nemzetközi jog magyar jogrendszerbeli helyének alkotmányos szabályozásáról' [On the constitutional regulation of the place of International law in the Hungarian legal system] in *Alkotmány és jogtudomány. Tanulmányok* [Constitution and Jurisprudence, Studies] (Szeged, 1996) p. 23.

[13] The expression 'generally recognized principles' of international law is applied for instance by the German basic law (Art. 25) when it provides the general principles of International public law is part of the federal law and as such it has primacy over the acts and will directly entail rights and obligations for the inhabitants of the federal territory. Under Art. 9 of the Austrian federal constitution, the generally recognised principles of International law form part of the federal law in effect. Pursuant to the Greek constitution, the generally recognised principles of International law take priority over contradictory legal provisions. Art. 8(1) of the Portuguese constitution states that the general and common law principles of International law constitute part of Portuguese law. By virtue of Art. 10 of the Italian constitution, 'the Italian law and order aligns with the generally recognized principles of International law'. The conclusion we can draw from these formulations is the absolute priority of the general principles of International law over Domestic law. Although Art. 29(3) of the Irish basic law also recognises the generally recognised principles of International law, but adopts them just as principles of conduct against other countries. From this draft, it follows that the enforcement of generally recognised principles of International law is possible only within the restrictions imposed.

[14] The expression was used by Perassi in his work *Lezioni di diritto internazionale* [Lectures on international law] (Padova 1957) p. 29. Being turned into general domestic law does not exclude at all that certain 'generally recognised rules' should be determined by distinct treaties (too), and in that respect distinct transformation should be made. E.g., the United Nations Charter and the Geneva Convention contain such principles. 53/1993. (X. 13.) AB határozat, (CC decision), ABH 1993, 323, 327.

[15] 53/1993. (X. 13.) AB határozat, (CC decision), ABH 1993, 323, 327.

[16] A. Bragyova, *supra* n. 11, at p. 13.

[17] The Constitution contains the expression 'jogállam', which is equivalent to 'Rechtsstaat' or 'rule of law'.

democracy and respect for fundamental rights, could be regarded as such constitutional limitations.[18] The Constitutional Court has set some limits to the automaticity of the process: thus, it required that customary international law and *jus cogens* – such as certain rules of international criminal law – should prevail exclusively in respect of the facts of the case and conditions specified under international law.[19]

The question of who will interpret the international norms in question may arise, as they must be applied according to their international law content.[20] However, this question does not cause any problems, as the principles of international law introduced into national law in this manner must be enforced within the Hungarian legal system, and such enforcement is clearly the task of national courts. Thus, the courts should arguably apply the general rules of international law in light of the facts of the case, as specified by international law. However, in practice it turns out that customary international law does not have a role in the case-law of Hungarian courts and that even international treaties are rarely applied.[21]

2.1.3 *'Acceptance' and 'assurance of harmony' – international agreements*

In order to ensure the harmony of international treaties with domestic law, Hungary takes, in accordance with Article 7(1) of the Constitution, a dualist point of view because of its requirement to assure harmony.[22] The method applied for the transformation of international treaties into domestic law is the special adoption or transfer that is applied in practice in the case of self-executing international treaties.[23] The other type is the special regular transfer. Special, as it is done through execution, and regular because the generally used (legislative) procedure must be applied. In the case of a non-self-executing norm, legislators are therefore required to create

---

[18] Cf. e.g., 11/1992 (III. 5.) AB határozat, (CC decision), ABH 1992, 77, 80. Petrétei, József, *Magyar Alkotmányjog I* [Hungarian Constitutional law I] (Budapest-Pécs, Dialóg Campus Kiadó 2002).

[19] Cf. 53/1993 (13. 10.) CC resolution, ABH 1993, 323, 335. In the case, the CC stated that 'it is a constitutional requirement that the exclusion of the lapse of culpability can be established exclusively to the crimes for which the culpability, according to Hungarian law in effect at the time of the commission of crime, had no statutory limitation. There is one exception, that is if the crime (facts of the cases) is (are) declared a war crime or crime against humanity by international law, or the statute of limitations (or its possibility) for those crimes is established by international law and Hungary is obliged to exclude the statute of limitations by an international obligation.' 53/1993 (13.10.) CC resolution, ABH 1993, 323.

[20] A. Bragyova, *supra* n. 11, at p. 19.

[21] Blutman, László's remarks. Kiss, Barnabás, *Az európai jog, a nemzetközi jog és a nemzeti jogrendszerek egymáshoz való viszonya* [The relationship between European law, International law and national legal systems] (Jogtudományi Közlöny 1998/3) p. 105.

[22] According to Németh Art. 7(1) is essentially dualist in character. Cf. Németh, János, Az európai integráció és a magyar Alkotmány [European integration and the Hungarian Constitution] in Bragyova András (ed), *Nemzetközi jog az új Alkotmányban* [International law in the new Constitution] (1997) p. 107. A legal system which does not take a stand on the legal status of international legal norms explicitly is necessarily dualist. A. Bragyova, *supra* n. 11, at p. 15.

[23] A treaty is self-executing if it complies with specified conditions: domestic law does not exclude direct jurisdiction, the addressee is concretely specified or may be specified, the treaty includes rights and duties drafted exactly.

the executive rules needed (rules creating new organs and verifying authority of duty or procedure).[24]

In light of the constitutional obligation to ensure harmony mentioned above, any norms introduced by either transfer technique will take the introducing provision's place in the hierarchy of norms. In this respect, international law is regarded as a special source of law, as it takes effect in domestic law not through the given organ exercising its legislative authority but in connection with the State's international relations.[25] Hence, if a strictly formalistic approach is followed under the relevant Hungarian regulations, international treaties are placed below the Constitution and above all 'secondary legal sources' (laws as well as other forms of state administration). How the relationship between international treaty obligations and domestic law is designed falls within the State's (legislative) competence. However, the problem with the Hungarian hierarchy of legal norms is that related rules are scattered. Rather than being included in a single specified act, (Constitution, Act on legislation) other provisions – e.g., the Act on the Constitutional Court – are also relevant. It would be preferable if the rank of international treaty obligations published in a Hungarian legal source (Act or Government decree[26]), and their relationship with domestic legal sources, especially with purely domestic[27] Acts and Government decrees were regulated in an Act (Constitution or the Act on legislation).

In relation to the place of provisions enacting international treaties in the hierarchy of norms, the first question is whether the international treaty enacted could affect the provisions of the Constitution. The answer is negative because of the Constitutional Court's competence to carry out an *ex ante* review of the constitutionality of provisions of international treaties.[28] If the Constitutional Court verifies the constitutionality of an international treaty, it cannot be ratified until the unconstitutionality is repaired.[29] The treaty enacted cannot have an effect on the Constitution because the Constitution requires two thirds of the votes of Members of Parliament for its amendment.[30] Thus the Constitution cannot be subject to an implied constitutional amendment. However, ending the unconstitutionality will in some cases probably take a long time, since an international treaty may be bilateral or multilateral and its amendment will require the approval of all the contracting parties.[31] Because of this, an appropriate constitutional amendment may be needed.[32]

---

[24] G. Zagrebelsky, *supra* n. 6, at p. 124, L. Bodnár, *supra* n. 12, at p. 24 and J. Bruhács, *supra* n. 2, at p. 87.

[25] J. Petrétei, *supra* n. 18, at pp. 170-171.

[26] Art. 9 of Act L of 2005 on the procedure in connection with the international treaties.

[27] I.e., a legal source not referring to an international treaty.

[28] Art. 1(1) of the Act on the Constitutional Court.

[29] Cf. Art. 36 of the Act on the Constitutional Court.

[30] Art. 24(3) of 46/1994 (IX. 30.) Parliamentary resolution on the Standing Orders of the Parliament (46/1994 (IX. 30.) (Ogy határozat az Országgyûlés Házszabályáról).

[31] Cf. the Reasoning of the Act on the Constitutional Court.

[32] Cf. 4/1997 (22. 01.) AB határozat, (CC decision), ABH 1997, 41. This solution is applied by the Spanish Constitution, since its Art. 95 states that drawing up a treaty containing a provision contradictory to the constitution requires a preliminary amendment of the constitution. It appears in the Reasoning connected to Act 2 of Bill No. T/4486.

The primacy of international treaties in the hierarchy of legal sources is specified under Act XXXII of 1989 on the Constitutional Court (CC Act). By virtue of the CC Act it is for the Constitutional Court to examine a conflict between national law and international treaties.[33] Article 45(1) of the CC Act expresses the legislature's will that domestic law should be examined on its conformity with an international treaty and that if the former does not comply with the provision promulgating the international treaty it must be revoked as unconstitutional. This means that the international treaty enacted in an act or Government decree is superior to other acts/decrees, other legal provisions and other legal instruments of state administration. Therefore the principle of *lex posteriori* will not prevail here. From this follows the absolute primacy of international treaties, which is simultaneously strengthened and weakened by the following provisions regarding the competences of the Constitutional Court. If an act enacting an international treaty conflicts with a legal norm of a higher level,[34] the Constitutional Court, pursuant to the CC Act, is not entitled to annul the former or the latter provision, but it will call upon the domestic organ that concluded the treaty or the domestic legislative organ to resolve the contradiction.[35] This is a carefully crafted solution that shows the intention to preserve the hierarchy of legal norms in the domestic legal system.

It follows from the above that the preservation of harmony between international treaties and domestic law is based on the principle of the primacy of treaties in the hierarchy of legal norms. However, this system does not fully ensure the enforcement of constitutional obligations.[36] Although the organ requested to resolve any contradiction between domestic law and a treaty is obliged to fulfil its duty within an appointed time, and if it fails to do so, the Constitutional Court will verify the non-compliance,[37] this obligation is not legally enforceable. Consequently, in practice there will be no harmony between the international obligation and domestic law; and the constitutional order specified under Article 7(1) of the Constitution will not prevail.[38] A solution to this problem requires the total assurance of the primacy of international treaties. This could be achieved by placing international treaties between the Constitution and the acts – a solution which is similar to that adopted by other States.[39] At present, the place of legal instruments promulgating international treaties in the hierarchy of legal norms is rather complicated.

---

[33] Art. 1(c) of the Act on the Constitutional Court.

[34] E.g., a treaty was published in a decree of the Government and it conflicts with an Act of Parliament.

[35] Cf. Art. 46(1) and (2) of the Act on the Constitutional Court.

[36] International obligations become constitutional obligations by virtue of Art. 7(1).

[37] Cf. Art. 47(2) and Art. 47(1) and (2).

[38] Nevertheless, it does not mean the obligation effective under international law would not bind the Republic of Hungary on the international level. Cf. J. Petrétei, *supra* n. 18, at p. 175.

[39] Other constitutions have similar provisions in connection with the decisions of international organisations and international treaties promulgated. The Dutch constitution (Art. 94), Portugal basic law (Art. 8), the Greek constitution (Art. 28(1), the Finnish basic law (Art. 55, the Spanish constitution (Art. 96) and Art. 55 of the French constitution provide that treaties and/or decisions of international organisations and acts promulgating these treaties or decisions have primacy over domestic law. Compared to these, by virtue of Art. 9 of the Polish constitution, the Republic of Poland recognises Interna-

In summary, it must be noted that international treaties containing a general obligatory rule of conduct should be enacted in a provision corresponding to their content. In this way they will be placed below the Constitution, and neither a provision of a lower level nor a subsequent provision of the same level may contradict them. Further, a provision of a higher level, except the Constitution itself, may not be contradictory to a promulgating provision.[40] Any contradiction that may arise should be resolved not by the repeal of the higher-level provision but through the amendment of the international treaty or amendment of the higher-level provision itself. The latter solution is more frequent in practice.

2.2 **Community law in the Hungarian constitutional system**

According to the CC Act, once an international norm has been enacted, the Constitutional Court can examine the constitutionality of laws and other legal instruments of state administration and whether they comply with the norm. According to this competence, the Constitutional Court, by means of an *ex post* review, can examine if laws or other legal instruments of state administration are contrary to the Constitution or not. Should the Constitutional Court declare a legal norm unconstitutional, it annuls it. As the Constitutional Court is entitled to interpret laws, it has interpreted the CC Act, including its own competences. In some cases it found that a competence should be interpreted restrictively, while in other instances a more active approach was taken and the competence in question was interpreted broadly. The practice of the Constitutional Court with regard to Community law is not yet wide-ranging. To date there have only been two decisions concerning this issue, which have provoked extensive debates in legal scholarship.[41]

2.2.1 *The first decision: international law, Community law and national law*

In 1997 the Constitutional Court examined its competence of *ex post* review of constitutionality[42] under Article 1(b) of the CC Act. Although this is not spelled out explicitly in the CC Act, the Court held that laws enacting international treaties can

tional law as binding the State. Under Art. 87, however international treaties and provisions ratified are enumerated within legal sources generally binding the state. For the review of certain constitutional provisions see also J. Németh, *supra* n. 22, at p. 91 and L. Bodnár, *supra* n. 12, at p. 25.

[40] E.g., the promulgating provision is a Governmental decree. If it contradicts to an Act of Parliament, the procedure is followed according to the Act on the Constitutional Court mentioned above.

[41] See, Kecskés, László, *Magyarország EU-csatlakozásának alkotmányossági problémái és a szükségessé vált alkotmánymódosítás folyamata.* [Constitutional problems of the Hungarian EU accession and the necessary process of constitutional amendments] (Európai Jog 2003/1); Vörös, Imre, *Az EU-csatlakozás alkotmányjogi, jogdogmatikai és jogpolitikai aspektusai.* [Aspects of the EU accession from the perspectives of constitutional law, legal dogmatics and legal politics] (Jogtudományi Közlöny 2002/9).

[42] Petitioner stated that it is unconstitutional that the CC Act permits only the *ex ante* constitutional review of international treaties. He suggested that the CC should examine the possibility of *ex post* review of promulgating acts of international treaties.

be subject to subsequent examination of constitutionality.[43] These types of laws are, basically, 'normal' acts that can be referred to the Constitutional Court for *ex post* review.

In its decision, the Constitutional Court found that *ex post* review can be extended to the review of the constitutionality of the international treaty becoming part of any law that transposes it. If the Court finds the international treaty or any of its provisions unconstitutional, it declares the unconstitutionality of the act promulgating the international treaty.[44] Interestingly, the Court specifically made the following consideration with regard to Community law:

> 'regarding the relation between international law and national law the dualist transformational system is gradually replaced by a monist system, the direct application of international treaties (international law). According to the so-called monist-adoptive conception, the concluded international treaties, which became part of the national legal system, have primacy over national law, without any enactment of the State. This system is forcibly required by European integration, and this is why those Member States of the EU that use the transformational system apply the EU legislation without transformation and guarantee priority to it, except in the case of the Constitution. [...] Consequently, constitutional courts exercise their power related to constitutional control of norms also in case of Community decisions, which automatically become part of the national legal system.'

The Court referred to the practice of the *Bundesverfassungsgericht*, declaring that

> 'the constitutional control over international treaties is done by the constitutional courts of those countries that follow the dualist transformational system regarding also international treaties that become part of the national legal system by this method. The German Constitutional Court, besides its "natural" exercise of competence of constitutional court related to the subsequent control of norms especially regarding the EU treaties, can not give up a part of its role to protect the constitution, and this role extends over the execution of any kind of sovereignty that is based on the constitution.'[45]

According to the decision of the Constitutional Court, 'the legislative power has to create harmony between the international commitments assumed in the treaties and

---

[43] Decision 4/1997 (22 January) of Constitutional Court. (CC decision) pp. 41-54. It was not obvious according to the former decisions. Cf. Decisions 30/1990 (XII. 15.) AB határozat, (CC decision), and 61/B/1992 AB határozat, (CC decision).

[44] According to Dec. 4/1997 (I. 22.) AB of the Constitutional Court, if any provision of an international treaty were found unconstitutional by the Constitutional Court, it would establish the unconstitutionality of the domestic statute which promulgated the treaty. The decision declaring unconstitutionality has no effect on the obligations assumed by the Republic of Hungary under international law. The legislator must harmonise the obligations assumed under international law and domestic law, and pending this process, the Constitutional Court suspends its proceedings concerning the determination of the date of nullification of the promulgating statute for a reasonable time (ABH 1997, 41).

[45] 4/1997 (I. 22.) AB határozat, (CC decision), ABH 1997, 51-52.

national law, even in case of the need for amending the Constitution.'[46] This decision can be seen as a landmark case in that the Constitutional Court expressly refers to the nature of Community law. The reference to the practice of the German Constitutional Court suggests that the Court considered the 'Constitution-protecting' practice of other European constitutional courts against Community law a good example for Hungary.

2.2.2 *The second decision: Community law*

The second decision is a result of a norm control procedure[47] based on the 1997 decision.[48] In this case, Article 62 of the Europe Agreement signed in Brussels on 16 December 1991 establishing an association between the Republic of Hungary and the European Communities and their Member States (the 'Europe Agreement') promulgated by Act I of 1994[49] was at stake. This provision provides for Community criteria for the authorities supervising the respect of competition law. The Constitutional Court had to make a decision about how these criteria can affect national competition law. The Court held that the Parliament can not implicitly amend the Constitution by concluding or promulgating an international treaty. International agreements can not be effective in the Hungarian legal system where their content would cause a violation of the Constitution. The treaty examined was unconstitutional because the article in question caused the direct effect of Community law criteria, even though at that time Hungary was not yet an EU Member State. As the source of application of these uncertain criteria had not been based on the decision of the Parliament, the legitimate public authority stated in the Constitution that their application violated the principles of popular sovereignty and the rule of law.

> 'In the present decision, the Constitutional Court had to form an opinion on how the legal criteria and principles of Community law may prevail in the Hungarian legal system, on the basis of Article 62 of the Europe Agreement and the Implementing Rules, in the legal field of prohibiting the restrictions of competition. Thus, the construction of enforcing the criteria referred to in Article 62(2) of the

[46] 4/1997 (I. 22.) AB határozat, (CC decision), ABH 1997, 41.

[47] 'The Constitutional Court established earlier that examining the procedure of adopting a statute that promulgates an international treaty – including a review of the powers, authorizations and procedures linked to undertaking the international obligation – is a question of constitutionality falling within the scope of powers of the Constitutional Court. The results of the review may, therefore, form a basis for establishing the unconstitutionality of the promulgating Act of Parliament.' [Dec. 4/1997 (I. 22.) AB, ABH 1997, 42, and in a similar sense, the judgment of the European Court of Justice; ECJ, Case C-327/91 *France* v. *Commission* [1994] ECR I-3641, 3678].

[48] 30/1998 (VI. 25.) 4/1997 (I. 22.) AB határozat, (CC decision), ABH 1998, 220-239 Also available in English: <http://www.mkab.hu/en/enpage3.htm>.

[49] 1994. évi I. törvény a Magyar Köztársaság és az Európai Közösségek és azok tagállamai között társulás létesítéséről szóló, Brüsszelben 1991. december 16-án aláírt Európai Megállapodás kihirdetéséről [Act I of 1994 on the publication of the European Aggreement on the association among the Republic of Hungary and the European Communitites and their Member States, signed on 16 December 1991 in Brussels].

> Europe Agreement as provided for by the Implementing Rules is in the focus of constitutional review. Accordingly, it is a question of constitutionality whether it is possible for the Hungarian Competition Authority to directly apply the norms of domestic law of another subject of international law, of another independent public authority system, and of an autonomous legal system that serves the purpose of regulating legal relations of public law, without having these foreign public law norms made a part of Hungarian law." The Constitutional Court points out that the said criteria of the Community's internal law are qualified as foreign law in respect of the application of law in Hungary, as the Republic of Hungary is not a Member State of the European Union. The underlying legal relations of a public law and official nature – providing for the obligation to assess matters according to Community law criteria – are directly linked to the sovereignty of the state: the right to prohibit the restriction of competition – similar to criminal law or the law related to offences – is within the scope of exclusive jurisdiction of the state authority due to its contents and way of enforcement. Extending beyond the principle of objective territoriality of regulations in this field of law is not acknowledged by international law either. Neither may such regulations be qualified as generally recognized rules of international law, thus they are not covered by the first sentence of Article 7(1) of the Constitution. [...] The Constitutional Court points out that – as a general rule – an international treaty with a generally binding content must be promulgated in an internal source of law in order to make the legal norm contained in the treaty applicable to Hungarian subjects of law. However, the constitutional concern raised by the petition actually lies in the fact that Article 62(2) of the Europe Agreement merely refers to the Community law criteria without having them presented in an international treaty or in the promulgating domestic legal norm.'[50]

It is clear that the Constitutional Court put up constitutional restrictions against Community law and did not let the Hungarian legal system open up to such criteria, the normative content of which is based on the regulations, decisions and related practice of the EU institutions. These reasons were consistent with the domestic legal system prevailing at that time: the Hungarian Republic was not an EU Member State.

One has to take into consideration that until accession, the practice of the Constitutional Court in relation to Community law was reduced to the examination of an ordinary treaty. As an EU Member State, it is obvious that the Constitutional Court has to deal with the supranational norms of Community law in another way. This means that, in accordance with the principle of 'Community loyalty', the Constitutional Court may not jeopardize the effect of rules (including rules of secondary community law) that were introduced or implemented constitutionally. In Hungary, the problem in this respect is that the constitution-making and legislative powers have modified neither the Constitution nor the CC Act in connection with the competences of the Constitutional Court. Therefore, the Constitutional Court

---

[50] 30/1998 (VI. 25.) 4/1997 (I. 22.) AB határozat, (CC decision), ABH 1998, 220-239 Also available in English: <http://www.mkab.hu/en/enpage3.htm>.

itself has to reinterpret its competences.[51] Two ends of possible directions of interpretation are the (values of) activism and self-restriction. If the Constitutional Court chooses activism, it can interpret its competences so that it is the guardian of Community law. This, however, could cause continuous frictions with Luxembourg. In case of restraint based on cooperation, the Constitutional Court would give up its competence under the CC Act in relation to the EU/EC treaties. It could also take the opportunity of asking for a preliminary decision when the constitutionality of a Community provision appears doubtful.

2.2.3 *The new constitutional status of Community law*

In light of the case-law of the Constitutional Court and other constitutional requirements of accession to the EU, the amendment of the Hungarian Constitution related to the country's accession to the EU was passed by the Parliament – as the constituent power – in December 2002 (Act LXI of 2002). The bill amending the Constitution, however, did not deal with all questions, and referred some of them to 'ordinary' legislation. In fact, the bill did not meet modern constitutional standards. Moreover, it damaged the requirement of stability. Because of its deficiencies the bill was revised before being put to Parliament, where it was adopted as Act LXI of 2002 on the amendment of Constitution (the 'Amendment'). This Act introduced a new Article 2/A into the text of the Constitution that took effect on the day of its promulgation. This Article reads as follows:

> 'By virtue of treaty, the Republic of Hungary, in its capacity as a Member State of the European Union, may exercise certain constitutional powers jointly with other Member States to the extent necessary in connection with the rights and obligations conferred by the treaties on the foundation of the European Union and the European Communities (the "European Union"); these powers may be exercised independently and by way of the institutions of the European Union. The ratification and promulgation of the treaty referred to in subsection (1) shall be subject to a two-thirds majority vote of the Parliament.'

From its place in the Constitution under the 'General Regulations', the authorisation article, as a general rule, influences other norms in the Constitution. This is in harmony with the principle of maintaining the consistency and coherency of Constitution.

---

[51] Since the Constitution and the CC Act have not been properly modified (the latter was not modified at all), the CC could examine the harmony of Community and domestic law according to Art. 15(c) CC Act. It is, however, evident from the decision of the Constitutional Court that it refrains from doing so (because this falls within the competence of the European Court of Justice). By virtue of Art. 1(c) CC Act, the Constitutional Court has competence to examine conflicts between domestic law and the EC Treaty as a traditional international treaty. This would not be a problem in itself, since there are constitutional courts for which this may be a constitutional issue, for instance the practice of the Austrian, Belgian and Italian constitutional courts. The Constitutional Court definitely wanted to have such conflicts resolved by courts of law and, finally, by the European courts, which is well demonstrated by point 1.1 of 1053/E/2005, CC Decision.

The European Article in the Amendment set aside the phrase 'transfer/confer of competence'. It emphasized the 'common' exercise of competence with Member States instead of the exercise of competence 'by the institutions'. However, in light of the dynamic evolution of EU law this distinction can be regarded as superfluous and misleading.

The new text of the Constitution sets out the aim of the transfer of competence (to take part as a Member State in the EU) and its limitations (to the extent of fulfilment of duties and exercising rights coming from the Treaties). The Amendment lacks elements which are contained in the constitutions of many Member States to protect sovereignty and fundamental constitutional norms. To that effect, the Amendment could have included a statement such as:

> 'If there is a need for amending the Constitution implied by the transformation of competences described in the Constitution, the amendment shall not amend the provisions of §1, 2, 8, 56 of the Constitution.'

This refers to the following constitutional values: republic form of state, democracy, rule of law, popular sovereignty, principle of public representation, fundamental rights, especially the recognition and the respect of the right to life and human dignity.[52]

In the meantime the Constitutional Court has held that it 'will not treat the founding and amending treaties of the European Union as international treaties even though they arise from treaties.' In the absence of material unconstitutionality, the Constitutional Court does not regard the collision of domestic law and Community law as a constitutional issue in itself. Apparently, this conflict is to be resolved by courts of law. The omission to legislate when such an obligation arises from a founding treaty does not result in the violation of Article 2/A in itself, and in order for this to become a domestic constitutional norm conflict, an extra condition is required, namely that the said omission establishes a substantial unconstitutional situation at the same time, in other words that the omission violates a constitutional norm containing a fundamental right, a fundamental obligation, a prohibition, a guarantee or a competence.[53]

3. The triangular relationship at the legislative level

Legal harmonisation has been a central element of Hungarian legislation for more than a decade. Since EU accession in 2004, Hungarian national law has had to take a different position as regards its approach to EC law. Since then, legal harmonisation

[52] So, following the solution of the German constitution, an 'Ewigkeits-klausel'-like phenomenon would have entered the Constitution, which, however, would not mean the general limit of the amendment of constitution, only the amendment in connection with the transfer of competence.

[53] Blutman, László and Chronowski, Nóra, *Alkotmánybíróság és közösségi jog: alkotmányjogi paradoxon csapdájában* [Constitutional Court and Community Law: falling into the trap of a constitutional paradox] (Európai Jog 2007/4) pp. 17-25.

has been carried out in connection with each newly adopted and published Community act. The whole process is regulated by Government decrees, but the emphasis obviously lies on the compliance with the provisions of the Constitution and Act XI of 1987 on Legislation.[54] As the Minister of Justice and Law Enforcement is responsible for guaranteeing the lawfulness of legislation, he issued Guideline No. 7001/2005 (IK. 8.) concerning law-harmonisation legislation[55] (the 'Guideline'). In what follows, we examine whether the Hungarian legislature fulfils its obligations stemming from membership of the EU.

3.1 Treaties establishing the EC

According to the Guideline,[56] the treaties establishing the European Communities do not formally require any incorporation, since they are sources of Community law. But as they are international treaties as well, they have to be published in the proper domestic legal instrument. This instrument is Act XXX of 2004 on the publication of the 2003 EU Accession Treaty.[57] Thus, primary Community (treaty) law was transferred into the Hungarian domestic legal system in 2004. Since then, from the viewpoint of Hungarian law, it is no longer international law or Community law, but purely national law.

3.2 International agreements concluded by the Community and mixed agreements

As regards international agreements concluded by the Community, the Guideline repeats the findings of the European Court of Justice (ECJ) on the nature and characteristics of these legal instruments in Community law and establishes that there is no need for transformation by a domestic legal norm.[58] The Guideline does not preclude the possibility that for implementing international agreements concluded by the Community, domestic legislation may be necessary. It distinguishes between agreements that have direct effect and those that do not. The Guideline establishes that if the conditions are not present for direct effect, there is a need for legislation,

[54] 1987. évi XI. törvény a jogalkotásról.

[55] 7001/2005 (IK. 8.) IM irányelv a jogharmonizációs célú jogalkotásról.

[56] Guideline, point 162.

[57] 2004. évi XXX. törvény a Belga Királyság, a Dán Királyság, a Németországi Szövetségi Köztársaság, a Görög Köztársaság, a Spanyol Királyság, a Francia Köztársaság, Írország, az Olasz Köztársaság, a Luxemburgi Nagyhercegség, a Holland Királyság, az Osztrák Köztársaság, a Portugál Köztársaság, a Finn Köztársaság, a Svéd Királyság, Nagy-Britannia és Észak-Írország Egyesült Királysága (az Európai Unió tagállamai) és a Cseh Köztársaság, az Észt Köztársaság, a Ciprusi Köztársaság, a Lett Köztársaság, a Litván Köztársaság, a Magyar Köztársaság, a Máltai Köztársaság, a Lengyel Köztársaság, a Szlovén Köztársaság és a Szlovák Köztársaság között, a Cseh Köztársaságnak, az Észt Köztársaságnak, a Ciprusi Köztársaságnak, a Lett Köztársaságnak, a Litván Köztársaságnak, a Magyar Köztársaságnak, a Máltai Köztársaságnak, a Lengyel Köztársaságnak, a Szlovén Köztársaságnak és a Szlovák Köztársaságnak az Európai Unióhoz történő csatlakozásáról szóló szerződés kihirdetéséről <http://www.complex.hu/kzldat/t0400030.htm/t0400030_1.htm – lbj1%22>.

[58] Guideline, point 165.

which is done, as a rule, at Community level. However, if there is an obligation to legislate, it is the Member State (Hungary) that has to approve the necessary legal norms according to its constitutional and other rules.[59]

As to mixed agreements, the Guideline concludes that, since Member States' competences are involved, an internal legislation process must take place. Thus the transformation is to be done via a domestic legal norm, as provided for by Act L of 2005. According to the Guideline, in most cases the powers of the Community or Member States are not strictly outlined. Thus, the internal transposition process must cover the entire international agreement, i.e., the complete agreement has to be enacted in Hungary. This technique may cause some uncertainty in terms of law enforcement, as the scope of Community competences may not be clear, but Member States cannot decide on this matter, as it is within the jurisdiction of the ECJ.[60]

As regards mixed agreements concluded by the 'old' Member States and the Community, some provisions of the Accession Treaty provide for the obligation of accession to these kinds of agreements (e.g., Article 6). As the Guideline states, the legal means of joining these mixed agreements are protocols, the conclusion of which is within the competence of the Council acting on behalf of the 'old' and the 'new' Member States. Therefore, Hungary does not need to sign and confirm the protocols, but must nonetheless enact them via a domestic legal norm. Thus, these mixed agreements must also be enacted,[61] even though some parts of the agreement have already become a part of the Community legal order.

3.3 Agreements concluded under the Second and Third Pillar

Points 173-176 of the Guideline contain provisions on the international agreements concluded under the EU's Second and Third Pillar. They take Article 34(2)(d) of the TEU[62] as a starting point, and determine that this provision enables a Member State to uphold and apply its own constitutional provisions. The Guideline also states that, as a consequence, the parties to these international agreements are the Member States. Thus Hungary has to apply Act L of 2005 with an additional proviso according to which the final determination of the international agreement is to be made according to the decision-making procedure of the Council of Ministers. Nonetheless, for acknowledgment of the binding effect and enactment and publication of the agreement the above-mentioned provisions of Act L of 2005 apply. The same rule applies to the international agreements concluded under Article 34(2)(d) of the TEU before Hungary's accession, as Hungary has undertaken to sign up to these treaties under Article 3(4) of the Accession Treaty.[63]

[59] Ibid., point 166.

[60] Ibid., points 167, 168.

[61] Ibid., point 172.

[62] [...] the Council may [...] d) establish conventions which it shall recommend to the Member States for adoption in accordance with their respective constitutional requirements. Member States shall begin the procedures applicable within a time limit to be set by the Council.

[63] Guideline, point 174.

The *Guideline* cites Article 24 TEU and concludes that the determination of the contracting party is controversial. As stipulated in the Guideline at point 175, neither the Union nor the Council has legal capacity under international law. Thus, the most convincing viewpoint is that the contracting parties are the Member States, which is strengthened by Article 24(6), which states *expressis verbis* that agreements concluded on this legal basis are binding on the institutions of the EU. According to the Guideline, Article 24 TEU simplifies the treaty-making procedure. It does not give legal capacity under international law to the EU, but only gives procedural competence in relation to the negotiation of the treaty in question. The Guideline requires that the treaty-making procedure regulated by domestic rules be followed. Thus, Hungary again has to apply Act L of 2005 with an additional proviso according to which the final determination of the international agreement is done in conformity with the decision-making procedure in the Council.

The same rule applies to the international agreements concluded under Articles 24 and 38 of the TEU before Hungary's accession, as Hungary undertook to sign up to these treaties under Article 6(1) of the Accession Treaty. Provisions of the TEU, however, have to be taken into account.[64] Joining these agreements is done by applying Act L of 2005. This means that a dualist method is applied, so each such agreement is enacted into a Hungarian legal norm, and therefore has no special features of treatment. By its enactment it becomes part of the Hungarian legal system.

In sum, it can be said that Hungary regards international agreements concluded by the Community as Community law, and does not seem to have the intention of upholding a dualist approach towards such international treaties. It is questionable whether, in case of mixed agreements, national enactment is required, since when the Council adopts this act, the agreement becomes binding for Hungary as Community law and can entail a direct effect within the Hungarian legal order. The Hungarian legislature seems somewhat over-insured so as to avoid any risk of non-compliance with international and Community law, as it follows the procedure applicable in case of transposition of international treaties into the national legal system and at the same time provides for the indication in the act that it contains rules that are in harmony with the relevant Community law provisions. Clearly, accession to the EU has resulted in many domestic law-making processes in accordance with the commitment undertaken in the Accession Treaty. It is imperative here to underline the fact that even though these Acts contain international, Community or EU law obligations, they are considered as normal domestic legal norms as they are enacted in a domestic legal instrument and do not have any specific position in the legal hierarchy. There is one exception, though, namely acts that have international treaty elements. The Constitutional Court has special competence in respect of these acts, and acts containing entirely or partly Community or EU law because in these instances the competence of the Hungarian legislature is considerably narrower. It is also vital to note that the principle of *lex posteriori derogat lege priori* cannot prevail regarding these kinds of legal sources.

---

[64] Ibid., point 176.

4. THE TRIANGULAR RELATIONSHIP BEFORE THE HUNGARIAN COURTS

It may be hard to assess the case-law of Hungarian courts, with the exception of the Constitutional Court as it does not belong to the normal judiciary system,[65] in light of the fact that there have not been many cases involving international or Community elements before the courts. Should a court deal with cases that have international relevance, it basically applies national (Hungarian) law. This is because, as has been outlined above, international treaties and sometimes Community legal norms also have legal effect in Hungary only once they have been enacted within a Hungarian legal norm.

The appraisal of case-law on the triangular relationship of international, Community and national law is also rendered more difficult because Hungary has been a Member State of the EU for only four years. Thus, it is not quite certain that judges have modified their way of thinking in adjudicating cases before them. One should not forget that judges reluctantly referred to international agreements even before EU accession. This practice could be justified by reasoning that, due to the dualist system, it is not necessary for the courts to apply international law as they are bound to apply national law, in which the international agreement was enacted. Thus, in judgments one can usually find that the judge has to apply a certain act relating to the enactment of a given international agreement, but one can rarely find any reference in the judgment to doctrines developed by international courts or other law-application bodies in connection with the international agreement.

4.1 Fundamental rights

The judicial approach to fundamental rights is largely determined by the fact that such rights are regulated in the Constitution itself.[66] Therefore international agreements governing human rights issues are part of the Hungarian legal system not only by their enactment by domestic legal norm, but also by the relevant provisions of the Constitution.[67] The provisions of the Constitution on fundamental rights are quite often present in judicial decisions.[68] References in court decisions can be classified as follows: 1) parties intend to strengthen their reasoning by referring to the Constitution, but the final judgment does not deal with the constitutional provision; 2) courts refer to the Constitution without clarifying the relevance of the cited provision of the Constitution for the case in question; 3) the Supreme Court[69] deals

[65] Moreover, its decisions (some translated into English) are available at <www.mkab.hu>, with proper search facilities.

[66] We consider rights as fundamental rights when they are recognised and guaranteed by the Constitution; we refer to rights as human rights when they are regulated and guaranteed at international level.

[67] Harmathy Attila, *Bírói gyakorlat – Alkotmány* [*Case law – Constitution*] (Magyar Jog 11/2004) p. 645.

[68] A. Harmathy, *supra* n. 67, at p. 642.

[69] The Supreme Court is situated at the top of the ordinary judicial system, while the Constitutional Court does not belong to the judicial system; the latter is the 'defender of constitutionality'.

with the relevant rule of the Constitution as a substantive part of the judgment, but it bases the reasoning itself on the particular rules of the given branch of law; 4) the basis of a judgment is the joint interpretation of the Constitution and the particular rules of a branch of law. The number of these types of decisions is, however, limited.[70]

In some judgments judges make reference to international human rights agreements, such as the International Covenant on Civil and Political Rights (ICCPR) and the European Convention on Human rights (ECHR). The ICCPR was brought into the Hungarian legal system by Law Decree No. 8 of 1976 on the enactment of the ICCPR,[71] whereas the ECHR was transposed by Act XXXI of 1993 on the enactment of the ECHR.[72] In the following, some examples will illustrate the practice of Hungarian judges in matters involving international elements.

In one case[73] the applicant filed an application to the Capital Court[74] for registration of a civil organisation he intended to establish. He attached all the necessary documentation, including the statute of the organisation, in which the founders declared that the aim of the organisation was to assist in the acknowledgement of the right of self-determination of homosexual people as a fundamental right. The Court denied the registration and demanded a completion of documents, stating that the name of the organisation (which contained the word 'gay') did not comply with the requirement of accuracy. According to the Court the documentation should contain the name and the age of the members because the Criminal Code does not allow minors to be a member of this kind of organisation. The founders submitted the documents again but without the requested modification of the name or the list of the names and ages of the members. The founders argued that these requirements are contrary to Articles 7(1) and 63(1) of the Constitution declaring the right to association[75] and the anti-discrimination clause of the Constitution,[76] Act II of 1989 on the right to association[77] and the ICCPR. After the denial of registration the

[70] A. Harmathy, *supra* n. 67, at p. 643.

[71] 1976. évi 8. törvényerejů rendelet a Polgári és Politikai Jogok Nemzetközi Egyezségokmánya kihirdetéséről.

[72] 1993. évi XXXI. törvény a az 1950. november 4-én Rómában elfogadott emberi jogok és alapvető szabadságok védelméről szóló Egyezmény kihirdetéséről l.

[73] BH 1995. 246, Legf. Bír. Kpkf. III. 25. 796/1994. sz.

[74] This is a court at second, in some cases at first instance, which has jurisdiction in the capital, Budapest. In certain cases its jurisdiction is exclusive.

[75] Art. 63. (1) On the basis of the right of assembly, everyone in the Republic of Hungary has the right to establish organisations whose goals are not prohibited by law and to join such organisations. (2) The establishment of armed organisations with political objectives shall not be permitted on the basis of the right of assembly. (3) A majority of two thirds of the votes of the Members of Parliament present is required to pass the law on the right of assembly and the financial management and operation of political parties.

[76] Art 70/A. (1) The Republic of Hungary shall respect the human rights and civil rights of all persons in the country without discrimination on the basis of race, colour, gender, language, religion, political or other opinion, national or social origins, financial situation, birth or on any other grounds whatsoever. (2) The law shall provide for strict punishment of discrimination on the basis of Paragraph (1). (3) The Republic of Hungary shall endeavour to implement equal rights for everyone through measures that create fair opportunities for all.

[77] 1989. évi II. törvény az egyesülési jogról.

founders referred the case to the Supreme Court citing the above-mentioned reasons in their plea for remedy. The Supreme Court confirmed the decision of the Capital Court, in which it denied the registration, holding that the right of association, under both the Constitution and the Act on association, can be limited, and that the limitation in the Act is in accordance with the ICCPR. Subsequently, the Court simply interprets Article 67(1) of the Constitution[78] and refers to the relevant provision of the Criminal Code. It makes no reference to the potentially useful decisions of the European Court of Human Rights. Thus, it can be seen again that it is the national law that is applied by the courts, even if it is, originally, an international rule.

In another case[79] the ICCPR was referred to by the Supreme Court in connection to the free movement declared in Article 12.2 of the ICCPR. Pursuant to this provision, everyone is free to leave any country, including his own. A defendant had failed to complete his military service[80] and had not been reported to a relevant military unit; instead he went absent without leave and illegally trespassed the Bulgarian-Turkish border, where he was caught. The defendant was then delivered to the Hungarian authorities. In the meantime, the Act XI of 1992 on the nullification of convictions for certain crimes against the State and public order committed between 1963 and 1989[81] was approved. The defendant submitted a petition for the nullification of his conviction, which was granted by the Capital Court. The Court argued that the illegal trespassing of the border had to be considered as an exercise of the right to free movement as declared in Article 12.2 of the ICCPR; thus the nullification under Act XI of 1992 was justified. The military prosecutor appealed, however, arguing that the trespass could not be regarded as an exercise of the right to free movement. This argument was accepted by the Supreme Court, which referred to Article 12.3 of the ICCPR:

> 'The above-mentioned rights shall not be subject to any restrictions except those which are provided by law, are necessary to protect national security, law and order, public health or morals or the rights and freedoms of others, and are consistent with the other rights recognized in the present Covenant.'

The Court also drew attention to the amended Criminal Code, which criminalized the failure to fulfil military obligations, pointing out that this provision was in accordance with the ICCPR.

In a third case[82] a defendant who could not speak or understand Hungarian was convicted. Under the judgment, the defendant was obliged to pay the cost of

---

[78] In the Republic of Hungary all children have the right to receive the protection and care of their family, and of the State and society, which is necessary for their satisfactory physical, mental and moral development.

[79] BH 1994. 579, Legf. Bír. Stf V. 665/1994. sz.

[80] At that time there was obligatory military service in Hungary involving the obligation to report to have personal data checked and then to join the army.

[81] 1992. évi XI. törvény az 1963 és 1989 között elkövetett egyes állam és közrend elleni bűncselekmények miatt történt elítélések semmissé nyilvánításáról.

[82] BH 1979. 1. Győr Megyei Bíróság Bf. 590/1977. sz.

interpretation and translation from Hungarian to German and vice versa. The County Court of Győr declared that this obligation was contrary to Article 14.3 f) of the ICCPR, which sets forth minimum guarantees in the determination of any criminal charge, including the 'right to have the free assistance of an interpreter if he cannot understand or speak the language used in court.'

A fourth case[83] dealt with the re-regulation of contact between children living in the United States and their father. The County Court made brief reference to Act LXIV of 1991 on the publication of the New York Convention on the Rights of the Child.[84] However, this was done by the County Court not because of the full awareness of the fundamental rights and best interests of the child. According to the Country Court, the problem was that the guardianship court[85] had not revealed all the facts of the case and had not acquired the declaration of the child on the contact. The Supreme Court, however, announced that it is not obligatory to acquire the declaration of the child on the contact either under the New York Convention, or under Act IV of 1952 on marriage and family and guardianship.[86] Again, the Court did not utilize the relevant case-law or doctrines available for these matters.

In this area it is difficult to find any triangular relationship between international, Community and national law. Rather, one can see that Hungary uses the dualist system towards international law and applies national law even if the ECHR could be seen as regional customary law[87] or as part of general principles of Community law.

4.2 The Europe Agreement

One can find some case-law dealing with Act I of the Europe Agreement, Community law (regulations) and the case-law of the ECJ. These cases can be broadly classified into two groups, i.e., cases in which the problem of applying Community law has occurred before and after the accession.

In a significant decision the Supreme Court held that the case at hand had to be decided according to laws in effect at the time of occurrence of the relevant legal procedure. Thus, the applicant referred in vain to an EC regulation, since at the time Hungary was not an EU Member State. Consequently, only the provisions of the Europe Agreement, and not the EC regulation, were applicable.[88] In another case, the Supreme Court also found that Community law cannot be applied to cases, or more precisely to the right to initiate a legal procedure, that occurred before the accession to the EU.[89]

[83] BH 1998. 154, Legf. Bír. Kfv. III. 27.669/1996. sz.

[84] 1991. évi LXIV. törvény a Gyermek jogairól szóló, New Yorkban, 1989. november 20-án kelt Egyezmény kihirdetéséről.

[85] In Hungary it is not a court but a special organ.

[86] 1952. évi IV. törvény a házasságról, a családról és a gyámságról.

[87] J. Wouters and D. Van Eeckhoutte, *supra* n. 1, at pp. 27-28.

[88] EBH 2005. 1375.

[89] Kfv.II.39.203/2004.

In a decision[90] of 4 December 2003, the Supreme Court, ruling only on the given case, referred to a decision of the ECJ.[91] It held that the latter's decisions did not bind the Hungarian courts, but legal principles expounded in its judgments were applicable provided that they could be founded on Hungarian law that was in effect.[92] In this way, the Supreme Court, making use of the quoted case-law of the ECJ, indirectly applied the Sixth VAT Directive to Hungarian VAT rules. This case demonstrates how Community legal sources may be applicable even before the accession.

At least one Hungarian county court has acknowledged the primacy of EC law, and in the case before it applied a Community regulation[93] and Act CXXVI on the implementation of the customs law of the Community.[94] By giving primacy to EC law, the accused persons were acquitted of smuggling, as under the relevant Community law their action could no longer be considered as a crime.[95]

4.3 Other matters

International covenants in international *transportation* by road, air or railway have been part of the Hungarian legal system since the 1960s and 1970s. The International Covenant on International Railway Transportation was enacted by Law Decree No. 9 of 1975,[96] the International Covenant on the Contract on International Transportation by Road was enacted by Law Decree No. 3 of 1971[97] and the International Covenant on International Transportation by Air, known as the Warsaw Convention, was enacted by Act XXVII of 1936, as modified by its Protocol enacted by Law Decree No. 19 of 1964.[98] In this field, courts have not been as reluctant to refer to the above-mentioned Covenants and solved the case applying the covenant almost solely.[99]

A number of problems arose in *criminal law* cases because of the application of criminal law provisions in international agreements, such as war crimes, protection of victims of wars, etc.[100] In these cases, the Supreme Court applied international provisions through the enacting Hungarian laws, in effect paying

[90] Kfv.I.35.057/2002/6.

[91] C-258/95. The reference and the interpretation may have been due to the reference made by the defendant in his claim.

[92] In the case it was the act on VAT.

[93] 2913/92/EEC Regulation.

[94] 2003. évi CXXVI. törvény a közösségi vámjog végrehajtásáról.

[95] County Court of Hajdú-Bihar 1.BF.982/2003.

[96] 1975. évi 9. tvr. a Vasúti Árufuvarozásról szóló Nemzetközi Egyezmény kihirdetéséről.

[97] 1971. évi 3. tvr. a Nemzetközi Közúti Árufuvarozási Szerződésről szóló Egyezmény.

[98] A nemzetközi légifuvarozásra vonatkozó, Varsóban 1929. október 12-én aláírt, az 1936. évi XXVII. törvénnyel kihirdetett egyezmény.

[99] See, BH 1983. 39, Legf. Bír. Gf. III. 30 424/1981. sz. on the application of CIM; BH 1995. 653, BAZ Megyei Bíróság 3. G. 22. 072/1993. – Legf. Bír. Gf. III. 34. 100/1994. sz. on the application of CMR and the Civil Code; BH 1997. 137, Legf. Bír. Gf. III. 30.01/1995. sz. on the application of the Warsaw Covenant and the Civil Procedure Act.

[100] EBH 1992/2. sz. 82, 83 cited by A. Harmathy, *supra* n. 67, at p. 645 and footnote 5.

attention to its nexus at the international law level.[101] One such decision[102] applied and interpreted the provision of an act enacting the Geneva Convention relative to the Protection of Civilian Persons in Time of War, and the act on criminal procedure relative to some crimes committed during the revolution and war of freedom of 1956.

It is apparent that there has been almost no interrelation between international and Community law in Hungarian case-law. This is probably due to the small number of cases dealing with international and Community law. As far as the relationship of national and Community law is concerned, the case-law before accession may indicate an awareness of the necessity of the future application of Community law on the one hand, and the proper law-harmonising activity of the legislature, on the other. After accession, one can recognise a tendency of parties to request that courts apply Community law, with varying success. Further, courts seem to make reference to domestic acts, thus referring to Community law indirectly, since the Hungarian acts refer to the relevant primary law source. Obviously, this practice will develop in the future with regard to Community legal norms having direct effect or being directly applicable.

5. Concluding remarks

The present contribution has examined the triangular relationship between international, Community and national law in Hungary. To do so, it was necessary to start with an interpretation of the relationship between international, Community law and national law from the perspective of constitutional law. The Hungarian Constitution attempts to regulate, not very successfully, this relationship in Articles 2/A and 7. It was found out that the Constitution neither determines the status of Community law in, or its relation to the Hungarian legal system, nor regulates explicitly the position of international law. What is clear is that, on the one hand, primary Community law (i.e., only treaty law) is to be handled according to the aforementioned articles, while on the other hand, the Hungarian legal system adopts a dualist approach towards international law. Thus, the Hungarian legal system is not particularly international-law friendly as far as international agreements are concerned.[103]

---

[101] A. Harmathy, *supra* n. 67, at p. 645.

[102] EBH 1999, 83.

[103] See, the criticism of these articles in more detail; Chronowski, Nóra and Petrétei József, *EU-csatlakozás és alkotmánymódosítás: minimális konszenzus helyett politikai kompromisszum* [EU accession and modification to the Constitution: political compromise instead of minimal consensus] (Magyar Jog 8/2003) pp. 449-466; Chronowski, Nóra, *Integrálódó alkotmányjog. Az Európai Unió és a Magyar Köztársaság alkotmányos rendszerének kapcsolata* [Constitutional law under integration. The relation between the European Union and the constitutional system of the Republic of Hungary], Ph.D. thesis, Manuscript (2004) p. 85.

Many experts have drawn attention to the deficiencies of the Constitution in connection with the nature of international law as a source of law in recent years.[104] Despite this, Article 7(1) of the Constitution has remained unchanged. It may be regarded as a serious omission that this section was not specified in 2002 together with the Amendment, and that a differentiated regulation of the features of Community law and international law, as sources of law, has not occurred. One has to take into consideration the fact that the founding treaties of the European Communities and the European Union and the Accession Treaties, though originally international treaties, are essentially supranational law.

Since we have taken a national-law perspective in this contribution, it can be said in conclusion that international agreements concluded by the Community are Community law, while customary international law remains international law for Member States[105] and thus for Hungary as well. Hungary for its part is ready to comply with Community law obligations, including the implementation at a legislative level of international agreements concluded by the Community. Techniques of enactment of mixed international agreements and reference to the relevant Community law provision are applied by the relevant national organs. As far as the case-law is concerned, it is difficult to evaluate due to the modest amount of Community-relevant case-law. Hungarian judges apply Community law through relevant domestic acts and sometimes by referring to the ECJ case-law, but rarely apply enacted international agreements and almost never apply doctrines developed at the international level. If the standpoint expounded in this contribution is correct, then it may also be said that the relationship between international, Community and national law can be characterised by the expression 'triangular' only from the perspective of Community law. From the perspective of Hungarian law, there exists only a dual relationship between international and Community law as 'foreign law' on the one hand and national law on the other.

[104] See for example, Bodnár, László, 'Alkotmányfejlődés és EU-csatlakozásunk' [Development of Constitution and EU Accession], in Bodnár, László (ed.), *EU csatlakozás és alkotmányozás* [EU accession and constitution making] (SZTE ÁJTK Nemzetközi Jogi Tanszék, Szeged 2001) pp. 5-11.

[105] This is an obvious generalisation; an examination of the constitutional provisions of all Member States would provide an accurate picture.

Chapter 10
UN SANCTIONS AND JUDICIAL REVIEW

Nikolaos Lavranos*

1. Introduction

The implementation of UN Security Council sanctions through the European legal order is a prime example of the europeanisation of public international law. This contribution will analyse the implications of the European Court of First Instance (CFI) rulings in the *Yusuf/Kadi* cases[1] – taking into account the most recent case-law of the CFI and the opinion of Advocate General Maduro in the *Kadi* case[2] – as well as the *Bosphorus* judgment[3] of the European Court of Human Rights (ECtHR) for the availability of judicial review at the European level for private parties affected by UN sanctions.

The starting point of this analysis is the fundamentally important principle of the right to judicial review against all acts of the European Community/European Union ('the EC' and 'EU', respectively), as established by the case-law of the European Court of Justice (ECJ). The CFI summarized this right as follows:

> '121 In this connection, the Court of Justice has stated that *access to justice is one of the constitutive elements of a Community based on the rule of law and is guaranteed in the legal order based on the EC Treaty in that the Treaty has established a complete system of legal remedies and procedures designed to permit the Court of Justice to review the legality of measures adopted by the*

* Dr jur.; LL.M.; Assistant Professor European Law and Senior Researcher International Law. This chapter has been written as part of the research project 'Interaction between International Law and national law' sponsored by the Netherlands Scientific Research Organization (NWO). This is a revised and updated version of my conference presentation. Many thanks to professors Erika de Wet, André Nollkaemper and Jan Wouters for their comments on an earlier draft text. The usual disclaimer applies.

1 CFI, Case T-306/01 *Ahmed Ali Yusuf and Al Barakaat International Foundation* v. *Council of the European Union and Commission of the European Communities* [2005] ECR-II 3533; Case T-315/01 *Yassin Abdullah Kadi* v. *Council of the European Union and Commission of the European Communities* [2005] ECR II-3649.

2 Opinion of AG Maduro in case C-402/05 P *Yassin Abdullah Kadi* v. *Council of the European Union and Commission of the European Communities*, of 16 January 2008, available at <http://curia.europa.eu/jurisp/cgi-bin/form.pl?lang=en>.

3 ECtHR, *Bosphorus Hava Yollari Turizm ve Ticaret Anonim Şirketi* v. *Ireland*, judgment of 30 June 2005, available at <http://cmiskp.echr.coe.int/tkp197/view.asp?item=1&portal=hbkm&action=html&highlight=bosphorus&sessionid=6612317&skin=hudoc-en>.

J. Wouters, P.A. Nollkaemper, E. de Wet (eds.), The Europeanisation of International Law

> *institutions* (Case 294/83 Les Verts v Parliament [1986] ECR 1339, paragraph 23). The Court of Justice uses the constitutional traditions common to the Member States and Articles 6 and 13 of the European Convention for the Protection of Human Rights and Fundamental Freedoms as a basis for the right to obtain an effective remedy before a competent court (Case 222/84 Johnston [1986] ECR 1651, paragraph 18).
>
> 122 *The right to an effective remedy for everyone whose rights and freedoms guaranteed by the law of the Union are violated has, moreover, been reaffirmed by Article 47 of the Charter of fundamental rights of the European Union*, proclaimed on 7 December 2000 in Nice (OJ 2000 C 364, p. 1). Although this document does not have legally binding force, it does show the importance of the rights it sets out in the Community legal order.'[4] [emphasis added]

The central question that will be examined is whether, and if so, to what extent judicial review against acts of the EC implementing UN sanctions is available at the European level and, ultimately, at the national level. The analysis begins by providing a legal framework explaining how UN sanctions are implemented in the Community legal order. This is followed by a commentary on some of the key statements of the CFI in the *Yusuf/Kadi* ruling in the light of the most recent developments, which will be combined with some remarks on the *Bosphorus* judgment of the ECtHR. Finally, the attention will turn towards the national law level, in particular the German Constitutional Court (*Bundesverfassungsgericht*, (BVerfG)) and its approach towards ensuring the right of judicial review against European acts.

2. The legal framework

In the past decade the use of sanctions against States and private parties has rocketed.[5] Whereas in the past sanctions were applied only against States or regimes, more recently the UN Security Council as well as the EU are using 'smart' sanctions that target specific individuals and private organisations. In particular, since the 'war against terrorism' has started, sanctions are targeting individuals and private organisations that are suspected of being involved with terrorist activities.[6] Sanction measures focus especially on the freezing of all financial assets of listed suspects in order to reduce their ability of financing and/or carrying out terrorist activities. However, sanctions are not limited to the freezing of financial assets.

---

[4] CFI, Case T-377/00 *Philip Morris* v. *Commission* [2003] ECR II-1 at paras. 121-122.

[5] See extensively, V. Gowlland-Debbas (ed.), *National implementation of United Nations sanctions: a comparative study* (Leiden, Martinus Nijhoff 2004; Id., *United Nations sanctions and international law* (The Hague, Kluwer Law International 2001).

[6] See, e.g., UN Security Council Resolutions 1333 (2000), 1373 (2001), 1566 (2004), 1611 (2005) all available at <http://www.un.org/terrorism/sc.htm>. Council Common Position 2005/427/CFSP of 6.6.2005 updating Common Position 2001/931/CFSP, OJ 2005, L 144/54; Common Position 2001/931/CFSP, OJ 2001, L 344/93; Common Position 2001/154/CFSP, OJ 2001, L 57/1; Council Regulation No. 2580/2001, OJ 2001, L 344/70.

Rather, they encompass a whole array of measures including, for instance, restrictions on travelling.[7]

After the UN Security Council has decided to impose sanctions, a so-called UN Sanctions Committee is established which supervises the proper implementation of the sanctions in the UN Member States. One of the important tasks of the UN Sanctions Committee in this context is the '(black)listing' of persons and organisations that are to be targeted by the sanctions. Blacklisting means that, on the basis of secret information received by intelligence services of UN Member States, the UN Sanctions Committee draws up a list of suspects to be targeted by the sanctions. Moreover, the UN Sanctions Committee is the only body that can 'delist', that is, remove the names of persons and organisations from the sanctions list. This is done once the UN Sanctions Committee decides unanimously that there is no longer any reason for the individual or organisation to be listed.

The EU, while not being a member of the UN, generally implements the sanctions imposed by the UN Security Council based on Chapter VII of the UN Charter by a two step procedure.[8] First, the EU adopts a common position within the intergovernmental Second Pillar of the Common Foreign and Security Policy (CFSP).[9] Second, in order to give legally binding effect to the common position, the EC adopts a basic Regulation within the First Pillar (the EC Treaty), which is directly applicable in all EU Member States.[10] The subsequent enforcement of the basic Regulation implementing the UN sanction within the EC is entrusted to the European Commission. The European Commission has in particular the task (and the power) of updating automatically the listing of suspected targets in accordance with the list of the UN Sanctions Committee. The Commission performs this task by issuing Commission Regulations.[11]

Thus, a 'communitarisation' of UN Security Council Resolutions within the Community legal order takes place. As a consequence thereof, UN sanctions as implemented by the EC/EU enjoy supremacy over all national law, including constitutional law, of the EU Member States. In addition, the Regulations – that is, the basic Regulation as well as the Commission Regulations – are directly applicable from the moment they are published in the Official Journal of the EU. It should be

[7] See, e.g., UN Security Council Resolutions 1636 (2005), 1591 (2005), all available at <http://www.un.org/Docs/sc/unsc_resolutions05.htm>.

[8] See extensively, N. Lavranos, *Decisions of International Organizations in the European and Domestic Legal Orders of selected EU Member States* (Groningen, Europa Law Publishing 2004); R. Wessel, *The EU's Foreign and Security Policy* (The Hague, Kluwer Law International 1999).

[9] See, e.g., Council Common Position 2005/440/CFSP of 13.6.2005 concerning restrictive measures against the Democratic Republic of Congo and repealing Common Position 2002/829/CFSP, OJ 2005, L 152/22.

[10] See, e.g., Council Regulation (EC) No. 1183/2005 of 18.7.2005 imposing certain specific restrictive measures directed against persons acting in violation of the arms embargo with regard to the Democratic Republic of the Congo, OJ 2005, L 193/1.

[11] See, e.g., Commission Regulation (EC) No. 84/2006 of 18.1.2006 amending Council Regulation (EC) No. 1183/2005 imposing certain specific restrictive measures directed against persons acting in violation of the arms embargo with regard to the Democratic Republic of the Congo, OJ 2006, L 14/14.

noted that the adoption and implementation of UN sanctions, in particular the listing of suspects, take place on a purely executive regulatory power basis. That is, neither on the international, European nor national level is there any involvement of a parliament or other supervisory body. In other words, the UN Security Council – amplified by the supremacy of Community law and direct application of the Regulations – directly influences the national law level and exerts direct force in the sense that the sanctions have to be executed by the national authorities purely on the basis of executive acts.[12]

It is clear that the implementation of UN sanctions through the Community legal order modifies the previously public international law nature of UN sanctions into measures that have obtained EC law characteristics such as supremacy over all national law and direct applicability. At the same time, since the UN sanctions are communitarised into EC law, the ECJ/CFI – which are responsible for the proper application of EC law – come into the picture as a forum to which suspects targeted by UN sanctions could potentially turn to for obtaining judicial review.

3. The CFI's *Yusuf/Kadi* rulings and the ECtHR's *Bosphorus* judgment

3.1 The CFI's *Yusuf/Kadi* rulings

It is not the purpose of this section to analyse the long and complex *Yusuf*[13] /*Kadi*[14] rulings of the CFI, which are currently pending in appeal before the ECJ.[15] Instead, some of the key statements regarding the hierarchy of norms and judicial review that are relevant for our purposes will be discussed in more detail.

In essence, the CFI considered itself not competent to review the validity or legality of UN sanctions since that would result into trespassing upon the prerogatives of the UN Security Council.[16] The CFI is only prepared to review UN Security Council Resolutions with regard to potential violations of *jus cogens*. Moreover, while the CFI explicitly recognised that there is no effective judicial review available at the international law level, which – according to the CFI – has been a deliberate choice of the UN Security Council, affected individuals or

[12] See generally, M. Bulterman, 'Oh, baby, baby, it's a wild world – Over terrorisme financiering, financiële sancties en rechtsbescherming' [Oh, baby, baby, it's a wild world – On financing terrorism, financial sanctions, protection of fundamental rights], 30 *NJCM-Bulletin* (2005), pp. 1069-1084.

[13] CFI, Case T-306/01 *Ahmed Ali Yusuf and Al Barakaat International Foundation* v. *Council of the European Union and Commission of the European Communities* [2005] ECR-II 3533.

[14] CFI, Case T-315/01 *Yassin Abdullah Kadi* v. *Council of the European Union and Commission of the European Communities* [2005] ECR II-3649.

[15] See, OJ 2006, C 48/11, the case is listed as C-415/05 P *Ahmed Yusuf* v. *Council* and OJ 2006, C 36/19, the case is listed as C-402/05 P *Yassin Abdullah Kadi* v. *Council*. See further, M. Karayigit, 'The Yusuf and Kadi judgments: The scope of the EC competence in respect of restrictive measures', 33 *Legal Issues of Economic Integration* (2006), pp. 379-404; C. Tomuschat, 'case-note on Yusuf/Kadi-judgments', 43 *CML Rev.* (2006), pp. 537-551.

[16] CFI, Case T-306/01 *supra* n. 1 *Yusuf*, para. 339.

organisations can use other, diplomatic means through their own governments in order to be delisted by the UN Sanctions Committee.[17] In addition, the CFI argued that the EC is bound by UN Security Council Resolutions *in the same way* as EU Member States.[18] Based on these arguments, the CFI concluded that individuals and organisations that are blacklisted cannot obtain judicial review before the CFI, unless *jus cogens* is violated.

These findings are in stark contrast with the otherwise fundamental rights-minded case-law of the ECJ and CFI. It therefore came as no surprise that the CFI was heavily criticised for essentially refusing to provide any effective fundamental rights protection.[19] Indeed, as will be discussed below in more detail, AG Maduro disagreed with the CFI's *Kadi* judgment, while even before his opinion was published, the CFI itself also realised that it was on the wrong track and thus began to revise its case-law.[20]

3.2 The ECtHR's *Bosphorus* judgment

A couple of months before the CFI issued its ruling in the *Yusuf/Kadi* cases, the ECtHR rendered for the first time a judgment on UN sanctions imposed against the Former Republic of Yugoslavia (FRY) that were implemented through EC legislation.[21] In this case, Bosphorus, a Turkish company, had leased a plane from the state-owned Yugoslav air carrier JAT. The plane was impounded by Irish authorities in accordance with the UN sanctions against the FRY that prohibited, *inter alia*, all air service and related activities when the plane was serviced in Ireland. Bosphorus first challenged the impoundment of the plane before Irish courts. At last instance, the Irish Supreme Court requested a preliminary ruling from the ECJ as to the legality of the Irish measures. The ECJ ruled that substantial limitations of the exercise of fundamental rights and Community law freedoms, such as the right to property and the freedom to pursue a trade or business, must be accepted for the sake of full effectiveness of UN sanctions.[22] Accordingly, the ECJ rejected the claim of Bosphorus by giving precedence to the full effectiveness (*effet utile*) of UN sanctions.

Since the judgments of the ECtHR in the *Cantoni,*[23] *Matthews*[24] and *Senator Lines*[25] cases, we know that the ECtHR is – in principle – prepared to indirectly review the conformity of Community law acts with the European Convention of Human Rights (ECHR).[26] Given the fact that the EC/EU is not a party to the ECHR,

---

[17] Ibid., paras. 314 et seq. and 340.

[18] Ibid., para. 243 (emphasis added).

[19] See, e.g., N. Lavranos, 'UN sanctions and judicial review', 76 *Nordic JIL* (2007), pp. 1-18.

[20] See below for a detailed discussion.

[21] ECtHR, *Bosphorus* v. *Ireland*, *supra* n. 3.

[22] ECJ, *Bosphorus Hava Yollari Turizm* v. *Council* [1996] ECR I-3953, paras. 22-23.

[23] ECtHR, *Cantoni* v. *France*, judgment of 15 November 1996.

[24] ECtHR, *Matthews* v. *UK*, judgment of 18 February 1999.

[25] ECtHR, *Senator Lines* v. *15 EU Member States*, judgment of 10 March 2004.

[26] See further, M. Breuer, 'Offene Fragen im Verhältnis von EGMR und EuGH' [Open issues regarding the relationship between the ECtHR and ECJ], 32 *Europäische Grundrechtszeitschrift* (2005), pp. 229-234; N. Lavranos, *supra* n. 8.

the ECtHR considers itself not competent to review Community law acts directly, but rather only the measures of EU Member States (which are parties to the ECHR) that implement the Community law acts.[27] As EU Member States are obliged to implement Community law, usually without being able to deviate from it, review by the ECtHR of national measures implementing Community law acts boils down to an indirect review of the Community law acts themselves.

On this basis, Bosphorus brought Ireland before the ECtHR for violating Article 1 of Protocol 1 of the ECHR on the right to property when the plane was impounded. In September 2001 the ECtHR admitted the case[28] and, after having transferred it to a Grand Chamber, it took until June 2005 before the ECtHR rendered its judgment.[29] In its *Bosphorus* judgment, the ECtHR again reasserted its competence to indirectly review Community law acts. However, since according to the ECtHR, the level of fundamental rights protection available within the EC is 'comparable' though not 'identical' to the one of the ECHR,[30] the ECtHR would exercise its jurisdiction regarding EC law acts only in cases in which the fundamental rights protection is 'manifestly deficient'.[31] Unfortunately, the ECtHR did not define what constitutes a 'manifestly deficient' fundamental rights protection. In any case, the system of judicial review within the Community legal order as applied and interpreted by the ECJ/CFI – prior to the *Yusuf/Kadi* rulings of the CFI – did not meet the conditions of being 'manifestly deficient'. Thus, the ECtHR is not willing

---

[27] The ECtHR stated in *Matthews* v. *UK*, *supra* n. 24, this point as follows: '32. The Court observes that acts of the EC as such cannot be challenged before the Court because the EC is not a Contracting Party. The Convention does not exclude the transfer of competences to international organisations provided that Convention rights continue to be "secured". Member States' responsibility therefore continues even after such a transfer.' In *Bosphorus* v. *Ireland*, *supra* n. 3, the ECtHR formulated this point as follows: '153. On the other hand, it has also been accepted that a Contracting Party is responsible under Article 1 of the Convention for all acts and omissions of its organs regardless of whether the act or omission in question was a consequence of domestic law or of the necessity to comply with international legal obligations. Article 1 makes no distinction as to the type of rule or measure concerned and does not exclude any part of a Contracting Party's "jurisdiction" from scrutiny under the Convention (*United Communist Party of Turkey and Others* v. *Turkey* judgment of 30 January 1998, Reports, 1998-I, § 29). 154. In reconciling both these positions and thereby establishing the extent to which State action can be justified by its compliance with obligations flowing from its membership of an international organisation to which it has transferred part of its sovereignty, the Court has recognised that absolving Contracting States completely from their Convention responsibility in the areas covered by such a transfer would be incompatible with the purpose and object of the Convention: the guarantees of the Convention could be limited or excluded at will thereby depriving it of its peremptory character and undermining the practical and effective nature of its safeguards (*M. & Co.* at p. 145 and *Waite and Kennedy*, at § 67). The State is considered to retain Convention liability in respect of treaty commitments subsequent to the entry into force of the Convention (*mutatis mutandis*, the above-cited *Matthews* v. *the United Kingdom* judgment, at §§ 29 and 32-34, and *Prince Hans-Adam II of Liechtenstein* v. *Germany* [GC], no. 42527/98, § 47, ECHR 2001-VIII).'

[28] ECtHR, *Bosphorus* v. *Ireland* , decision on admissibility of 13 September 2001.

[29] ECtHR, *Bosphorus* v. *Ireland, supra* n. 3; see also, S. Douglas-Scott, 'case-note on ECtHR's Bosphorus-ruling', 43 *CML Rev.* (2006), pp. 243-254.

[30] ECtHR, *Bosphorus* v. *Ireland*, n. 3, para. 155.

[31] Ibid., para. 156.

to provide for effective judicial review against UN sanctions that have been implemented by the EC and EU Member States except in very unusual circumstances.

In sum, it can be concluded from the above that neither the CFI nor the ECtHR are prepared to review Community law acts implementing UN sanctions unless *jus cogens* is violated or the fundamental rights protection within the EC is 'manifestly deficient' – whatever that may mean.[32]

The question obviously arises: how can this conclusion be reconciled with the fundamental right to judicial review against all Community law acts, as quoted in the beginning of this contribution? By way of analysing the *Yusuf/Kadi* and *Bosphorus* rulings in a more general context, an attempt is made to answer this question below.

4. Analysis

4.1 The application of UN Charter provisions to the EC/EU

From the outset, I would emphasize that whatever creative line of argument is used, at the end of the day the fact remains that the EC/EU is not yet a member of the UN and therefore not formally bound by UN Security Council Resolutions – at least not in the same way as EU Member States, all of which are also Member States of the UN. This submission could be challenged by arguing that, on the basis of Articles 25, 48(2) and 103 UN Charter, the EC/EU is legally bound to implement UN Security Council Resolutions.

However, it is clear from their text that Articles 25[33] and 103[34] UN Charter are addressed to UN Member States only, and are therefore binding solely on them. Thus, all UN Member States must comply with UN Security Council Resolutions and must set aside other conflicting treaty obligations in order to implement those Resolutions. Clearly this obligation does not apply to the EC/EU, even though there are examples where UN Security Council Resolutions also call upon non-UN Member States to execute those Resolutions.[35] In other words, non-UN Member States may choose to implement UN Security Council Resolutions – as the EC/EU regularly does – but non-UN Member States are certainly not legally bound to do so. Thus, while Article 103 UN Charter imposes a legal supremacy of UN law on UN Member States, it does not impose such a supremacy upon the EC/EU. This opinion

---

[32] See generally, C. Costello, 'The Bosphorus ruling of the ECtHR: Fundamental rights and blurred boundaries in Europe', 6 *Human Rights Law Review* (2006), pp. 87-130.

[33] Art. 25 UN Charter reads as follows: The Members of the United Nations agree to accept and carry out the decisions of the Security Council in accordance with the present Charter.

[34] Art. 103 UN Charter reads as follows: In the event of a conflict between the obligations of the Members of the United Nations under the present Charter and their obligations under any other international agreement, their obligations under the present Charter shall prevail.

[35] See, e.g., UN Security Council Resolution 661 (1990), available at <http://www.un.org/Docs/scres/1990/scres90.htm> and recently UN Security Council Resolution 1681 (2006), available at <http://www.un.org/Docs/sc/unsc_resolutions06.htm>.

is in contrast with various authors of Simma's Commentary on the UN Charter.[36] For instance, Delbrück, commenting on Article 25 UN Charter, states that 'the binding force of decisions of the UN Security Council under Art. 25 UN Charter may extend to non-members', although at the same time he admits that there are limits to an extension of the binding force of UN Security Council decisions on non-Member States, such as States enjoying the status of permanent neutrality which 'may not be obliged to comply' with such decisions.[37] Regarding more specifically the binding effect on the EC/EU, Bernhardt, commenting on Article 103 UN Charter, refers to Article 30(6) of the Vienna Convention of 1986 on the law of treaties between States and international organisations or between international organisations, which provides that in case of conflict between obligations under the UN Charter and obligations under a treaty, the UN obligations shall prevail.[38] However, while it cannot be denied that the Vienna Convention of 1986 has some value as an expression of customary international law, it must be emphasized at the same time that the EC/EU has not signed the Convention and that it has not yet entered into force. Thus, it cannot be argued – in my opinion – that Article 30(6) of the Vienna Convention of 1986 imposes supremacy of UN law over EC law. This is especially so because the Community legal order must be considered to be an own legal order that is distinct from the international legal order.[39] As a consequence thereof, the EC/EU can and indeed has determined internally its own hierarchy of norms in which it did not place the UN Charter at the top.[40] Rather, within the Community legal order, the generally accepted hierarchy of norms places the EC/EU Treaties, including the ECHR,[41] at the top as the supreme law of the land within the EC/EU and its Member States. International agreements and decisions of international organisations (IOs) that have become integral part of the Community legal order follow. Then comes secondary EC law (Regulations and Directives), and at the lowest level national (constitutional) law.[42] Consequently, even if one would accept that Security Council Resolutions are binding on the EC and have become

[36] B. Simma (ed.), *The Charter of the UN – A Commentary* (Oxford, Oxford University Press 2002).

[37] J. Delbrück, Commentary on Art. 25, in B. Simma, *supra* n. 36, Art. 25, para. 19.

[38] R. Bernhardt, Commentary on Art. 103, in B. Simma, *supra* n. 36, Art. 103, para. 5.

[39] In Case 26/62 *Van Gend & Loos* [1963] ECR 95, the ECJ stated: 'The conclusion to be drawn from this is that the *Community constitutes a new legal order of international law* for the benefit of which the states have limited their sovereign rights, albeit within limited fields, and the subjects of which comprise not only Member States but also their nationals.' (emphasis added). While in Case 6/64 *Costa* v. *ENEL* [1964] ECR 1141, the ECJ stated that: 'By contrast with ordinary international treaties, *the EEC Treaty has created its own legal system* which, on the entry into force of the Treaty, became an integral part of the legal systems of the Member States and which their courts are bound to apply.' (emphasis added).

[40] See, T. Hartley, *EU Law in a Global Context* (Cambridge, Cambridge University Press 2004) pp. 131 et seq.

[41] Since the judgment in ECJ, Case C-112/00 *Schmidberger* v. *Austria* [2003] ECR I-5659 we know that the ECHR is placed at least at the same level as the EC/EU Treaties and may under certain circumstances even enjoy supremacy over primary EC law.

[42] See for details, N. Lavranos, *supra* n. 8.

integral part of the Community legal order, they still would not enjoy supremacy over the EC/EU Treaties. Rather, they would in any case have to be in conformity with the highest norm within the Community legal order, the EC/EU Treaties. Thus, while the ECJ has acknowledged that secondary EC law should be interpreted as far as possible in light of the international obligations of the EC,[43] this clearly does not mean that UN Security Council Resolutions necessarily enjoy supremacy over the EC/EU Treaties, including fundamental rights as contained in the ECHR.

Then there is of course Article 48(2)[44] UN Charter, which requires UN Member States to effectuate UN Security Council Resolutions also through the international agencies to which they are members. In other words, EU Member States are also to ensure the implementation of UN Security Council Resolutions through the adoption of the necessary measures within the EC/EU. That is especially so since the EC/EU has obtained exclusive competence regarding external trade, including the imposition of sanctions on the basis of Articles 301 and 60 TEC. Moreover, as the CFI stated in its *Yusuf/Kadi* rulings, Article 308 EC must be used as an additional legal basis for the imposition of 'smart' sanctions against specific individuals and organisations.[45] Accordingly, it is clear that the EC/EU is competent to adopt the necessary measures for implementing UN Security Council Resolutions by virtue of the EC/EU Treaties and despite the fact that the EC/EU is not a member of the UN. In fact, the EC/EU has been implementing UN sanctions

---

[43] See, e.g., Case C-162/96 *Racke GmbH* v. *Hauptzollamt Mainz* [1998] ECR I-3655, in which the ECJ stated: '45 It should be noted in that respect that, as is demonstrated by the Court's judgment in ECJ, Case C-286/90 *Poulsen and Diva Navigation* [1992] ECR I-6019, paragraph 9, the European Community must respect international law in the exercise of its powers. It is therefore required to comply with the rules of customary international law when adopting a regulation suspending the trade concessions granted by, or by virtue of, an agreement which it has concluded with a non-member country.' Of course, the question arises whether UN Security Council Resolutions could be considered to be rules of customary international law, which in my view is not the case. In Case C-61/94 *Commission* v. *Germany* [1996] ECR I-3989, the ECJ explicitly stated that: '52 When the wording of secondary Community legislation is open to more than one interpretation, preference should be given as far as possible to the interpretation which renders the provision consistent with the Treaty. Likewise, an implementing regulation must, if possible, be given an interpretation consistent with the basic regulation (see ECJ, Case C-90/92 *Dr Tretter v Hauptzollamt Stuttgart-Ost* [1993] ECR I-3569, paragraph 11). Similarly, *the primacy of international agreements concluded by the Community over provisions of secondary Community legislation means that such provisions must, so far as is possible, be interpreted in a manner that is consistent with those agreements.*' (emphasis added). This applies to international agreements concluded by the EC, which is not the case for the UN Charter, and to secondary EC law (Regulations and Directives) and thus not to primary EC law (EC/EU Treaties). So the question arises whether this obligation to interpret Community law as far as possible in the light of international obligations of the EC is also – by analogy – applicable to UN Security Council Resolutions. In my view that is in principle possible, although it certainly does not imply any kind of supremacy over primary EC law, including ECHR.

[44] Art. 48 UN Charter reads as follows: 1. The action required to carry out the decisions of the Security Council for the maintenance of international peace and security shall be taken by all the Members of the United Nations or by some of them, as the Security Council may determine. 2. Such decisions shall be carried out by the Members of the United Nations directly and through their action in the appropriate international agencies of which they are members.

[45] See, R. Wessel and R. van Ooik, 'case-note on Yusuf/Kadi', 54 *SEW* (2006) pp. 230-246.

for many years.[46] In this way EU Member States fulfil their obligations arising out of Article 48(2) UN Charter.[47] Thus, one could speak of an indirect binding effect of UN sanctions on the EC via its Member States and on the basis of Article 48(2) UN Charter. Indeed, this position is in line with the view of Bryde/Reinisch, commenting on Article 48 UN Charter, who state that

> 'Article 48 (2) correctly creates a legal duty for the UN members in other organizations, since only these members – not the other organizations themselves – can be bound by the Charter. Since the UN's universal membership guarantees that UN members can exert a commanding influence in (almost) all international organizations, such an indirect approach to other international actors seems to be sufficient.'[48]

Clearly, this binding effect cannot be equalized with the formal binding effect of UN sanctions on EU Member States. Therefore, it is in my view not correct to state – as the CFI did in its *Yusuf/Kadi* rulings – that the EC is bound in the same way as EU Member States by UN sanctions. It is precisely for this reason that the whole line of argument of the CFI falls apart. The CFI (and ECJ) is not part of the UN machinery and therefore is able – and indeed required by EC law – to exercise its task of providing judicial review and determining the compatibility of secondary EC legislation (Regulations) that implement UN Security Council Resolutions with primary EC law (EC Treaty and fundamental rights as enshrined in the ECHR).[49]

Indeed, in its recent judgment in the *MOX plant* case,[50] the ECJ strongly emphasized that

> 'an international agreement cannot affect the allocation of responsibilities defined in the [EC/EU] Treaties and, consequently, the autonomy of the Community legal system, compliance with which the Court ensures under Article 220 EC.'[51]

In this sense, the CFI was required by virtue of Article 220 EC to protect the autonomy of the Community legal order by reviewing the EC Regulations implementing UN sanctions and their compatibility with the highest legal norms, that is, the EC Treaty and the ECHR. In this context, I would like to emphasize that this

---

[46] See also the very useful website of the EU on all EC/EU legislation that is currently in force regarding sanctions <http://ec.europa.eu/comm/external_relations/cfsp/sanctions/measures.htm>.

[47] B.-O. Bryde and A. Reinisch, Commentary on Art. 48, in B. Simma (ed.), *The Charter of the UN – A Commentary*, Vol. I (Oxford, Oxford University Press 2002) Art. 48, para. 9.

[48] B.-O. Bryde and A. Reinisch in B. Simma, *supra* n. 36, para. 10.

[49] See generally, M. Payandeh, 'Rechtskontrolle des UN-Sicherheitsrates durch staatliche und überstaatliche Gerichte' [Judicial review of the UN Security Council by national and international courts], 66 *ZaöRV* (2006), pp. 41-71.

[50] ECJ, Case C-459/03 *Commission* v. *Ireland* [2006] ECR I-4635; see generally, N. Lavranos, 'The MOX plant and IJzeren Rijn disputes: Which court is the supreme arbiter?, 19 *Leiden JIL* (2006), pp. 223-246.

[51] ECJ, Case C-459/03 *Commission* v. *Ireland* , *supra* n. 50, para. 123.

review would only concern the EC implementing measures and not the UN Security Council Resolutions themselves, since in my view only the International Court of Justice (ICJ) would be competent to review UN Security Council Resolutions.[52] Accordingly, the CFI could and should have reviewed the compatibility of the EC implementing measures with the EC Treaty and fundamental rights without reviewing the legality of UN Security Council Resolutions as such. Indeed, the fact that there is no judicial review available on the international plane allowing individuals to challenge the legality of being listed – as the CFI itself acknowledged in its *Yusuf/ Kadi* judgments – should have compelled the CFI to exercise its jurisdiction. This is especially so in view of the paramount importance of access to judicial review as one of the fundamental rights ensured within the Community legal order.[53] In this context, it is important to note that the CFI was not required to 'delist' Yusuf and Kadi when exercising its jurisdiction, but rather to conclude that by failing to include an effective system of review of listed suspects, EU Member States failed to meet minimum fundamental rights standards as protected by the EC Treaty and ECHR. Thus, while the Member States remain obliged by virtue of UN law to implement UN sanctions, they are at the same time obliged by virtue of EC law and ECHR law to ensure that the decision of being listed is open to review by an independent body – be it the CFI, ECJ or any other suitable court. In other words, the question is not whether or not the Member States are obliged to implement UN sanctions through the EC/EU, but rather how the Member States do this, in particular how they ensure that minimum procedural rights – which are generally applicable within the EC – are also applied to the implementation of UN sanctions. Therefore, there is no conflict between the obligations of EU Member States arising out of UN law and EC law. Consequently, the argument that Article 307[54] EC would be applicable and thus would enable EU Member States to set aside EC law, i.e., fundamental rights, is irrelevant in this context. The only problem that may arise for EU Member States is having to explain to the UN Sanctions Committee that its decisions on who is listed are subject to judicial review at the European level. If that causes diplomatic problems for EU Member States it is their responsibility to ensure that a system of review is established at the UN level. Therefore, it

[52] See, e.g., B. Sabahi, 'The ICJ's authority to invalidate the Security Council's Decisions under Chapter VII: Legal romanticism or the rule of law?', 17 *New York International Law Review* (2004), pp. 1-52.

[53] See the quote cited at the beginning of this contribution.

[54] Art. 307 EC reads as follows: 'The rights and obligations arising from agreements concluded before 1 January 1958 or, for acceding States, before the date of their accession, between one or more Member States on the one hand, and one or more third countries on the other, shall not be affected by the provisions of this Treaty. To the extent that such agreements are not compatible with this Treaty, the Member State or States concerned shall take all appropriate steps to eliminate the incompatibilities established. Member States shall, where necessary, assist each other to this end and shall, where appropriate, adopt a common attitude. In applying the agreements referred to in the first paragraph, Member States shall take into account the fact that the advantages accorded under this Treaty by each Member State form an integral part of the establishment of the Community and are thereby inseparably linked with the creation of common institutions, the conferring of powers upon them and the granting of the same advantages by all the other Member States.'

must be concluded that the CFI failed to respect and effectively guarantee the fundamental right to judicial review and thus not only violated primary EC law but also ECHR law.[55]

The CFI quickly realised that this conclusion is not acceptable and revised its case-law in subsequent cases involving UN sanctions freezing the financial assets of individuals.

The *Ayadi* case[56] allowed the CFI to re-examine its approach adopted in the *Yusuf/Kadi* cases. While the CFI essentially confirmed the main findings of its *Yusuf/Kadi* judgments,[57] it made several interesting remarks regarding other possible rights of affected individuals to challenge their listing or request a de-listing.

The CFI turned its attention in particular to the Guidelines for the UN Sanctions Committee that were adopted by the UN Security Council. According to the CFI, the UN Security Council intended with the adoption of the Guidelines to take into account as far as possible the fundamental rights, in particular the right to be heard, of the persons listed by the UN Sanctions Committee.[58]

The Guidelines do not confer a right to the affected persons to be heard directly by the UN Sanctions Committee. Instead, they contain only procedures on how affected persons have to address their own State to request a re-examination of the listing and how the requested State has to address the UN Sanctions Committee in order to start the re-examination procedure. In other words, it is essentially part of the diplomatic protection afforded by a State to its own nationals. Despite the fact that such a request to the UN Sanctions Committee is entirely in the discretion of the State and does not, in principle, grant any rights to individuals, the CFI seemed to attach great importance to the Guidelines in two ways.

First, the CFI argued that the Member States of the UN Sanctions Committee are under a legal obligation to act in good faith during the re-examination procedure and are required to cooperate fully with the UN Sanctions Committee.[59] More specifically, the petitioned government, which is best suited to ensure the effectiveness of the procedure for removal from the list, is – according to the CFI – obliged to review all relevant information supplied by the affected person and then has to approach the other UN Member States.[60] Moreover, particular obligations are im-

---

[55] In Case C-112/00 *Schmidberger* v. *Austria* [2003] ECR I-5659, the ECJ repeated again the fundamental importance of the ECHR that even prevails primary EC law. Nonetheless, the situation of non-availability of judicial review seems to be comparable to the one regarding the lack of judicial review of Community law and its conformity with WTO law. See on this aspect, N. Lavranos, 'The Communitarization of WTO Dispute Settlement Reports: An Exception to the Rule of Law' 10 *EFA Rev.* (2005), pp. 313-339.

[56] Case T-253/02 *Ayadi* v. *Council* [2006] ECR II-2139; see also, N. Lavranos, 'case-note on Ayadi', European Human Rights Cases 2006, pp. 1171-1191.

[57] Case T-253/02 *Ayadi* v. *Council* [2006] ECR II-2139, para. 116.

[58] Ibid., para. 140.

[59] Ibid., para. 142.

[60] Ibid., para. 143.

posed on EU Member States.[61] Indeed, since EC Regulations implement UN sanctions, the CFI qualified the possibility of presenting a request of re-examination to one's own government referred to in the Guidelines as 'a right guaranteed not only by those Guidelines but also by the Community legal order.'[62] In addition, this right also flows from the European Convention of Human Rights.[63]

As a consequence thereof, EU Member States must ensure as far as possible that affected persons can present their case before the competent authorities of the petition State, while at the same time Member States are not allowed to refuse to initiate the re-examination procedure solely because the person affected could not provide all relevant information.[64] Moreover, EU Member States are obliged to act promptly to ensure that a case is presented without delay and impartially to the UN Sanctions Committee.[65] In other words, the CFI imposed several concrete legal obligations on the Member States to ensure that listed persons and organisations are effectively able to make a request to their home State, while at the same time that State is obliged to ensure that such a request is properly examined and brought before the UN Sanctions Committee.

Second, the CFI apparently derived from the Guidelines of the UN Sanctions Committee in conjunction with Community law and ECHR law, a legal right for the affected persons and organisations against their home State to have a re-examination procedure started before the UN Sanctions Committee.

Indeed, the CFI reminded us that affected persons have the possibility to bring an action for judicial review based on the domestic law of the petitioned States,

> 'indeed even relying directly on the contested [EC] regulation and the relevant resolutions of the UN Security Council which that [EC] regulation puts into effect, against any wrongful refusal by the competent national authority to submit their cases to the UN Sanctions Committee for re-examination and, more generally, against any infringement by that national authority of the right of the persons involved to request the review of their case.'[66]

Moreover, in line with the general case-law of the ECJ, in the absence of Community procedural law, national procedural rules for effectuating rights conferred by Community law cannot be less favourable than those governing rights which originate in national law and they cannot render virtually impossible or excessively difficult the exercise of rights conferred by Community law.[67] In other words, affected individuals must have the possibility to let a refusal of a petitioned government to make a request for a de-listing to the UN Sanctions Committee be reviewed by a domestic court.

---

[61] Ibid., para. 144.
[62] Ibid., para. 145.
[63] Ibid., para. 146.
[64] Ibid., paras. 147-148.
[65] Ibid., para. 149.
[66] Ibid., para. 150.
[67] Ibid., para. 151.

Thus, the CFI attempted to compensate the obvious and acknowledged lack of effective judicial review at the international and European law level by imposing specific legal obligations on EU Member States to handle any petition for requesting a delisting from the UN Sanctions Committee properly and by ensuring that affected persons can turn to domestic courts to review the way diplomatic protection was afforded. This ruling represented a major shift of the CFI's position as adopted in its *Yusuf/Kadi* rulings.

The CFI continued on this new path in its *OMPI* judgment[68] by distinguishing the *OMPI* case from the *Yusuf/Kadi* cases on the basis of the following reasons:

> '99 It is, moreover, appropriate to mention the aspects which distinguish the present case from the cases which gave rise to the judgments in *Yusuf* and *Kadi*, where it was held that the Community institutions were not required to hear the parties concerned in the context of the adoption and implementation of a similar measure freezing the funds of persons and entities linked to Osama bin Laden, Al-Qaeda and the Taleban.
>
> 100 That solution was justified in those cases by the fact that the Community institutions had merely transposed into the Community legal order, as they were required to do, resolutions of the Security Council and decisions of its Sanctions Committee that imposed the freezing of the funds of the parties concerned, designated by name, without in any way authorising those institutions, at the time of actual implementation, to provide for any Community mechanism whatsoever for the examination or re-examination of individual situations. The Court inferred therefrom that the Community principle relating to the right to be heard could not apply in such circumstances, where a hearing of the persons concerned could not in any event lead the institution to review its position (*Yusuf*, paragraph 29 above, paragraph 328, and *Kadi*, paragraph 29 above, paragraph 258).
>
> 101 In the present case, by contrast, although Security Council Resolution 1373 (2001) provides inter alia in Paragraph 1(c) that all States must freeze without delay funds and other financial assets or economic resources of persons who commit, or attempt to commit, terrorist acts or participate in or facilitate the commission of terrorist acts, of entities owned or controlled directly or indirectly by such persons, and of persons and entities acting on behalf of, or at the direction of, such persons and entities, it does not specify individually the persons, groups and entities who are to be the subjects of those measures. Nor did the Security Council establish specific legal rules concerning the procedure for freezing funds, or the safeguards or judicial remedies ensuring that the persons or entities affected by such a procedure would have a genuine opportunity to challenge the measures adopted by the States in respect of them.
>
> 102 Thus, in the context of Resolution 1373 (2001), it is for the Member States of the United Nations (UN) – and, in this case, the Community, through which its Member States have decided to act – to identify specifically the persons,

[68] Case T-228/02 *Organisation des Modjahedines du peuple d'Iran (OMPI)* [2006] ECR II-4665.

> groups and entities whose funds are to be frozen pursuant to that resolution, in accordance with the rules in their own legal order.'[69]

As a result of this difference between the *OMPI* case on the one hand and the *Yusuf/ Kadi* cases on the other hand, the CFI was able to come to the following conclusion:

> '107 Since the identification of the persons, groups and entities contemplated in Security Council Resolution 1373 (2001), and the adoption of the ensuing measure of freezing funds, involve the exercise of the Community's own powers, entailing a discretionary appreciation by the Community, the Community institutions concerned, in this case the Council, are in principle bound to observe the right to a fair hearing of the parties concerned when they act with a view to giving effect to that resolution.
>
> 108 It follows that the safeguarding of the right to a fair hearing is, as a matter of principle, fully applicable in the context of the adoption of a decision to freeze funds under Regulation No 2580/2001.'[70]

In other words, in the *OMPI* judgment the CFI introduced a distinction as to whether the names are put on the freezing list by the UN Sanctions Committee or by EU Member States. If the latter place the names on the list full judicial review by the CFI is available, whereas if the former places the names on the list there is no judicial review available.

While such a distinction allowed the CFI to provide for judicial review in some cases, it makes this right entirely dependent on factors which are unpredictable and thus arbitrary and discriminatory. That is especially the case because at the end of the day all names are provided for by UN Member States and their intelligence services to the UN Sanctions Committee. Therefore, this distinction does not do away with the still lacking right of full judicial review.

As the CFI itself realised this, it continued to strengthen the procedural rights of individuals targeted by UN freezing sanctions in its subsequent *Sison*[71] and *Al Aqsa*[72]-rulings, which (rightly so) barely have any resemblance with its *Yusuf/Kadi* judgments. Accordingly, the CFI concluded that:

> '219 The applicant has not only been unable effectively to make his views known to the Council but also, given the lack of any statement, in the decision originally challenged or in the contested decision, of the actual and specific grounds justifying those decisions, has not been placed in a position to make good use of his right of action before the Court, given the aforementioned links

---

[69] Ibid.

[70] Ibid.

[71] Case T-47/03 *Sison* v. *Council*, judgment of the CFI of 11 July 2007, available at <http://curia.europa.eu/jurisp/cgi-bin/form.pl?lang=en>.

[72] Case T-327/03 *Stichting Al-Aqsa* v. *Council*, judgment of the CFI of 11 July 2007, available at <http://curia.europa.eu/jurisp/cgi-bin/form.pl?lang=en>.

> between the guarantees of the rights of the defence, of the obligation to state reasons and of the right to an effective legal remedy. It is to be borne in mind that the possibility of regularising the total lack of a statement of reasons after an action has been brought is now considered in the case-law to be prejudicial to the rights of the defence and is therefore prohibited (see paragraph 186 above).
> […]
>
> 226 In conclusion, the Court finds that no statement of reasons has been given for the contested decision and that the latter was adopted in the course of a procedure during which the applicant's rights of the defence were not observed. What is more, the Court is not, even at this stage of the procedure, in a position to undertake the judicial review of the lawfulness of that decision in light of the other pleas in law, grounds of challenge and substantive arguments invoked in support of the application for annulment.
>
> 227 Those considerations cannot but lead to the annulment of the contested decision, in so far as it concerns the applicant.'[73]

Thus, the CFI reversed its flawed case-law within a timeframe of two years. That the CFI's *Yusuf/Kadi* case-law was indeed unacceptable from the point of view of Community law was confirmed by the Opinion of AG Maduro in the appeals proceeding of the *Kadi* case.[74]

AG Maduro was radical in his dismissal of the reasoning of the CFI in the *Kadi* case. First of all, he underlined that the EC is a legal community that respects the rule of law and fundamental rights. Secondly, he explained that the EC is not automatically obliged to follow UN sanctions; rather it is EC law and in last instance the ECJ which decide how to implement international obligations. In doing so, legal principles of EC law and fundamental rights must be observed. Legal protection against acts of EC institutions and the Member States are part and parcel of these fundamental rights that the EC and therefore also the CFI and ECJ need to protect. The AG concluded that the CFI ruling needs to be set aside and that the EC Regulation should be annulled in regard to the applicant Kadi. He also suggested that the ECJ should make use of the possibility of giving final judgment in this case, rather than refer the matter back to the CFI. In short, he finds that UN sanctions can only be implemented if legal protection is sufficiently warranted. It is hoped that the ECJ will follow the opinion of the AG and puts an end to the flawed legal reasoning of the CFI.

In sum, it can be concluded from the above that judicial review against UN sanctions is in practice very difficult to obtain from the ECJ/CFI – unless the ECJ completely overrules the CFI's case-law. Moreover, the ECtHR seems somewhat reluctant to step into this lacuna. In essence, it seems that the ECtHR applies a sort of '*so lange*' test (as long as) regarding the review of Community law acts which is quite similar to the test applied by the BVerfG concerning the review of the consti-

---

[73] Case T-47/03 *Sison* v. *Council, supra* n. 71.

[74] Opinion of AG Maduro in Case C-402/05 P *Yassin Abdullah Kadi* v. *Council of the European Union and Commission of the European Communities*, of 16 January 2008, *supra* n. 2.

tutionality of Community law with German constitutional law.[75] This '*so lange*' test means that as long as the EC/EU provides a level of fundamental rights protection that is comparable to that of the ECHR, as is currently the case, the ECtHR will – in principle – not review (indirectly) Community law acts. This hands-off attitude of the ECtHR leads us finally to the national law level, which could provide for judicial review as *ultima ratio*.[76]

4.2 National courts as *ultima ratio*

Whereas at first sight, one would think that due to the supremacy of EC law and ECJ/CFI case-law over national law and national courts, national law and national courts are of little help, the recent debate between the ECJ and the BVerfG illustrates that national courts will not always follow blindly and automatically the exclusive authority of the ECJ. The debate between the ECJ and the BVerfG concerns the legal nature and effect of the Third Pillar in general and Third Pillar Framework Decisions in particular.[77] So, while the following section does not relate to UN sanctions, it illustrates a possible means by which national courts could act as the ultimate protector of fundamental rights when European courts fail or are unwilling to do so. It will become apparent that the ECJ and the BVerfG have very different opinions on the legal status and effect of Third Pillar Framework Decisions, which has also consequences for the issue of whether, and if so, to what extent national courts still have jurisdiction to decide on the validity of Framework Decisions independently from the ECJ, and thus would be able to deviate from the ECJ.

In the *Pupino* case,[78] the ECJ and AG Kokott[79] rightly emphasized the strong similarities between EU Framework Decisions and EC Directives, i.e., legally binding on Member States as to the results, which require the national courts of the Member States to interpret national law as far as possible in the light of the EU Framework Decision and thus accept the unity and consistency of the whole European legal order.[80] This implies that Third Pillar Framework Decisions enjoy – just as EC Directives enjoy – supremacy over national law, and also that the ECJ

---

[75] See generally, N. Lavranos, 'Das So lange-Prinzip im Verhältnis EGMR und EuGH' [The So-lange-Principle in the relationship between the ECtHR and ECJ], 41 *Europarecht* (2006), pp. 79-92.

[76] See the interesting insights of former BVerfG-judge Jaeger who is now ECtHR-judge: R. Jaeger, 'Menschenrechtsschutz im Herzen Europas' [Fundamental rights protection in the heart of Europe], 32 *Europäische Grundrechtszeitschrift* (2005), pp. 193-204; E. Hey, R. de Lange, and P.A.M. Mevis, 'De transnationale dialoog tussen rechters: verschillende interpretaties van Europese en nationale grondrechten' [The transnational dialogue between judges: different interpretations of European and national fundamental rights], 80 *Nederlands Juristenblad* (2005), pp. 1734-1736.

[77] See, C. Tomuschat, 'Ungereimtes – Zum Urteil des BVerfG vom 18.7.2005 über den Europäischen Haftbefehl' [Unresolved issues – on the German Constitutional Court's judgment on the European Arrest Warrant], 32 *Europäische Grundrechtszeitschrift* (2005), pp. 453-460; M. Adam, 'Die Wirkung von EU-Rahmenbeschlüssen im mitgliedstaatlichen Recht' [The effect of EU Framework Decisions in domestic law], 16 *Europäische Zeitschrift für Wirtschaftsrecht* (2005), pp. 558-561.

[78] Case C-105/03 *Maria Pupino* ECR [2005] I-5285.

[79] Opinion of AG Kokott in Case C-105/03 *Maria Pupino* ECR [2005] I-5285.

[80] See already N. Lavranos, *supra* n. 8, Chapter 5.

has final jurisdiction to interpret the validity and legality of Third Pillar Framework Decisions.

In contrast, the BVerfG, in its ruling concerning the implementation of the EU Framework Decision on the European Arrest Warrant[81] (published shortly after the *Pupino* judgment of the ECJ), emphasized the differences between the more democratically and judicially controlled supranational First Pillar and the predominantly intergovernmental Third Pillar with much less developed democratic and judicial control mechanisms. As a consequence thereof, while the BVerfG has accepted in its *bananas* judgment[82] the final authority of the ECJ regarding the First Pillar, in its *European Arrest Warrant* judgment it did not accept the final authority of the ECJ regarding the Third Pillar. More specifically, the BVerfG underlined that the legal effect of EU Framework Decisions cannot be equalised with that of EC Directives, i.e., superseding completely the fundamental rights enshrined in the German constitution.[83] Thus, the BVerfG concluded that EU law cannot limit the fundamental rights guaranteed by the German constitution.[84] Therefore, the BVerfG continues to retain a reserve jurisdiction regarding Third Pillar measures.

While not agreeing with the view of the BVerfG that EU law (Third Pillar) is part of the public international law order rather than being part of the Community legal order, what is important to note for our purposes is the willingness of the BVerfG to continue to exercise its jurisdiction in spite of the exclusive jurisdiction of the ECJ in policy areas that are much less democratically and judicially controlled than the First Pillar. In other words, the BVerfG does not accept that it has to act like a 'robot' and follow blindly and automatically the ECJ without reserving some of its jurisdiction as a back-up system should the European system fail to provide sufficient protection of fundamental rights. It is exactly for these reasons that national courts must exercise their jurisdiction and provide judicial review against acts implementing UN sanctions when the European courts (ECJ/CFI and ECtHR) fail or are unwilling to exercise their jurisdiction effectively. After all, in a democratic society based on the rule of law, every individual should be able to effectively challenge all measures adopted by governmental organs before a proper court.

5. Conclusions

From the preceding discussion the answer to the question raised at the beginning appears clear: the current absence of judicial review against UN sanctions before the European courts (ECJ/CFI and ECtHR) cannot be reconciled with the fundamental right to judicial review that is to be ensured by the European courts. Until the current case-law is modified to the advantage of affected individuals, national

[81] BVerfG, 2 BvR 2236/04 (European Arrest Warrant), judgment of 18.7.2005, available at <http://www.bundesverfassungsgericht.de/entscheidungen.html>.

[82] BVerfGE 2 BvL 1/97 (bananas), judgment of 7.6.2000, available at: <http://www.bundesverfassungsgericht.de/entscheidungen.html>.

[83] BVerfG, 2 BvR 2236/04 (European Arrest Warrant), judgment of 18.7.2005, para. 80.

[84] Ibid., para. 118.

courts of EU Member States are seemingly the last hope. Indeed, De Wet and Nollkaemper have argued that national courts should – as *ultima ratio* – review UN Security Council Resolutions since the ICJ does not provide for any judicial review for individuals.[85] Similarly, since the European courts (ECJ/CFI and ECtHR) apparently only provide judicial review in extremely limited cases, national courts are called upon to take up this task and fulfil the legal obligations arising out of the ECHR. Indeed, as the BVerfG rightly pointed out, the exercise of jurisdiction by domestic courts is particularly relevant for Third Pillar legal measures that are adopted under the intergovernmental regime, with its very limited democratic and/or judicial control mechanisms. In my view, the same applies even more so with regard to UN Security Council sanctions that have been implemented by EC/EU measures, since they are adopted under a regime that contains even less democratic and/or judicial control mechanisms.

On a more general level, the analysis of the CFI's *Kadi/Yusuf* rulings showed that the CFI was clearly mistaken – from the point of view of Community law – to assume that EC/EU is bound by UN Security Council Resolutions in the same way as EU Member States. The CFI was equally wrong to place UN law at the top of the hierarchy of the Community legal order, thereby granting UN law supremacy over primary EC law. The bottom line remains that the EC/EU is not a member of the UN and therefore is able – and indeed required by its own indispensable basic principles – to ensure that fundamental rights and the rule of law are always respected. That is exactly the message of AG Maduro.

Even though it must be admitted that in its most recent case-law, the CFI has made quite a turnaround towards protecting fundamental rights more seriously, it must be emphasized that the CFI continues to fail to provide judicial review in case the UN Sanctions Committee places the names on the freezing list. However, it seems to me that it is only a matter of time until this case-law will be applied in all cases involving UN sanctions, since it should not matter for the level of effective protection of fundamental rights who is providing the names for the freezing list. In sum, it can only be hoped that the ECJ will follow AG Maduro, thereby bringing the protection of fundamental rights back where they belong.

However, should the CFI/ECJ fail to protect fundamental rights appropriately – as has been clearly the case in the *Yusuf/Kadi* cases, domestic courts remain obliged to step in and fill up this lacuna. Indeed, that is exactly what AG Mengozzi recently has argued in his Opinion in the *Segi* case, which involved so-called 'EU-autonomous sanctions'.[86]

In sum, it can be concluded that whereas at the beginning of the europeanisation of UN sanctions, fundamental rights were systematically sacrificed for the sake of the

[85] E. De Wet and A. Nollkaemper, 'Review of Security Council Resolutions by national courts', 45 *GYIL* (2002), pp. 166-202.

[86] Opinion AG Mengozzi in Case C-354/04 P *Gestoras Pro Amnistia et al.* v. *Council* and Case C-355/04 *Segi et al.* v. *Council* [2007] ECR I-1579.

'war against terrorism', now it seems that the times have changed by putting the protection of fundamental rights first, especially a genuine right to judicial review against all acts.

Chapter 11
EUROPE, AMERICA AND THE 'UNITY' OF INTERNATIONAL LAW

Joost Pauwelyn*

1. Implications of 'europeanisation' of public international law for the unity of international law: the question, and what asking it implies for Europe

Is international law 'europeanised'? If so, what are the implications of such 'europeanisation' for the unity and coherence of international law? To the neutral observer, international law could be europeanised on at least two levels:

(1) Europe may have a particular impact on, or approach to, international law that distinguishes it from the rest of the world;
(2) European courts in Luxembourg or the Member States, or both, could be receiving, applying and interpreting international law in a manner that is different from non-European courts or international tribunals.

At both of these levels (Europe writ large v. European courts), the link between the europeanisation of international law, on the one hand, and the debate on unity or fragmentation of international law, on the other, is readily made:

(1) If European courts apply and interpret international law in one way, the risk arises that other courts – be they international tribunals or national courts outside Europe – take a different view. This could be seen as a threat to the unity of international law, in the sense of different courts interpreting the same international law differently (section 2).
(2) Similarly, a distinct European approach to international law raises the specter of fragmentation, in particular, a European versus an American view of international law (section 3).

* Professor of International Law, Graduate Institute of International and Development Studies, Geneva. Some ideas in this chapter have been further developed in a book entitled *Optimal Protection of International Law, Navigating between European Absolutism and American Voluntarism*, forthcoming with Cambridge University Press, 2008.

J. Wouters, P.A. Nollkaemper, E. de Wet (eds.), The Europeanisation of International Law

The fact that Europeans even ask the question – i.e., does a European model of international law threaten the unity of the international system? – unearths a more fundamental underlying current in European international law circles: A post-modern anxiety to openly defend and export a 'European' model of international law.[1] This reluctance is fed by the critical legal scholar's charge that '[i]nternational law is a European tradition ... [which] imagines itself as universal'[2] and fears of neo-colonialist reproaches especially by developing countries, of the kind that Europe would normally direct against so-called American unilateralism or imperialism.[3]

In the United States, in contrast, defence of national interests and a US model of international law are unabashedly pursued.[4] Even so-called internationalists within the US legal academy argue for US commitment to international law as a means to promote US values and hegemony.[5] The fact that the United States, including its courts, might thereby exert a distinct influence on international law is seen as a plus, even a goal, not a threat to the 'unity' of international law. Witness recent discussions in the United States on the Alien Tort Statute[6] and the applica-

[1] On this European model, see Jeremy Rifkin, *The European Dream, How Europe's Vision of the Future is Quietly Eclipsing the American Dream* (New York, Penguin 2004).

[2] Martti Koskenniemi, 'International Law in Europe: Between Tradition and Renewal', 16 *EJIL* (2005) pp. 113-124, at p. 113.

[3] For a perfect anecdote confirming such European fears, see Philippe Sands, *Lawless World: America and the Making and Breaking of Global Rules* (New York, Viking Penguin 2005), recounting his visit to Tehran University and talk there about the *Pinochet* case. Sands decided to simply recount the facts of the case for fear that 'the Court's decision not to recognize Pinochet's claim to immunity would be taken as a further example of the colonialist/imperialist tendency endemic in British culture, including its legal culture, and an inability to refrain from meddling in the internal affairs of Chile, another state' (at p. 223). To Sands' great surprise, however, in students' reactions to the talk, 'criticism was directed not at the House of Lords but at me, why did I not embrace the case as a great moment for international law and the cause of human rights? ... It was striking that international law had provided a common language to explore complex moral and political issues faced by just about every country in the world' (at p. 224). Similarly, talk about human rights or environmental protection in the world of international trade is too often and easily portrayed as a Northern hegemonic agenda imposed on poor Southern countries. But clearly, even if such talk is at times thinly disguised protectionism, it is not as if developing countries are waiting to violate human rights or have a value-system or unstoppable urge to torture or enslave their people and to pollute their surroundings.

[4] See Jack Goldsmith and Eric Posner, *The Limits of International Law* (New York, Oxford University Press 2005), whose theory is that 'international law emerges from states acting rationally to maximize their interests, given their perception of the interests of other states and the distribution of state power' (at p. 3).

[5] See Leila Nadya Sadat, 'An American Vision For Global Justice: Taking The Rule Of (International) Law Seriously', 4 *Washington University Global Studies Law Review* (2005) p. 328, at p. 331 ('the United States needs to take its commitment to the rule of law to the global stage, thereby playing to American strengths, enhancing American legitimacy and moral authority, and perpetuating the leadership role that the United States has historically exercised in the conduct of international affairs. As the hegemon presiding over – and benefiting the most from – the global economy, the United States has both a vital interest in maintaining the stability of that system and a responsibility to ensure that the system is fair').

[6] When, for example, the scope of the *Alien Tort Statute* is discussed in US legal academia, the pros and cons of American courts enforcing international law at the request of aliens and mostly against aliens center around the language and history of the statute, US federalism and constitutional law and US national interests in the world, *not* the risk of US courts expressing a distinct view of international

tion of international law by the US Supreme Court.[7] Both debates center on the extent to which international law encroaches on US sovereignty. That 'American' applications of international law might threaten the 'unity' of international law is never mentioned.[8]

Along similar lines, Europe ought to overcome its post-modern anxiety, realise that the 'European model' has much to contribute to the future development and shaping of international law and without regrets pursue a 'European' agenda based on European values and interests.[9] Frontal attacks on US foreign policy, including a Europe-wide position against a particular candidate in US Presidential elections, have proven to be counter-effective. The better approach would be to engage the United States with equal weapons, that is, with a positive European agenda steadfastly pursuing European values and interests. For Europe to define and defend such European agenda will, in the long-term, strengthen rather than undermine the unity of international law. For one thing, it will remind us how much Europe and America continue to have in common both in terms of values and the challenges they face.[10]

Crucially, however, any such European agenda must avoid the extremes of European idealism, or what I will call European normativism. Of equal importance,

---

law and thereby disproportionately contributing to the future of international law and threatening its 'unity'.

[7] See, for example, Thomas H. Lee, 'The U.S. Supreme Court as Quasi-International Tribunal: Reclaiming the Court's Original and Exclusive Jurisdiction over Treaty-Based Suits by Foreign States against States', 104 *Columbia Law Review* (2004) p. 1765, arguing that the US Constitution grants original jurisdiction to the US Supreme Court for claims by foreign countries against individual US states and invoking as one of the main arguments in favour of such jurisdiction the prospect that the US Supreme Court could thereby become the *primus inter pares* of international tribunals. Contrast this to Piet Eeckhout, 'Judicial Enforcement of WTO law in the European Union', 5 *JIEL* (2002) p. 93, pointing out, as an argument to *deny* direct effect, that by giving direct effect to WTO law, the ECJ could easily become the most important court for the interpretation of the WTO and in doing so could in fact come into competition with the WTO Appellate Body.

[8] At most, the openness, for example, of the US Supreme Court to enforce certain international norms under the *Alien Tort Statute* is seen as an attempt by the US judiciary to amplify its powers as against other domestic actors. See Julian Ku and John Yoo, *Beyond Formalism in Foreign Affairs: A Functional Approach to the Alien Tort Statute*, University of California at Berkeley School of Law, Boalt Hall Public Law and Legal Theory Research Paper Series, Research Paper No. 652141 (2005), at p. 2 ('We believe that the Court was reluctant to end federal judicial participation in the development and enforcement of CIL for unstated functional, policy, or pragmatic reasons, which have also been unexplored in the academic debate').

[9] As Koskenniemi puts it (*supra* n. 2, at p. 115): 'The fact that international law is a European language does not even slightly stand in the way of its being capable of expressing something universal. For the universal has no voice, no authentic representative of its own. It can only appear through something particular; only a particular can make the universal known. A danger and a hope are involved. The danger is that of mistaking one's preferences and interests for one's tradition – and then thinking of *these* as universal, a mistake we Europeans have often made.'

[10] Even the late Jacques Derrida, shortly before his death, pointed at Europe's return to the tradition of international law and institutions as the world's best hope: G. Borradori, *Philosophy in Times of Terror, Conversations with Jurgen Habermas and Jacques Derrida* (Chicago, University of Chicago Press 2003) at p. 116-119). For a view stressing the commonalities between Europe and the US, see Timothy Garton Ash, *Free World* (New York, Random House 2005).

it must skirt the excesses of American realism or what I will refer to as a purely transactional approach to international law. Taking these realist and idealist extremes seriously – that is, Europeans taking American critiques of international law seriously and Americans honestly examining the 'European dream' – and subsequently finding a middle ground between the transactional and normative approach to international law, and developing the American and European model, is one of the greatest challenges for us international lawyers in the 21st century. We must move beyond the shouting games over the International Criminal Court and the Kyoto Protocol,[11] and end the *débat de sourds* between Kantian cosmopolitans based in Europe and the increasingly vocal conservative international legal academy in the United States. This chapter is a modest attempt in that direction.

2. Is the application of international law by European courts a threat to the unity of international law?

This section does not discuss the appropriateness of European courts (be it the European Court of Justice (ECJ), or domestic courts) applying or giving 'direct effect' to public international law, be it customary international law, WTO law, the European Convention on Human Rights or the Biodiversity Convention. Doing so raises serious questions of democratic legitimacy, especially if international law is automatically supreme to all domestic law. In addition, direct effect goes to the heart of the balance of powers, first, internally between the judiciary and the legislative/executive branches of government and, second, externally between countries giving direct effect to international law and those that do not.[12] Rather, this section assumes that European courts do refer to international law – be it through direct application or the method of 'consistent interpretation' of domestic law with international law[13] – and queries the impact of such reference on the unity of international law.

The perspective adopted in this section is, therefore, a purely international one, that is, from the perspective of international law, is the risk of inconsistent

---

[11] For a stimulating example, see Jutta Brunnee, 'The United States and International Environmental Law: Living with an Elephant', 15 *EJIL* (2004), p. 617 and most of the other articles in that issue's Symposium on the United States and International Law.

[12] Along those lines, I have expressed doubts about giving direct effect to WTO law in domestic courts. See Joost Pauwelyn, 'The Transformation of World Trade', 104 *Michigan Law Review* (2005) pp. 1-66, available at <http://www.law.duke.edu/fac/pauwelyn/pdf/world_trade_6nov04.doc> (describing the lack of direct effect of WTO law in domestic courts as an 'exit option' for WTO Members which enabled the strengthening of the WTO dispute process, limits the need for 'voice', facilitates political agreement on new WTO rules and offers a democratic safety valve) and Joost Pauwelyn, 'A Typology of Multilateral Treaty Obligations: Are WTO Obligations Collective or Bilateral in Nature?', 14 *EJIL* (2003) pp. 907-951, especially at p. 948 (arguing that WTO provisions are bundles of bilateral relationships, not collective or *erga omnes partes* obligations; as a result, flexibility in their implementation and remedies scheme is permissible and may actually operate as a democratic safety valve).

[13] See, for example, ECJ, Case 104/81 *Hauptzollamt Mainz* v. *C.A. Kupferberg & Cie KG a.A.*, [1982] ECR 3641 and ECJ, Case C-106/89 *Marleasing SA* v. *La Comercial Internacional de Alimentación SA*, [1990] ECR I-4135.

interpretations (in particular, between European courts and international courts) a valid reason for domestic courts and/or the ECJ not to refer to public international law?

2.1 A more effective international law outweighs the risk of inconsistent interpretations

At a most basic level, to argue that the application of international law by European courts threatens the unity of international law[14] is like saying that the application of Dutch law by Amsterdam courts threatens the unity of Dutch law.[15] Of course international law should applaud its application in European courts. It extends the relevance and impact of international law from the international to the domestic scene. As the domestic legal system is backed-up by a more effective enforcement mechanism, it also strengthens the implementation of, and compliance with, international law. From that perspective, the risk of inconsistent interpretations is only a side effect, a potential cost that is dwarfed by the immediate benefits of a more robust international law.

After all, what is the alternative? For European courts not to apply international law at all, because of the risk of inconsistent interpretations? Thus presented, one may be choosing between two evils: either (1) apply international law and risk inconsistent interpretations or (2) ignore international law altogether.[16] In my view,

[14] See, for example, in respect of the ECJ applying WTO law, A. Rosas, 'Annotation to C-149/96, Portugal v. Council', 37 *CMLR* (2000) p. 797, at p. 812 ('Interpretations on individual provisions handed down by various national courts could pose serious problems for the overall system, notably as there is no possibility for national courts to obtain a ruling by the WTO bodies that are in charge of dispute settlement'); M. Bronckers and P.J. Kuijper, 'The WTO in the European Court of Justice', 42 *CMLR* (2005) p. 1313, ('One must admit that serious practical problems may arise in relation to the coordination of interpretation. The lack of any equivalent for the preliminary ruling procedure in the WTO could lead to great inequality between the members of the organisation in the implementation of the WTO rules'); A. von Bogdandy, 'Legal Equality, Legal Certainty, and Subsidiarity in Transnational Economic Law', in A. von Bogdandy, P.C. Mavroidis, and Y. Mény (eds.), *European Integration and International Co-ordination* (The Hague, Kluwer Law International 2002) pp. 13-37, at p. 30 et seq. (arguing that the risk of divergent judicial interpretations is one of legal equality) and M. Krajewski, *Verfassungsperspektiven und Legitimation des Rechts der Welthandelsorganisation (WTO)* [Constitutional perspectives and legitimacy of WTO law] (Berlin, Duncker & Humblot 2001) at p. 63 et seq. and p. 270 (pointing at the absence of a mechanism to settle discrepancies between WTO dispute rulings and national court rulings on WTO provisions as a reason to exclude direct effect of WTO law in all Members of the WTO).

[15] Dutch law does, of course, have a Supreme Court. Yet, this Supreme Court does not intervene in all cases and the fact that multiple courts in Holland apply and interpret one and the same Dutch law is not normally seen as a big issue.

[16] This reminds me of the choice that WTO panels must make: either (1) apply WTO law together with other international law (e.g., environmental or human rights treaties) and risk making the wrong or an inconsistent interpretation of those treaties, or (2) apply WTO law in a legal vacuum and completely ignore other international law. If one is a human rights activist, for example, should not the former approach be advocated? See Joost Pauwelyn, 'The Role of Public International Law in the WTO: How Far Can We Go?', 95 *AJIL* (2001) pp. 535-578 and Joost Pauwelyn, *Conflict of Norms in Public International Law, How WTO Law Relates to Other Rules of International Law* (New York, Cambridge University Press 2003).

however, from the standpoint of international law,[17] the cost-benefit analysis is readily made: rather bolster the implementation and effectiveness of international law and accept the risk of contradictory interpretations, than live a life of complete neglect in the legal venues that matter the most (i.e., domestic courts).

With sovereignty concerns in mind, and to facilitate acceptance of international norms on as wide a base as possible, international law has always accepted a degree of discretion when it comes to its implementation in domestic law (witness the freedom of nations to adopt either a monist or a dualist approach). The risk of inconsistent interpretations fits within this long-recognised discretion.

To argue that, for unity's sake, the interpretation of international law should be the exclusive domain of international courts and tribunals is, therefore, more of a hegemonic project to defend the turf of international lawyers against the intrusion of domestic actors,[18] than an agenda to defend international law as such.[19] It reminds one of the human rights activist arguing against the application of human rights treaties by WTO panels,[20] or of the International Court of Justice (ICJ) judge crying foul at the creation of specialised international tribunals for fear that such tribunals may hold a different view on general international law and thereby undermine the unity of the system.[21]

---

[17] This calculus from a standpoint other than that of international law (e.g., looked at from the perspective of domestic law) may, of course, be different. Weighing concerns of democratic legitimacy and balance of powers pointed at earlier, one may well conclude *not* to give direct effect to international law. See *supra* n. 12.

[18] P.J. Kuijper (formerly European Commission official and Director at the WTO) emphasized, for example, the existence of a distinct WTO dispute mechanism and the threat of inconsistent interpretations as arguments to deny direct effect of WTO law in the ECJ (see *supra* n. 14). Given his position within the European Commission, one could, indeed, argue that by submitting such arguments he tried to protect the power of the European Commission against ECJ interference, and to keep the WTO level (where the European Commission enjoys extensive powers and discretion) distinct and separate from the domestic EC legal system (where the Commission is subject to more stringent checks and balances). The same could be said about A. Rosas' Annotation, *supra* n. 14 (written at a time where he was still a European Commission official, not an ECJ judge as he now is). Recall, however, that I am skeptical about giving direct effect to WTO law, but not because of an alleged risk of inconsistent interpretations (see *supra* n. 12).

[19] See Martti Koskenniemi, *Global Legal Pluralism: Multiple Regimes and Multiple Modes of Thought*, Harvard Presentation, 5 March 2005, 5 ('Unity is a hegemonic project. It seeks the predominance of *my* perspective, *my* institution. Against this, we are accustomed to depicting the world – or some aspect of it – as oppressively homogeneous, ruled by a totalizing logic of power, globalization, empire').

[20] See *supra* n. 16 and contributions in Thomas Cottier, Joost Pauwelyn and Elizabeth Burgi, *Human Rights and International Trade* (New York, Oxford University Press 2005). Although application of human rights by WTO panels would clearly bolster the impact of human rights, quite a number of human rights activists have, however, argued against such approach. They want to reserve 'their' domain of human rights exclusively to human rights bodies and fear the hijacking of their turf by trade lawyers who, in their view, would interpret human rights with a free-trade bias.

[21] See Judge Jennings, 'The Role of the International Court of Justice', 68 *BYIL* (1997) p. 58, Judge Schwebel, *Address to the Plenary Session of the UN General Assembly* (26 October 1999) and Judge Guillaume, *The Proliferation of International Judicial Bodies: The Outlook for the International Legal Order*, Speech to the Sixth Committee of the UN General Assembly (27 October 2000), both available at <http://www.icj-cij.org/icjwww/ipresscom/iprstatement.htm>.

2.2 The bright side of 'judicial competition' and its prerequisites: judicial curiosity, dialogue and tolerance

That reference to international law may occasionally lead to inconsistent rulings on the same question of international law is not necessarily the end of the system of international law. On the contrary, it may be an engine for reflection, refinement and further development of international law. After all, in domestic legal systems as well, different lower courts may issue inconsistent interpretations on the same question of domestic law and it often takes years or decades for the highest court to intervene, the court often waiting until the discussion has sufficiently matured.

The absence of a preliminary or advisory ruling system linking domestic courts to the relevant international tribunal and, *a fortiori*, a type of Supreme Court for international law, means that the international system may lack the clarity and hierarchical structure of the internal European system (where national courts of the Member States can request preliminary rulings on questions of EC law from the ECJ, an ECJ which is, moreover, generally seen as hierarchically superior to domestic courts). At the same time, the unstructured interaction between domestic and international courts, and domestic courts amongst themselves, avoids supremacies that are carved in stone and enables a healthy judicial competition in which the best interpretation is likely to surface (along the lines of 'regulatory competition' or the 'laboratory of ideas' tolerated, even encouraged, in the 50 states of the United States). In most, if not all, cases the benefits of this flexibility outweigh the costs of strict hierarchy, a hierarchy which would, first, be difficult to set up (imagine the United States or France agreeing to the establishment of a World Supreme Court) and, second, costly to implement as it would stifle diversity between States and between the different branches of international law.

In addition, preliminary references by national courts from (potentially) 190 countries to, for example, the ICJ or the WTO Appellate Body would risk long delays, overburdening those international tribunals and, perhaps most important of all, raise questions of democratic accountability and sovereignty far beyond those currently expressed against international organisations.

Today's multi-layered governance structure – national, international and transnational – is of such complexity that clear-cut hierarchies between institutions have become illusive.[22] In that sense, the messy interaction between domestic and international courts – with its inherent risk of contradiction – may be a blessing (that stimulates change and refinement of international law) rather than a curse (that would somehow undermine the very foundations of international law).[23] What is needed to nurture this interaction between courts on issues of international law is

[22] See Gunther Teubner and Andreas Fischer-Lescano, 'Regime Collisions: The Vain Search for Legal Unity in the Fragmentation of Global Law', 25 *Michigan Journal of International Law* (2004) pp. 999-1046.

[23] See in this respect Christian Joerges' theory of 'deliberative supranationalism' to replace the current EU supremacy approach (Christian Joerges, *Rethinking European Law's Supremacy: A Plea for a Supranational Conflict of Laws*, on file with author).

not strict hierarchies or delineated reference systems, but an open and robust judicial dialogue premised on a minimum of judicial curiosity and tolerance toward other legal regimes and actors.[24]

As much as strict unity smells of hegemony (in our case, as pointed out earlier, international lawyers protecting their turf against domestic actors or specialised international tribunals), equally, self-contained fragmentation (here, refusal by courts to take account of other international rules or rulings) is often inspired by a superiority complex or hegemonic project. Closing one's doors to international law – as the ECJ arguably did in the 1972 *Dyestuffs* judgment[25] or the GATT did in the 1990s *Tuna/Dolphin* cases[26] – can easily be interpreted as an attempt to give identity and autonomy to 'my' regime as one that towers above all others.

2.3 Three techniques to avoid inconsistent interpretations

Finally, the risk of truly divisive and lasting inconsistencies of interpretation can be mitigated, if not altogether avoided, by three commonly used techniques.

First, one court (say, the ECJ) can refer to the rulings of other courts (say, the ICJ, the European Court of Human Rights (ECtHR), or the WTO Appellate Body). For example, in recent cases where the Luxembourg courts referred to customary international law, such as *Poulsen*, *Racke* and *Opel Austria*,[27] reference was made to ICJ judgments. In relation to the European Convention on Human Rights (ECHR), the ECJ has also been 'careful to ensure that its case-law on fundamental rights conforms to the case-law of the European Court of Human Rights.'[28] Although such 'reference' must not automatically imply 'deference', deviation ought to be rationally explained so as to enable and foster judicial dialogue, as the Ap-

---

[24] Even within the EC system such tolerance without strict rules is at play, especially between the ECJ and the Member States' highest constitutional courts (see the *Solange* case-law and J.H.H. Weiler's notion of 'constitutional tolerance').

[25] ECJ, Case 48/69 *Imperial Chemical Industries Ltd.* v. *Commission of the European Communities* [1972] ECR 619.

[26] Tuna – Dolphin I, Panel Report of 3 September 1991, DS21/R and Tuna – Dolphin II, Panel Report of 20 May 1994, DS291R.

[27] ECJ, Case C-286/90 *Anklagemyndigheden* v. *Peter Michael Poulsen and Diva Navigation Corp.* [1992] ECR I-6019; ECJ, Case C-162/96 *A. Racke GmbH & Co.* v. *Hauptzollamt Mainz* [1998] ECR I-3655 and CFI, Case T-115/94 *Opel Austria GmbH* v. *Council of the European Union* [1997] ECR II-39.

[28] Jan Wouters and Dries Van Eeckhoutte, *Giving Effect to Customary International Law Through European Community Law*, K.U. Leuven University, Institute for International Law, Working Paper N. 25 (2002) at 28, with footnote 118 referring to specific cases such as ECJ, Case C-270/99 P *Z* v. *European Parliament* [2001] ECR I-9197, para. 24 (process within a reasonable period); ECJ, Case C-274/99 P *Connolly* v. *Commission of the European Communities* [2001] ECR I-1611, paras. 39, 41, 49 and 51 (freedom of expression). See also H.G. Schermers, 'European remedies in the field of Human Rights', in C. Kilpatrick, T. Novitz and P. Skidmore (eds.), *The Future of Remedies in Europe* (Oxford, Hart 2000) p. 205, at p. 205 ('Notwithstanding the absence of any formal binding Treaty commitments, the Court of Justice in fact considered the Community bound by the Convention. For the interpretation of the Convention it takes the interpretation by the European Court of Human Rights into account, and in fact it follows its case-law wherever possible').

peals Chamber of the International Criminal Tribunal for the Former Yugoslavia did when disagreeing with the ICJ's standard of control required for state attribution.[29]

A second tool to avoid inconsistent interpretations is for European courts to seek expert advice on the relevance and meaning of public international law and other treaties, preferably from the bodies in charge of those particular treaty regimes. Along those lines, WTO panels, for example, seek the advice of other international organisations and secretariats on a regular basis (e.g., the Codex Alimentarius Commission, WIPO or the World Customs Organization).[30]

Third, where national courts of one treaty party (say, the ECJ) consistently apply, for example, certain WTO provisions in deviation from WTO rulings, or contrary to what another WTO Member considers the correct interpretation, such other WTO Member can always challenge the national court practice directly before a WTO panel. In the *Matthews* case, the ECtHR as well has, at least implicitly, expressed a willingness to control the compliance by EU institutions with the ECHR on the premise that EU Member States, all of whom ratified the ECHR, cannot evade their obligations through the EC.[31]

In the end, the idea of an organic, interactive dialogue between courts may be too much for traditionally trained European civil lawyers who regard hierarchy and strict divisions of competence as the hallmarks of a legal system. The approach may be more palatable, though, for common law lawyers. This brings me to the next level of this chapter, namely the apparent or real contrast between a European and an American approach to international law and its impact on the unity of international law.

3. Is there a European and an American approach to international law? If so, does this threaten the unity of international law?

This section summarises the conventional view of a stark divide between a European and an American approach to international law. It also offers examples to indicate that this divide may be less severe than usually thought. Most importantly, the section uses the example of the reception of international law in domestic courts in Europe and the United States to illustrate that transatlantic positions on international law have been, and continue to be, influenced as much by relative power and internal institutional features that change over time and apply equally across the Atlantic, as by an inherent substantive disagreement between Europe and America on international law. The section ends with a research agenda to find adequate middle ground between the largely theoretical but analytically useful extremes of a strictly

[29] *Prosecutor* v. *Dusko Tadic*, International Criminal Tribunal for the Former Yugoslavia: In the Appeals Chamber, Case No. IT-94-1-A (15 July 1999).

[30] See Joost Pauwelyn, 'The Use of Experts in WTO Dispute Settlement', 51 *International And Comparative Law Quarterly* (2002). pp. 325-364.

[31] ECtHR, *Matthews* v. *United Kingdom*, judgment of 18.2.1999 [GC].

normative approach to international law (European idealism) and a purely transactional view of international law (American realism).

3.1 Conventional wisdom on a European versus an American approach to international law

Although there is, obviously, not one single European view, nor necessarily one single American view on any particular question, conventional wisdom holds that, generally speaking, Europe and the United States have fundamentally different approaches to international law, what it is and what it can achieve. Whilst European governments agreed to lock themselves into a new EU Constitution, the 2004 Presidential candidates in the United States gained their biggest applause when pledging not to be constrained by the UN or any other 'global test'.[32] Europe championed the creation of the International Criminal Court (ICC) and adherence to the Kyoto Protocol, the United States continues to object to both. European courts, both in Luxembourg and in the EU Member States, have long accepted the idea of referring to foreign and international laws, including the supremacy of EC law. In contrast, the slightest nod to foreign and international norms by American courts is critically received as an abdication of US autonomy.[33]

Based on the same generalisations, international legal scholarship is equally divided across the Atlantic. With limited exceptions, European legal scholars approach and analyse international law in largely the same way they analyse domestic law. They take its independent normative value and constraints for granted and often make abstraction of politics and power. In Europe, the need for cooperation

[32] For a representative sample, see Robert Kagan, *Paradise and Power: America and Europe in the New World Order* (New York, Knopf 2003) and Jeremy Rifkin, *The European Dream: How Europe's Vision of the Future is Quietly Eclipsing the American Dream* (New York, Jeremy P. Tarcher Penguin 2004).

[33] See, most eloquently, the dissents by Justice Scalia in *Roper* v. *Simmons* (03-633) 112 S. W. 3d 397 ('Though the views of our own citizens are essentially irrelevant to the Court's decision today, the views of other countries and the so-called international community take center stage ... More fundamentally, however, the basic premise of the Court's argument – that American law should conform to the laws of the rest of the world – ought to be rejected out of hand') and *Sosa* v. *Alvarez-Machain* (03-339) 542 U.S. 692 (2004) 331 F.3d 604 ('The notion that a law of nations, redefined to mean the consensus of states on *any* subject, can be used by a private citizen to control a sovereign's treatment of *its own citizens* within *its own territory* is a 20th-century invention of internationalist law professors and human-rights advocates ... We Americans have a method for making the laws that are over us. We elect representatives to two Houses of Congress, each of which must enact the new law and present it for the approval of a President, whom we also elect. For over two decades now, unelected federal judges have been usurping this lawmaking power by converting what they regard as norms of international law into American law'). See also the Bill introduced before the US House of Representatives in March 2004 whose only provision was that judicial determinations regarding the meaning of the laws of the United States should not be based in whole or in part on judgments, laws, or pronouncements of foreign institutions unless such foreign judgments, laws, or pronouncements are incorporated into the legislative history of laws passed by the elected legislative branches of the United States or otherwise inform an understanding of the original meaning of the laws of the United States (108th Congress, 2d Session, H. Res. 568).

and international governance is mostly a given, the question is only how best to legitimise it. In this exercise many Europeans see the need to 'constitutionalise' international law in pursuit of the Kantian ideal of cosmopolitan law separated from politics as far as possible (hence, an extreme example of what I call the European normative approach to international law).[34]

In the United States, in contrast, the academic picture is quite different. With limited exceptions, the debate of whether international law is really law remains as hot as ever.[35] In addition, many scholars (in particular, the current younger generation of international lawyers) regard international law as merely a pattern of behaviour that is driven by self-interested, rational actors and reflected in law, not constrained by law.[36] From this perspective, international law can, at best, be explained as a patchwork of contract-type, cost-benefit analyses aimed at enhancing economic welfare or political support at home. On this view, countries can pick-and-choose from this patchwork depending on the national interest of the day and the 'coalition of the willing' which can be found to support it[37] (hence, what I call the American transactional approach to international law). In this exercise, international cooperation, if feasible and needed in the first place, must be legitimised by national sovereignty, preferably through the interface of domestic, democratic politics. If not, international law is 'unacceptable to a free people'.[38]

3.2 Counter-examples

Although the above-explained transatlantic divide over international law surely has truth to it, counter-examples are available. At a most basic level, the claim that 'international law is a European tradition' is certainly true when considering its 17th century founders (such as Grotius) and its subsequent development from the Treaty of Westphalia up to World War I. Evaluating the 20th century, however, there can be no doubt that the main instigator and staunchest defender of the international system was the United States. Without US leadership, there would not have been a UN, World Bank, IMF or, for that matter, WTO as we now know it.

Evaluating some of the specifics of EC-US positions, within the WTO, for example, European governments have dragged their feet as much as (if not more than) the United States when it comes to implementing adverse dispute rulings (consider only the *Hormone beef*[39] and *Bananas*[40] disputes). The conduct and tac-

---

[34] See, for example, E.U. Petersmann, *Constitutional Functions and Constitutional Problems of International Economic Law* (Fribourg, Westview Press 1991).

[35] See John Bolton, 'Is There Really 'Law' in International Affairs?', 10 *Transnational Law and Contemporary Problems*, (2000) pp. 2-48 and E. Posner, 'Do States Have A Moral Obligation to Obey International Law?', 55 *Stanford Journal of International Law* (2003) p. 1916.

[36] See *supra* n. 4.

[37] See Richard Pearl, 'United They Fall', *The Spectator*, 22 March 2003.

[38] J. Bolton, *supra* n. 35, at 9.

[39] EC – Hormones, Appellate Body Report, adopted 13 February 1998, WT/DS26/AB/R.

[40] EC – Bananas, Appellate Body Report, adopted 25 September 1997, WT/DS27/AB/R.

tics of the EC in its relations with potential accession candidates,[41] the countries with which it negotiates association agreements and its former colonies[42] are, in turn, not that different from those engaged in by the United States at a worldwide level, the only difference being that the EC operates from a regional hegemonic position, the United States as the world's hegemon.

Equally, although their domestic constitutions point in that direction, domestic courts in Europe have failed to take customary international law seriously and hardly ever apply it in practice.[43] More prominently, the ECJ's refusal to give 'direct effect' to WTO agreements has been severely criticised by most European law scholars. Some of those scholars have also voiced disagreement with the ECJ's restrictive application of customary international law.[44]

Conversely, if one takes the Bush administration's quest for individual freedom in all corners of the world at face value, it might be mistaken for Kant's liberal theory of international law as, according to one prominent Kantian international lawyer, 'Kant includes freedom (respect for individual autonomy under the rule of law) as the first tenet of international ethics.'[45]

Equally, any attempt to read beyond the critique of international law by an increasingly skeptical US legal academy,[46] shows just how receptive US courts, in particular the US Supreme Court, have been toward foreign and international law. *Lawrence* v. *Texas* (2003),[47] for example, declared unconstitutional state laws prohibiting homosexual sodomy, in part, by considering decisions of the ECtHR. *Sosa* v. *Alvarez-Machain* (2004)[48] left the door open for suits by aliens against alien or US individuals or companies based on claims of violation of

---

[41] See the EC's demand that Croatia hand over suspects to the ICTY before accession talks can start.

[42] See the EC's imposition of countervailing duties just a few days after it signed the EEA agreement with Austria in *Opel Austria*; the EC's negotiation of free trade agreements with ACP countries, to replace the Lomé Conventions, as well as the EC's new scheme to grant preferences to developing countries (so-called GSP) where extra benefits are conditioned on accession by the developing country concerned to a series of human rights, labor and environmental agreements. All EC association agreements equally have a human rights and democracy clause, conditioning EC benefits to compliance with human rights and democratic values.

[43] See Jan Wouters, 'Customary International Law before National Courts: Some reflections from a continental European perspective', 4 *Non-State Actors and International Law* (2004) pp. 25-38 (at p. 25: 'When looking into the application given by national courts to customary international law in continental Europe, one cannot escape to find a paradox, namely a remarkable difference between the general rule and its actual application').

[44] J. Wouters and D. Van Eeckhoutte, *supra* n. 28, at pp. 21-22.

[45] Fernando R. Teson, *A Philosophy of International Law* (Boulder, Westview Press 1998) at p. 3, and also at p. 7: 'The Kantian thesis, then, can be summarized as follows: observance of human rights is a primary requirement to join the community of civilized nations under international law'. Violation of human rights can, in other words, form the basis for intervention into the domestic affairs of another country.

[46] Although surely, Koskenniemi's lament that '[t]he international law professor is an almost extinct species at United States law schools' (see *supra* n. 2, at p. 117) must be an exaggeration.

[47] *Lawrence* v. *Texas* (02-102) 539 U.S. 558 (2003) 41 S. W. 3d 349.

[48] *Sosa* v. *Alvarez-Machain*, *supra* n. 33.

> 'a norm of international character accepted by the civilized world and defined with a specificity comparable to the features of the 18th-century paradigms we have recognized [i.e., violation of safe conducts, infringement of the rights of ambassadors, and piracy].'

In *Simmons* v. *Roper* (2005),[49] the majority cited foreign sources of law – including provisions of the International Covenant on Civil and Political Rights for which the United States has tabled an explicit reservation, and the Convention on the Rights of the Child, which the United States has not even ratified – as further support for the Court's own views of what punishments violate the Eighth Amendment ('cruel and usual punishments', in cases ordering the death penalty for anyone under 18 years old). In another instance Bush himself went as far as ordering his native Texan courts to respect the ICJ decision in *Avena*.[50] As a recent study on more than 200 years of Supreme Court practice in the area concludes,

> 'the Court's citation of foreign sources of law in recent years is not "unprecedented" as Justice Scalia implies, but ... citation to foreign sources of law is increasing in the modern era.'[51]

Finally, when so-called neo-conservatives in the United States make statements such as 'claims that "international law" has binding and authoritative force ultimately ring either hollow or unacceptable to a free people',[52] are they not taking international law more seriously than traditional European scholars? By raising what are, in my view, valid questions of democratic accountability in the making and enforcement of international law, and in giving unconditional direct effect and supremacy to international law over domestic law, at least those conservative US scholars have realised that modern international law has changed considerably: it really matters (i.e., penetrates the realm of day-to-day domestic affairs) and is for real (e.g., is increasingly enforced). Hence, 'a free people' must continuously ex-

---

[49] *Roper* v. *Simmons*, *supra* n. 33.

[50] *Case Concerning Avena and Other Mexican Nationals (Mexico* v. *U.S.)*, Merits (31 March, 2004). If only to subsequently retract from the Optional Protocol to the Vienna Convention on Consular Relations (Optional Protocol Concerning the Compulsory Settlement of Disputes, 24 April 1963, 21 UST 325, 596 UNTS 487) granting the ICJ jurisdiction over the United States (which, of course, is the US' full right and must therefore be distinguished from the earlier decision to respect US obligations then binding on the US). See *George W. Bush, Memorandum for the Attorney General* (28 February 2005): 'I have determined ... that the United States will discharge its international obligations under the decision of the International Court of Justice in the [*Avena Case*], by having state courts give effect to the decision in accordance with general principles of comity in cases filed by the 51 Mexican nationals addressed in that decision'.

[51] Calabresi, Steven G. and Dotson Zimdahl, Stephanie, 'The Supreme Court and Foreign Sources of Law: Two Hundred Years of Practice and the Juvenile Death Penalty Decision' (April 2005) at p. 10, on file with the author), adding at 1-2: 'The depth of the support for citing foreign sources of law suggests that the movement to do this is just beginning and will only gather force over time. In the wake of *Simmons*, the debate on the Court is no longer over whether to cite foreign sources of law but over when and how to cite them. This portends a sea change in the Court's doctrine'.

[52] J. Bolton, *supra* n. 35, at p. 9 (emphasis added).

amine the content and legitimacy of this new, crucial layer of regulation. To stick to the old European normative position that State consent is legally binding (*pacta sunt servanda*), hence international law must always be complied with, over and above domestic law, under-estimates either the importance and effect of modern international law, or the need for democratic or other legitimising controls over the law-making exercise. Suffice it to point to the popular rejection of the new Constitution for Europe in French and Dutch referenda as proof that this proposition is valid not only in the United States.

3.3 Might the transatlantic divide be influenced more by relative power and internal constitutional features than by inherent, substantive differences?

That European and American attitudes toward international law are inspired more by temporal elements (such as one's power-position at the time, or the degree of one's constitutional development), witness the striking similarities in both Continents' original position. Indeed, the founding fathers of both the EC and the United States expressed very strong commitments to the international legal system.

At the time it was concluded, the Treaty of Rome was after all a treaty part of, and concluded under, international law. Article 300(7) of the EC Treaty confirmed, for the purposes of 'domestic' EC law, the binding nature of treaties concluded by the EC with other countries. In early ECJ case-law, moreover, the Court granted direct effect to treaties concluded by the EC (*Haegeman* in 1974 and *Kupferberg* in 1982[53]) and recognised the supremacy of international treaties over EC and Member States' legislation.[54]

In the United States, the Supremacy Clause of the Constitution explicitly states that, together with the Constitution itself and US federal law, 'all Treaties made, or which shall be made, under the Authority of the United States, shall be the supreme Law of the Land.' This Clause was a sharp departure from the traditionally dualist British position regarding treaties, where treaties did not have the status of municipal law until implemented by statute. In addition, this time in line with English common law, the United States also incorporated customary international law as part of the law of the land (now part of so-called federal common law). As Bronckers and Kuijper recently remarked, therefore, at their origin, '[b]oth constitutional systems are monistic'.[55]

What explains this concurrence? In my view, it is the fact that, at these respective time periods, both the EC and the United States were fledgling institutions that were relatively weak and needed to confirm their commitment to the

---

[53] ECJ, Case 181/73 *R. & V. Haegeman* v. *Belgian State*, ECR [1974] 449 and ECJ, Case 104/81, *supra* n. 13, *Kupferberg*.

[54] Note, however, that the early ECJ was less open toward *customary* international law, i.e., a type of international law over which EC institutions have less control. See *supra* n. 25.

[55] M. Bronckers and P.J. Kuijper, *supra* n. 14.

international system, first, to reassure outsiders and, second, to confirm their newly granted powers as against competing domestic actors.

In an attempt to explain the EC's early commitment to international law, Bronckers and Kuijper refer to

> 'positions based on questions of principle and legal reasoning, which were of great importance in giving the relation between Community law and the agreements concluded by the Community a solid legal foundation in a period in which the Community was still a relatively weak actor on the international stage.'

In their view,

> '*Kupferberg* was a typical product of a certain period, in which the Community had just started to win its position in international relations ... In such a relatively weak position it is often seen as safest to be closely guided by (international) law. And this seemed all the more obvious, because this was (still) the period in which the Court clearly held a dominant position among the institutions.'

Indeed, by giving direct effect and supremacy to treaties concluded by the Community, the ECJ not only increased its own powers, it also elevated the Community institutions as a whole in their power struggle with the Member States. This was done, especially by highlighting the Community as an actor on the international scene capable of concluding treaties with direct effect and supremacy in the domestic legal systems of the Member States.

Explaining, in turn, the US Supremacy Clause, Carlos Vazquez submits that 'the repeated violations of treaties by the states [in particular, the Treaty of Peace with Great Britain] was a prime concern of the Framers who gathered in Philadelphia.' He hastens to add, however, that

> 'it was merely one facet of a more general problem: the Articles [of Confederation, preceding the US Constitution] lacked a mechanism for enforcing any of the acts of the central Government, or the Articles themselves. The absence of such a mechanism was a principal reason for the Framers' decision to draft a new Constitution rather than amend the Articles.'[56]

In other words, the US Constitution's strong commitment to treaties was inspired, first, by an attempt to impose federal authority over the states and, second, to avert international friction caused by the newly-created US; in particular, friction caused by states' treaty-violations, which would be attributable to the federal US.[57]

---

[56] Carlos Vazquez, 'The Four Doctrines of Self-executing Treaties', 89 *AJIL* (1995) p. 695, at p. 698.

[57] See also T.H. Lee, *supra* n. 7 ('The acute danger to the young, weak Republic's trade and peace posed by individual state defections from U.S. treaties in the late eighteenth century inspired the framers to vest the Supreme Court with this original jurisdiction [over claims by foreign states against states part of the US under international law] despite the possible lack of reciprocity ... It was only in 1934, when America's great-power status in the world balance was incontestable, that the reasons for the

In sum, when relatively weak on the international scene and pressed to establish one's powers against competing internal forces, it should come as no surprise that actors strongly commit to international law, first, to gain respect in, and protection from, the international community and, second, to utilise the international scene as a platform for the aggrandisement of one's own identity and powers.[58]

Consider how much this situation has changed since those early founding years, both in the EC and in the United States.

Summarising the case-law on the question of 'direct effect' of WTO law before the ECJ (especially after *Portugal* v. *Council*[59]), Piet Eeckhout concludes that the EC system can now safely be defined as 'dualist'.[60] At the same time, the ECJ continues to give direct effect to other treaties, including economic association agreement and preferential agreements such as the Lomé Convention. For Bronckers and Kuijper the reasons for this evolution are clear:

> 'it can be questioned, twenty years on [i.e., after Kupferberg in 1982], whether some of these answers [giving direct effect and supremacy to treaties] were not too much focused on matters of principle, and in fact belittled issues that only the larger, more powerful Member States (France!), which were more exposed to international power politics, were aware of ...
>
> All this has now changed. The Community has become an important factor in international relations. Particularly in the WTO, where it was 'present at the creation' and so an 'original Member', it has become a significant power and is also itself better capable of standing up to the power politics of others. Moreover, the Court's position in relation to the other institutions within the Community has changed. In this situation, an adjustment of the Kupferberg case law, particularly regarding the WTO, is understandable and necessary.'[61]

Court's original and exclusive jurisdiction over treaty-based suits brought by foreign states against States were completely forgotten').

[58] Note, however, the somewhat contradictory argument that the *rejection* of international law by the ECJ in certain early cases can be seen as an attempt to distinguish the EC regime from ordinary international law and thereby to confirm the 'separate legal order' and identity of the EC. Timmermans, for example, argues that the ECJ's initial reticence to apply customary international law in *Dyestuffs* (1972) can largely be explained from its efforts to safeguard the autonomy of EC law *vis-à-vis* international law. See C. Timmermans, 'The EU and Public International Law', 4 *European Foreign Affairs Review* (1999) pp. 181-194, at p. 181-183. In my view, the force of this argument is rather limited, in particular to the systemic issue of defining the EC treaty as setting up a separate, quasi-domestic legal order (first proclaimed in *Van Gend & Loos*), which is distinct from the substantive question of commitment by the EC to international law. Moreover, the argument does not explain the opposite move in the ECJ's reception of treaties, from *Kupferberg*'s enthusiasm to *Portugal* v. *Commission*'s skepticism. But see Robert Uerpmann, *International Law as an Element of European Constitutional Law: International Supplementary Constitutions*, Jean Monnet Working Paper 9/03 (2003) (insisting that recent ECJ case-law rejecting direct effect for WTO agreements, and the EC's refusal to ratify the ECHR, are continued attempts to define the identity and autonomy of the EC legal system as against international law).

[59] Case C-149/96, *Portugal* v. *Council* [1999] ECR I-8395.

[60] Piet Eeckhout, *External Relations of the European Union, Legal and Constitutional Foundations* (New York, Oxford University Press 2004) at p. 302 et seq.

[61] See *supra* n. 53.

Explaining the continued reception of so-called asymmetric treaties (such as the Lomé Convention where, in essence, only the EC opens its market, without much reciprocity) or closer integration agreements (such as association agreements and Free Trade Agreements where both parties promise open trade), Rosas refers to the EC's relatively strong power position in both of these specific treaty settings:

> 'granting the latter types of bilateral agreements direct effect is much easier even if the other Contracting Party does not reciprocate, as first of all it has been the intention of the EU to grant its special partner some specific rights and advantages, and secondly as the EU would in any case have the economic and political means to encourage compliance by the other Contracting Party.'[62]

It will not escape the reader that the above power-based positions, as well as the ECJ's own reasons for denying direct effect to WTO law – based on concerns of internal and external balance of powers,[63] in particular, so as to maintain the scope for maneuver (read: position of power) of the EC executive to delay or negotiate a way out of compliance – are very familiar to any observer of US practice in the field, where deference to the executive and legislature, and questions of sovereignty and democratic legitimacy have long played a predominant role.[64] Much like Piet Eeckhout in the EC, Curtis Bradley in the United States now talks of 'our dualist constitution'.[65]

Indeed, in the United States, rather than directly incorporating treaties as the supreme law of the land (as envisaged in the Supremacy Clause), the presumption now is that treaties are not self-executing, if only because in over 90 per cent of cases the US Executive and/or Congress explicitly deny direct effect when ratifying or implementing the treaty.[66] The Uruguay Round Agreements Act of 1994, for example, explicitly precludes direct effect of WTO law in US courts.[67] In a recent Court of Appeals ruling, even the so-called 'Charming Betsy' doctrine of consistent interpretation of US law with international law was put aside.[68] In addition, customary international law and its reception in domestic US law, traditionally through

---

[62] See *supra* n. 14, at p. 813.

[63] Discussed *supra* text at n. 12.

[64] See Andrea Bianchi, 'International Law and US Courts: The Myth of Lohengrin Revisited', 15 *EJIL* (2004) p. 751.

[65] Curtis Bradley, 'Breard, Our Dualist Constitution, and the International Conception', 51 *Stanford Law Review* (1998-1999) p. 529.

[66] See C. Vazquez, *supra* n. 56.

[67] URAA 1994 Section 102(c)(1): 'No person other than the United States – (A) shall have any cause of action or defence under any of the Uruguay Round Agreements or by virtue of congressional approval of such an agreement, or (B) may challenge, in any action brought under any provision of law, any action or inaction by any department, agency, or other instrumentality of the United States, any State, or any political subdivision of a State on the ground that such action or inaction is inconsistent with such agreement' (Uruguay Round Agreements Act, Pub. L. No. 103-465, 108 Stat. 4809). See John Barcelo, *The Status of WTO Rules in Domestic Law – An American Perspective*, draft, June 2004 (on file with the author).

[68] *Corus Staal* v. *Department of Commerce*, US Court of Appeals for the Federal Circuit, 04/1107, 21 December 2004.

federal common law, has become a true obsession amongst US international law scholars. Given its contested automatic incorporation in US federal law, streams of law review articles continue to be devoted to the topic.[69] As federal common law normally prevails over inconsistent state law, scholars defending state rights have happily joined the bandwagon against applying customary international law in US courts.

In sum, the reception of international law both in the EC and the United States started from strikingly similar (monist-like) positions. Moreover, the current EC and US positions continue to share very similar preoccupations with power relations, sovereignty, democratic legitimacy and balance of power between the judiciary and the executive/legislature to deny direct effect to international law (with both gradually moving to a dualist-type conception). Driving this argument to its extreme, the main difference between them is, in the end, that the EC is powerful in only a limited set of circumstances (in particular, external trade, where it denies direct effect), whilst the United States speaks from a power position in almost all areas (hence, driving a wedge between international and domestic law in almost all fields). The same power consideration, together with a persisting EC need to confirm its still relatively new powers as against competing internal actors (in particular, the Member States), might also explain the EC's continued commitment to those areas of international law where the EC remains relatively weak, in particular, treaties outside the trade field (such as the Biodiversity Convention in the *Biotech Inventions* case[70]) and (albeit with limitations) customary international law (in *Racke* and *Opel Austria*[71]).

Put differently, when Europe talks of its commitment to international law, or heralds the supremacy and direct effect of international law, it may partly be doing so based on its normative, idealist approach to international law. However, another explanatory factor is that Europe speaks from a position of relative weakness and is, therefore, quite keen to see everyone (including its more powerful partners) commit to international constraints.[72] In addition, as the EC is not a sovereign State but remains an international institution with strict internal controls by its Member States. Also when the EC operates externally, for the EC to commit

---

[69] Starting with C. Bradley and J. Goldsmith, 'Customary International Law as Federal Common Law: A Critique of the Modern Position', 110 *Harvard Law Review* (1997) p. 815

[70] Panel Report on EC-Biotech, adopted 21 November 2006, WT/DS291/R.

[71] See *supra* n. 27.

[72] For elements of European weakness even in the field of trade (thus partly explaining the EC's commitment to, for example, the strengthened dispute process of the WTO), see Theofanis Christoforou and Allan Rosas, *A preliminary assessment of nearly ten years of participation by the European Union in the WTO dispute settlement system*, on file with the author: 'the EC, despite the fact that it enjoyed at that time exclusive competence in external trade ... has not always been capable, from a structural and internal organizational point of view, of exploiting effectively this power, especially when countermeasures and retaliatory action were contemplated ... EU action in the external trade field is, more frequently than not, based on the lowest common denominator of the positions expressed by the Member States or it takes a considerably long period of time to be framed and adopted. Powerful third countries, like the US, could fairly easily apply the 'divide and rule' strategy to bring standstill in, and even destroy the cohesion of, the decision-making process in the Council'.

itself even to WTO constraints (where the EC does speak from a powerful position) is relatively easy: as the EC is already committed to principles of transparency and non-discrimination through its internal structure, it is easier to accept the same constraints as they are imposed from Geneva, especially if it means that the EC's trading partners will do the same and thus operate from an equal level playing field.[73]

Conversely, in the United States power relations and domestic sovereignty are not the only factors at play. In the United States, much like in Europe, a prominent place remains reserved for normative impulses and value-laden references to, for example, the ideal of individual freedom or the international community (as in recent US Supreme Court rulings referring to, for example, 'norms of international character accepted by the civilized world'[74] or Bush's reference in the *Avena* determination to 'general principles of comity'[75]).

In short, Europe and the United States play the same game, within the same framework and with the same reflexes. Differences in their position have to do more with relative strength and constitutional framework, than substantive transatlantic disagreements.

3.4 The search for a middle ground between the normative European and the transactional American approach: a research agenda

The previous section illustrates that, though theoretically appealing, the divide between European idealism (normativism) and American realism (transactionalism) is less outspoken in practice. Europe has demonstrated a healthy dose of realism itself (witness, in particular, the ECJ case-law on the effect of WTO law), and the United States is not, and has never been, an antithesis to international law (witness its historical role since World War II, the surge of references to international law by the US Supreme Court and the Bush foreign affairs agenda centered around Kantian ideals of freedom).

Nonetheless, the juxtaposition of a European and an American approach to international law remains analytically useful. It can serve as a framework within which to critically assess the two extremes of idealism and realism and to find a balanced middle ground between them.

---

[73] See T. Christoforou and A. Rosas (ibid.): 'issues of transparency, legitimacy and good governance are raised quite frequently and with even more rigor against trade measures and actions proposed by the European Commission for adoption by the EU ... There is little doubt, therefore, that these internal structural and organizational problems have played and still continue to play a prominent role in constraining EU's behavior internationally ... It appears, therefore, that for the EU, in order to be able to complete effectively its mission internally and still be an efficient international player, there was a greater need to rely more frequently on consensual policy-making and the rule of law. This is considered necessary in order to balance the divergent trade and economic interests and rally the support of its Member States, as it cannot apply in its internal decision-making process pure power politics. In other words, the EU was and still is in a much greater need of an international trade regime that is based on principles, norms, rules, and judicial supervision, for both internal and external legal reasons, than individual nation states'.

[74] *Sosa* v. *Alvarez-Machain*, *supra* n. 33.

[75] See *supra* n. 50.

Consider, for example, the risk of inconsistent interpretations discussed in section 2. The normative European approach validly raises this concern (a non-issue in American transactionalism). Yet, the normative approach may go too far and sacrifice a less than homogenous application of international law only to safeguard the system's sacred unity and hierarchical relation to domestic legal systems. American transactionalism – in particular, concepts such as 'regulatory competition' – can temper this extreme and lead to the proposals centered on the notion of judicial tolerance suggested in this chapter. Equally, the question of whether to give direct effect to international law, discussed in section 3, would receive a resounding 'yes' under the European normative extreme: international law is legally binding, so what is the problem with giving effect to it in domestic courts? Such a principled position – though raising valid points of moral commitment and legal predictability – must, however, be tempered by the democratic legitimacy and balance of powers concerns of the transactional, American approach to international law. This should happen, however, without falling into the extreme of this transactional approach (such as construing international and domestic law as hermetically sealed-off compartments or denying any legally binding effect to international law).

This research agenda is, in my view, one of the greatest challenges for us international lawyers in the 21st century. Rather than threatening the unity of international law, it is absolutely necessary to pursue this agenda – including a more outspoken European agenda – to preserve the long-term integrity of the international legal system. As Anne-Marie Slaughter put it in 2002:

> 'If the U.S. can recognize that international law does have a crucial role to play and the EU can recognize that many traditional international rules and institutions must now be modernized, they have a tremendous opportunity to work together to strengthen the global legal order.'[76]

4. Conclusions

The application of international law by domestic courts does not threaten the unity of international law. The risk of inconsistent interpretations, or one national court applying international law inconsistently with other national courts or the relevant international tribunal, is not a reason to deny application of international law before domestic courts. There may be other reasons to do so, based on democratic legitimacy, internal balance of powers or reciprocity with other nations. Nonetheless, the risk of fragmentation or inconsistent interpretations is not one of them.

From the perspective of international law, the risk of inconsistent interpretations is far outweighed by the benefits of a more effective international law. In addition, it may have a bright side, namely the refinement and further development of international law through 'judicial competition'. The multitude of layers and

[76] Anne-Marie Slaughter, *The Future of International Law: Ending the US-Europe Divide*, Crimes of War Project, September 2002, available at <http://www.crimesofwar.org/sept-mag/sept-home.html>.

concerns raised by today's format of international governance are too complex to be constrained in strict hierarchies and preliminary reference schemes. Instead, judicial curiosity, dialogue and tolerance are the best recipe to nurture the integrity and further development of international law.

Courts can, in particular, avoid inconsistent interpretations by referring to the rulings of international tribunals and requesting expert advice from international organisations. Moreover, when serious inconsistencies do persist, other treaty parties can challenge the national court practice before the relevant international tribunal. Calls for either strict unity (for example, to reserve WTO interpretations to the WTO level alone) or self-contained fragmentation (for example, for the ECJ or WTO panels to reject any reference to international law allegedly to maintain their autonomy) can easily be reduced to hegemonic projects.

In turn, the definition and pursuit of a European agenda or European approach to international law does not threaten the unity of international law. Rather than negative attacks on how other nations (read: the United States) should not approach international law, Europe must offer its own, positive agenda on how to view and refine the international system. Europe must shed its reluctance to define, and aggressively pursue, this agenda based on European values and interests. Doing so will remind everyone how much Europe and America continue to have in common. Indeed, when scratching the surface of today's conventional wisdom of Europe as the defender of international law and America as its antithesis, the attitudes, mental framework and reflexes as well as prevailing concerns are strikingly similar across the Atlantic. Both countries, in particular, have strongly committed to international law when relatively weak on the international scene and pressed to establish their powers against competing internal forces, first, to gain respect in, and protection from, the international community and, second, to utilise the international scene as a platform for the aggrandizement of their own identity and powers. Most differences in approach are, therefore, explained not by inherent, substantive disagreements between Europe and the United States, but rather by relative power positions and internal constitutional features.

Given those transatlantic similarities, one of the greatest challenges for us international lawyers in the 21st century will be to unearth these convergences and to find answers to the common questions of, for example, the democratic accountability and legitimacy of international law raised both in Europe and the United States. This requires an appraisal of both the extremes of what I called the strictly normative approach to international law (European idealism) and the purely transactional view of international law (American realism). Yet, to maintain the long-term integrity of international law what is needed is a balanced middle ground between those two extremes.

TABLE OF CASES

International

European Court of First Instance

European Court of Justice

National

INDEX